THE PEACEMAKING STRUGGLE: MILITARISM AND RESISTANCE

Ronald H. Stone and Dana W. Wilbanks, Editors

THE PEACEMAKING STRUGGLE: MILITARISM AND RESISTANCE

Essays Prepared for the Advisory Council
on Church and Society of the
Presbyterian Church (U.S.A.)

Ronald H. Stone and Dana W. Wilbanks, Editors

UNIVERSITY
PRESS OF
AMERICA

LANHAM • NEW YORK • LONDON

Copyright © 1985 by

University Press of America,® Inc.

4720 Boston Way
Lanham, MD 20706

3 Henrietta Street
London WC2E 8LU England

Co-published by arrangement with
The Council on Theology and Culture
and The Advisory Council on Church and Society
of the Presbyterian Church (U.S.A.)

ISBN (Perfect): 0-8191-4773-7
ISBN   (Cloth): 0-8191-4772-9

All University Press of America books are produced on acid-free
paper which exceeds the minimum standards set by the National
Historical Publications and Records Commission.

PREFACE

This volume is a collection of essays on the relationship of Christian faith to the issues involved in the contemporary struggle over the meaning of resistance to militarism. It is intended as a resource to help the Presbyterian Church (U.S.A.) face the question of an appropriate response to the responsibilities and limits of Christian citizenship in a society increasingly faced with the dangers of militarism.

Presbyteries, local churches and the General Assembly are being asked to provide guidance as institutions of the church to individual Christians on civil disobedience, draft resistance, tax resistance and other forms of action regarding militarism. This work may help them in their reflections on the meaning of conscience and corporate church response to these questions.

A steering committee of Beth Lewis, George Stroup, W. Dean Hopkins, Kermit Johnson, Ronald H. Stone, and Dana W. Wilbanks guided the definition of the project. Staff of the Presbyterian Church including Dean Lewis, Gaspar Langella, Robert Smylie, and Gail Hastings Benfield participated in the process. The work was done for the Advisory Council on Church and Society in consultation with the Council on Theology and Culture.

The shape of the project was given by the General Assembly of 1983's request for work on resistance to taxes, the ethics of the justifiable war tradition, the question of non-violent strategies for social change, and the issue of paramilitary developments. As the work developed it was cast in the context of the ethics of a just peace and what the present time required as an authentic church response.

Developments in the church like the Geneva Presbytery's discussions about civil disobedience and the Presbytery of the Western Reserve's concerns over tax resistance encouraged the project to face the issues of corporate church responsibility. Local church involvements with the Sanctuary movement and the General Assembly's endorsement of the Sanctuary movement gave another dimension to the work. The Peacemaking Program's nurturing of the peacemaking ministry among congregations has resulted in countless expressions of peacemaking in Presbyterian congregations.

The project generated many fine studies which could not be included in the volume. These studies will assist in informing the church discussion as the church moves toward decision on the problems of the limits of Christian obedience to the state in a militaristic society. Almost all of the studies here were commissioned explicitly for this project. Acknowledgment and appreciation for permission to use Robert McAfee Brown's essay, "1984: Orwell and Barmen," is given to *The Christian Century* (August 15-22, 1984, vol. 101, No. 25, 770-774), and to *The Seventh Angel* in which a shorter version appeared; Orbis Books granted permission to use Allan A. Boesak's "Divine Obedience" excerpt from *Black and Reformed*, and "Jesus Christ the Life of the World" was made available by the *Reformed World* (September, 1984, pp. 232-238). *Church and Society* granted permission for Robert F. Smylie's "What About the Russians?''; Vincent Harding granted permission for his essay previously entitled, "To Wrestle and Dance: Black History and the Perils of Equal Opportunity," which had appeared in *The National Leader*.

The editors' deep gratitude is extended to Ms. Iris Lowe of Pittsburgh Theological Seminary who did the preliminary work on the manuscript.

The title emphasizes "peacemaking" which is an ongoing, deepening ministry of the church. The term "struggle" indicates that these are studies in process. Each essay is finite, but the process with each author and the church continues. The volume is a stage in our journey as individuals, a church, a nation, and a world. The editors want to encourage the process, not to stop it at a particular point. Militarism threatens our world and calls forth a broad engagement with its threat. Resistance is part of our response to the threat. The study and practice of resistance has its fuller meaning for Christians in the context of prayer, community, ecumenical life, service, and the politics of peacemaking.

CONTENTS

CONTRIBUTORS

1. Herbert Meza is Pastor of Fort Caroline Presbyterian Church in Jacksonville, Florida.
2. Edward Leroy Long, Jr. is Professor of Christian Ethics and Theology of Culture at Drew University Theological and Graduate Schools.
3. Robert F. Smylie is Associate for Peace and International Affairs, the Program Agency of the Presbyterian Church (U.S.A.).
4. Barbara G. Green is Associate Director of the Washington Office, Presbyterian Church (U.S.A.).
5. Richard J. Barnet is co-founder and co-director of the Institute for Policy Studies.
6. Vincent Harding is Professor of Religion and Social Transformation at the Iliff School of Theology.
7. Lamar Williamson, Jr., is Professor of Biblical Studies at Presbyterian School of Christian Education.
8. George R. Edwards is Professor of New Testament at Louisville Presbyterian Theological Seminary.
9. Donald Gowan is Professor of Old Testament at Pittsburgh Theological Seminary. Ulrich Mauser is Dean of the Faculty and Professor of New Testament at Pittsburgh Theological Seminary.
10. Robert McAfee Brown is Professor of Theology and Ethics at the Pacific School of Religion.
11. Nancy Lukens is Associate Professor of German at the College of Wooster.
12. Allan A. Boesak is Chaplain at the University of Western Cape in South Africa and President of the World Alliance of Reformed Churches.
13. Cynthia M. Campbell is Assistant Professor of Theology and Ministry at Austin Presbyterian Theological Seminary.
14. Ronald H. Stone is Professor of Social Ethics at Pittsburgh Theological Seminary.
15. Kermit D. Johnson, Chief of Chaplains U.S.A. (retired), is Associate Director of the Center for Defense Information.

16. Dana W. Wilbanks is Professor of Christian Ethics at the Iliff School of Theology.
17. Walter E. Wiest is Professor of Philosophy of Religion at Pittsburgh Theological Seminary.
18. W. Dean Hopkins, Cleveland lawyer, is legal counsel for the Presbytery of the Western Reserve.
19. Liane Ellison Norman is founder and director of the Pittsburgh Peace Institute.
20. Douglas Mitchell is a community relations representative for the City of Pittsburgh Commission on Human Relations.

Introduction to

THE PEACEMAKING STRUGGLE: MILITARISM AND RESISTANCE

The maker of heaven and earth has through the teaching and action of Jesus Christ claimed us as peacemakers. God's saving love is adequate to give to humanity the fullness of a just peace in which all interacting dynamically would nurture each other. From our creation we are blessed, but the restoration of that blessedness to our war-torn world requires more serious engagement than we have given.

We are by our nature peacemakers, but in our fallenness we are bent strongly toward war making and making ready for war. Out of our *yes* to the beautiful creation God has given us for peace, we must now say *no* to the forces that make for war. Our *yes* to God is in gratitude for God's saving love, our *no* to war is said to the forces that deny the reality of that love and its commandments.

The increasing commitment to peacemaking in the Christian churches is antithetical to the deepening militarism of the world. Militarism is understood as a worldwide phenomenon. It is subject to many different definitions. Militarism is viewed by the editors as expressed in three dynamic movements which characterize the present:

1. The nuclear arms race, the proliferation of nuclear weapons capacity, and the development of other arms of mass destruction.
2. The trade in conventional weapons, and the spread of military approaches to social problems.
3. The spread of technologies and of training in repression of internal opposition.[1]

These tendencies reinforce a process of the "militarization" of society, but the editors' focus is on militarism as it has moved beyond policies of defense or the struggles against injustice or the gaining of independence under the limits of a means of "last resort."[2] Militarism represents the current extreme developments of military power and the too easy reliance upon military power in situtations of difficult international relations.

The 1980s have seen both a deepening concern for peace and an escalating arms race. The churches have made bold calls for disarmament and policies of

[1]

reconciliation through exchanges and negotiations. They have supported the work of international organizations as a move to reduce international anarchy. However in crisis after crisis the resort to force has thwarted negotiations. Cynicism about international organizations has been encouraged by the U.S. which previously helped develop them. The churches have called for peacemaking emphases throughout their life. The struggle within the church is to find means or patterns of Christian practice that are adequate to the call for peacemaking in the increasingly militarized world.

This volume of essays builds upon the peacemaking call of the churches in their ecumenical work. It particularly grows out of the Presbyterian tradition represented in *Peacemaking: The Believers' Calling* (1980). Christian peacemaking concerns are very broad. They include the vital preaching of the Word, the proper ministry of the sacraments, the upbuilding of Christian community, and the development of peoples through the service ministry of the church. The equipping of Christians to engage in the public policy formation of their countries and to engage in the politics of peacemaking is central to the vocation of peacemaking, the work of Christians with others in voluntary organizations to struggle for peace is crucial to the task. Peacemaking is naturally an ecumenical task and the restoration of peace to a divided church is important to the work of peacemaking. In addition to all of the above, more and more Christians are uniting in taking actions, some legal and some illegal, to protest their government's militaristic policies. The committee which was appointed to guide the work of this project for the Presbyterian Church (U.S.A.) learned in hearings at the 1984 General Assembly that Presbyterians have joined others in engaging in tax resistance and civil disobedience in opposition to U.S. policies. Presbyterians who are engaged in civil disobedience and tax resistance have asked their church for counsel, support and guidance in their actions. Other Presbyterians have talked with the editors about their withdrawal from military service and their conscientious change of vocation out of work directly related to weapons of mass destruction.

The editors consider that various actions of selective withdrawal from aspects of cooperation with the military system may be described as resistance to militarism. Such decisions are not made without struggle. Likewise, people who are committed to cooperation with government as a necessary aspect of society find civil disobedience and tax resistance difficult modes of action. Resistance has many meanings. The editors use it in a broad sense to include actions against militarism as defined above. Resistance often involves struggles with conscience and with courage. Its modes may include a spectrum from demonstrations, civil disobedience, support for the Sanctuary movement for refugees, tax resistance, draft resistance, the vocational withdrawal from the military or war-related occupations, and working within one's vocation to oppose militarism. The editors recognize that all Christians will not agree about the appropriateness of many of these actions. Moral ambiguity which often surrounds human actions is particularly real in questions of this nature. It is hoped that the essays will help Christians answer the question: What does obedience to God call us to do in this situation? If the direction of governmental policies is to rely more and more upon the threat of world destruction and upon the actual use of armed forces, what are we as Christians to do?

The answer is both a corporate decision for the church and a personal, deeply existential question for each Christian. The volume begins with Herbert Meza, pastor of the Fort Caroline Presbyterian Church in Jacksonville, Florida, telling his personal story. He has moved from the consciousness of a soldier to a peacemaker in a journey he calls, "Getting Used to a Large Idea." The editors asked Edward Leroy Long, Jr., one of the architects of *Peacemaking: The Believers' Calling* which in 1980 launched the peacemaking priority in the then United Presbyterian Church in the U.S.A., to write on a just peace. His essay focuses mostly on the conceptual changes that the church will have to go through to move from justifying war to pursuing a just peace. His "The Mandate to Seek a Just Peace" represents the new theology of a just peace that must develop if our churches are to contribute something fresh and distinctively Christian to the debate over national direction. Barbara Green's "A Theology of the Enemy" draws upon her experience in the German Democratic Republic. Her work has inspired others to work on this theme which has been more developed in Europe than in the United States. The further refinement and development of our images, theologies and ethics of the enemy is one of the central intellectual tasks of Christian peacemaking work.

Reformed theology and practice is historically activist. It assumes that the Christian life is involved in both personal and social transformation. It has a high respect for the state and it says *yes* to the state as a provider of order, the protector of the people, the source of justice for the poor, and the enabler of the weak. It also says *no* to the state when the inevitable temptations of absolutism, imperialism or militarism are surrendered to by the state. Because the state practice is so necessary to life and because the temptations are so prevalent, Reformed persons should expect at various times in their life to support and to resist the state. The question emerging for many Christians is, should they resist their states? Should they in obedience to God resist in Poland, in the U.S.S.R., in Korea (South or North), in the Philippines, in El Salvador, in Nicaragua, or in South Africa? What about resistance in the U.S.A.? The answer will depend both upon our reading of the situation and our affirmation of our theological-ethical heritage.

The Present Situation

Church statements on the present situation emphasize its momentous nature. It is perceived as a time of crisis. The combination of the deteriorating relations between the two superpowers and the worldwide arms race is perceived as fraught with danger to the whole human race.

The U.S.A. and the U.S.S.R. are temporarily locked in a race which decreases their security. The amount of time between political decision and international destruction decreases. The latest installation of U.S. missiles in Europe and counter-moves by the U.S.S.R. increased the psychological pressures immensely and the weapon capacity marginally. Each new American system will be matched by a Soviet system in a few years. Now we are on the brink of militarizing space which will bring weapons of mass destruction to within one hundred miles of any site on earth. The tendencies of hostility and arming tend toward war. They must be stopped, for the very meaning of humanity is at stake.

How long a world filled with alienated human beings, misshapen nation states and international anarchy can avoid major conflict is not known. But the tendency toward belligerent militarization in such a world threatens to bring the conflict.

Citizens of the U.S.S.R. will have to find ways to encourage creative action from their leaders, if we are to avoid the doomsday events that are probable. Our responsibility, however, is to find ways to prompt acts that will end our rush toward the end. The U.S.A. as the predominant power and the financial and technological leader of the world will have to lead the way out of this treadmill of death. Avoidance of the conflict to be sure will require cooperation and creativity from the Soviets, but we must begin here.

Belligerent militarism on the part of the U.S.A. is encouraged by several factors. There is the obsession with national security analyzed in its contemporary expression in Richard Barnet's essay, "The National Security State." The American experience with this is largely a post-World War II development. It expresses itself both in a policy of enforcing domestic controls on the citizenry and in expending the national wealth on preparations to deter a war with the U.S.S.R. or to fight such a war. The national security state is, in Barnet's judgment, less a result of the Soviet Union than a memory of Hitler. In a world of total war it is believed the U.S.A. must be prepared. The national security state concept is a refinement of the military-industrial complex idea. It originally was associated with the obsessive militarization of some poor totalitarian societies. Increasingly, its applicability to the U.S.A., which sponsors many of the other national security state systems, is becoming clear. Obviously, a major purpose of national governments is to do what they can in an insecure world to provide security. Barnet shows why in the case of the modern world the attempt to build security through militarism is inappropriate.

Militarism in the present situation impacts black people differently than it does white people. Vincent Harding has contributed an essay that shows how black people are equal in pursuing American political objectives abroad but unequal at home. Poor blacks disproportionately serve as the frontline troops of a country that projects its power abroad. Peace is inseparable from justice, and domestic poverty produces soldiers for war directed against poor populations abroad. Harding convincingly shows that the use of American military might promises but does not and cannot promote justice domestically. Rather, now it relies on injustice for its foot soldiers or cannon fodder.

The present tendency for the state dominated by national security to prepare for suicide is fed by the money available, the lure of scientific and technological developments, ideological struggle, and over-respect bordering on idolatry for the state.

Military spending is not good for the economy as it drains money to nonproductive aspects of the economy and away from services and capital investment that improve the economy. However, military spending is very good for certain interest groups in the economy. In both the Soviet Union and the U.S.A. powerful interest groups push for increased spending on the military to further their own interests. According to the International Institute for Strategic Studies, global spending for arms was $790 billion in 1983. Competition for scarce revenues is inevitable, but like other tendencies in society, too much expansion of one sector is destructive of the rest of society.

The lure of the scientific imagination to think of new possibilities is a reality. The work of the pure mathematician or the pure biologist engaged in pursuit of truth or vocational fulfillment is used for weapons development. If the military interests have the major claim on the national purse strings, the quest for scientific truth is financed by and for military interests which may be founded not on truth but on mad fearfulness. The mathematicians, scientists and technicians bear a special load of responsibility as their lives' energies are invested in preparing world holocaust.

The tendency for humanity to invest its particular way of organizing society with ultimate meaning is exemplified in the ideological dimensions of the Cold War. Proud communists and proud capitalists both claim more for their respective forms of social organization than either can deliver. Both systems are rooted in the historical facts of their society, and American capitalists can do no more to reform Russia than Russian communists can do to communize the U.S.A. But in their human insecurity and pride, human beings judge others by their own standards. So the virtues of one's system are magnified and the vices neglected while the reverse is the fate of the other system. This egocentricism is, of course, often transcended, but in a world becoming less secure because of militarism the transcendence becomes difficult, particularly politically. In the Soviet Union criticism, particularly Western-sounding criticism, is ruthlessly repressed, and outbreaks of repression occur in the U.S.A., also.

The ideological hatred rooted in the insecurity common to all humans fuels the belligerent militarism. It tends to root policy in fear, not reality. It tends to absolutize the evil of the other; it makes it more possible to think of inflicting intolerable evil upon another people.

Throughout history people have invested their political systems with great meaning. Naturally the political organization of a country is important. In the modern world that which happens in the political arena can decisively affect other arenas of society. However, those who have political control tend to overestimate their value to society. They tend to want adulation, and in the broad sweep of human history they have usually claimed adoration as participants in divine sanction.

In both of the superpowers it is difficult for citizens to resist the temptation to idolize the state and its policies. In the Soviet Union obedience is demanded and political criticism is not a major Russian tradition. The experience of religious and intellectual challenge to the state is less developed in the Soviet Union than in the Western democracies. In the U.S.A. criticism is expected, but fundamental critique of the policy of the national security state has been muted. This passivity is rooted in the tendency to trust the government and to give it loyalty, particularly in matters of national security. It is the issue of the belligerent militarism of the national security states that threatens our children and our human meaning. Can a policy of citizen dissent change the direction of the states? The modern state has become almost like a god. As Thomas Hobbes saw at the emergence of the modern period, out of fear of each other we have created a modern Leviathan. At what point do traditions of cooperation with the modern Leviathan border on placing our ultimate trust in the state? If we are called by the reality of the present situation to consider dissenting from our present system's trust in the state, we had better look to our theological foundations.

The Biblical Heritage

The Bible has shaped our conscience on the questions we are considering. Through its use in devotions, in sermons, in prayers and in study it has formed many of our attitudes. However, to throw Biblical light on the question of non-cooperation with the state, we must take the question to the Bible itself. Not all relevant passages can be considered here, but G. Ernest Wright (formerly professor at Harvard Divinity School) responded to a question about civil disobedience in the Old Testament: "The most significant figures of Scripture all seem to resist established legal authority in some manner."

One of the best tales of resistance is of the Hebrew midwives' resistance to Pharaoh in Exodus 1:15-22. The Pharaoh's attempt to limit the growth of the Hebrew people by putting their male babies to death is thwarted by the chicanery of the Hebrew midwives whose names are remembered as Shiphrah and Puah. They defied the command of their sovereign and lied to him so that the children might live. In the next chapter Moses himself is saved by more defiance of the sovereign, this time the resistance to authority involves even the Pharaoh's daughter and his own household. Moses, of course, saved through an act of defiance, is later used by God to defy the state openly and to lead his people to freedom. The author of the Letters to the Hebrews connects Moses' salvation from death and his leadership of resistance against the Egyptians directly to faith.

A case of resistance leading to revolution is in I Kings 12. Solomon's son, King Rehoboam, was urged to lower the taxes that Solomon had imposed for his court and building projects. Rehoboam refused and threatened to increase the tax load. According to the text, the Lord then brought about a "turn of affairs" that resulted in Jeroboam leading the tribes away from allegiance to Rehoboam and founding Israel in Bethel. Jeroboam's own form of worship as an alternative to Jerusalem also received prophetic criticism, but the division of the Kingdom held, with only little Benjamin remaining allied to Judah and the house of David.

Micaiah represents the figure of the prophet who says *no* to the king. Throughout the Old Testament the prophet representing God's Word challenges royal authority and is punished for speaking God's Word. Micaiah in I Kings 22 warns Jehoshaphat of Judah and Ahab of Israel that their campaign against the Aramaeans will be disaster. It is not a clear case of religious spokesman against royal authority, for it is also an intra-religious struggle. All the other prophets promise success. For his negative prophecy Micaiah goes to prison. In defying his prophetic *no* Ahab and Jehoshaphat go to battle and to defeat. It costs Ahab his life, " . . . and the dogs licked up the blood" (I Kings 22:38).

Esther's bold breaking of the law began the reversal of fortunes which saved them from pogrom under Persian rule. Her statement of purpose to save her people represents the best spirit of action against law to save life: "I will go to the king, although it is against the law; and if I perish, I perish" (Esther 4:16).

John Calvin grounded his understanding of religious resistance to governmental decrees in reflections upon the book of Daniel. The young Hebrews under the Persians and the Medes simply refused to follow the orders of the emperor in matters of worship. Shadrach, Meshach and Abednego refused the command of Nebuchadnezzar to worship and honor the royal idolatry. Similarly Daniel refused to stop praying to his Lord, defying a royal edict. These were rescued from punishment by God's action. This non-compliance when ordered to violate one's faith has been a model for much Christian resistance to religious persecution. The willingness to endure persecution for faith has also, as in Daniel, often been an argument for honoring the faith that has strengthened adherents in the face of persecution.

There is a theme of God requiring resistance to the government in the Old Testament. It is, of course, only one theme. The motif of covenant obligation binding the Hebrews together as a mutually supportive people is a prominent theme. The covenant is made before God; after the Hebrews accept kingship, the ruler is obligated to God. Protestant political thought rests much of its foundation upon the idea of a covenant of the people together, and then the people covenanting with a sovereign who is obligated before God to respect the covenant. The ideas of resistance to the sovereign never disappear. The forms of resistance mentioned in the Old Testament reappear in the New Testament: resistance to save the children, resistance to taxes, breaking of a law to save a people, and religious resistance to idolatry.

The question of the challenge of the Messiah's authority to political authority haunts the New Testament. From the birth narratives of Jesus to his execution as "King of the Jews," political authorities from Herod to Pilate are threatened by Him. His ministry is in the context of Jewish parties agonizing over their relationship to Rome. The gospels reveal the context of their writers struggling with the antagonism of synagogue and church after the Roman destruction of Jerusalem. Paul writing before the destruction of Jerusalem and before the Neronian persecution understands the ethics of subordination to the state in one way. The author of Revelation, writing much later, sees Rome's destruction and the victory of the cosmological Messiah over the persecutors of His people.

The New Testament is both more inner and more eschatologically oriented than the much larger Old Testament. Consequently, in political thinking stemming from the Reformed branch of the church, the Old Testament has received more use. But the insistence that the Old Testament is more political does not mean that the New Testament is innocent of political involvement and implications. Much of this less-political character of the New Testament is simply due to the fact that Rome occupied the land. Jews normally were not citizens, they were not subject to military service, and they had little political clout. The state in the New Testament is provisional, it lasts for a while to maintain order. It is not absolute, though Revelation reveals its absolute pretensions.

The central actors of the New Testament all defy the authorities sufficiently to be imprisoned or executed. The New Testament, though focusing on the inner person and focusing on eschatology, is set in a political storm. The ringing statement of Peter, "we must obey God rather than men," is from one who struggled with the political meaning of his beloved Jesus. Peter would not only question Jesus, he would, under pressure, deny him after defending him with a sword. Peter would not only defy the authorities to preach Christ resurrected, he would with God's help escape from prison twice.

The essays by Lamar Williamson, Jr., and George R. Edwards bring us to an encounter with the New Testament treatment of political authority and resistance, particularly tax resistance. Edwards deals with the difficult passages of Mark 12:13-17 concerning taxes to Caesar and Romans 13:1-7 on subordination to authority. Williamson discusses these texts also but develops principles of ethics from the New Testament which have led him to tax resistance. The Edwards paper, "Biblical and Contemporary Aspects of War Tax Resistance," moves from an analysis of the scholarly debates about taxes in the New Testament to his own reasons for contemporary advocacy of tax resistance. The Williamson essay presents more of a New Testament-based principled ethic in "Limits on a Christian's Obedience to the State" before making recommendations for church action on the issue.

The essay, "Shalom and Eirene," by Professors Gowan and Mauser is quite different in intention than the works by Williamson and Edwards. They recognize that, though the Christian peace movement has adopted the Hewbrew word *Shalom* for peace, work remains to be done in explicating the meanings of peace in the Old and the New Testaments. Their essay is a dialogue between an Old Testament scholar and a New Testament scholar on the meaning of peace in the Bible. Their essay makes clear the richness of the Biblical meanings of peace and also the need for theological work to make clear the meaning of peace in our time in continuity with the Bible.

Church History

The New Testament concludes with the struggle between the cosmological Christ and the corrupted Roman state. This struggle has shaped Christianity so that even today wild interpretations of *Revelation* which neglect the historical context of the book still confuse Christian political ethics. In this book only those that have refused the demands of the state are regarded as Christ's.

In response to an inquiry about civil disobedience in the early church, the late Roland Bainton of Yale Divinity School responded: "From Nero to Constantine, any adherence to Christianity was civil disobedience, even though punished only intermittently."[3]

The Christians of the early church, until it was legalized under Constantine, prayed for the emperor, paid taxes, and lived lives of exemplary citizenship, but they urged their followers to resist demands for worship or ultimate allegiance to the state's deities. Christian resistance to the imperial cult led to persecution, and to martyrdom occupying a central place in the life of the church. Although they generally refused military service, after 170 A.D. there is evidence of Christians serving Rome in the army. Edward Leroy Long's and Ronald H. Stone's essays both survey the evolution of Christian thought about war and peace from the early church to the modern period. It is of interest to our subject that early Christian resistance is one of the two major reasons for Christian absence from the military in those early centuries. Christian conscience forbade in many cases the honoring of the deities and the worship of the emperor required by military service. That restraint on Christians' serving in the armed forces was removed with the Christianizing of the empire; the ethic of love, however, still restrained many from taking up the sword. The early church said *yes* to the order of the Roman empire, but *no* to the religious practices which legitimated the empire and expressed its claim to absolutism.

The *no* to empire became much more muted after the empire began to be allied with the church. Monasteries and ascetics still separated from the state, but the church embraced it. In the East where the empire was strong enough to survive to the fifteenth century, the rulers tended to dominate the church. In the West where the empire dissolved, the church tried to rally forces of order and to restore civilization. In the emergent church-feudal blended society, the church under strong leaders sometimes said *no* to the princes for the freedom of the church, but the *no* to military practice was very muted and confined to small witnesses. The alliance between the church and militarism reached a zenith in the crusades of the middle ages.

Long before the church was involved in the barbaric slaughter that accompanied the crusaders' conquests in Constantinople and Jerusalem, the church's complicity with armed force was established. The same Augustine who, out of an ethic of love (see: Ronald Stone's essay, "The Justifiable War Tradition") could reluctantly sanction armed defense, eventually came to excuse the application of armed force against heretics. Crusades approved by the church were carried out against non-orthodox Christian groups, but also against Christian peoples (e.g., the Norman conquest of England in 1068). The church sought through the techniques of the Truce of God and the Peace of God to limit violence, but it was too involved in the use of violence to protect its own temporal interests to be an effective peacemaker. Similarly in the European conquest of the world from the fifteenth century until the twentieth, the church complied with the imperial needs of the European powers. It had its own missionary interests, but these were vitally compromised with the worldly motivations for wealth and empire. Here and there a prophetic voice from within the church, like Father Bartolome de las Casas in Central America in the sixteenth century, would protest against the subjection and murder of the native inhabitants. But basically religious legitimacy in the name of Christ was bestowed upon the European conquest of others.

The uneasy alliance between spiritual and temporal authority that characterized the Middle Ages resulted in many struggles between the spiritual and temporal rulers. But in the eleventh century the Pope could claim to be under God, the source of both temporal and spiritual authority. The claim could not hold, however, and the far-reaching claims of the Pope contributed to the conflict that exiled Hildebrand, even from Rome. Secular rulers were limited by custom, by law, and by the power of the church. The church was at least a co-equal, if not the rightful sovereign, in this long, complex period of Western history. The legal thought of Thomas

Aquinas (1225-1274) laid the grounds for much of Catholic constitutional theory limiting the role of temporal authority. His claim that positive law was dependent upon divine law and natural law has, in our own time, been the ground for Christian resistance to unjust positive laws.

The Protestant Reformation tended to pit the new religious movement against the old order. Martin Luther (1483-1546) justified the refusal to obey the commands of the sovereign when they violated God's will ("we must obey God rather than men," Acts 5:29). His high view of scriptural authority also led him to avoid resistance on the grounds of Romans 13 ("There is no authority but by act of God, and the existing authorities are instituted by Him."). Disobedience to the authorities? Yes, when they violated God's law. Resistance to the authorities? No, at least he avoided resistance until very late in life. Finally, he was persuaded that the Emperor's move into Germany to persecute the reformation was illegal, and on the advice of lawyers he agreed that constitutionally resistance to the illegal action of the emperor was legal. Then he could justify armed resistance to the emperor. Later, Calvinist-armed resistance to the sovereign often borrowed from theological arguments developed on Lutheran ground.

John Calvin (1509-1564) tried to restrain his followers from revolution. He also taught that impious commands of the sovereign were not to be obeyed. The authorities were constituted by God and were to be honored, though civil servants had a duty to resist their princes if they acted contrary to the law. His followers in the Netherlands, France and Scotland were to push the implications of his positive attitude toward government much further. In all those lands historical forces pushed Calvinists into revolution and they succeeded in the United Netherlands and Scotland. The early Protestant revolutionaries acted out of the need to defend the true or Protestant faith against blasphemy and idolatry. But by the 1570s in French Protestant political theory, the grounds of revolution were the supposed original freedoms of the people and their rights under natural law.[4]

Calvinist political theory developed in subsequent centuries until its positive view of the state, grounded in covenantal language with its Old Testament roots and founded in revolution, could be expressed in the U.S. Constitution. It underwent substantial change on its way to supporting popular revolution in John Locke's *Two Treatises of Government* from John Calvin's disobedience to the sovereign in *The Institutes of the Christian Religion*.

The Reformed view of the emerging states was positive. The leaders of the states were, of course, sinners and often foolish, but the state was the dike of God against sin. Order was precious and the vocation of a public office holder was in John Calvin's thought to be respected above all other vocations. There was no romantic anarchy or idealistic perfectionism in Calvinist political wisdom. Still, in its beginnings it recognized the duty to disobey on religious grounds. Soon it was driven in honoring that God is Lord of the conscience to resist and then overthrow tyrannical-idolatrous regimes. The conception of a covenant between the people and God for the ordering of their lives led to the idea that the sovereign could be overthrown if the ruler violated the covenant. The covenant's meaning was grounded both in the constitutional history of the realm and in the natural rights of the citizens. So the grounds were laid not only to resist unjust laws, but to depose sovereigns. George Buchanan (1506-1582) carried the right to depose sovereigns as far as any Calvinist thinker and, of course, he did it for Scotland where Calvinists succeeded in deposing the Queen in 1567.

The historical material reveals only that Protestant Christians like their Catholic counterparts are free morally to resist or to replace governing orders which act against the purposes of the constitution or religious faith.

The year 1984 was the fiftieth anniversary of the Barmen Declaration, which is affirmed as a confession of the Presbyterian Church. The Barmen Declaration was made in the face of the claims of a state to dominate Christian conscience. The essays by Robert McAfee Brown and Nancy Lukens both examine this confession's relevance to us in our time. Are we at a time where the claims of the belligerent, national-security state forces us to confess our opposition and to move into a stance of resistance against the distortion of our state? Robert McAfee Brown reveals the dangers of Orwellian trends in the U.S. of 1984. The need for today's Christians to find their way to say *no* as the Barmen Christians found their way to say *no* is affirmed. Nancy Lukens uses Barmen as a mirror to help us see our own complicity in national evil that has religious dimensions. She then illustrates the formation of a Christian style of resistance with the Sanctuary movement. Obviously, many Christians individually have taken stances of non-cooperation with the belligerent policies of the state. The Presbyterian Church (U.S.A.) in its General Assembly (June, 1984) reaffirmed the religious appropriateness of sheltering refugees. These essays on Barmen call us to consider the appropriateness of a Christian church stance of resistance to military belligerency.

Reformed Christianity has produced both its oppressors and those who in the name of Christ resisted oppression. The Reverend Allan A. Boesak, a Black Reformed minister and theologian, is president of the World Alliance of Reformed Churches. He also has accepted appointment as an International Peacemaker of the Presbyterian Church (U.S.A.). Here he presents his address to the World Council of Churches in Vancouver, 1983, and a letter to the Minister of Justice of South Africa. The theology of the first with its inseparable union of peace and justice is illustrated by his practical action of resistance in his letter to his government. The letter is reprinted with permission from Orbis Press as it is included in his book *Black and Reformed*. Permission for "Jesus Christ the Life of the World" is from *Reformed World* (Geneva).

Christian Ethics,
United States Policy and Resistance

As one of the needs of the Presbyterian Church expressed in the request of the General Assembly was to study the relevance of the just war teaching to the contemporary situation, several essays were undertaken in this area.

Cynthia M. Campbell argues that the just war tradition demonstrates the immorality of the use of nuclear weapons. She examines just war teaching in both the work of Protestant ethicist Paul Ramsey and the American Roman Catholic Bishops' Pastoral Letter. She finds the Roman Catholic position more adequate and she accepts that "deterrence is an acceptable policy, they argue for the interim." However, clearly for her the just war theory shows that nuclear war is not justifiable war. Ronald Stone and Kermit Johnson both affirm just war theory as the conventional moral discourse of the Western world about war. They recognize that it has been criticized (see: e.g., the comments by George Edwards on just war), but they regard it as the most adequate set of criteria for moral reasoning about war by non-pacifists. Stone's paper deals more with the origins of just war theory. Kermit Johnson's paper deals with the detailed application of the theory to contemporary U.S. policy. Johnson finds current nuclear policy failing the tests of just war theory. Stone focuses on the intention behind nuclear deterrence and explains that deterrence depends upon the willingness to engage in monstrous evil, perhaps the most objectively evil act ever perpetrated by humanity. They both, therefore, reject nuclear deterrence and present U.S. nuclear policy as immoral. Their reasoning brings them to a clear unequivocal *no* to U.S. nuclear policy.

Dana Wilbanks examines the deterrence strategy and its fundamental presuppositions or doctrine. Not only does deterrence subject humanity to unacceptable risks of failure, it is morally flawed at the foundational level. Security must be provided for in alternative ways. He concludes that deterrence must be overcome so humanity can begin to work seriously on disarmament, because the doctrine of deterrence itself prevents disarmament.

All four essays in Christian ethics reveal the growing consensus expressed at the Vancouver World Council of Churches Assembly in 1983 that Christians must repudiate false security based on nuclear armaments.

The essay, "A Christian Ethic of Resistance in a War-Making Society," moves from all we have previously considered towards analysis of Christian response. Walter Wiest surveys possible Christian responses to our militarized·society. The commitment to peacemaking is assumed. The ethical issues of the essay revolve around whether one is called beyond politics and a personal lifestyle of peacemaking to resigning from war-related vocations, civil disobedience, and tax resistance. If the conclusions of the previous work are correct that present U.S. policy threatens human existence, then extraordinary means of resisting the evil may be called for at this time. The editors do not intend to suggest that any one form of Christian resistance to the belligerent militarism of the U.S. is required. They believe, however, that Christians need to be considering appropriate forms of resistance to militarism.

W. Dean Hopkins, the legal counsel for the Presbytery of the Western Reserve which has over a period of two years faced the implications of a specific case of tax resistance by one of its pastors and wrestled with the problems involved in tax resistance, analyzes the problems associated with the non-payment of taxes as a form of resistance to militarism. Lamar Williamson and George Edwards, two biblical scholars engaged in tax resistance, have addressed the theological, biblical and ethical issues in the Biblical Perspectives section. The essay, "Resistance to

Taxes for Military Purposes,'' raises the questions before the church at the present time. Certainly the Presbyterian Church (U.S.A.) will defend the rights of conscience of its members to resist in this way. Whether the church will, as an institution, find this a wise and prudent form of action for corporate support is now before the church for decision. The committee developing these essays found the World Peace Tax Fund to be an exciting possibility for meeting the needs of conscience of some of our members. Unfortunately, its movement toward reality in legislation has not developed very far in Congress. Under present legislation there seems to be almost no possibility of the Supreme Court recognizing the rights of conscientious refusal to pay taxes. It is clear that some Presbyterians will refuse to pay taxes as a form of protest. The enormity of the evil they are acting against will require most Presbyterians to support their moral right to such a protest, even if they do not adopt it themselves.

Given that the present policies threaten human existence, can we achieve a reasonable degree of security? The easy reliance upon armed force has obscured the development of thought about non-violent means of defense. Liane Norman, peace activist and founder of the Pittsburgh Peace Institute, presents the case for non-violent means of defense in her essay. Martin Luther King, Jr., advanced beyond Gandhi in the application of non-violent means of social change as the major tool for change in racist policies and laws in the U.S.A. Non-violence became a method for some of the thoughtful and the brave to change power structures. Norman argues that non-violence is the necessary, safer alternative to our present policies which threaten nuclear Armageddon.

The present crisis pushes in on all of our consciousness. It is an ultimate situation. The character of the situation forces itself into religious language and religious symbolism. While striving to remain responsible under the present pressure we must also attend to extremism which threatens our society. There is the extremism of the religious right which expresses itself in a rampant American nationalism. This extreme nationalism projects its own fears and fantasies onto the presumed enemy and regards the U.S.S.R. as totally evil. This nationalism blessed with religious fervor has made inroads into our national politics. To the extent that governmental leadership depends upon it, the nation is unable to negotiate seriously with the Soviet Union about our ultimate danger.

There are even more virulent forms of religious nationalism haunting our public life. These are present in the burgeoning paramilitary movements in the U.S. Douglas Mitchell, a Presbyterian minister and expert in extremist political and racist movements, has prepared an analysis of the religious extremist and paramilitary convictions. The social struggle in religious terms is with extremist groups of the right as well as with the militarized bellicosity of the national security state.

Our ultimate hopes and fears influence our politics. The editors believe the Christian faith is best represented by an attitude of trust. The introduction began with an affirmation of God's creation. We mean that the source of all life is trustworthy. The eschatologies of the paramilitary extremists influence them to believe there will be a war with communists in the U.S.A. We regard this as foolishness

[13]

based upon misread scripture, fear, and absolutism in political life. They have a right to read scripture by their own conscience; it is their threat to public peace that encourages our advocacy of opposition to their practice. Hal Lindsay, Jerry Falwell and occasionally President Ronald Reagan have advocated a form of nuclear Armageddon theology which has no basis in scripture and is disastrous in its implications for life.[5]

The hopes of these editors are in *Shalom*. We reject nuclear war readings into scripture written in the Roman empire. We affirm the traditions of fulfillment in peace which reach their height in Isaiah 2:4:

> He shall judge between the nations
> and shall decide for many peoples
> And they shall beat their swords
> into plowshares,
> And their spears into pruning hooks;
> Nation shall not lift up sword against nation,
> Neither shall they learn war any more.

Its parallel in Micah 4 adds:

> But they shall sit everyone under
> his vine and under his fig tree
> And none shall make them afraid;
> for the mouth of the Lord of hosts
> has spoken.

Through peacemaking, which includes the upbuilding of justice, the structuring of order, the overcoming of militarism with resistance and politics, God's hopes for human fulfillment can be more approximately realized in our history. The vision is of humanity aware of God's presence with us. The blessing for the struggle is of God with us as Jesus said:

> "Blessed are the peacemakers
> for they shall be called children of God."
> (Matthew 5:9)

ENDNOTES

1. "The Consultation on Militarism" of the World Council of Churches (Montreux, Switzerland, 1977) in José-Antonio Viera Gallo, editor, *The Security Trap* (Rome: IDOC International, 1979), p. 127.
2. *Ibid.*, p. 117.
3. Quoted in Richard W. Bauer, Carol Meier, Richard E. Moore, Henry Carter Rogers, *A History of Civil Disobedience: In Defense of the Reverend Maurice McCrackin*, n.d., mimeographed, p. 14.
4. Quentin Skinner, *The Foundations of Modern Political Thought*, II (London, Cambridge University Press, 1978), p. 338.
5. Jerry Falwell, "Nuclear War and the Second Coming of Jesus Christ" (Lynchburg: Old-Time Gospel Hour, 1983); Hal Lindsay, *The 1980's: Countdown to Armageddon* (New York: Bantam Books, 1981).

INTRODUCTION

The documentation for President Ronald Reagan's nuclear theology is in Ronnie Dugger, "Does Reagan Expect a Nuclear Armageddon," *The Washington Post* (April 8, 1984), pp. C1, C4.

A detailed discussion of nuclear Armageddon theology is Robert G. Clouse, "The New Christian Right, America, and the Kingdom of God," *Christian Scholar's Review,* XII, No. 1 (1983), pp. 3-16.

Peacemaking

GETTING USED TO A LARGE IDEA

Herbert Meza

The first fact of my spiritual journey in the odyssey of peace begins in a Cuban ghetto. The life I entered, by birth, was an immigrant's view of a Quixote world. That view was shaped by Hispanic logic which, to the uninitiated, may sometimes appear to be paradoxical. The paradox has to do with a sense of solidarity with people everywhere, simply because they are people, simply because they are part of the human drama, and on the other hand, with a profound sense of personal uniqueness. John MacKay tells, somewhere, a story which describes this uniqueness. MacKay met a Spaniard once who told him that every Spaniard went around thinking he had a paper in his pocket which entitled him to do whatever got into his head. This is not to be confused with stubbornness. It is rather the individuality of heroic men and historic women whose unending obstinacy blurs into legend the pages of Hispanic history and literature and is poignantly captured in Don Quixote's phrase,

"Yo se quien yo say!"

This affirmation of self-awareness and its uncontrollable yearning for the heroic is what initiated me into the concept of solidarity and the awareness of others also engaged in the classic struggle against the tragic sense of life. In that sense, I suppose my journey began in my genes. This cultural inclination reflects the enigma of the Latin psychic, which North Americans always fail to comprehend, the sense of fatalism, heroic fatalism (Si Dios quiere?) and the sense of celebration so ably captured by Gabriel Garcia Marques in his masterpiece, *One Hundred Years of Solitude*. The dignity of the individual is a revered precept among Hispanics. It transcends culture and represents the essence of solidarity.

This Hispanic temperament is not easily defined. It is and always has been a mentality fraught with contradictions; violent passion offset by stoicism; the bravura of machismo coupled with gentleness and sentimentality; the degradation and the sanctification of woman in a single breath. There is a dynamic that lives within us that nourishes an insatiable creativity, full of sorrow and beauty, full of self-affirmation and a yearning for solidarity. Poets and prostitutes, priests and politicians, prophets and peasants, all creatures of this unbridled reality, we have had to ask little of imagination; but our crucial problem is that we are not believable and this has contributed to our sense of solitude and solidarity.

The second fact of the journey has to do with Jesus Christ. Hispanics have always responded more readily to individuals *(caudillismo)* than to ideologies. Our history has been shaped by strong men and women. It is a shame, in my judgment, that the United States seeks to find the mirror image of American democracy in Central America when it should be looking for heroic leaders. Latin American history has been shaped by cruel dictators, flamboyant conquistadores, Spanish viceroys, inspired guerilla fighters, and crusading bishops and priests. It is a culture held together by the sheer force of personality. Latins understand and respond to heroic leadership. When, as a young man of sixteen, I was first introduced to Jesus Christ, I wanted to gallop off on a horse somewhere and be a hero for Christ. He, Christ, appealed to every instinct in my being. That Galilean stirred something within me, so drugged by the culture I was seeking to become a part of, that I had to struggle to keep it alive; something that I found and still find, that the realist of our day cannot and will never understand. That has been, by the way, the ultimate test of my faith, i.e., to live without being understood (solitude). But that elan vital within me that longed to fight a dragon and rescue a damsel was tired of the plodding sanity of our times and the devotion to security and success. I was stirred to life by a Galilean, some called him deluded, who raised up a vision of a Kingdom, a hope, a dream of brotherhood and sisterhood, and peace on earth. As I look back, that's where it begins, this call to peacemaking.

> To follow a man who was unimpressed
> by status, and felt at home with little children.
>
> Who ran demons off a cliff and spinned
> the dream of a kingdom to come.
>
> Who broke up a funeral and catered
> a wedding with good wine.
>
> Who saw life and world as it might
> be and said, "Why not!"

Thus, I have been conditioned by faith and culture to live by the romance of providence. I have never known how one develops that, or if it can be developed, but it began for me in the awareness that there is a vision we do not manufacture, we merely lay hold of it. There is a truth we do not possess, it possesses us; there is a way which is not ours but God's. I have discovered that those who are caught up in this romance become fearless in the face of the unknown, untouched by the harsh realities that throw themselves at them; and crushed by the soft innocence of those they wound, they are toughened by adversity and tenderized by tears.

That is why I have never really felt at home in American culture. The American experience turns us all into zealous bookkeepers, or as Saul Bellow wrote:

"The life of every citizen becomes
a business. This is one of the
worst interpretations of the meaning
of life that history has ever seen.
Man's life is not a business."

Daniel Bell, Harvard social historian, blames this love affair with the consumption ethics (Adam Smith's enlightened self-interest) as the reason for the loss
of solidarity which makes men and women brothers and sisters to one another. He
says, by the way, that our hope lies through regrasping those experiences which
give us a tragic sense of life, of life lived on the knife edge of finitude and freedom;
and religion becomes the most revolutionary of all forces.

My mother taught me by example much of how I feel about life. Unlike most
recent arrivals from Cuba, she came to this country not seeking asylum, but looking for a promised land whose logo was a statue of liberty and whose creed was
inscribed on the base of that monument. She saw America from the under view and
fell in love with that dream. Widowed early and alone, she was one of the pioneers
to join a labor union in the cigar-making industry and, in the process, lost her job.
But her courage was contagious, and I admired her from the beginning. To save
streetcar fare, five cents in those days, I would ride her to work in West Tampa on
my bike, her quiet dignity never shaken. Her words were always of the future;
always of *la humanidad*. She taught me a kind of courage that I was to encounter
later during the turbulent days of my ministry in Washington, D.C. I specifically
recall greeting a group of Texas farm workers who had walked all the way from
Texas to dramatize their need. We housed them at the Church of the Pilgrims, a
church which voluntarily gave its life and strength and buildings on behalf of hurting people during those difficult, and yet glorious, years. I spoke to a tough-
looking, weather-beaten, soft-spoken Mexican one morning, cautioning him about
how to behave before a Congressional committee. And he said something that I had
heard from my mother on that bicycle classroom:

"If I'm already sleeping on the
floor, don't caution me about falling
out of bed."

I had almost forgotten that I had once learned that lesson. When one has
nothing to lose, one has arrived at the ultimate stage of freedom. I suppose that's
why the poor are often so threatening to those who have so much to lose. I've
always felt poor in that way. I've never had any allegiance or owned any sense of
security to anyone or anything except what I've felt to be just and decent. As I've
tried to find a reason for this feeling, I keep going back to my youth. I cannot
forget, indeed, I choose not to forget. Growing up, having to deal with prejudice,
taught me that lesson. I remember once going to a swimming club in Sulphur
Springs, Florida, right outside Tampa, and seeing a sign which read;

"No dogs or Latins allowed!"

We tore that sign down and dared anybody to do anything about it. We were ready to fight and, in my judgment, it was a just thing to do. I often wondered what Christ would have done on such an occasion. That, by the way, is why I often wonder if I am a true pacifist. I know I am a nuclear pacifist. Nuclear war solves nothing, but rather endangers the whole creation. War, as we have understood it, has already been abolished. The extravagant and uncontrollable yearning for national security has left us all with less security, nervous and depressed. I take issue with the idea that some evil is so necessary, that it is no longer evil. Nuclear war is evil! But here I am not consistent, though perhaps I never felt consistency was a virtue . . . another one of those Hispanic paradoxes.

But I feel such a deep sense of solidarity with those who live under the bondage of prejudice and oppression in abject poverty and misery. I consider that to be a form of violence. Who am I to deny that violence may be a legitimate response to that kind of violence? The moral decision I leave to the oppressed, with the admonition that "the revolutionist without love," to quote Ché Guevara, "is likely to be the next oppressor." I have wondered that if there is no peace without justice, and if justice is not possible without violence, is there a role for violence? That question is still open for me. Had I lived in a Latin or Central American country, I probably would have been a revolutionist.

But in my own mind, I am quite sure that I cannot accept a world half-fat and half-famished, where God is on the side of the privileged few. Stories, sometimes, tell the essence of our lives. I remember a story I read somewhere of the French liner, Champollion, which sank in a heavy sea. Only a few life boats were able to be launched and they were quickly filled. When those struggling in the water tried to climb into the already filled boats, those aboard would cut off their hands with hatchets. One person who had been in one of the boats put in words what I have accepted as my own,

> "I refuse to take a place in a boat
> in which there is room only for a
> limited number of people."

I decline to accept the dehumanization of people on any basis.

That, in my judgment, is the tragedy of this country. We stand today as the self-proclaimed leader of the unhumiliated world over against the vast majority of the earth's humiliated people. As black historian Vincent Harding has phrased it:

> "One of America's most critical blind areas is in the realm of understanding the oppressed, the wretched of the earth. Our vaunted experience of virtually unbroken success, our alabaster cities undimmed by human tears, our movements into the strange joys of corporate capitalism . . . have cut us off from the rest of the world."

Much of what I feel today is because I refuse to forget my roots. My theology is not so much systematic as it is sympathetic. I have felt that Calvinism with its great emphasis upon the sovereignty of God has very often played into the hands of those who would prefer to make God the author of the status quo, which is Latin for "the mess we're in." Our theology could profit from a different angle of vision. At this point, liberation theology has made sense to me. It is a corrective both to Hegelian dialectics and Calvinist predestination.

It was natural that I should enter the Marine Corps. That would prove to be the third variable in my journey. I did so at seventeen. At eighteen, I had already earned two Purple Hearts and a commanding officer's citation. (Marines are very hesitant to give medals, as we all have learned in the Grenada fiasco.) It was natural, I say, because I continued to be so vulnerable to the heroic; and I say that without shame or without boast. I know that the Holy Spirit is supposed to lead us to larger parishes and more stature and increased income, but it's never worked that way for me. Somehow, with one exception, I have always been drawn to those areas of challenges, to frontiers. So it was natural for me to "join up" as soon as I got out of high school, immediately after Pearl Harbor. My mother had to sign my application and she did so with no reservations but with great reluctance. A year later she was to get a telegram that I had been killed in combat. It was a week before the error was corrected and in that week, with her quiet dignity and her breaking heart, she paid her dues proudly for being part of the most unusual political experiment in political science, the United States of America. She never regretted having lost a son and having offered another one. When the second telegram came with new information that I was wounded and not killed, she accepted that too as part of a larger plan. Her sense of drama and providence were always impeccable.

At nineteen, I killed an enemy soldier in hand-to-hand combat. That event was the genesis of much that I feel about war. We were lying in our foxhole, having been warned not to move, and to shoot at anything that moved. The enemy was infiltrating through our lines, clad in G strings and grenades. In the middle hours of the night, tired after a long session on my stomach, I turned and lay on my back. At the same moment, while my hands were at my side and my rifle lying flat on my stomach and chest, an infiltrator rolled over into my foxhole, landing on top of me, on top of my rifle, with my hands constrained by the force of his weight and the sides of the foxhole. We struggled quietly for fear of calling attention and its consequences. I managed to reach down to my leggings where I carried my knife, an ugly, huge and balanced weapon of multiple uses. Bringing it up from my legs, I thrusted it upwards. There was a soft explosion of air entrapped in his body cavity, a pitiful sound, not a cry or a grunt, but the kind of sound which conveys resignation and dignity. That's how it sounded to me. With his blood oozing upon me, I shoved him out of the foxhole and spent the rest of the night in the most agonizing retreat of my life. In the morning, I sought his body, cold now, and with the added indignity of having soiled his brief garment. I searched for some identity and found a little picture of a beautiful woman. I kept that picture in my wallet for the rest of the war and I still have it today, the only evidence of things not seen but beginning to appear. Late that day, in a bomb crater, I sat by myself to eat my C-rations. It was a crater made by one of our shells. As I ate, the sand below my feet, finding a vacuum beneath it, began to sift much like the sand in an hourglass. Suddenly a hand was exposed. Buried beneath this debris was a broken body. I transformed my C-rations into communion elements, and there, with an enemy who also had offered up his body, I celebrated the first step of that journey which I have called the odyssey of peacemaking . . . an odyssey which began to make more sense in the ensuing years.

In those postwar years, the island we had liberated was restored to the enemy. Another atoll was obliterated in a nuclear experiment, our former enemies have become our friends, and in recent time we are quarreling with them because they refuse to arm themselves after we disarmed them. Why does it take a war to transform enemies into friends? It's becoming harder to recognize our enemies without a program. The Vietnamese war was fought to prevent the domino theory of Communist expansion. Ronald Reagan, at that time, vowed perpetual vigilance and enmity against China and eternal allegiance to Taiwan. At the very moment I write this, he is drinking a toast to eternal friendship with China.

Why is it I killed that father-brother-son-lover? I have come to see now the truth that man is the only animal that kills for an idea and, in the process, turns his truth into ideologies not to be used but defended. And, in the process, ideologies become easy coverups for self-interest. Freedom, which we are fond of citing, has gone the way of ideology . . . "The freedom in this sick and melancholy time of ours has become, not a thing to use but a thing to defend" (Archibald MacLeish). Where is the freedom that we have misplaced among our convictions? Where is the force we have lost in the forms?

So that in our defense of the idea of freedom, we have supported every cruel dictator in Latin and Central America, oppressive and inhumane forces that have denied real freedom, making easy assumptions that all unrest is due to Communist conspiracy, making Communism better than it is, giving it the best lines. Our blind ideology has robbed us of the ability to see authentic forces of liberation and freedom. It's an old script, blaming outside agitators. Just a few years ago, when the public schools were being integrated, I walked with a group of black children to their first integrated school in Texas City, Texas. The First Presbyterian Church of that city, of which I was pastor, had remained very calm. We were the first church to integrate in Galveston County, and it had taken place without much trauma. I have had the good fortune to follow some very able pastors in the two churches where I served during those trying years. In Texas City, my predecessor had been Dave Currie, a wonderful and courageous maverick. From him I had learned to attend union meetings even though my church was full of Monsanto and Union Carbide management folks. But as I walked with the children on that emotional morning, under the watchful eye of the local police, some of whom I knew, the epithets were always followed by, "go back to where you came from, Pinko, we don't want your kind here." I have always marvelled how all racial unrest was blamed on outsider agitators, discounting years of humiliating prejudice and civil rights denial, discounting over a hundred years of slavery.

Our blind anticommunist ideology has robbed us of so much truth. That is what happens when freedom becomes a code word for self-interest. We deny our own freedom by not daring to live beyond self-interest. Chinese Communism is acceptable, but not Cuban or Nicaraguan. Today the strongest ideology which motivates this country is anticommunism, even though it is practiced selectively. It is being suggested, that in order to be patriotic, we must not only hate the Soviets, but we must not even appear soft on Communism; thus creating a conditioned reflex in which leaders, including church leaders, outdo each other in terms of bellicosity, and the positive, more reconciling voices of moderation are drowned out in a chorus of "better dead than red." Developing then is a national policy which suggests that the more aggressive attitude the U. S. presents, the better the detente, locking us up in a syndrome of escalating fear and hate which must sooner or later produce the fatigue which leads to chaos.

And that, I think, is the moment and the temptation we face; and it is incumbent upon the church to demythologize the role of ideologies and bring to government the wisdom and restraint of truth. More than ever the nation needs the church, particularly a church with a clear vision of its Lord and a clear understanding of Christ's concern for people.

And that is the most important struggle going on now. It is the struggle for the soul of the nation. Theology is of supreme importance now. The rising tide of conservative and fundamentalist churches have been falling over themselves to enlist in the "Swiss guard of the power elite." Whether we realize it or not, theology and theological perspectives have become of extreme importance. The ideologies, both in the church and outside the churches, like to simplify the things they fear while deadening their moral sensitivities. Reducing truth to ideology for the sake of confronting crises seems to me to be the very thing that produces crises. For a fanatic is a person who loses his way and redoubles his efforts. That was the fourth variable of my journey. For the same force that drove me to the heroic led me to fundamentalism. I wanted to be a hero; I became a bore in the process.

I went through a period in my life, very early, when I embraced fundamentalism. In a desire to be heroic and truly committed, I became dogmatic. That is the simplistic way of proving your commitment with the least effort. Intolerance was a badge I wore in those days as a mark of distinction. I deepened my commitment by narrowing my mind. As I look back now I can count the number of people who were patient with me and kept trying to enlarge my perspective. I owe them, an anonymous host in the main, a debt of much gratitude.

The fifth major variable of my personal journey into peacemaking took place after my graduation from Union Theological Seminary in Richmond, Virginia, in the summer of 1952. I had planned to go to Japan as a missionary, having gone through such a profound experience in combat; but at that time, the Board of World Missions had been looking for someone to go to Portugal as the first Presbyterian Church U.S. missionary, or fraternal worker, as we preferred to call ourselves. Because of our Latin background, we were invited to go to Portugal, and we finally accepted.

And so, after much trouble in arranging our visas, we sailed for Portugal, my wife and small child aboard the Italian liner Saturnia, traveling third class, September 19, 1953. After a year in Lisbon, learning the language and doing other interim assignments, we were sent to the island of Madeira where that little Protestant community was experiencing some difficulties. We arrived with three barrels of clothes to distribute to the poor who were always in our congregations. To our

[25]

surprise, we were attacked in the local press as missionaries who had arrived in Madeira, with gifts of clothes and money, to make "rice Christians." Needless to say, I was first angry and then angrier. I went to the local press with my side of the story and they wouldn't print it. I tried to get a handbill printed to distribute in the street with an "evangelical defense," but nobody would take the printing order. I learned then how power corrupts and ecclesiastical power corrupts worst of all. I was learning that church and state can commit adultery with each other in the name of privilege. I was slowly coming to the realization that there had to be a higher loyalty than accommodation. I began to hope and pray that I would never love my church or my country so indulgently that I would withhold the truth from them. To make matters worse, I sent to the mainland, to Lisbon, to get my handbill printed in which I asked the local priest to give me a chance to tell my part of the story or even to debate me. Few places would let me display the handbill, and no one ever answered my challenge.

I know now that, in that island, I learned a lesson which is still very close to me. Oppression can take many forms; the worst oppressions are those committed in the name of religion and patriotism. There has to be a supreme loyalty by which these lesser loyalties are held in place. I was becoming a citizen of another Kingdom.

And this brings me to the final chapter. In 1968, I accepted a call to the Church of the Pilgrims. Again I had the good fortune of following one of the most able men in the church, Randy Taylor. But 1968 was a year of enormous frustrations.

My generation, if at all honest, must certainly know the temperature and climate of despair. Those of us who came back from the Second World War were not exactly prepared for the kind of world that had come about.

Wearied with two world wars, many of us came back secure in the knowledge that the nation should and would be placed in good hands, that a less cynical generation, with a worldwide point of view and a large dimension of idealism, tested and refined in the fires of modern warfare, would be given the helm of the ship of state.

The General who led us to victory was given the joy of leading us into peace. Our enemies were rehabilitated, our returning soldiers honored and we all began to build a new world! At the beginning of the decade, John Fitzgerald Kennedy came to Washington as President of the United States, and Camelot began to take shape. Pope John XXIIII opened the windows of the Church and a rushing mighty wind filled all the house for the first time in almost four hundred years.

Our youth began a pilgrimage to the uttermost parts of the world, asking what they could do for their new friends, and their number was legion. And we began to reach for the moon.

A King came riding into Washington in the summer of 1963 with his dream and his message of peace. He bore the Christian name of Martin Luther, and on the day when the nation's eyes were focused on the Lincoln Memorial, the crime rate was the lowest Washington, D. C., had ever known.

In the fall, two shots rang out, and the young President died, and our hopes were bruised. I remember the words I spoke to a gathering of citizens at a football stadium in Texas:

My dear fellow citizens:

John F. Kennedy has entered upon the new frontier. He is in the presence of an ancient Pioneer who also spilt His blood upon a street in the glad morning of His youth. Our President is dead. Even now he lies in silence. And yet in death he is more eloquent than in life. He, that wanted to get his country "moving again," has moved us profoundly by his sacrifice. He that asked nothing of his country, gave all to it. An assassin's weapon has robbed us of his vigor, but not of his vision. Hate has triumphed over life, but only briefly, for you cannot assassinate a memory with a spent bullet.

But they were only brave words. We knew something had happened! Hopes began to be frayed. Dynamite exploded in a Birmingham Sunday School class; Selma, Alabama, saw hopes clash with a way of life in which hopes were limited. Watts rioted and Detroit and then on the 4th of April, 1968, another shot rang out in Memphis, Tennessee, and the fires of hell reddened the skies over Washington, D.C. The world in which my parish existed went hysterical. In mid-afternoon came a traffic jam as workers headed for their homes in flight. Then came an incredible emptiness, like the end of something. Along with darkness came looting, burning of buildings, and open anger. Hope was making her exit and wrote one reporter:

"Only the White House shone with imperturbable beauty, a strange island in a sea of madness."

In the meantime, the tragic war in Vietnam kept getting worse and the generals were asking for more soldiers. And as a result, a tired and weary nation, hesitant and faltering, offered up its safest leadership and crowned its mediocrity . . . and in the process the configuration of the nation was defaced by the machinations of its government . . . and we faced the greatest watershed of our brief history.

And the youth of the land, without Camelot, departed into "far countries" looking for themselves. And none of us was left untouched. And the theologians, of all people, were saying God was dead!

In retrospect I have thought that we ought to be grateful for the calamities of our day. They have shattered many illusions which were keeping us from the truth about ourselves. Our deep racial hatred had once again brought us to the edge of violence. Assassinations had revealed that deep flaw in our character so devoted to violence. And the war, the Vietnam war, revealed other things. War does one thing pitilessly: it holds up, before the eyes of the society that is waging it, the essential reality upon which that society is based. It is a cruel mirror. What the Vietnamese mirror showed us was that we had entrusted ourselves to a new belief in power. Watergate became a reflection. Our highest faith now was in the government machine. It had to be defended at all cost, even the cost of coverup. The spirit had been bypassed. It was in a coma! Frustration began to set in, in the national psyche. The nation was suffering the equivalent of an emotional breakdown. It did not know which America it wanted to be—Camelot or Memphis—the America that saw herself in terms of narrow interest and expansionist terms or the America that saw herself in terms of a way of life that would give inspiration to people. The aggressive, assertive concept was dramatically being subjected to challenge by a humbler interpretation of America's greatness. During my years in Washington, with the increasing awareness that the growing military and economic interventions in Central and Latin America were not accidents, the dramatic exposure of the Pentagon papers, and with the confessions of the CIA, I began to see my role more in terms of exposing our sense of self-righteousness, more in terms of the *other* American dream. The one based on power had proved too tempting, too available as a rationalizing cover for the misuse of American power. The challenge we faced then, as now, was a challenge to our self-understanding.

And that is why Vietnam became such a significant watershed in modern American history. For in that conflict America's soul was struggling for self-understanding. For without anyone wanting it, we stumbled into a military confrontation where the issue of what vision would define our actions came to a head. In a moment of uncertainty, tempted to rely upon our overwhelming power rather than upon our intelligence, we succumbed in part to the temptation. Bewildered, unnerved, without any immediate success, we were at the edge of an abyss, the depth of which no one knew, and in this struggle for the soul, we suffered the immolation of the true American spirit. We are still convalescing from that psychological crisis, and the struggle goes on this time in Central America.

And that has been my pilgrimage. It has not been easy. In the process I experienced a tragic, humiliating divorce and the loss of my family. More than once I have been on the verge of despair and repeatedly have lived with a sense of failure and solitude. I have lived without a sense of success or acceptance, and only in the last few months, after marrying a bouyant and strong Christian woman, have I begun to experience some tranquility of the soul. But I have never really felt at home, in any one moment or any one place. As Kazantzakis says, "My journey has been my home." I have committed as much of myself as I could to as much of God as I have discovered along the way. But the thing that has sustained me has been a lesson I learned from the Spanish mystic Miquel Unamuno. "Most men," he wrote once, "are Don Juans about ideas. What we should do is find a large idea, marry her, and set up housekeeping with her." That is what has happened to me. And I have come to the conclusion that, for those of us who love humanity, we must not be satisfied to serve the power of any one nation. We must insist on a larger idea, particularly in this nuclear age. For those of us who have seen that idea in Jesus Christ, we must remember that in the complexity of this modern world, only a tough-minded and resolute determination to think all things through in the light of the revelation of God's purpose, and in the style and love of Jesus Christ will see us through. For the world is too small for anything but love, and too dangerous for anything but truth.

THE MANDATE TO SEEK A JUST PEACE

Edward Leroy Long, Jr.

The world in which we live places an ever-increasing reliance upon the routine possession of military weaponry as a means by which one group keeps another group from having its way. The result is an arms race that creates fear and distrust between the major powers and among all the smaller countries whose fate depends so heavily upon what the major parties do. So accustomed have we become to this state of affairs that we have almost forgotten times when nations kept modest armed forces prepared to defend their own borders against unexpected attacks, but geared up for full scale conflict only when international conditions grew ominous or when a declaration of war required the full-scale pursuit of military campaigns.

While we do not say we are in a state of war—indeed, we sometimes call our involvement in this state of affairs "peace-keeping"—most of the economic priorities and the prevailing psyche of the nations more nearly resemble a state of war than a condition of peace. This situation is further complicated by the fact much of the conflict is also carried on in covert ways—most of which have the earmarks of warfare except for the formal declaration that hostilities exist. Hence it is entirely plausible to suggest that we are living in a warring world and that we are one of the chief participants in the raging conflicts that plague the globe today.

We may also think of ourselves as being in a state of war because we have an identifiable group upon whom we fasten our distrust and against whom we mount our continual hostility. That group has a different political perspective than we do— though curiously its system has been built upon a philosophy set forth by a writer who was reared and lived in the socio-political sphere of which we are a part. Each of the major sides in the present conflict has beliefs and rituals that give it the qualities of a total worldview, in fact, the qualities of a religion—even though, strictly speaking, one professes to be atheistic but has many devout believers in its midst who hold onto their faith at some risk, while the other professes to be religious but is highly secularized and has great segments even of those who profess religion who take their convictions lightly. Each side regards human freedom differently. One stresses the importance of keeping individuals protected from state interference in private lives. The other stresses the importance of being free from

[29]

economic want and is willing to subordinate individual liberty in order to pursue what it believes to be a better way of life.

Each group regards the other as aggressive in seeking to spread its point of view outside of its borders. Each group does things that make the other group apprehensive, things that range from verbal condemnations of the other's way of life to interference in the affairs of countries which have had long and friendly relationships with the other side. Each group sends military aid to smaller sovereignties that will align themselves with it and often works by covert means to support insurgency—insurgency that undermines the political stability of regimes that will not become its puppet. Each group believes that its socio-economic system can counteract and overcome the injustices that are rampant in a world where the rich are very affluent and the poor are very miserable, though one appeals more to the need for freedom from interference by government as the crowning mark of a great society and the other professes a greater concern for the elimination of gross inequities and for the publically arranged alleviation of misery and distress.

Perpetual Conflict

The relationship between these two groups has become one of endemic and perpetual conflict, into which we have slid almost without intending to do so. The conflict is global in its range and all-encompassing in its dimensions. Unlike many previous conflicts it is not confined to one or two identifiable "issues" or points of disagreement. Indeed, it is not merely a military kind of battle that we experience, but a total interaction between political and economic systems. Almost every breach of order that develops in the world, whether in the Middle East, in Southeast Asia, even on a small island off the coast of South America, is seen as but a part of this larger conflict. To be sure, we did not so interpret the brief skirmish that once raged between the French- and English-speaking parts of our neighbor Canada as part of this great conflict, nor the hostilities between Catholic and Protestant parties in Northern Ireland—but otherwise there has hardly been an international altercation or an internal rebellion anywhere in the globe during the last three decades that hasn't been interpreted in terms of the Cold War between two major parties, and responded to accordingly. This has prompted us to scurry, sometimes in overt "policing actions" and more often in covert ways, to every point of friction or possible ignition in the world in the effort to control the outcome of the situation to our advantage. This has been explained and justified as keeping the head domino in a string from falling down and starting the collapse of the whole line. The things we have done in responding to this state of affairs have not been national defense in the traditional sense of warding off attack. They have been national defense only in a more ideological sense of trying to keep a whole world under our influence. We have thus become involved in something like war on a most extensive scale, even though we think of it as keeping peace.

Unlike the traditional concept of war, which thinks in terms of redressing a particular grievance, settling a specific issue in dispute, or overcoming the power of a particular enemy to cause mischief so that both parties can live at peace afterwards, the conflict in which we now find ourselves offers no remedy, no solution, no prospects of termination. We accept it stoically for the long haul and plan to exist this way indefinitely. We make fear the foundation of our existence and hostility the handmaiden of our policies. We have no constructive plan for a future to come after the present tensions are resolved because we do not believe the tensions should be overcome. If we do have a thought about the eventual outcome of all this, it is only that in some way the other side will give up, suffer a tremendous calamity, or disappear from the political scene. There is no talk of establishing justice, no exploration of what might come about to provide something more enduring and enriching for all the children of the earth—merely the intention to keep things at bay in a world that is split apart into two great camps, neither of which believes it is important to learn to live in harmony with the other.

This situation premises no possibility of change, gives no encouragement to those who aspire to better international relations, and overarches the human venture with the lurking suspicion of futility. Moreover, the danger in the present situation is compounded by the fact both sides possess weapons that, if used at all, can destroy the very fabric of civilization itself—not merely to overcome the threats which the other side can pose. This situation affects us deeply. Even our children— those we brag about as being heirs of freedom and blessed with so much opportunity—often lack hope and frequently escape into chemically induced stupors or into lives of narcissistic indulgence. While our leaders tell us we are lucky to have peace—deep in our hearts we know that they are only crying, "Peace, peace, when there is no peace."

This total globalization of conflict is unprecedented. It follows in a series of different postures which America has had as a nation. For many years we manifested an isolationism characterized by a localized concern for our own national destiny. We have come out of that but in a way that has made us a party to conflict and polarization rather than to cooperation and good will in the world. We have become more like a great colossus than a freindly neighbor—feared at least as much as we are respected.

Our Moral Tradition

The moral categories which we have for understanding and dealing with this situation were born of very different circumstances. Terms like just war and international cooperation were generated under less ideological conditions. This adds to our problems, since we are as bankrupt in our ideas for handling the experience of perpetual tension as we are badgered by the difficulties with which it confronts us. Yet, we do have to think about this situation with the moral categories at our disposal. We cannot jump by some Herculean leap out of one framework of moral thinking into another any more than we can escape from our present set of circumstances into a more peaceful world by wishful thinking. We do have to start our reflection about the present situation with those understandings that have been developed about international morality in different circumstances even though such understandings by themselves cannot possibly provide the means for thinking our way through and beyond the present strange kind of conflict in which we find ourselves.

Recognizing that, we will first take note in a brief and cryptic fashion of the different ways in which the Christian community has across the years responded to the problems of conflict and violence in the world. We shall then inquire whether it is possible to extrapolate from that body of reflection a new and creative way of responding to the circumstances into which we have wandered.

The first three centuries of the Christian movement were lived in a situation not altogether dissimilar to the conditions that face us today. The political and social world known to the Christians was a heavily militarized culture marked by the iron rule of Rome over its subject countries. The rule of Rome provided something of a bulwark against barbarism, even though Rome could not identify that barbarism as threatening from one single place, and there was no single great counter-power to challenge the dominance of the Empire. The peace which the rule of Rome offered to the ancient Mediterranean world depended upon the exercise of an unquestionable superiority of military power as the foundation of order.

In this situation the prevalent attitude of the church for the first three centuries was a refusal to be involved in the military operations that maintained the kind of peace offered by Rome. The church remained faithful to an ethic of love and reconciliation in circumstances over which it had little influence. That faithfulness expressed itself as a pacifism that withdrew from participation in the exercise of military office. The early Christians refused to bear arms or to burn incense at Caesar's altar. Tensions between the Christian movement and the Roman authorities resulted—even persecutions. Like every military establishment, Rome was driven to demand conformity to her agenda. Those who would not take part in the violence upon which Rome's exercise of military peacemaking depended were bound to be considered disloyal. Many Christians considered it idolatry, and not merely the violation of an ethical ideal, to be involved in supporting the military enterprise of the Roman state, and they willingly paid the price that was extracted of those who resisted the demands that were made for the performance of military duty.

We do not know what would have been the fate of Western society had the pacifist position of the early Christians remained intact as the main witness of the church. Perhaps the church would have been snuffed out as another fruitless protest against the behavior of the governing authorities. Perhaps a very different kind of Western society would eventually have emerged—a society less dependent upon military coercion as the foundation of its political order. We do know that Constantine extended official recognition to the Christian movement, and thus cajoled a great majority of Christians to participate in the maintenance of the state through the exercise of power. We also know that the pacifist position remained a minority witness in the church throughout the entire history of the West. Perhaps that witness has helped us from ever taking the use of power to be the highest moral norm—to be exercised without qualms and in a mood of complacent arrogance. At least the presence of the pacifist position as a minority witness in the Christian West has kept us from succumbing completely to a view that power is ultimate and treachery commendable in the conduct of political affairs.

There are many Christians today who consider that the only legitimate way of responding to the ever-increasing reliance upon military ways of dealing with the world is to refuse to be a party to that way of ordering international life in the present world. These are the Christians who are active in disarmament movements, who sit down in protest at the entrance gates to factories that manufacture the weapons of death, who withhold some or most of the taxes that are channeled into the support of arms and secret operations, and who protest the panoply of ritualistic nationalism which does so much to keep the whole agenda an object of public adulation. Because our society is more free and democratic than was that of Rome, the persecution such people suffer is somewhat more subtle and less bloody than that experienced by the early Christians—but it is a kind of persecution nevertheless. Alas, the kind of protest they have mounted has no more proven able to dent the policies of present-day rulers than the refusals of the early Christians brought about a change in the behavior of Rome. However, there is always some faint possibility that in a democratic society public protests based on moral convictions can bring about changes in policies.

We do not know all the motives that led the Emperor Constantine to grant official recognition to the church or all the factors that led Christians to accept a new relationship to the Empire. Did the two sides simply get tired of being at loggerheads? Did Constantine believe that acceptance would insure Christian blessing for, rather than opposition to, his policies? Did the Christians come to believe that by controlling the exercise of coercive power they could insure its proper use and thus overcome the problems associated with it? While answers to such questions may ever elude us, we do know some of the moral stances that ensued. In the subsequent life of the church, now a partner rather than a critic and outcast of the empire, at least two different ethics of war attracted the allegiance of the majority of Christians. One of these became manifest some centuries after Constantine, when many Christians felt impelled by a zealous righteousness to go East to free the Holy Land from its Muslim captors. This produced the ethic of the crusade. This ethic reverses the pacifist position. Instead of looking upon war as a contradiction of Christian morality it makes the use of war an instrument for the achievement of a righteous purpose; instead of looking upon military force as a contradiction of the Christian ethic of love, it sees the bravery of the soldier as a noble trait and an instance of exemplary obedience; instead of thinking that the destiny of the church is dependent upon spiritual fidelity and integrity, it assumes that the faith must be defended against all enemies by the same means as the political order defends its life against those who would threaten it. The crusade mentality needs an identifiable enemy—usually one that can be charged with being an infidel or adhering to a false religion rather than merely being a political adversary.

The ethic of the crusade has always been in the side wings of Western history, sneaking out occasionally to coalesce religious fervor with patriotic zeal. For instance, the first world war was fought with the full sanction of religious idealism. Pulpits became recruiting posts; the belief that one decisive onslaught against "the Hun" would make the world safe for democracy was widespread; the settlement that followed was punitive and retributive as it sought to reduce the nation that was considered to have caused the war to abject penitence. Whenever wars are fought in the name of a moralistic idealism, in which the knights of righteousness are pitted against the devils of evil, it is difficult to avoid a crusade mentality.

The ethic of the crusade is still in the wings, ready to pop out under certain conditions to make any conflict into a simple contest between the forces of right-eousness and the forces of evil. It is most likely to come out when the case for a conflict needs ideological bolstering because the strategic circumstances do not in themselves demonstrate the absolute necessity of taking action. The ethic of the crusade is still functional in nationalistic jingoisms that believe everything depends upon the victory of one side—that pits the godly against the godless, the righteous against the demonic, the believers in freedom against the enemies of freedom. In the contemporary situation the ethic of the crusade is most likely to appear in the guise of civil religion or in that type of politically conservative evangelicalism that has been so enamored with individualistic salvation that it has developed little or no sophisticated social sensitivity. Thankfully, the ethic of the crusade has become a thing of the past in the social understanding of most mainline denominations, even as it has been expunged from most scholarly political thinking about the legitimacy of warfare and violence as means of seeking discrete national goals. But that doesn't prevent it from appearing in the body politic.

A crusade ethic is not interested in questions of justice, but rather only in justifying the use of force for the destruction of an enemy. To be sure, every crusader believes that the cause which attracts one's supreme loyalty and demands the supreme sacrifice is a justified cause. But thinking about what is justified in that sense is quite different from thinking about what is just, a fact that becomes far more evident when the teaching of the just war is examined in contrast to the ethic of the crusade.

In contrast to the ethic of the crusade, the tradition of the just war has developed criteria for judging the legitimacy of any particular resort to war. It started as early as the thinking of Saint Augustine and was extended for several centuries until it became a crucial tradition and carefully elaborated position by the time of Saint Thomas Aquinas. It was given even more explicit and sophisticated explication in thinkers such as Francisco de Vitoria in the sixteenth century. The tradition of the just war makes both the decision to engage in war and decisions whether or not to use particular methods in the conduct of war subject to moral scrutiny. Certain clear and potentially decisive criteria have emerged in just war teaching for judging the moral standing of a particular conflict. The decision whether or not to engage in conflict is subject to tests such as the following: Is the proposed action to be taken only after all other means of settling a dispute have been exhausted? Is the action declared by a legitimate political authority? Does the proposed use of military action promise to preserve or enhance a structured order and/or does it contribute to the furthering of a greater justice? Is the war entered with the right attitudes, in the spirit of righting a social wrong and not in a mood of vindictive anger or in the spirit of vengeance? The legitimacy of war is also subject to certain tests about the means by which the conflict will be pursued. Can the means used be kept under moral restraint? Can damage to noncombatants and innocent bystanders be avoided or kept to a minimum? Is the harm likely to be inflicted proportional to the good likely to be achieved? Will the rules of war, for instance, those that call for the fair treatment of war prisoners, be observed? Whereas the ethic of the crusade finds no difficulties with wars that are fought mainly for self-aggrandizement or in an effort to advance one's own cause, the ethic of the just war insists that war is to be used only for the furtherance of a greater justice for all parties concerned, even if one of those parties must be temporarily held in check by the use of force in order to become willing to submit to the conditions that make for that greater justice.

As a matter of practice, just war teaching has been far more elaborate in theory than functional in practice. Until quite recently, its main use was to legitimize rather than to curtail conflicts. For centuries there were few, if any, instances when the teaching of the church about just war had the practical consequences of actually preventing a conflict from beginning or of bringing any conflict that was seen to violate the moral criteria to a halt. Yet, the framework of scrutiny and judgment that was developed has always carried with it the possibility that at some particular time it would be employed to judge a war morally unacceptable.

The failure of just war teaching to exercise controlling judgments over the actual conduct of war was evident right up through the second world war. The saturation bombing of major cities that was carried out in that war could easily have been seen as stretching just war teaching beyond its elastic limit, yet few Christian voices were raised to say so. The idea of demanding an "unconditional surrender"—which robs an enemy of any hope of remaining an autonomous agent ready to act justly under conditions of defeat—was hardly the stuff of which a just war is made. The use of an atomic bomb—indeed two atomic bombs—against centers of civilian population was an act that was premised on the maximization of terror as the stuff of warfare rather than on just war standards of what is legitimate in military operations. Except for those with pacifist convictions such things were generally accepted as the terrible price of engaging in war under modern conditions. But they also constituted actions that prompted the whole world to conclude that there are no restraints on what nations—even the professedly peace-loving nations—will do for victory once they have entered a war. The legacy of "total war"—that is, war that is pursued without any moral restraints—is very much a part of what makes the present situation with which we have to deal so vexing. It is difficult to commend a set of moral restraints to nations that still have vivid memories of a war in which all such restraints were treated as subordinate to the achievement of victory by all the parties involved.

Much rethinking has occurred since the victories produced in Europe and Japan by the conduct of war according to those premises. Less by intention than by revulsion, the experience in Vietnam has caused a deep seated re-examination of the conduct of war. The disproportion between the depth of the destruction and the paucity of the political objectives attained raised the problem of proportionality in stark terms. It seemed senseless to hurl quantities of Agent Orange at forests and napalm at helpless people when the political situation remained as unresolved and tenuous as it did in those circumstances. Not everyone used the technical jargon to analyze the situation. Many were simply revolted by the carnage. But, for one of the few times in Western history, the phrase "unjust war" became a functional element in actually prompting one side to withdraw from a conflict.

It would be overly sanguine to suppose the moral lessons of that experience have penetrated deeply into the consciousness of the nation. There are still those who feel that if only we had—crusade-like—escalated the bombardment we would have avoided the need to give up the fight. They will argue that all we needed to do was to unleash the military without restraints. On the other side, there are those who realize that the Vietnam conflict showed us the fruitlessness of military operations, however technologically massive, that are conducted without the context of a political system that can make the success of those operations a source of some viable public system of justice and order. A war cannot be just if it merely destroys evil. It can only be just if it brings about the possibility of positive achievements.

The second development that has caused a re-examination of the pertinence of just war teaching has been the ever-increasing potential for destruction embodied in nuclear weapons. The nuclear arms race has raised the stakes in starting a conflict to the point where almost everything that constitutes the basis of civilized order may be destroyed in the initial interchanges between two parties. The Roman Catholic bishops have seen this fact very clearly, and their pastoral latter of May 3, 1983, entitled *The Challenge of Peace: God's Promise and Our Response,* has pointed to the moral problem with utmost urgency. Can any war fought with nuclear weapons ever be just? Can deterrence that is based upon the intention to use nuclear weapons for the purpose of keeping others from using such weapons ever be morally justified, except perhaps on a very temporary and provisional basis? While the nuclear arms race is less easy to sense as a danger than the violence and horror of jungle warfare when pictured on a television tube, the problems it poses for the morality of the just war may be even more momentous.

If the direction taken by military strategy in Vietnam was a portent of the futility that will be encountered in all counter-insurgency operations carried on against peoples whose social context is different from ours, and if the nuclear arms race demonstrates a predicament into which all schemes of deterrence will fall if they seek merely to maximize the threat of destruction, then just war thinking has come to the limits of its contributions to our understanding of the morality of conflict. Under such conditions war can never be an act of justice in a sense that warrants continued confidence in its moral legitimacy. Perhaps a deliberate effort to revert to the use of conventional weaponry to make discrete and controllable strategies possible might give some additional life to the belief that war can be justly conducted, but as long as we are faced with the kinds of developments which have marked recent history the need for new modes of thinking becomes imperative.

The Just Peace

Most of the thinking that has just been reviewed deals with the kind of responses that have to be made after discontent and conflict have intensified to the point where hostilities have broken out or where nations have amassed great capacities to destroy others. This is the case whether the moral outlook is one that holds war must be repudiated, that argues war pursued vigorously enough can be an instrument for insuring the triumph of righteousness, or that war may be used in the service of justice if it can be kept in moral bounds. All thinking about war comes into play after the social and political situation is allowed to deteriorate and war seems to be the only possible outcome. Even just war teaching, which is profoundly concerned about justice, conceives of justice as something that gets established by the legitimate and proper exercise of force for curbing wrong behavior.

The passion of the political realist to emphasize the need to keep potential evildoers in check by the mounting of a credible capacity to destroy them utterly does not need to be augmented in our age. Perhaps that was required in a time when the society was more isolationist and religious impulses were more pacifist. Reinhold Niebuhr thought so and wrote his pivotal book *Moral Man and Immoral Society* (Charles Scribner's Sons, 1932). But even in that book, which argues so strongly for taking power seriously in dealing with the relationships between nations, Niebuhr warned against making coercion, self-assertion, and conflict into the only guides to action. As Niebuhr phrased it:

A too consistent political realism would seem to consign society to perpetual warfare. If social cohesion is impossible without coercion, and coercion is impossible without the creation of social injustice, and the destruction of injustice is impossible without the use of further coercion, are we not in an endless cycle of social conflict? If self-interest cannot be checked without the assertion of conflicting self-interests how are the counter-claims to be prevented from becoming inordinate? And if power is needed to destroy power, how is this new power to be made ethical? If the mistrust of political realism in the potency of rational and moral factors in society is carried far enough, an uneasy balance of power would seem to be the highest goal to which society could aspire. If such an uneasy equilibrium of social forces should result in a tentative social peace or armistice it would be fairly certain that some fortuitous dislocation of the proportions of power would ultimately destroy it. Even if such dislocation should not take place, it would probably be destroyed in the long run by the social animosities which balance of power creates and accentuates.

[And then there follows this observation which Niebuhr made of the world condition at the time he wrote his book, but which we might reiterate about the world condition in our time, perhaps with some different nuances in reporting the details but with even greater cogency as to the diagnosis of the predicament.]

The last three decades of world history would seem to be a perfect and tragic symbol of the consequences of this kind of realism, with its abortive efforts to resolve conflict by conflict. The peace before the War was an armistice maintained by the balance of power. It was destroyed by the spontaneous combustion of the mutual fears and animosities which it created. The new peace is no less a coerced peace; only the equilibrium of social and political forces is less balanced than it was before the War. The nations which pretended to fight against the principle of militarism have increased their military power, and the momentary peace which their power maintains is certain to be destroyed by the resentments which their power creates. (p. 231f)

We must find a quite different way of dealing with human affairs than the one that governs the present policy making of the nations. Such a new outlook will start with a premise that justice is a social condition that contributes to harmony and order, that justice is less the system of restraints imposed by force than the condition of social well-being that makes conflict less likely to occur. Such a different way of thinking might be called the doctrine of a just peace. It directs attention to the needs, hopes, and aspirations of people, and is concerned to think how their needs can be cared for, their personhoods and communities respected, and their liberties cherished. In peace thinking, justice becomes the means of eliminating conflict before it erupts, of avoiding the conditions that lead to rancor and hostility if allowed to go uncorrected.

There is afoot in our time, not least among thoughtful Christians, a still embryonic realization that such an innovative way of thinking is sorely needed. For instance, in 1975 the General Assembly of the Church of Scotland declared that the doctrine of the just war is no longer relevant to our modern situation. A group of Scottish Christians, concerned to affirm something positive rather than merely reject something inadequate, met together to develop their thinking about the nature of a just peace. The results of their work were summarized by Peter Matheson and published in 1979 under the title *Profile of Love* by the Christian Journals Limited of Belfast, Ireland, and in 1981 under the title *A Just Peace* by Friendship Press of New York. While much of this reflection is better related to the situation in the British Isles, the model provided by the effort is one that American Christians ought to be taking seriously. Repudiating the debates between pacifist and non-pacifist as useless, the report of this group called for a new effort to think about how to achieve peace.

The spirit in which the British group sets forth that agenda is reflected in this quotation from its report:

Peace *is* within our grasp, and our greatest stumbling-block lies not in the vested interests in war and violence—massive as they are—but in the soft-centeredness of our own concept of peace. "Just leave us in peace", is the instinctive reaction of most of us, most of the time, when disasters loom. We just want to be left alone, to be left 'in peace'. This is only human and very often understandable.

The Christian analysis of reality, however, and the Christian hope offer us a potent antidote to this soft-centered concept of peace. They help us to see that peace is indivisible, that we, in our small and shrinking world, cannot buy our peace at the cost of the wretchedness of others. For the Bible peace and righteousness walk hand in hand. We will have to invite our neighbours in the Second World of Communism, and the Third World of the developing nations, and the Fourth World of urban deprivation in the West, to come together with us in the global village council and work out a *just peace*. We inhabit a grotesquely unjust world. Unless we redress its imbalances, peace will slip out of our grasp again. (p. 14)

Closer to home, though also speaking from a Reformed church perspective, Nicholas Wolterstorff has provided an extensive exploration of what is entailed in bringing peace and justice together. In his book *Until Justice and Peace Embrace* (Erdmann's, 1981), he speaks about the conditions of *shalom*—the biblical vision of the blessed life. Shalom is based upon the creation of right relationships—right relationships between people and God as their ultimate source of meaning and hope, right relationships between human beings in their communities, and right relationships between human beings and nature. All these relationships must be just, that is, they must be righteous and harmonious, before we can expect human life to become what it has been destined to be in the purposes of God. The divine mandate involves both the impulse to utilize the benefits of the created world for human well-being and the mandate to loose the chains of injustice that oppress the disadvantaged around us. To ignore either mandate is to undercut the possibility of peace.

The Mennonite leader, Maynard Shelly, in his book *New Call for Peacemakers* (Faith and Life Press, 1979) elaborates on the many ways in which Christians must repudiate violence but also work for social and economic justice all over the globe. He sums up his observations by suggesting that "dismantling the demonic establishment of militarism will be of little value if the causes of war in human need and injustice are not overcome." (p. 68) Frederick Herzog underscores the contributions of the United Church of Christ to this same chorus. In *Justice Church: The New Function of the Church in North American Christianity* (Orbis Books, 1981) he explores the 1978 statement of a study group of the church which emphasized God's justice and the need of the church to be a people that is "called in covenant to join God's struggle for the new age of justice." The Roman Catholic bishops, in their pastoral letter on nuclear weapons, quoted with approval these words from Pople Paul VI: "Peace cannot be limited to a mere absence of war, the result of an ever precarious balance of forces. No, peace is something built up day after day, in the pursuit of an order intended by God, which implies a more perfect form of justice among men and women." (Paragraph 234b) A key consultation held in Baden, Austria, in 1970, which brought together representatives from both the World Council of Churches and the Pontifical Commission on Justice and Peace, put the same truth this way: "Peace is . . . inseparable from the achievement of justice in human life, provided that justice is understood in the Biblical sense, not as the administration of a set system of laws but as the activity of God, raising up the poor and outcast, vindicating the victims of oppression and saving men from their sins for new life with each other and with him. Justice means the establish-

ment of the disadvantaged in the full rights and possibilities of their humanity."
(Peace: The Desperate Imperative, p. 9) Members of the Presbyterian Church will
find all these ideas gathered together in a forceful overview in the position paper
approved by the General Assembly and issued in 1980 under the title, *Peacemaking: The Believers' Calling.*

To be sure, a just peace will not consist merely of justice, however important
justice is to its establishment. There must be candor and integrity—the very antithesis of the covert intrigue and clandestine operations that have become the stock and
trade of modern nations in their pursuit of power and advantage over each other.
There must be patience with those who do not always behave in the best of ways;
there must be a willingness to sacrifice as much to enable people to live together in
harmony as there has been a willingness to make sacrifices to obtain victory in war.
There must be compassion toward those in need. There must be a renewed cultivation of sophisticated diplomacy and international statecraft. Christians who are
concerned about a just peace must become as vigilant as sentinals on military duty,
as brave as the stoutest warrior, and as dedicated to the task as the most devoted
soldier. They must call up short the truculence and bombast with which the leaders
of the nations perpetuate the condition of hostility by which we find ourselves
surrounded.

American Christians have the task of becoming better informed and increasingly critical of the tragic contradictions between the professed ideals of their nation and its actual record in world affairs. We profess to be a nation of law and an
advocate of the rule of law in human relations, but in 1982 we sided with only four
other countries of the world in refusing to agree to the Law of the Sea Treaty. We
profess to be defenders of human rights, but have yet to ratify either of the covenants designed by the United Nations to further the implementation of human rights
around the globe. We profess to be humanitarian but we lead a small minority of
industrial countries that refuses to negotiate seriously on the demands of the Third
World for a new international economic order; we profess to believe in international cooperation but we threaten to withdraw our financial support from international bodies that take positions we do not approve; we profess to believe in the
adjudication of issues by courts of law, but announce in advance that we will not
even accede that the World Court has the jurisdiction to condemn a military move
we might make in Central America. These are not the postures of which just peace
can be made and until our attitudes are changed our record will not be one that
inspires the nations to seek peace.

In the course of this paper we observed that Christian teaching about the just
war was not particularly effective in stemming the tide of crusade-like behavior in
the nations. Perhaps a Christian understanding of the demands to seek a just peace
will be no more effective against the massive pressures of a world in which all sides
believe themselves dependent upon the techniques of war as the only means of
seeking survival. But that does not abrogate the calling to advocate just peace as the
essence of discipleship, for Christians were never called to be successful if that
required apostasy of their deepest convictions. Perhaps peacemaking cannot be

successful in any nation at the present time. Perhaps Christians will need to disassociate themselves from their societies in order to make a witness of last resort against a culture that contradicts so much they believe is right. But if any hope of transformation, any significant possibility of the redemption of the world is to be kept alive, then it will be important to seek a peace with justice with every resource at our command, and with a love which does not let the world go to ruin in the destructiveness of its own folly.

The Enemy

WHAT ABOUT THE RUSSIANS?

Robert F. Smylie

"What about the Russians?" "What about the Russians?" The question is heard at every turn. Is the issue disarmament? The response is: "What about the Russians?" Is the concern human rights? The response is: "What about the Russians?" Is there anxiety about the future of the Third World? The response is: "What about the Russians?"

Who are these people who dominate our thinking? What is their country like? What is their history? What are their concerns and anxieties? Are they human or demonic? What has been the relationship of the United States to their country? Why are we locked in conflict? Are Americans partly afraid because we cannot answer these questions?

The questions are important, and though there are many other world/global forces and problems, none appears as dominant as this. The confrontation between the United States and the Soviet Union—often put as the conflict between the superpowers—shapes or sets the context for almost every other issue. Indeed, many world problems reflect or are by-products of the bipolarization implicit in this confrontation. Looked at in a different way, the resolution of many global issues is impossible without the full cooperation of both powers. In this sense, the power and greatness of the Soviet Union cannot be isolated, ignored or irradicated without peril to all.

Some observers state the question differently. For them the issue is "What about the Communists?" For these people this question is the same as that of the power and greatness of Russia. It is the contention of this presentation that that is another matter with its own implications. Communism is an ideology, complex in statement, diverse in application. Discussion of Communism usually generates more heat than light. The Soviet Union is a great country with great power and extensive influence. Obviously it has ideological influences and complex value patterns. But it is the country and not simply the ideology that we deal with.

In gospel terms there is a dividing wall of hostility between the United States and the Soviet Union. In psychological terms, "they" are the enemy. What then do we do with the biblical injunctions that tell us peace has to do with breaking down

[45]

dividing walls, that remind us that discipleship has to do with loving our enemies?

What follows are some reflections on the subject: "What about the Russians?" These are presented as a series of propositions designed to stimulate rethinking United States-Soviet relations. This discussion is meant to be suggestive, *not* definitive.

I. Three Worldviews

PROPOSITION: *Our worldview is influenced by three dominant perceptions: Machiavellianism, Manichaeanism and Statism.*

These shape our thinking in general and, subsequently, our perception of the Soviet Union. The first two are political. The third is a very practical matter.

First, we Americans tend to be Machiavellian, that is, we see power as the primary social value. Relationships are determined in terms of power, and our goal is to maximize power. Since the most obvious form of power is military, we have tended to militarize all other values and assume that we can resolve most of the world's problems with militaristic responses.

Second, we Americans tend to be Manichaean. Manichaeanism is an expression of dualism wherein everything is seen in terms of good and/or evil, black and/or white. We see this dualism as characterizing human relations in our world. The implications of this are numerous for our own life and our understanding of the Soviet Union. The historic "isolationism" of the United States was rationalized because we did not want to be involved in an evil world. Leaving the European evils behind, and using the protection of two oceans, Americans thought they could do what God wanted: build a new Jerusalem, a new Israel, a paradise in the wilderness. Consequently, in all our historic conflicts we have perceived ourselves as good.

The near genocidal treatment of the Indians (Native Americans), the enslavement of the Blacks for two centuries, the importation of Chinese to build railroads, and our imperial ventures in Puerto Rico and the Philippines have hardly dimmed this view. We have viewed the rest of the world with suspicion. This kind of thinking lends itself to a bipolar view, which is expressed in U.S.-Soviet relations. What the Soviet Union does is evil. What we do is good. Simple!

For a long time this kind of a worldview led the United States to tell the rest of the world, particularly developing Third World countries, that they had to choose sides. If you are not on our side, you are obviously with "them." This style of thinking has shaped our anticommunist rhetoric, ideology and policy. It has shaped the way we view war in terms of total victory (or unconditional surrender). It also tempts us to flirt with total annihilation. It is the basis for the aphorism "better dead than red." The concept of "limited war" cannot convey the absoluteness of the conflict between good and evil.

An irresistible illustration will bear out this point. The Undersecretary of State for Security Assistance concluded an address to the Aerospace Industries Association about arms transfer and the national interest as follows:

> We [the United States] are the last best folk on Earth; and we have no responsible choice but to act accordingly.

I know that conservatives are often accused of being simplistic; and as a self-confessed, card-carrying member of that fraternity, I might as well confess that I harbor the simplistic notion that on the world's stage today it is possible to divide the principal actors between the good guys and the bad guys; and we might as well understand that the bad guys are serious and playing for keeps.

A few years ago that great American philosopher, Leo Durocher, made the observation that good guys finish last. It is the intention of this Administration to prove him wrong. *(Current Policy,* Number 279, May 21, 1981)

What does that kind of thinking do for world peace?

The third conception is of a different nature. We take it for granted that the nation-state system is the dominant political form in our world, both for the organization of power and the organization of conflict. The nation-state system embodies the concept of national sovereignty; the nation-state is responsible only to and for itself. The key concerns of nation-states are power, interest and security. Ideology may influence these considerations but seldom displaces them. As power is thought of most frequently in military terms, the concept of national sovereignty has provided the foundation of modern military structures. A country wants a military establishment strong enough to preserve internal order in case of rebellion, to protect itself from aggressive actions abroad, and to project itself abroad in order to protect vital interests. In itself, this is never enough. A country also needs an economy that is strong, healthy and capable of growing with a growing population and its needs. A country needs skilled diplomacy to protect its interests in the give-and-take of international negotiations where political agreements are reached. While it is obvious to see and justify such needs as we reflect on our own society, it is often only grudgingly that we understand that other countries, including the Soviet Union, may be operating with the same basic premises about the nation-state system.

II. An Interdependent World

PROPOSITION; *We live in an interdependent world.*

Interdependence has several dimensions. For Christians, interdependence is theological in its origins and is an integral, though distorted, part of our Christian tradition. We believe the world was created and is sustained by God. We believe that Jesus the Christ came to save the whole world, not just part of it. The essential nature of the church throughout its history is ecumenical. It is worldwide in nature, transcending political and economic barriers.

In practical terms we are increasingly aware of the interdependence of the world, politically, economically and culturally. This becomes more evident with worldwide instantaneous communication. We know, or think we know, what occurs in Moscow, Baghdad or Beijing at the switch of the television set. Air travel makes all major parts of the world reasonably accessible and potentially vulnerable. At the turn of the previous century something could happen in Russia and we would not know of it until long after the event. Modern telecommunication has changed the character of international relations and responsibility.

We are also growing increasingly interdependent in economic terms. U.S. dependency on trade, raw materials, etc., including oil for energy, shapes our attitudes and relationships around the world. Growing trade difficulties and the necessity to maintain our balance of payments in times of inflation, unemployment and high oil prices increase our anxiety. The "practical" dimensions of our interdependent world are also seen in the growth of both functional and political international organizations. The United Nations umbrella covers about eighty different international organizations necessary to help regulate, manage and solve problems with global implications. In many of these organizations the United States is a full cooperating partner with the Soviet Union.

Finally, our interdependence takes on a sobering, eschatological form. Because of the development of nuclear weapons we share with others the possibility of global annihilation, having "progressed" beyond the capacity of genocide to omnicide. In the event of a major nuclear war the whole world would be affected. This interdependence of annihilation must be faced and understood.

What does interdependence mean in terms of U.S.-Soviet relations? It means that we have the choice of competing and/or cooperating with the Soviet Union in this interdependent world but that we do not have any chance to live in isolation. We share the temptation to control and destroy the other, but no such chance exists without risking the destruction of the interdependent world.

It should be noted that interdependence is probably seen by more Americans as a threat than as an opportunity. The sense of vulnerability to the perceived whims of OPEC, and the rhetoric that the emergence of a Marxist-Leninist regime anywhere in the world directly threatens U.S. interests, particularly during times of economic unrest, give us the feeling that we have lost control. Soviet reluctance to play a more creative role in world affairs reflects its own paranoia. In fact, neither society is prepared for interdependence intellectually or psychologically. How long will the common human fears of the unknown, of freedom, of change keep us from creative response to the possibilities of global community?

III. A Revolutionary World

PROPOSITION: *We live in a revolutionary world.*

What is meant by "a revolutionary world"? Simply that massive political, economic, technological and social change is occurring in Africa, Latin America, Asia, Europe and even in our own society. The processes of change are continuous, unavoidable without repression, and frequently unnerving. The world, since 1945, has seen the breakup of the historic empires of Britain, France, the Netherlands, Spain and Portugal. A hundred new states have come into existence. While political revolution has been successful, many of these new countries are still wrestling with the socio-economic revolution. In areas where the colonial or imperial power vehemently opposed independence, liberation movements often turned to the socialist countries for assistance. The economic revolution from subsistence or colonially-dependent colonies has been uneven—often regressive—and shaped by a multitude of factors including the question of reasonable economic viability in some of the smaller societies.

[48]

The knowledge explosion most often seen in technological terms, breaking down earlier limits of activity, creates revolutionary scenarios for humanity's future while at the same time widening the socio-economic power gaps between those who are able to participate in the activity and those who are marginalized.

The religious revolution has also set in motion dynamic changes that will not be ended soon, such as the militant resurgence of traditional religions—often linked with aggressive nationalism—in the Middle East and in Asia.

We have to learn better how to live and adjust in this changing world. Some of our problems in the United States flow from our failure to understand the revolutionary nature of our time. This is partly because we fail to understand the original revolutionary nature of our own society. Our revolutionary history has impacted the rest of the world. Therefore our constant counter-revolutionary response to contemporary revolutions is often justly considered inappropriate. Too often we oppose change by supporting repressive regimes, thus increasing militarization, violence and counter-violence. Only if change can be manipulated for our own self-interest do we help bring it about.

On the other hand the Soviet Union appears to other countries to be supportive of their revolutionary efforts to free themselves from colonial rule or economic dominance. Because the United States has taken the reactionary role, in the view of many Third World countries, the Soviet Union has been regarded as the primary revolutionary force in the world. Indeed, the U.S. tends to react as if every revolution bears the label: "Made in Moscow."

IV. The Largest Country in the World

PROPOSITION: *The Soviet Union is a big country; its "bigness" helps shape its role in the world and how we respond to it.*

In simple terms this land mass, which extends from Central Europe to the Pacific Ocean, contains over 8.5 million square miles. It stretches for 5,500 miles from one end to the other, and its widest point, from north to south, is over 2,700 miles. Indeed, containing one-sixth of the land mass of the world, it is the largest country. New York is closer to Moscow than Moscow is to Velen, the Soviet's eastern-most city. The United States has four continental time zones; the Soviet Union stretches across twelve time zones.

Two-hundred-sixty-million people live in that land, the third largest single population in the world. Its composition includes twenty-two major ethnic groups, with sixteen major languages. Two important religious traditions govern the spiritual life of the people. One is the Russian Orthodox Church. What most Americans do not realize is that there are somewhere between 40 and 50 million Islamic people who live in the southern tier of Soviet republics, a fact that may dominate the future of the Soviet Union.

For the most part we also do not realize the limited usefulness of this huge land mass. Only 15 percent is suitable for agricultural purposes, partly because a good portion of it is frozen year-round. If you look at the globe, most of the land mass of the Soviet Union lies in the same zones as Canada and Alaska. Therefore, Soviet agricultural problems are not only bureaucratic but also geographic in nature. On the other hand, the land contains vast mineral resources. The Soviet Union, by some estimates, is the world's largest oil producer. It has abundant natural gas, iron and coal. It is also the world's largest producer of manganese and chromium, the second largest producer of gold, and produces around 12 percent of the world's copper.

One other geopolitical fact must be noted. The Soviet Union has eleven contiguous neighbors with which it must cope plus many other near neighbors. The United States is fortunate because it has only two: Canada to the north and Mexico to the south. But the Soviet Union, in its own short life, has had struggles with most of its eleven neighbors. This reflects the Soviets' inheritance from the longer history of Russia. The U.S.S.R. has struggled with China. It has had centuries of war with Turkey. The European portion of the Soviet Union has been overrun numerous times by European invaders, partly because there are few natural geographical barriers preventing land invasion from Europe. The geography of the country provides the rationale for extensive defense forces.

This fourth proposition has obvious implications. The Soviet Union is a big place. Its "bigness" provides the source of its strength but also contributes to its major problems. It is indeed one of the world's great countries and has legitimate economic, psychological and security needs. We need to recognize and accept that.

V. Common Traditions

PROPOSITION: *The United States and the Soviet Union have more in common than our ideological rhetoric would allow us to accept.*

Both societies are deeply rooted in Christian civilization. The question of whether Marxism is a Christian heresy must be addressed elsewhere. The fact is that Russian history is inseparable from the history of the Russian Orthodox Church. This Orthodoxy still persists among the people and deeply influences their culture and their lives. The faith and traditions are very much alive. Religion is not simply something of the older generations that will die when they die.

Both political systems were born in revolution. The revolutions, however, were different. America's revolution was fought against an absentee master, namely the British empire. Much of its social revolution had taken place before the political revolution occurred. Therefore the revolutionary experience in the United States was quickly consolidated. In contrast, the Soviet revolution was against an authoritarian system with power reaching into every aspect and structure of Russian society—including the church. Therefore, a costly civil war delayed consolidation. The results were devastating and long-lasting. The United States experienced a successful revolution but seems to have abandoned its revolutionary heritage. The Soviet Union has not completed its own revolution but still seeks to project its revolution around the world.

Both countries have long traditions of isolation. The roots of American isolation have already been mentioned. For a century and a half we thought that we were living apart from the world. We benefited from flows of people, capital and goods. We expanded across and beyond the continental bounds, but somehow we thought that we stood alone. Russian history also has been isolated but often through ostracism rather than by choice.

Both countries are pluralistic. Americans, however, have been conditioned to think of the Soviet Union as a monolithic society. Still, no two other countries in the world have such incredible ethnic and racial mixtures. The United States has absorbed different populations, having difficulty primarily where race has been involved. Various ethnic groups have been merged, in time, into our Anglo-Saxon melting pot, that is, into a system dominated by the English language and English political traditions. This provides a veneer over the rich pluralism of the population. The Soviet Union has generally perpetuated ethnic differences. The various republics have largely preserved their languages and cultural heritages. On the whole, though, one might submit that neither society has successfully coped with problems of disaffected minorities.

Both societies have pluralistic political systems: the U.S. has states, the U.S.S.R. has republics. Both also have a party system. The formal governmental structures are organized at every level. Representation occurs up to the highest governing bodies of the land. The party systems differ, but even "one party" systems have their own internal dynamics (as our Southern tradition should have taught us). Obviously, end results differ.

Both societies are secular in their orientations despite deep religious traditions. Materialistic goals are mixed with idealistic goals. Soviet secularism has been shaped by an ideological atheism that has evolved as a reaction to the centuries of the Orthodox Church's linkage with Czarist oppression. While the U.S. has linked Christianity with the free enterprise system and democracy, a secular consumerism and militant nationalism have become our actual dominant modes of thought.

Both countries are addicted to nuclear weapons. Each appears committed to the mutually reinforcing thesis that the only thing the other side understands is *force*.

One hardly has to add, in this context, that both sides are vulnerable. Neither side can protect itself from the devastation of all-out nuclear war. Both countries also seem to need external enemies to justify their behavior patterns. That is, as long as one country perceives and maintains another as its enemy, it can justify near-limitless national sacrifices, as in domestic spending and projects for "defense" purposes.

VI. Historic Differences

PROPOSITION: *There are commonalities, but there are also major historic differences between the United States and the Soviet Union.*

The United States never had a feudal past but it *did* have a slave past. The Soviet Union never had a colonial past while the United States did. The United States, for over a hundred years, has generally had friendly neighbors and therefore "open" borders. The Soviet Union for most of its history, has had hostile neighbors and therefore insecure borders.

The impact of World Wars I and II differed greatly in each, despite the fact that in both wars both countries shared the same enemy. In World War I Russia was disgraced, devastated and dismembered. In World War I, for the first time, the United States tested its virility in the world arena and came away proud, if not arrogant, and sure that it had won the war in Europe. Following World War I, the United States led the way toward diplomatically isolating the new Bolshevik government that had come to power in the 1917 Russian revolution.

The United States emerged from World War II with its homeland undamaged, a booming economy, and the sole posssessor of the atomic bomb. The Soviet Union, also a "victor" in that war, lay in ruins. Over twenty million Russians had been killed. A monument on the highway just outside Moscow symbolizes the tank barriers that finally prevented the German tanks from reaching the Kremlin wall. The war's devastation included the destruction of 30,000 factories, 13,000 railroad bridges and 137,000 tractors. One-half of the coal and steel production had been ruined. Victory was costly indeed, and the horrifying memories are still a fundamental emotional reality to the survivors and the general Soviet perspective on war. Underscoring the differences in experience, the United States within a few years helped rearm West Germany.

VII. The Russian Struggle for Security

PROPOSITION: *Russian-Soviet history has been characterized by a struggle for security.*

Russia has struggled for survival and security. Created in the ashes of World War I, the Soviet Union questionably may never have felt (or been) secure. The Soviets know full well the devastation of war. They have never known the sense of secure borders. Western Europe has always been hostile and has been the launching ground for major invasions. China has been an historic enemy. The border is long and porous. If one looks at the distribution of Soviet troops, one finds that a large percentage of their troops are dispersed along the Chinese border. As China strengthens its position economically, its likelihood of becoming a superpower increases. This creates, for the U.S.S.R., the need to divide its defense resources between its *two* fronts, west and south.

The Soviets are also vulnerable to devastating missle attack from each leg of the United States' triad system. One Trident submarine carries enough power to destroy every Soviet city of over 100,000 people. That is only *one* Trident submarine and the Navy is planning the construction of a fleet of some eight Tridents! The Soviets know that there is no way they can prevent this kind of threat, and their ability to destroy us does not diminish that anxiety.

Their insecurity has other roots as well. The Eastern European countries, members of the Warsaw Pact and COMECON, are basically unreliable in a crisis situation. For thirty-five years these countries have been restless to the point of revolting against Soviet dominance. This only serves to increase the vulnerability of the Soviet Union. We are witnessing this tension in Poland today. Further anxiety is generated by the Islamic fervor which infects several neighbors bordering the Soviet Union. The United States has viewed the Islamic revolution in Iran as a threat to its interests. Fifty million Soviet Muslims might be infected by that Islamic resurgence if it spilled over the border into five or six of the republics. It could help instigate a break-up of the Soviet Union and is a threat to its interests. Internally, there also exists a social insecurity in the U.S.S.R. because of its inability to satisfy the expanding desires and needs of its own people and those of its Eastern European partners. The greater population remains constantly dissatisfied with its circumstances over which they have little control.

Understanding this constant insecurity, both internal and external, might help Americans comprehend the Soviet Union and its patterns of behavior.

VIII. The Struggle for Economic Development

PROPOSITION: *Soviet history has been characterized by a struggle for economic modernization.*

The Soviet Union's second major struggle has been for economic development. Russia was in the early stages of industrialization when the Soviet Union was formed. Since then, its history has been marked by an incredible effort to catch up and complete the modernization process. In this it has had the United States as a stimulus.

Economic modernization involves the application of scientific, technological and managerial knowledge to the productive system of a society. It has to do with the way the factors of production (resources of land and raw materials, labor, capital, knowledge, etc.) are organized in order to increase the productive capacity of the society. The quality, quantity and mobility of those factors establish some of the parameters for the economic process. Motivation and values establish others.

Economic modernization requires capital formation, which means the ability to transfer resources from patterns of consumption to productive use, i.e. increasing the capacity to produce more goods.

The primary economic-political decision in the Soviet Union was probably influenced as much by Russian autocratic history as by communist economic analysis. The Soviet Union adopted an "economic command" model. Two basic patterns followed: the first pattern involved *centralized* planning regarding the allocation and use of the factors of production. In the Soviet case, there is a central authority, currently working through a series of five-year plans to determine what is to be produced, how much, and how it is to be distributed. The second pattern involved *state* ownership of the major/basic means of production. In this pattern the state also became the primary source/agent for the accumulation of capital.

Other crucial decisions followed in Soviet economic development. First, priority was given to investment in the industrial or capital goods sector—that which was perceived as necessary for subsequent economic growth. This involves the ability to extract raw materials from nature, to transform them into primary/capital goods, e.g., factories, machinery, energy and the basic infrastructures of transportation and utilities.

Second, the primary source of capital formation was to be, perhaps of necessity, based on internal sources. It was accomplished through expropriation of private wealth, and through control of wages and prices whereby resources were and have been withheld from consumption for capital investment. Through selective development, and through the exploitation of natural resources, wealth was accumulated which could then be invested as the central planners determined. Unlike early modernization in the United States and contemporary developing countries, little capital was available to the Soviets from external resources (either through loans, investment, grants or surplus from trade).

Third, the agricultural sector was initially both neglected and exploited. Wealth was extracted from the agricultural sector, prices were controlled, income limited and new investment was almost non-existent.

The Soviet Union's agricultural sector is an enigma. There is a larger area of arable land than in the United States, yet it is a smaller percentage of total land. The productivity of the arable land is limited by numerous factors: insufficient rainfall, shorter growing seasons, for example. Therefore, Soviet land has not been as productive as land in the United States.

The organization of the agricultural sector involves a combination of state farms (20,800) and collective farms (26,000). A large percentage of the population is engaged in agricultural pursuits (26 million in the Soviet Union versus 3.7 million in the U.S.). The same central planning system also sets the goals for the agricultural sector.

Little attempt was made in the early decades to modernize the agricultural sector through mechanization, fertilization, irrigation and scientific research. Certain aspects of central planning have proven totally inappropriate for efficient agricultural production, and recent attempts to improve agricultural output have proven inadequate. Thus, whether massive investment or extensive reform will change the picture is unknown.

Fourth, the Soviet Union has made the decision that it will allocate as much of its economic resources as necessary to attain and maintain military strength and capacity sufficient at least to keep it on a par with the United States. This has been accomplished by depriving the Soviet consumers of additional personal benefits beyond the meeting of essential basic needs.

The Soviet economic experience has and can be evaluated several ways. It is easy to point out the difficulties in meeting consumer demand and agricultural production and, therefore, label it a failure. On the other hand, the Soviet Union has managed to achieve such economic growth as to be considered the second most productive country in the world, and its military strength is second only to that of the United States.

It may be helpful to remember that modernization in the U.S. occurred under a different set of historical and practical circumstances. In a sense, the growth of the United States and the industrial revolution were movements that took place hand in hand. In the Soviet Union, modernization was imposed on a static, post-feudal society with immense problems inherited from and rooted in its past history.

IX. The Struggle for Identity and Direction

PROPOSITION: *Soviet history has been characterized by a struggle for identity and direction.*

The Soviet Union's third struggle has been for identity and direction. The tensions have been deep, the costs in human life and suffering often high. The

Soviet Union has been torn between two traditions. On the one hand, there is the heritage of an ancient culture embodying a messianic vision that identified Moscow as the third Rome, the preserver and transmitter of Christian civilization following the declines of Rome and Constantinople. On the other hand is Marxism, an imported revolutionary ideology embodied in the Third International and adopted by Lenin for the Russian context. Will the second phenomenon ever destroy the first? Will they remain in tension? Or has the Communism of the Soviet Union become the secular expression of the messianic mission, whose purpose is to facilitate the creation of a new world through the molding of the just society?

When the struggle is paraphrased in these terms, it obscures the historic tension found in the meeting of Eastern and Western cultures with divergent worldviews. This struggle is further complicated when the pragmatic demands of the state with its immense economic responsibilities are hampered by ideological constraints.

The Soviet Union is embroiled in its own "identity crisis": the tensions between the real and the ideal; the contradictions besetting an ideology that envisages a perfect, just society—free from the totalitarianism of the past but in practice an authoritarian, repressive system which is as constricting as that of the Czarist regimes; and the suspension between the rich civilization of the past and the yet-to-be fulfillments of a great society. These characteristics mark a society searching for its own being.

X. Erratic Relations between the Two Powers

PROPOSITION: *The history of relations between the United States and the Soviet Union has been erratic.*

During World War I, Woodrow Wilson, then President of the United States, hesitated to join the Allies because of the undemocratic nature of the Czarist system. When the February-March (1917) Revolution occurred, Wilson overcame his reservations. By April he had moved the United States into the war on the side of the Allies. The sixth of his famous "Fourteen Points" welcomed Russia "into the society of free nations under institutions of her own choosing."

The November (Bolshevik) Revolution, however, cooled Wilson's ardor. The Bolsheviks sought a separate peace with the Germans through the March 1918 Treaty of Brest-Litovsk. The treaty, however, left Russia at the mercy of the Germans. Seeking to prevent a transfer of German forces to the West and simultaneously to keep their supply lines open, the Allies directly intervened. British forces landed in Russia in the north at Murmansk and Archangel, and Japanese forces landed at Vladiovostok in the Far East. They were joined in time by American forces and those of other Allies. The British supported anti-Bolshevik activities and considerable fighting occurred in the spring of 1919 between the Allies and the Bolsheviks. The Allies abandoned Murmansk and Archangel in September 1919, almost a year after World War I was over. The Japanese held Vladivostok until October 1922.

A civil war in Russia, with the White Army (those seeking restoration of the old regime) fighting against the Red or Bolshevik Army, ended with a Bolshevik victory and the emergence of the new society, called the Union of Soviet Socialist Republics. Economic chaos, starvation and a struggle for power culminated in the emergence of Stalin, religious persecution and the wholesale turnover of social institutions.

Meanwhile, the United States was caught up in the "Red Scare," an ideological confrontation fanned by U.S. Attorney General A. Mitchell Palmer, who conducted mass arrests and the deportation of members of the newly established Workers' Party in the U.S. With such anxieties, the United States refused to recognize the new Soviet government for over a decade, doing so only in 1933 after Franklin Roosevelt became president.

Eight years of uncertain relations followed, during which time the United States went through the throes of its worst economic crisis, torn between the temptations of socialism and fascism. Those same years in the Soviet Union were marked by Stalin's great purge (1934-38) and the resurgence of a militant atheism aimed at destroying the church. Thus, our reluctant alliance with the Soviets in 1941 not only had to overcome our reactions to Stalin's excesses but the baffling pact between Hitler and Stalin in 1939, the Soviet's war with Finland and the brutal division of Poland. The threat of a triumphant Nazism drew both countries together, not eliminating their mutual suspicions but at least neutralizing them for the duration.

The Cold War began almost immediately after the end of World War II. The "iron curtain" shut off Eastern Europe. Only after Stalin's death in 1953 did a thaw occur. Both crisis and rapprochement characterized the years under Khrushchev, years which included the Cuban missile crisis, America's escalation of the Vietnam conflict and the Soviet repression of the Czechoslovakian revolution. Détente became the policy framework under Nixon and Kissinger, embodied in the Helsinki Accords. The currently revived cold war is repetitous of past years—using the same rhetoric but with increased stakes in terms of the potential costs of a nuclear confrontation.

One might say that the history of U.S.-Soviet relations has been marked by unnecessary hostilities (always based on worst-case scenarios) and unwarranted expectations (excitement at the slightest glimmer of hope). Sometimes these patterns have been shaped by events of global significance. Other times, the dynamics of domestic politics in each society have stimulated the confrontational spirit.

XI. Human Rights

PROPOSITION: *Americans, preoccupied with Soviet violations of human rights, are often unconscious of the ways they deny Soviet human rights.*

Americans have valid reasons to be concerned about patterns of Soviet behavior that are abhorrent to our traditions, particularly as we see these patterns resulting in the violations of human rights which are dear to our own thinking and are protected by the Universal Declaration of Human Rights. In the Soviet Union these violations or denials tend to take place basically in the realm of civil and political rights—areas where we generally feel most comfortable and assured that they are upheld in our society. The Soviets respond accusing us of violating the rights of minorities and of denying economic and social rights for large numbers of our peoples.

Americans view dimly and with appropriate alarm the suppression of Soviet dissidents, the limitations on the voluntary political activity of Soviet citizens, and the persistence of punitive labor camps. For sixty years, American Christians have seen the direct and indirect suppression of the church in the Soviet Union as violative of our basic premises of religious liberty. Our response, indeed, has been so intense that some are not even willing to accept the fact that the church has survived in any way except as a tool of the state.

To remind ourselves that the patterns of human oppression are a recurring part of a Russian/Slavic history dominated by authoritarianism does not lessen our abhorrence of these new forms of denying Soviet citizens the political-civil rights we enjoy and take for granted.

To remind ourselves that all societies, in the process of rapid change and stress, including our own, tend to curtail if not suppress the freedom of individuals—often justified as temporary expedients for the good of the order—does not diminish our urge to ask, "How long, how long?"

To remind ourselves that we have been and are prepared to intervene in other societies around the world if we believe our own interests are at stake (the Middle East and Central America) does not soothe the negative vibrations that continue to emanate from historic events in Czechoslovakia, Hungary and Poland.

But our preoccupation with Soviet violations of human rights masks our own subtle denial of Soviet human rights. We have a hard time thinking of Soviet leaders and citizens as human beings. The tendency of Americans is to view Soviets as either superhuman or inhuman: the first stems from an inflated estimate of Soviet military capabilities, usually related to the U.S. military budget process which measures Soviet expenditures based on U.S. equivalent costs; the second originates in stereotypical, prejudiced perspectives which universalize the worst evidences of Soviet historic behavior. The clichés are familiar: "They are all the same!" "They have never changed!" "They *cannot* be trusted!" (Or its variation: "They *can* be trusted—to do us in.")

In part we deny the Soviets their humanity—the right to be human, to be viewed as individuals with personal worth and integrity, the right to suffer, to hope, to have pride, to have consciences. More modest voices are heard to say with a different kind of inconsistency: "We have nothing against the Russian people—only their government." What remains unsaid is that we are still willing to destroy the people *because* of their government.

In part we suspend history, denying the basic understanding of the social sciences. History is the record of change. Do we assume that the Soviet Union is capable of transcending history? If it is a totalitarian state, does that condemn it to this condition forever? The social sciences tell us that societies are all in continuous process of change both from internal and external factors. When we attribute Soviet military behavior, for instance, to a statement by Lenin sixty years ago, we are implying that the intervening years have made no difference to Lenin's descendants, that they are incapable of reexamining their position in the light of new realities.

To say "they cannot be trusted" is to judge a whole people by the real or alleged actions of but a few. It is also to forget that trust is a relational quality dependent on the building of mutually affirming experiences and behavior. This phrase also implicitly suggests that the United States can be trusted. While this may be our self-image, there are many around the world who say the United States cannot be trusted either.

Reconciliation can begin with the acknowledgement and acceptance of the other's humanity. If our anthropology convinces us of the sinful nature of humanity, then we should at least acknowledge that corruptibility is not confined to the other. If our theology speaks to us of forgiveness, then we should at least grant the possibility of God's forgiveness to the other as well.

XII. Religion in the Soviet Union

PROPOSITION: *Americans, caught up in their anxiety about "atheistic godless Communism," have lost sight of the religious heritage of the Soviet peoples and have discounted the role of religion in Soviet life.*

So accustomed are Americans to thinking of the evils of Communism that the historic staying power of the church is denied. This is partly because their Orthodox tradition appears to be remote from our own experience. It is also partly because we have been long accustomed to reports of religious persecution in the U.S.S.R. A range of opinion is heard: surprise to encounter a church which is alive and growing; skepticism that assumes the existing church is but the tool of the state; self-righteousness that argues that the only true Christians are dead or in prisons! But the fact remains that millions of Christians in the Soviet Union continue to believe and worship despite the long history of difficulty and current restraints.

The Islamic factor in Soviet life has seldom been noted in America's public consciousness. The Islamic populations there number around 45 million, the sixth largest Muslim population in the world. They include forty nationalities, mainly in six republics in the southern tier. Currently accounting for 17 percent of the Soviet population, it is the fastest growing group and is projected to account for 25 percent by the year 2000. Muslims provide one third of the military recruits and the largest pool for industrial labor (raising questions about the location of Soviet industrial growth). In all of the history of religious persecution in the Soviet Union, the Muslim populations have been basically unaffected, because Islam has expressed itself more in cultural than in religious terms. Yet therein lies a potential problem for Soviet stability: namely, a latent nationalism, capable of being explosive if affected by the spreading Islamic fervor and militancy in Iran, Iraq and the other Middle Eastern countries. One cannot understand the significance of the Soviet action in Afghanistan apart from this dynamic context.

The Jewish population has posed a different kind of problem for the Soviet Union. More widely dispersed through Russia, the Jewish population was not treated in the same way as other "national" groups. The Jewish populations were generally European in origin. Their pre-Soviet history is marked with persecutions. Yet Jewish leaders were often Marxist in their thinking, and the Soviet Union was an original supporter of the State of Israel. In the conflict of loyalties and international politics, Soviet immigration limitations affecting Jewish migration have been a subject of much controversy.

Because of an appropriate concern for religious liberty, the United States has attempted on occasion to make good relations with the Soviet Union dependent on Soviet guarantees of religious liberty. These attempts have been less than successful. Three illustrations may be noted. In 1933, when the United States negotiated the recognition of the Soviet Union, one of three conditions dealt with religious freedom. While the Soviet Constitution guaranteed religious freedom, President Roosevelt wanted the Soviet Union to assure religious liberty for American citizens living in the Soviet Union. The agreement, however, did little to help insure more liberties for Soviet citizens.

Again, in 1941, the United States debated giving Lend-Lease assistance to the Soviet Union, which was then barely surviving against the Nazi invasion. Since the U.S. categorically aided the other Allied nations without reservation, its reluctance in the Soviet case could only serve to antagonize relations. Did our hostility towards Hitler ultimately overcome our antipathy to Soviet Communism? It did, but not until Soviet officials tendered guarantees of greater religious liberty.

And recently, the Jackson-Vanik Amendment making trade benefits to the Soviet Union contingent on relaxed immigration procedures for Soviet Jews has brought a negative response from the Soviet Union. Hence trade and immigration have both been curtailed. Neither our ignorance of Soviet religious traditions nor misguided attempts to coerce the Soviets on religious matters serve either society.

XIII. Three Common Assumptions

PROPOSITION: *Three commonly held assumptions by Americans about Soviet expansionism, about Soviet military growth, and about the Soviet economy need considerable qualification.*

These can be illustrated as follows.

1. Soviet Expansionism

First, we hear repeatedly, inside and outside government, that the Soviet Union has continuously and aggressively expanded since the end of World War II, fulfilling a plan for world domination. This accusation is perpetuated without historical verification or critical analysis. The accusation reflects a limited view of history and an inflated response to Soviet pretensions to world power. Further, it is seldom viewed contextually with the actions of other countries in the same or parallel circumstances.

During World War II, the Soviet Union, invaded by Nazi Germany and its East European partners, was able to halt those forces finally at the gates of Moscow. The Soviet armies, turning the tide, drove the Axis forces out of their own country and captured much of Eastern Europe as they drove the Nazis back into Germany.

Their record since then is mixed—not conspiratorial as often portrayed.

Germany was temporarily divided into occupational zones by agreement among the Allies; disagreements have perpetuated that division—most vividly symbolized with the Berlin Wall. Latvia, Lithuania and Estonia were reincorporated into the Soviet Union as republics, which corrected from the Soviet perspective the results of World War I, when those territories, long a part of Russia, were separated from the Soviet Union. Through an agreement involving the U.S., the Soviet Union withdrew its troops from northern Iran in 1946, only later to have the agreement nullified by the Shah. Though Austria and Finland had been closely linked with the Nazi regime, the Soviet Union withdrew its troops from both countries in 1955. It should be noted that the Soviet Union never militarily controlled the Communist states of Yugoslavia and Albania and its control in both is limited, in the first instance by an independent nationalism and in the second by a more rigid ideological totalitarianism.

The Soviet Union has consolidated its influence over East Germany, Poland, Czechoslovakia, Hungary, Romania and Bulgaria, not by direct rule but through treaties and pro-Soviet regimes reinforced by the military and economic agreements of the Warsaw Pact and the COMECON. One of the most controversial situations was Czechoslovakia. In the final days of World War II the Soviet Army, by agreement, occupied Prague. The National Front government which was formed was allied to the Soviet Union and the strongest party was the Communist Party. When this relation appeared to be threatened in 1948, the Soviet Union consolidated its position by a brutal use of force. This use of extreme force to prevent change was repeated again in Hungary in 1956 and in Czechoslovakia in 1968. Even with heavy Soviet influence the circumstances in these countries vary greatly.

The fact is that nowhere in Europe beyond those end-of-war locations has the Soviet Union expanded. The withdrawals are seldom acknowledged. Critics of the Soviet's natural desire to protect its European buffer tend to forget that the United States, also, by a series of treaties and other arrangements, continues to maintain a large military presence in both Japan and West Germany, where those same war memories and similar defense concerns exist.

Soviet influence in other parts of the world has been mixed. Its occasional success is often due less to the skill of Soviet policy than to the ineptness of American policy. Studies have shown that Soviet influence was at its height in the 1950s and that there has been little momentum since. Of 155 or more countries in the world, the Soviet Union has once had influence in 35. Presently it has influence in 19. The Soviet Union has lost previously held influence in such places as the People's Republic of China, Egypt, Indonesia and India. Apart from its own population and productivity, the Soviet Union influences only about six percent of the world's population and five percent of the world's gross national product. A study by Ray Cline, a former C.I.A. official, indicates that 70 percent of the world's power balance is pro-West and China, and only 20 percent pro-Soviet. Whatever the rhetoric, the Soviet expansion is not as drastic as claimed though it is able to extend its influence far more extensively than before.

2. Soviet Military Growth

Second, we attribute responsibility for the arms race to the Soviet Union, using the rhetoric: "They have only one goal—world conquest!"

An honest assessment of the facts in the nuclear arms race shows the Soviet Union has been in a constant catch-up position. In all but two major developments in either nuclear technology or in delivery systems, the U.S. has been ahead of the Soviet Union. Briefly, the record shows that the United States exploded its first weapons on Hiroshima and Nagasaki in 1945. The Soviet Union did not conduct its first tests until 1949. In 1948 the U.S. introduced the intercontinental bomber capable of delivering nuclear payloads to the Soviet Union. The Soviet Union followed suit seven years later in 1955. The United States developed the hydrogen bomb in 1954, the Soviet Union in 1955. In 1960, the U.S. produced the first nuclear-powered submarine capable of sea-launched missiles (SLBM). The Soviet Union entered the waters with theirs eight years later. In 1966, the U.S. increased the number of warheads a missile could carry; the Soviet Union followed in 1968. These warheads were called MRV's and each missile carried three warheads. The U.S. further refined the multiple-warhead technology by introducing the Multiple Independently Targetable Re-entry Vehicle (MIRV) in 1970, the U.S.S.R. in 1975.

In only two developments has the Soviet Union been ahead, but these have interesting implications. The ICBM was developed by the Soviet Union in 1957 and by the U.S. in 1958. With the ICBM the Soviet Union achieved a possibility the U.S. already had, namely, the ability to deliver nuclear weapons to the other's homeland. (The U.S. had had intercontinental bombers with nuclear warheads since 1948.) The ABM developed in 1968 by the Soviet Union and 1972 by the United States was defensive in purpose. Its military benefit was questionable, and its political benefit neutralized when the ABM Treaty, in effect, ended further developments.

United States' MX and Cruise missile technology will be matched by the Soviet Union. It is also clear that technological achievements do not insure permanent strategic advantages, rather, they fuel the arms race into evermore dangerous levels. The history of the arms race is clear. Interpretations of the arms race, however, vary widely.

3. The Soviet Economy

Third, Soviet economic achievement is often denigrated—readily labeled a failure. The ideological and psychological advantage of this is, of course, obvious. We thereby prove our system right, theirs wrong! The result is more self-congratulation than illumination. (This is a strange satisfaction for an economy plagued by severe problems: inflation, stagnation, high unemployment, massive debts, and persistent pockets of poverty.)

But by what measure do we see success or failure and for what motive do we make the choice of measurements? What ingredients or factors are included or excluded in the comparison?

Any critical examination of the Soviet economy will reveal many problems, difficulties, yes, even irrationalities. Some of these are rooted in the system, others in circumstances. However, let us keep in mind the most obvious. The Soviet Union is today, by most measures, the second most productive society in the world, and the Soviet Union ranks high in the provision of basic necessities for its people. It also supports one of the world's largest military establishments, in a manner rapidly being simulated by the United States, at great cost to other sectors of the economy. It has accomplished this despite the fact that in 1917 it was still predominantly an undeveloped economy, despite the setbacks of World War I, the ravages of the long civil war that followed, and the incredible material devastation that occurred during World War II. Further, its reconstruction efforts were without the support from the immense U.S. economic investments that Japan and West Germany received.

The point here is not to glorify the economic achievements of the Soviet Union, but to avoid the folly and complacency of an inadequate, deceptive analysis. The Soviet Union is neither ten feet tall nor a crippled midget. It can produce and it can still allocate its economic resources to achieve social goals, though on a selective basis. The United States' tendency to distort reality in its description of the Soviet Union hurts the U.S. more than it does the Soviet Union.

XIV. Misguided Policies of the U.S.

PROPOSITION: *United States attitudes toward the Soviet Union have often, if not consistently, resulted in sterile, misguided policies and practices vis-à-vis the Soviet Union itself, Western Europe, China and the Third World in general.*

Full exploration of this thesis would demand a book, but several things may be noted here: First, regarding the Soviet Union itself, United States policy has been shaped by ideas of containment, denial and punishment.

The containment policy, operative even in World War II, has assumed an unrelenting drive by the Soviet Union toward a goal of world domination. Containment has meant the prevention not only of Soviet military expansion but of their economic, social and political influence as well. The NATO alliance accomplished this in Europe. Efforts to duplicate it elsewhere have been less viable—such as METO and SEATO. The containment doctrine applied in other spheres has had incredible consequences. The Korean and Vietnam wars were wars of containment: "Communism must be stopped regardless of cost." Even "détente" has been discussed as a containment strategy, in which the Helsinki Accords were interpreted as a legalized delimitation of the Soviet sphere of activity.

The policy of denial has included denial of legitimacy (the right to be) and of access (the right to participate). Let me illustrate only briefly. Members of the Reagan Administration have argued that the Soviet government is illegitimate, having come into power by revolution, and therefore has no rights. The U.S. condemns the Soviet Union for preventing its citizens from traveling, while simultaneously it refuses to allow Soviet scientists and scholars the right to meet with their American peers. Thus, the policy becomes hypocritical and self-defeating. Exclusion from trading channels furthers antagonism not freedom.

The punitive policy, in current practice, sets up the U.S. as the arbiter of good behavior with the right to punish the Soviet Union when it steps out of line. Our boycott of the Moscow Olympics was punishment for the Afghanistan invasion. Opposition to the Soviet pipeline has been defined by Reagan as punishment of the Soviet Union for the situation in Poland (hardly the real reason for U.S. opposition to the pipeline).

One other foreign policy pattern must be noted. The U.S. tends to interpret and respond to most events in the Third World as if they were intrinsic to the East/West conflict, totally ignoring or distorting the historic, economic and social sources of those events and problems. When we refer to people's movements as Marxist-oriented, left-wing or Moscow-backed, we relieve ourselves of the necessity for more careful analysis. Thus we often oversimplify complex situations and respond to them inappropriately.

XV. Our Christian Responsibility

PROPOSITION: *The Christian community bears the major responsibility for breaking down the dividing wall of hostility between the United States and the Soviet Union, for creating a new dynamic, a new relationship between our two peoples.*

A new understanding and relationship is indeed needed. In a sense we have come full circle. How can we break down the dividing wall of hostility? How do we make our enemies our friends? For do this we must. The *practical* reason is clear. Failure to establish détente and eventual rapport between the United States and the Soviet Union can only mean an increasing risk to the survival of humanity. In a sense this practical reality carries with it its own moral imperative.

But who will lead the way? One does not assume that Christians alone are capable of such leadership. Enlightened government leadership and self-interested business leadership are capable of bringing about changes in attitudes, policy and practice. Both should be encouraged at every opportunity to bring about constructive change—taking the initiative for such ends. But there is little to indicate at this point in time that the stimulus will come from government leaders. The business community seems reluctant or divided enough to be unwilling to *lead,* though many are actively seeking change.

The church, therefore, has a particular motivation and a peculiar role. Reconciliation—breaking down walls that divide—is a Christian responsibility and an imperative expression of our faith and our calling as peacemakers.

The Confession of 1967 called the United Presbyterian Church:

. . . to practice the forgiveness of enemies and to commend to the nations as practical politics the search for cooperation and peace. This requires the pursuit of fresh and responsible relations across every line of conflict, even at risk to national security, to reduce areas of strife and to broaden international understanding.

In *Peacemaking: The Believers' Calling* (General Assembly, 1980) we are reminded:

By God's grace we are members of a world community, and can bring our global insights and peacemaking to our particular settings. By God's grace we are freed to work with all people who strive for peace and justice, and to serve as signposts for God's love in our broken world.

It is because we are a people of faith that we are free to ask the question: "What about the Russians?" We seek answers, not motivated by fear but because of our faith. We trust, not in the Russians but in Jesus Christ and his forgiving, reconciling power. The gospel message is that the dividing wall of hostility is to be broken down by the one who is our peace. In the blood of Christ we are made one, yes, even with the Russians. Our hostility is ended in the cross as we are reconciled to God and each other. The paradox remains: Can we reconcile ourselves with that reconciliation?

A THEOLOGY OF THE ENEMY

Barbara G. Green

This is going to be a restricted, truncated Christian anthropology. It does not include an examination of who *we* are as a nation of immigrants, many of whom came for religious reasons, of who we are as a nuclear superpower, or of who we are as a nation which could perpetrate at the same time democratic idealism and slavery. It focuses on that sector of the human community which we call our enemies. It is a broken question because it leaves out "who are we?", and focuses on "who are they?". Already the question itself has begun to deny the gift of Christ's reconciliation, because it assumes that the world can be divided into "we" and "they." It is, however, what I will try to do, because I believe there are some things which the Christian community can and must say about enemies.

In the early summer of 1977, my first year of a five-year term as liaison from the National Council of Churches to the churches in the German Democratic Republic (GDR), I attended a day-long rally of some 3,000 church-related young people out on a large meadow near Potsdam in the GDR. In the course of the morning's program, I had been introduced as an ecumenical guest from the U.S.A. During the lunch break, a high-school-aged youth from the GDR came up to me and said, "There are two Russian soldiers standing over there behind the stage platform. They have heard that there is an American here, and they would like to meet you. Will you come talk to them?" I thought to myself, "Good heavens! Real live Russian soldiers! What on earth do they want with me?" But I swallowed hard, made very sure that the people who had brought me understood where I was going in case I should be eaten alive and not reutrn, and followed the boy some distance across the field and around the stage.

There were two men in the familiar olive uniforms with red shoulder patches and red stars. On closer look they turned out to be two 18-year-old boys. We communicated roughly through gestures and some school-book Russian, and learned fairly quickly that these two were not ethnic Russians. They came from one of the Asian republics in the Soviet Union, Russian was not their native language, they were both away from home for the first time, some 2,000 miles far away in a strange country where they couldn't communicate. What they most wanted in life

[65]

was to get their two-year stint over with and be able to go home. They asked me about myself; I tried to say that I was a minister, but the only Russian word that my GDR friend could think of that even came close to "minister" was the word for an Orthodox priest. This seemed to have some very startling impact on the two soldiers, as I could offer neither of the two long black items they knew to be prerequisites of that office: a cassock and a beard! The whole encounter was over before very long, yet it was for me an experience of humanizing the enemy which has truly stayed with me. Those fear-inspiring creatures, Russian soldiers, turned out to be a couple of homesick teenagers.

Who is the enemy? The English word "enemy" comes from the Latin word *inimicus,* as does the French equivalent *L'ennemi* and do similar stems in the other Latin languages. *Inimicus* comes from *in + amicus,* meaning "not friendly," "hostile." The German word for "enemy," *der Feind,* comes from the same Old High German root as the English word "fiend," and means "a hating one," "a hostile one." The Russian word means "hating one, hostile one." And most moving to me, the ancient Greek word used in the New Testament comes from the adjective, "hated"; so that the New Testament commandment to love one's enemies actually reads, "Love the ones you hate." The point is that at that level of collective subconscious in which the origins of language are rooted, at least in the Western language families, the concept of enemy is defined only in terms of a hostile relationship. An enemy has no organic reality in nature within a given species, like parent or child. A person is an enemy only because there is somewhere another person who perceives the first one as such.

This definition only in terms of subjective perception strikes me to be in startling contrast with our frequent assumptions about the objective reality of the enemy. Our military training, for example, is full of assumptions that, of course, the enemy is out there and is as real as the force of gravity.

Enemies do not come only in neatly organized groups of nations or states. Any individual or group perceived to be threatening, hostilely competitive or otherwise frightening easily becomes labeled Enemy. In the mid-1970s the West German Protestant churches set up a working group to spend the next five years studying the notion "enemy." Their motivation, as strange as that now seems, was not the Soviet threat, nor the burdens of superpower conflict in their lives, nor even a struggle with a Nazi past. Rather, a wave of political kidnappings and terrorist activity within the Federal Republic had led people to begin to talk about *Staatsfeinde,* enemies of the state within the state itself, and the church people decided they better work on the concept of "enemy" as part of that domestic problem.

All this not withstanding, the game where the stakes are highest in the poker of human hostility is that of collective, national enemies. All through human history states or national groups have set out to systematically conquer or destroy each other. In our time the stakes in this game are higher than ever before. The chips cost us globally some $600 billion annually in military expenditures, including some $50 billion in global conventional arms exports, not to mention the incalculable costs in human suffering. The wager is for nothing less than the very survival of human civilization itself. These are terribly high, fatefully high stakes for anything as precarious, as chameleon-like as human perceptions of enmity.

One paradox is that unless people have had direct experiences of occupation, of plundering or forcible evacuation or rape, or of persecution, they tend to have a relatively low investment of personal hate in another people defined as their national enemy. The fear and hate from such experiences are as much results of national enmity as they are a cause. Even when personal suffering has been experienced, people are able to distinguish between the collective entity which brought them their grief and individuals belonging to that group who may themselves be powerless or even fellow victims. Many Arabs distinguish between the state of Israel as their enemy and the Jewish people as people.

Another paradox typical of our own national experience in the twentieth century is the seeming historical arbitrariness in the shifts of our perception as to who are our enemies. In the 1940's the Russians were our friends and allies and the Germans were our mortal enemies. Forty years later, the Germans are our friends and allies and the Russians are our enemies. I remember a personal experience of this when I was a very new seminary student in West Germany. I was adopted by a dear family in Heidelberg, the father of whom is about my own father's age. He is a gifted amateur musician, and over the course of those years he unfolded to me wonderful treasures of his beloved Bach. I remember several times sitting beside him poring over some score or manuscript and thinking: Here is this man giving me such a gift of access to this music. If he and my own father had met each other on the street forty years ago, they would have been forced by the constraints of that time to try to murder each other. What madness!

Please forgive my turning to the Europeans so much in all this. My having lived there eight of the last eleven years inevitably tilts the balance of my own experience in that direction. What I hope is that, as in any major experience of international community, those years have planted in me a commitment to challenge nationalist exclusivism and enemy stereotypes wherever they may appear. Certainly, Americans who have tried to understand and care about Japanese people, Koreans, Vietnamese, people of the Middle East, or Africa, or Latin America, or a host of other places can give witness far more eloquently than I to the profound experience of unmasking inherited definitions of an enemy by learning to know and to cherish the specific humanity of the other people.

What fuels our perceptions of enemy? What keeps them going, even as specific historical enemies come and go? In some of the technical literature on the subject there is a good deal of reference to a nation having needs for its enemies, for example, to justify certain social structures or to bring people together. Carl Schmitt, a German lawyer writing in the 1920's and 1930's suggested that a healthy country needed a good strong enemy for its own purposes, as that could create a strong national spirit.[1] Carl Schmitt's ideas were obviously ripe to be taken up and exploited by the Nazis in their ideology in later years, as indeed they were.

George Kennan has interpreted the recent deterioration in U.S.-Soviet relations to be related to an American need for an external scapegoat enemy:

Observing then, in the years of the late 1970's and early 1980's, the seemingly inexorable advance of this hysteria of professed fear of and hostility to the Soviet Union, but finding so little objective reason for it, I could only suspect that its origins were primarily subjective; and this seemed to me to suggest something much more sinister than mere intellectual error: namely, a subconscious need on the part of a great many people for an external enemy—an enemy against whom frustrations could be vented, an enemy who could serve as a convenient target for the externalization of evil, an enemy in whose allegedly inhuman wickedness one could see the reflection of one's own exceptional virtue.[2]

Kennan goes on to suggest that all this represents ". . . a situation of immense, immediate, and—what was most tragic—quite unnecessary danger."

Even though developments in counterforce, first-strike, and limited "usable," "controllable" nuclear weapons technologies have seriously obscured clearly recognizable policies of defensive deterrence in the U.S., according to all the official rhetoric even of the Reagan administration, our entire national security policy is fundamentally based upon the strategy of deterrence. Its sole aim is to prevent war by deterring it. The word "deterrence" is derived from the same Latin word as "terror": *terrere,* meaning to frighten or terrify. Deterrence works by frightening war away, by making the consequences of war so terrible that an enemy would be frightened away from starting one. In order for the doctrine to function, it essentially requires something or someone to be worthy of being frightened off. It requires that something or someone be defined as the enemy, in order that it or they can be scared away, so that we may have national security. Certainly not all of the complex national competitions in international relations can be reduced to this scheme. I suggest, however, that the very essence of deterrence doctrine requires the identification of an external enemy, and that as long as our national security policy is based on it so centrally, we are trapped into maintaining the threatening nature of our perceived enemies, in order to be able to frighten them off.

One possible chance out of this dilemma is suggested through the findings of the Palme Commission report, *Common Security.* The central finding of that independent international commission is that: "In the modern age, security cannot be obtained unilaterally. . . . The security of one nation cannot be bought at the expense of others. . . . We face common dangers and thus must also promote our security in common."[3] The danger of global nuclear war has become so devastating, that it is much worse than anything any one particular national enemy could do to another. The arms race, the danger of war itself, has become a threatening enemy. If we must have an external enemy in order to frighten it away again, then perhaps the runaway arms race itself, together with the growing danger of new nuclear proliferation, the international trade in conventional arms and the exacerbation of local and regional conflicts which all feed it, is the single enemy most worthy of our mightiest efforts to scare it away again. It is an enemy which unites us across national borders and political blocs, and gives us some hope of understanding what is at stake in our finding common security.

Falling short of that in our sinfulness and shortcomings, we continue to seek and (of course) find national enemies, whom we must deter. What are the characteristics of these enemies we find? One is that we do not know them very well. National enemies are remote—we may have deliberate or *de facto* embargoes on news or cultural exchange with them, so we have no real opportunity to get to know them very well. Modern weapons technology shores up that feeling of distance and remoteness even in a battlefield situation. Enemies may seem strange or different; enmity along racial lines is captive to the human capacity to fear that which is different. The whole pop culture of danger from alien space invaders (not to mention the video games industry dependent on it) both feed on and nourish our willingness to fear the alien. While I am no fan of homogeneous commercialization in our society, I do rejoice that a few years ago our children acquired in E.T. at least one symbol, one role model that something which is initially perceived to be alien, ugly!, and threatening, is discovered to be not only non-threatening, but capable and worthy of love, as well as endowed with dignity and extraordinary gifts.

On the other hand, many of the most tragic wars of our time are fought in familiarity, by peoples in proximity or sharing social characteristics. Some of the bitterest family battles are those entrenched repetitive patterns of behavior long familiar to all sides. Collective fratricide was a terrible feature of the U.S. Civil War, where families were split and brothers fought brothers. In Northern Ireland, Irish fight Irish; in the Iran-Iraq war, Muslims fight Muslims; and in Beirut, people in adjacent streets fight each other. Estrangement, alienation out of familiarity, is even more treacherous than strangeness.

We dehumanize our enemies; we make of them either superhumans or subhumans. A former deputy mayor of Jerusalem, Meron Benvenisti, reports of the 1982 war in Lebanon that the Israeli army took extensive archives on Palestinian culture and history from the PLO's Palestine Research Center in West Beirut. He comments:

> This was not only to destroy them as a political or military power, but to take from them their history, to erase that because it is troublesome. This was a profound need or urge not to allow the Palestinians to be a respectable or historic movement.
>
> The process of dehumanization is a product of all such conflicts. We are in a twilight war. There are no trenches, and there is no front, so you have two levels of interaction, one adversarial level, the other neighborly. Who are they? It's very complicated, because if you are at war, you must dehumanize your enemy, because if not, then you are a murderer.[4]

Enemies feed on each other; they spur each other on. Richard Barnet suggests that enemies draw weakness from each other, that they become like each other in negative characteristics. The Soviet Union acquires a thriving military-industrial complex, for example, and the U.S. acquires an ever-greater commitment to government secrecy.

Finally, we theologize our enemies. We assume that our enemies are, in fact, also God's enemies. Probably every religious group in the world is at least somewhat vulnerable to that projection. German soldiers in World War I had engraved on their belt buckles: "God is with us." We are all too familiar with the slogan aimed toward the Soviet Union of fighting godless Communism, even that the godlessness of Communism makes it an incorporation of the anti-Christ in history. South Africa feels that it must protect itself as the last "truly Christian" nation from the total onslaught of godless Communism.

The Old Testament contains many examples of identification between Israel's enemies and God's enemies.

> Do I not hate them that hate thee, O Lord?
> And do I not loathe them that rise up against thee?
> I hate them with perfect hatred;
> I count them my enemies.
> Search me, O God, and know my heart!
> Try me and know my thoughts!
> And see if there be any wicked way in me,
> and lead me in the way everlasting!
>
> (Psalm 139:21-24)

At the same time Israel is never permitted to identify its enemies totally with God's enemies. Too many times God sends word to Israel one way or another, usually through a prophet, that Israel's particular enemy at hand is part of God's plan. God uses Israel's enemies to correct Israel's own sinfulness. When Israel shows pride and arrogance of heart,

> So the Lord raises adversaries against them,
> and stirs up their enemies,
> The Syrians on the east and the Philistines on the west
> devour Israel with open mouth
>
> (Isaiah 9:11-12)

> Woe to those who . . . turn aside the needy from justice
> and rob the poor of my people of their right,
> that widows may be their spoil,
> and that the fatherless their prey!
>
> (Isaiah 10:1-2)

> Ah, Assyria, the rod of my anger, the staff of my fury!
> Against a godless nation I send him,
> and against the people of my wrath I command him,
> to take spoil and seize plunder,
> and to tread them down like the mire of the streets
>
> (Isaiah 10:5-6)

Of course, this does not mean that Assyria gets off the hook for its own wrongdoing, just because it is God's tool in Israel:

> When the Lord has finished all his work on Mount Zion and on
> Jerusalem he will punish the arrogant boasting of the king of Assyria
> and his haughty pride.
>
> (Isaiah 10:12)

And so Israel is instructed not to be afraid of the Assyrians when they come and beat them with rods and staffs.

> For in a very little while my indignation will come to an end, and my anger will be directed to their destruction.　　　　　　　　　(Isaiah 10:25)

We are on pretty shaky ground when we try to convince ourselves that our enemies are God's enemies; much less when we try to convince God of that! They may, in fact, be God's instruments directed toward us. When the sixtieth anniversary of the Soviet Union's Great October Revolution was celebrated in the socialist bloc in 1977, all elements of the German Democratic Republic's society were expected to make some contribution to the festivities, even the Christians. Some Christians responded to that occasion by saying, "That revolution has nothing to do with us." Others responded by saying, "That revolution is for us a call to repentance. If we as Christians had lived up to our own principles of justice and compassion, then there would have been no need for a Communist revolution." Indeed, the fundamental ideological Marxist-Leninist critique of religion includes the criticism that religion is wrong because it does not live up to its own ethical standards in its own terms.

All of this division into friends and enemies, all of this polarization into hostile national groups denies the Biblical message of the commonality of all humanity. We all share the commonality of being God's creatures as part of the human family—of being God's children. We share in common stewardship of nature and its resources, although in these days that stewardship has turned into patterns of bitter competition and exploitation for limited resources.

We share in common that we are all sinners before God; none of us is exempt from the title of sinner. Evil has a small corner in all of our souls. All of us have at least a minimal capacity to be in a human relationship of enmity, to hate and be hated. Martin Luther wrote about this: "If we want to drive away our closest enemy, the one who does us the most damage, then we should drive away and kill ourselves. For we have no more destructive enemy than our own hearts."[5] One of the great insights of the Mahatma Gandhi was to understand that in order to change the world around one, one must first change oneself. To overcome the evil around us, we must overcome the evil within us.

As sinners we all stand before God in judgment. God has not turned over the final capacity to judge us, God has kept it. God puts a limitation on how we judge our enemies and how we condemn those whom we have vanquished by saying, "Final judgment is not yours to make. I will keep it as my prerogative." Jesus tells a parable (Matt. 13:24-30, 36-43) in which a man sows good seed in his field and while he is asleep, an enemy comes and sows weeds among the grain. The man's servants want to pull out the weeds, and the man forbids them to do so, saying that the good grain will be pulled out and lost with the weeds. Both should wait in the field until the harvest, when the Son of God will send his angels out to gather them in. Human servants, not even God's human servants, are finally to separate the grain from the weeds, are to decide ultimately final judgment over each other.

[71]

Finally, we share the commonality of Christ's act of reconciliation and the offer and commandment for human reconciliation which comes with it. Simeon proclaims in the temple:

for mine eyes have seen thy salvation
which thou hast prepared in the presence of all peoples,
a light for revelation to the Gentiles,
and glory to thy people Israel.

(Luke 2:31-32)

Salvation and reconciliation are intended to be for all people, not only those who are on *our* side of human tension and human conflict. No mud-spattered, tear-stained human foible can tarnish the shining truth of that gift and that offer of reconciliation.

As I have shared some of these thoughts on subjective perceptions of human enemies and commonality of humanity under God with Christians from Third World countries, their response has been a dissatisfied one: "This human projection is inadequate as a theological description of the oppression against which we struggle." That oppression is: capitalism, global imperialism uninhibited in its interventionalism, the military-industrial complex, the profit drive—there are many names. In any case, it is something bigger and stronger and more devious and deadly than a collection of mere mortals.

As I struggle to find a theological category for this, I light on Paul's references to the powers and principalities in Romans, Ephesians and Colossians. Back then, the principalities and powers were a pantheon of small gods, forces, fallen angels, demons, idols—deeply entrenched factors in the cosmos with which one had to reckon. It is not terribly difficult to find idols in our time usurping the place of worship in our hearts. At the 1979 "Choose Life" consultation of church leaders from the U.S.A. and U.S.S.R., Professor Bruce Rigdon identified three of these:

1. The autonomous momentum of technology;
2. The military-industrial complex and related military spending;
3. Narrow nationalism.[6]

All of them are human creations to which we give homage.

But even since 1979 there is a sense of demons at work in our international affairs due in Dale Bishop's phrase to "the obsessive demonology" of the Reagan administration. Demonic rhetoric has reached new heights in our public debate. Reagan's March 1983 Orlando speech to Evangelicals called the Soviet system the "source of all evil in the world," implying that it is therefore worthy of our worst accusations and worst strategic planning for terrible destruction. It elicited an unprecedented response from the Patriarch of the Russian Orthodox Church, who took an advertisement in the *New York Times* to protest. In discussion some of us are quite careful to differentiate between the people of the Soviet Union and its government, and some ascribe the same care to the current U.S. administration. I am not so sure even that distinction is afoot in the country at large as a result of the steady stream of obsessive demonology.

For example, a career diplomat in the Soviet embassy reports he was driving through the Midwest, and turned on his car radio at five past the hour to get a local weather report. After reporting local conditions, the weatherman began to give brief reports from around the world: "In Bombay it is 85 degrees and sunny, in Buenos Aires it is 75 degrees and rainy, in the Soviet Union there are sub-freezing temperatures *and they deserve it,* in Berlin it is 45 degrees and cloudy." The diplomat reported this with some visible pain as an attack on the humanity of his compatriots. My guess is that after these three years of obsessive demonology our country has more people willing to wish sub-freezing temperatures, economic hardship or collapse, or even nuclear annihilation on the peoples of the Soviet Union than we church folk are willing to admit. This very fact is in itself demonic. I cannot yet well articulate just how these modern forms of powers and principalities fit with the theological concepts of human free will and responsibility. But, I am becoming increasingly convinced that our efforts to understand our enemies theologically are simply inadequate without some consideration of powers and principalities.

What, then, is the special Christian witness to be to the hates and fears in which we all are trapped? "God did not give us a spirit of fear but a spirit of power and love and a sound mind." (2 Tim. 1:17). The spirit that God gives us is not the spirit of fear, not the spirit of deterrence, or of despair, or of cowardice, but the spirit of strength and love.

> You have heard that it was said, "You shall love your neighbor and hate your enemy." But I say to you, love your enemies and pray for those who persecute you, so that you may be children of your Father who is in heaven; for he makes his sun rise on the evil and on the good, and sends rain on the just and on the unjust. For if you love those who love you, what reward have you? Do not even the tax collectors do the same? And if you salute only your brethren, what more are you doing than others? Do not even the Gentiles do the same? You, therefore, must be perfect, as your heavenly Father is perfect.
>
> (Matt. 5:43-48)

Love your enemies! Love the ones you hate! It is the real enemy here, the one who does not return your love—by any stretch of the imagination—who is to be loved. In response to the feeling that I do not know anyone in that hostile relationship toward me, Martin Luther commented: "Whoever teaches that they have no enemy resisting them or anyone after revenge against them should not imagine that they are a thorough and righteous preacher of the word of God!"[7]

God has given us the spirit of strength and love. Loving one's enemy is an asymmetrical thing to do. It carries no obligation for the enemy to be loved; it has no strings attached; it has no guarantee of mutuality. In fact, the enemy being loved will probably remain full of hate and fear and remain the enemy. It is you who will be changed by the loving.

Augustine even calls a loving spirit one of the criteria for the conduct of a just war. Wars may have to be waged, but they must not be waged in a passion of hate or a desire for revenge. "No one indeed is fit to inflict punishment save the one who has first overcome hate in his heart. The love of enemies admits of no dispensation, but love does not exclude wars of mercy waged by the good."[8]

Bonhoeffer, in his meditations on the Sermon on the Mount in *The Cost of Discipleship*, calls loving one's enemies an *extraordinary* thing to do. By *extraordinary*, he is referring to the *more* in the text (v. 47). What a haunting question Bonhoeffer lifts up from that passage: "What *more* do you do?" Doing more means for Bonhoeffer a "better justice" than the Pharisees and the others are capable of. That which is natural, love of family or friends or one's own people, is the same for Christians and non-Christians. What is explicitly Christian beyond what is natural is this extraordinary love of one's enemies. This "better justice" is the *act* of discipleship.

God gives us the spirit of power and love *and* a sound mind. Loving one's enemies makes wisdom possible. Hatred blinds, it paralyzes the one hating, it distorts perception and behavior. It makes the hater see the mote in someone else's eye when she or he cannot see the beam in their own. In the Book of Proverbs (9:6) Wisdom herself, Sophia, invites us to "Leave simpleness, and live, and walk in the way of insight." It is not for nothing that *Prudencia* is one of those old cardinal virtues. Bishop Albrecht Schönherr of the GDR wrote

> Prudence requires a clear head, a head not dependent on temptations and anxieties, on seductions or threats. Prudence excludes both thoughtless pessimism and blind optimism.
>
> The spirit of prudence teaches us to think about the entirety of things. Today we know better than we used to that the whole world is a great network of special interests and dependencies. Seeing only my own small world is not prudent.
>
> The spirit of a sound mind reminds us that we must live together with other people in the future, as well as in the present. It causes us to think about insuring them sufficient conditions to live in the future.[9]

Prudence—a sound mind—wise behavior gives content and meaning to loving the enemy. At this point, I am very indebted to Carl-Friedrich von Weizsacker, the West German physicist and philosopher, who has introduced the notion of "loving one's enemy intelligently" as a concept. In a paper given to the 1980 Conference of European Churches Helsinki Consultation in Madrid, he said

> love of our enemies in practice starts with our coming to understand our enemies. Even then they will probably remain our enemies, they will continue to fear us and therefore to hate us. But at least we shall then begin to avoid making the gestures which constantly give them the impression that they are justified in fearing and hating us. Only then shall we be in a position to make them understand the extent to which they themselves have in the past acted in such a way that we were bound to fear them and therefore be misled into hating them. . .
>
> If anyone can, Christians should be able to love their enemies intelligently, to understand the motivation of their opponent and thus to prepare a

readiness for compromise. They can help to reduce fear and hatred in the nations and to build up understanding. They can urge governments to undertake negotiations over the dangerous problems with the aim of precise, practicable agreements.[10]

Love enables wisdom and wisdom gives content, not to mention political relevance to love, nourishing each other in a spiral of hope. This seems to me to be the single most exciting thing about loving one's enemies. Our Christian commandment to do so is not an invitation to suicide or an invitation to naive foolishness, but it is an invitation to hope because it is an invitation to and an enabling of wise behavior.

What are some of the ways this works out in practice? Well, it must be worked out afresh over and over again. A startling example takes place in the Old Testament, when Saul, the king of Israel, has come to perceive David as a competitive enemy for the throne and sets out to find and kill David. After a considerable cat-and-mouse chase, Saul unwittingly wanders into the cave where David and his men are hiding, and David, in a deliberate symbol of benevolent intentions, chooses not to kill Saul when he has the opportunity. When David is able to prove to Saul that this happened, Saul's hostility is disarmed and they are reconciled (and, incidentally, David acquires the power.)

The Swiss professor Hans Ruh, remembering Kant's categorical imperative to behave in such a way that it would be a good thing if everyone behaved that way, has developed a categorical imperative for disarmament, which seems to me to be a political translation of loving one's enemy intelligently.

Each military bloc must develop, reveal and practice a strategic plan designed to ensure that *my opponent can recognize that my conception of security also takes account of the security of my opponent.*

Another way to express this is

Arm only in such a way that the other can copy you exactly without your feeling threatened by this.

Or

Devise your armaments policy in such a way that it can at any time become everybody's principle and action.[11]

One of the recommendations which religious leaders made in their statement addressed to their governments at a conference in Moscow in May 1982 is "to enforce a moratorium on all hostile rhetoric."[12] Unmasking hostile and inflammatory rhetoric is certainly part of loving one's enemy intelligently.

One powerful expression of loving one's enemy intelligently in our troubled time is the witness in the leadership of the Middle East Council of Churches. Their thinking goes something like this: yes, our existence is threatened in a hostile environment (similar to Israel's self-perception). But in contrast to the response of the Phalange, which is: we must hold on to what we have; they say, we must not seek to grab power at the expense of the others, because that was not Jesus' way.

His way was the ultimate powerlessness of the cross. We can live with the Muslims, even at a disadvantage, and that is preferable to either fighting or moving. The presence of our community is our witness; our goal is not so much to convert individuals to our own religious fold as to seek the conversion of history to more justice in the sense of Jesus' ministry. What a disarming witness for that place!

Both the churches and the governments of the two German states have taken up the Palme report; the churches understand it to be a politically viable translation of the Biblical commandment to love one's enemy. In the last German/German summit conference between Helmut Schmidt and Erich Honecker, they developed the notion of "security partnerships," by which they mean partnerships across bloc lines and without threatening or disturbing existing alliances. In a declaration released at the June 1983 West German *Kirchentag,* entitled "For a New Politics of Security in Europe," several prominent church people East and West said that they would "learn to understand security partnership as a political translation of the Biblical commandment to love one's enemy."

What about the Soviet Union? Certainly, one good way *not* to love one's enemy intelligently is to declare categorically that they are the source of all evil in the world. That hardly inspires disarming confidence in the enemy toward our powers of perception. Instead, as an early draft of the U.S. Catholic Bishops' Pastoral Letter put it, perhaps "we also need to see the other as potentially more than an adversary. . . . Soviet behavior in some cases merits the adjective monstrous, but neither the Soviet people nor their leaders are monsters; they are human beings created in the image and likeness of God." Not to succumb to hysteria is to behave intelligently. We can seek the specific humanity of the peoples of the Soviet Union by not breaking off travel and trade, and by taking advantage of every opportunity for academic and cultural exchange. We can study the history, cultures, and languages of the Soviet Union, including their literature, especially the remarkable fiction of two contemporary Soviet authors: Chingis Aitmatov and Valentin Rasputin.

Always, we do things out of our Christian mandate to do *more* than non-Christians by loving our enemies. We have no promise from God that we shall be protected from our enemies. But even we are not left alone. God does give us the promise of sustenance as we have been given by God a sound mind to guide our behavior and the spirit of strength and love with which to fill it.

ENDNOTES

1. Carl Schmitt, "Der Begriff des Politischen," *Politische Wissenschaft,* Heft 5 (Berlin 1928).
2. George Kennan, *The Nuclear Delusion: Soviet-American Relations in the Atomic Age* (New York: Pantheon Books, 1982), p. xxii.
3. The Independent Commission on Disarmament and Security Issues, *Common Security* (New York: Simon & Shuster, 1982), p. 12.
4. Quoted in *New York Times* (February 20, 1983).
5. Martin Luther, *Gesammelte Schriften,* Weimar edition, III, 34.
6. Unpublished Bible study on the book of Colossions.
7. Martin Luther, *Gesammelte Schriften,* Weimar edition, V, 262.

8. Quoted in Roland Bainton, *Christian Attitudes toward War and Peace* (Nashville: Abingdon Press, 1960), p. 97.
9. Unpublished sermon, Berlin, 1980.
10. Conference of European Christians Occasional Paper, No. 12 (Geneva, 1980), pp. 73, 75.
11. Conference of European Christians Occasional Paper, No. 12 (Geneva, 1980), p. 85.
12. Final Document of the World Conference of Religious Workers for Saving the Sacred Gift of Life from Nuclear Catastrophe (Moscow, 1982), p. 12.

The Present Situation

THE NATIONAL SECURITY STATE

Richard J. Barnet

Over the past two generations a set of national security institutions has taken root in American soil that has transformed the government of the United States and its relationship to its citizens. These institutions are of two sorts: One threatens the security, even the survival, of other states in the name of national defense, and the other defends against enemies within by resort to secrecy, propaganda, and surveillance on a scale unprecedented in time of peace. As the twentieth century draws to a close both the United States and the Soviet Union appear to have become obsessed with national security, each unable because of its internal structures to establish durable, peaceful relations with the other. The search for security by the superpowers has not been notably successful for either side. By any measure the United States today is far less secure than in 1945 despite the expenditure of roughly three trillion dollars for the military establishment. The Soviet Union is also fifteen minutes away from annihilation and neither its leaders nor its people give much evidence of feeling secure. In both countries leaders assert the unprovable proposition that their national security efforts have prevented catastrophic war.

There is nothing new about the effort to achieve national security by military buildups and war. For almost five hundred years the primary function of the nation-state has been defense. Leaders have traditionally defended their territory by expanding it—acquiring foreign bases, colonies, and imperial possessions—and by carrying out pre-emptive attacks against potential attackers. Czarist Russia and Soviet Russia have at critical points followed this pattern. But this traditional approach to security does not take account of profound changes in the international economy and in the nature of war. In a world of nuclear missiles no nation can defend its territory in a literal sense. Nor can it insulate its economy from the world economy, particularly if its government is democratic. It was not until the Second World War that the United States which heretofore had maintained small military budgets and a modest regular army, experienced a dramatic change in its world-view. From then on this country has operated on the assumption that it faced a permanent national security emergency that had to be handled primarily by military means. Ironically, this shift in American thinking occurred at a moment when war was becoming an increasingly dubious political instrument.

Even by 1910 military operations had become too destructive on all sides to be a rational route to national security. In that year Norman Angell wrote *The Great Illusion* in which he correctly predicted that in any future European war the victors would turn out to be hardly better off than the vanquished. Britain and France emerged victorious from the world war eight years later but they had lost millions of lives and their empires were in dissolution. Their second victory twenty-five years later in World War II completed the process of imperial decline. Though the United States came out of World War II the most powerful nation on earth, perhaps, briefly, the paramount nation of all time, it has not won a decisive military victory since 1945 despite the trillions spent on the military and the frequent engagement of its military forces. Even its greatest successes in the use of force, the clandestine para-military operations in behalf of the Shah of Iran in 1953 and against the government of Guatemala in 1954 did not produce either political stability or lasting pro-U.S. regimes. Ironically, militarism, what Clausewitz called the use of force "contrary to common sense," is a natural, if pathological, reaction to the frustrations of a world in which war rarely accomplishes its intended purposes.

What Raymond Aron labelled "the century of total war" began with the First World War. Unlike earlier times, wars and preparation for war were no longer the projects of kings, dukes, and knights. Preparation for war had become the project of the whole population. Civilians became primary targets. This process of engaging the whole population in war had its culmination in the atomic bomb. The discovery and use of nuclear weapons has led to frantic efforts to make war-making power a useful political instrument once more. To fit the atomic bomb into the century of total war required the rehabilitation of limited war. How else could a nation maintain a permanent deterrent threat to the adversary without demoralizing its own population? The myth of limited war has been crucial in the nuclear age ever since the Soviets exploded their first atomic bomb. Robert McNamara's early conception of the Vietnam War was that, like the covert operations of the 1950's in Iran, Guatemala, and in Indochina itself, it could be pursued without mobilizing public anger. "The greatest contribution Vietnam is making—right or wrong is beside the point—" he said in 1966, "is that it is developing an ability in the United States to fight a limited war, to go to war without the necessity of arousing the public ire." Mobilization of the society for "national security" has become the substitute for total war.

The Legacy of World War II

The principal institutions of the national security state are a legacy of World War II. The global war against the fanatical nationalism of Germany and Japan proved to be a permanent jolt that transformed the United States government, the relationship of the government to the society, and the society itself. In 1939 the federal government had about eight hundred thousand civilian employees, 10 percent of whom worked for what we now call national security agencies. In keeping with a long tradition, prewar America had a small standing army, spent 1.4 percent of the gross national product on defense, had a handful of foreign bases, and strong suspicion of militarism. A sense of security nurtured by two vast oceans was reflected in moral attitudes of political leaders that are now considered hopelessly quaint. In the interwar period a U.S. Army chief of staff could veto plans for an airplane because it was immoral to bomb civilians. A secretary of state could reject plans for an intelligence operation because "gentlemen do not read each other's mail." And just before World War I a president (Woodrow Wilson in 1915) could fly into a rage upon discovering that the army actually had contingency plans for fighting wars.

The National Security Act of 1947 made permanent the national security focus that had dominated the war years. A National Security Council was established to mobilize the resources of government, and through government the resources of the economy for "national security," but nowhere was national security defined. The Central Intelligence Agency was created with a broad and substantially secret mandate to protect the national security through spying and covert paramilitary operations that have included the spreading of disinformation, bribery, and the planning of assassination. Most of the wartime bases were retained and their number expanded as the Cold War developed. The wartime proposal of Charles Wilson of General Electric that the United States maintain in peacetime a "permanent war economy" was put into effect. Relations between the federal government and heavy industry, especially high technology industry, that had turned the country into the "arsenal of democracy" were retained largely intact under the theory that there would never again be time to start industrial mobilization from scratch as in 1939.

Thus was born what President Dwight Eisenhower called the "military-industrial complex." The balance of power within the federal government was fundamentally altered. The New Deal agencies concerned with social security, development, and economic justice lost the lion's share of the budget and the power to shape national priorities to those agencies with one mandate or another to protect national security. Indeed, key non-military expenditures such as the interstate highway system secured the necessary congressional support only by being presented as security expenditures. (The citizen was encouraged to believe that he could escape the bomb by getting on one of the clogged "evacuation routes.") Considerable research was carried out in civilian institutions with the financial support of the military establishment and the result was the rise of what Eisenhower referred to as a "scientific-technical elite" heavily dependent on the Pentagon. The nation's colleges and universities became, in the words of the President of Michigan State, "bastions of our defense." Intellect had become, as the President of the University of California put it, "an instrument of national purpose. . . "

In the Century of Total War the search for national security became all pervasive. No environment from the depths of the ocean to the outer reaches of space to the inner recesses of human consciousness was off limits; the preparation for war would go on wherever the human imagination could conceive a "vital interest" or a military mission. Research on chemical and biological weapons proceeded even in the face of tabus, international agreements, and unilateral declarations of restraint on the ground that possible violations by the enemy of minimal civilized standards for conducting warfare justified pre-emptive research. Any "gap" between the horrifying weapons of the adversary and our own was deemed a mortal vulnerability. Virtually any lacuna in military potential could produce the panic needed for stepped-up appropriations. The fact that existing stockpiles of nuclear weapons, poisons, and strangulating gases were already more than sufficient to obliterate all human life provided little comfort. The most implausible predictions of a weapons "breakthrough" by the enemy could produce whole new generations of lethal technology. Even thoughts were a potential battleground. The CIA experimented secretly with mind-altering drugs on unsuspecting subjects.

Before World War II the managers of the large corporations, moved by traditional conservative concerns, were suspicious of industrial mobilization for war. The military was wasteful and unproductive. The government would become too involved with business; military procurement is by definition an effort in government planning. But the wartime experience proved highly profitable for business. The federal government became a steady customer, not overly fussy about quality, relaxed about being overcharged, and generous with subsidies for research. It soon became a fundamental tenet of the national security state ideology that military expenditures, provided they did not exceed some arbitrary percentage of gross national product, could not be harmful to the economy. Indeed the beneficial effects were immediately apparent. The Korean War mobilization, the Vietnam War mobilization, and the current Reagan military buildup all fueled economic growth, recovery from recessions, and were helpful in reducing high levels of unemployment.

In a national security state the economy is perceived as a weapon. Its potential for massive military buildup and its ability to stay on the frontier of technology are crucial to the theory of deterrence on which national security in the nuclear era depends. Only a growing economy that is willing to tithe to the military year after year adequately projects the national will to survive, according to the theory. More and more the arms race has become a spending race. A weapons system is procured not to provide a significant new military capability but to put the adversary to the expense of trying to counter it. Reagan administration officials have publicly advanced the thesis, contrary to considerable historical evidence, that heating up the spending race will induce the Soviets, because of their economic problems, to make important concessions.

In a national security state the military budget becomes the key planning instrument through which billions of dollars can be injected into the national economy and targeted to specific industries and regions. Under a capitalist system in which market forces are supposed to be the primary organizers of economic life, the domain of national security is the uniquely legitimate arena for continuous, massive government intervention. But in the process the society becomes dependent on military production as an economic stimulus and creator of employment.

Although the New Deal conception of the state was quite different from that of the national security state, in one respect the Roosevelt era paved the way. It established the legitimacy of the activist state and the inevitability of big government.

The idea that government should act as the rudder of the society went against the American grain. Though the federal government was always far more intervention-ist than legend had it, it was not until the New Deal that welfare, educational, and service functions once the exclusive province of the private market, the family, the church, or local community were considered legitimate Washington concerns.

At the same time it was only in World War II that the United States became an integrated continental nation. Technological developments including the airplane, business machinery, and marketing techniques created a national market for almost anything. The experience of war was a national unifier. Millions who joined the army left their small towns forever. The black migrations from the South changed the face of the industrial cities. Television hastened the process that Hollywood and the radio networks had begun, the creation of a coast-to-coast popular culture. The downplaying of regional differences and the homogenization of culture through increasingly centralized control of the media facilitated the growth of the national security state. The new popular attitudes toward the federal government nurtured by the New Deal and Truman's Fair Deal cut away at traditional suspicion of big government. At the same time the libertarian strain of American conservatism with its hostility to centralized power gave way to anticommunism. Mainstream conser-vatism remained as ideologically opposed to big government as ever without being troubled by the ever-expanding national security establishment.

The operative worldview of the national security state pre-existed anti-Communism. Indeed what we call anti-Communism is a simplification of a set of precepts, fears, and strategic notions that would be part of our political culture had Marx and Lenin never caused any trouble. The nation exists to preserve its power. Power can never be preserved unless it grows. Like a human organism a state is either developing or declining. The purpose of power is to acquire more power. Power is defined as the ability to bend others to your will, for in a hostile world nothing can be accomplished unless predatory forces are held in check by fear. Ironically the paranoid rhetoric and menacing posture of the Soviet Union lent credibility to a national security worldview, the intellectual antecedents of which are to be found in the geopolitical writings at the beginning of this century of such influential strategists as Mackinder, Kjellen, and Mahan.

At a time when Stalingrad was still under siege and it would have taken a lively imagination to conjure up a Soviet threat of world domination, United States mili-tary planners had already begun planning a huge postwar military machine. The stimulus was not the Soviet Union but a worldview in which the planners assumed a revived Germany and Japan. The hostile Soviet Union as the focus of American fears came later. Indeed, the document assumed that the Soviet Union was an ally, not an enemy. As the war ended the Army wanted a ground force capable of expanding to 4.5 million men within a year. The Navy thought it wanted to keep 600,000 men, 371 major combat ships, 5,000 auxiliaries, and a "little air force" of 8,000 planes. The Air Force wanted to be a separate service that would have a 70-group force with 400,000 men.

The national security worldview was shaped less by the Soviet Union than by the memory of Hitler. The national security state was legitimized in large measure by the sense of national guilt at not having marshalled the superior military might of the democracies in time to avert the catastrophe of world war. The lesson of the Hitler time was taken to be that peace not based on the dynamic preparation for war and the timely threat of military action was a naive and dangerous illusion. The existence of the bomb made the possibility of a new Hitlerian *blitzkrieg* even more dangerous and placed a premium on averting war by pre-emptive threats of mass destruction. The disadvantages of democracy in maneuvering in this perilous environment were apparent to American leaders. As the Cold War began Dean Acheson worried that the isolationist sentiments and hatred of war of the American people would inhibit the national security establishment in making credible the threats needed to make deterrence work. You could not be a superpower in the nuclear age if leaders felt hamstrung by phlegmatic or fearful populations. The Hitlers of the future were always waiting to test the will of the Number One Nation. To marshal public support for nerve-testing "crisis management," the managers of the national security establishment created for them a reality that was, as Acheson himself once put it, "clearer than truth."

Indeed, one constant theme in the national security literature is concern for the weak nerves of the American people. In the Century of Total War the will of the people is a critical national weapon, particularly so when the only "defense" is a deterrent strategy based on convincing the adversary that the leader has the popular backing to threaten national suicide. The ideology of the national security state denies the possibility of peace based on anything other than a permanent arms race. Even arms control which is unenthusiastically accepted within the national security establishment assumes the continuation of a qualitative arms race. Though there was an earlier American tradition of seeking peace through legal arrangements—the legacy of Elihu Root, John Dewey, Herbert Hoover, William Borah, and others—the experience of Hitler made it easy to disparage images of a peace based on an international legal order or on strong international organizations such as the United Nations. Idealism and cowardice had produced World War II; realism demanded that the American people settle for what John Kennedy in his inaugural address called a "hard and bitter peace."

The State of Permanent War

The national security state structures could not accomplish their task unless the American people were socialized to accept the idea that the only peace possible is a form of permanent war. Conflict is not resolved; it is managed. "Small" battles as in Korea or Vietnam are fought to prevent cataclysmic ones. Rival intelligence agencies stalk one another every day in a continuing "back-alley war" of propaganda, espionage, and assassination in the service of secret purposes. When I was a freshman at Harvard in 1948, the president of the university, James Bryant Conant, told us that our generation was fated never to know peace. If we were lucky, we would live out our lives in a twilight zone—neither war nor peace.

The sacrifice for national security is made legitimate by the image of The Enemy. How much of a sacrifice the United States has made for national security is hard to calculate but even the obvious costs have been heavy. Besides the trillions

spent, the energy, imagination, and talent of millions of people have been channeled into the quest for security. But in the process the American people, if polls
are to believed, have lost hope even in the possibility of a world from which the
threat of nuclear annihilation has been banished. The institutionalized hopelessness
offered by the national security state exacts a psychic toll, particularly on young
people, as recent research by psychiatrists such as John Mack and others suggests.

From the first the ideology of the national security state actually reinforced
feelings of insecurity among the American people because it assumed the existence
of a never-ending threat. The name of the threat might change—China moved from
being a focus of even greater evil than the Soviet Union to its present status of
quasially—but a threat of one sort or another to justify the never-ending flow of
resources to the military was now a fixture of American life. It is one of history's
great ironies that at the very moment when the United States had a monopoly of
nuclear weapons, possessed most of the world's gold, produced half the world's
goods on its own territory, and laid down the rules for allies and adversaries alike,
it was afraid. When Dean Acheson gave a speech in 1950 declaring that the United
States must create "situations of strength" the nation was not only the strongest
power on earth but it was stronger in relation to other nations than it would ever be
again. After the expenditure of the trillions of dollars the U.S. would end up having
less influence over external events than it had before the arms race began.

One reason for this is that the ideology of the national security state distorts the
meaning of security by defining it in primarily military terms. The source of American power and influence at the end of World War II was not so much its military
might as the promise of its economic and technological development and the admi-
ration in much of the world (extending even to Mao's China and Ho Chi Minh's
Vietnam) for our democratic institutions. In the economic potential and the promise
of liberty lay the great comparative advantage of the United States. By choosing to
measure power in military terms, that is the means to coerce others, the nation
offered competition in the one field of combat in which it was easiest to match it.

Thus fear has been a weapon for mobilizing the American public, but it has
had a boomerang effect. To secure ever-increasing revenues for the national security establishment it has been necessary to keep dramatizing the threat and so the
psychic rewards of the military buildup, the sense of increasing safety, are never
available. In an arms race no one ever wins and it is never safe to stop. The heavy
economic sacrifice and the inevitable infringement on traditional liberties demanded by the national security state are legitimized by the enemy. An enemy
worthy of the world's most powerful state and richest society must be an evil
empire, a threat not only to the nation but to all humanity. The heavy sacrifice of
traditional American values inherent in the militarization of our society, the rise in
secrecy, official deception, and the employment of so many to plan mass destruction and so few even to think about alternative approaches to peace is rationalized
as a last ditch defense of civilization itself.

The Soviet Union has played the role of enemy as if they were reading from an
American script. It has given inspiration, legitimacy, and support to the national
security state in the United States just as the United States has cooperated in rein-

forcing paranoid fears within the Soviet Union which Kremlin leaders use to legitimize their own rule. Official atheism and continued harassment of Christians and
Jews in the Soviet Union make it possible to enlist popular support for an ongoing
anti-Soviet crusade by touching the deepest feelings of people in the United States.
The repression of non-Russians, Poles, citizens of the former Baltic states, and
other ethnic minorities well represented in the United States lends authenticity to
the official U.S. picture of the Soviet Union. The belligerent statements of Soviet
leaders from Khrushchev's "we will bury you" to the more cautious invective of
today's leaders help to make the official American characterization of the "Soviet
threat" credible. Soviet clumsiness and defensiveness in handling a disaster such as
the shooting down of the Korean airliner in 1983 made it easier for the Reagan
Administration to charge and millions of Americans to believe, contrary to the
evidence, that the top leadership had ordered the deliberate massacre of civilians.

The predictable Soviet military buildup which has enabled them to match each
major U.S. innovation in lethal technology within five to seven years—the atomic
bomb, hydrogen bomb, ICBM, MIRV, and cruise missile were all developed here
first—has made it easy to arouse popular alarm in the United States. As the military
spending on both sides has increased, the Soviets have indeed become more of a
threat in the classic military sense: their capabilities for destroying the world are
becoming more impressive year by year. Thus the implied promise of the national
security state has never been fulfilled. Because leaders in the United States have
regularly asserted since 1946 that "the language of force" is the only language the
Soviets understand, one might have expected the Soviet threat to decline as the
U.S. investment in the military rose. But the opposite has been the case. After
almost forty years of an escalating arms race the will and capability of the Soviet
Union to compete has been proved again and again. The Soviet Union, which was a
severely damaged, economically backward Eurasian power with a record of cautious military deployments outside its own territory, except for the adjacent territories overrun in the war against Hitler, can now destroy the United States and as a
consequence of its steady buildup now deploys a formidable ocean-going navy, an
invading army in Afghanistan, and a sizeable military presence in Syria. There is
nothing in its recent history to suggest that under increasing U.S. military and
ideological pressure it is prepared to be more accommodating to the United States.
If indeed it is true that military force is the only language they understand, they
understand it differently from what American taxpayers have been led to expect.

Why was the United States, which was at the zenith of its power in the late
1940's when the Cold War began, so fearful? American leaders did not fear a
Soviet invasion of Western Europe, much less of the United States. They did not
fear a fight over what later came to be called the Third World; Stalin could hardly
have been less interested in poor countries that were unready and unsuited to tight
control from Moscow. The fear that swept Amerian leadership at the very moment
of American preeminence was ideological, not military. In 1946 President Truman
and his advisers worried about the health of the American economy. The unemployment rate in 1939 was 18% and many economists predicted a return to depres-
sion once the stimulus of wartime spending came to an end.

At the same time the Soviet Union, about which little was widely known, enjoyed considerable prestige as the radical alternative to Hitlerism. Capitalism in Europe had been discredited. Communists had fought bravely in the resistance. American leaders worried about the power of left-wing politicians and intellectuals in the U.S. and Europe to subvert pluralist democracy rooted in capitalism. Totalitarianism—the all-powerful state resting its power on the manipulated fanaticism of mass organizations—seemed to be on the march. The Communist Party of the Soviet Union had engineered a state as ruthless as Hitler's but it seemed even more formidable to some American officials such as James Forrestal because it promised not a demonic "new order" but a beguiling dream of justice and abundance. Thus the challenge of the Soviet Union was perceived to be one primarily of ideas. Their vaunted divisions, most of which had actually been secretly demobilized, assured them they would get attention for their ideas. The Soviets had a mastery of propaganda and an "organizational weapon" to make people believe their dubious claims. If Soviet divisions ever marched west, it would be because some subversive minority called for them. But the power and prestige of communism in Europe quickly crested. By 1946 communists were out of government everywhere and in the United States left-wing forces suffered crushing setbacks in the early postwar years in struggles within the U.S. labor movement. By 1948 with the debacle of Henry Wallace's campaign for the presidency on the Progressive Party ticket the ideological defeat of the left within the industrial world was complete.

Yet the fear in the United States was greater than ever. Stalin did enough—the brutality of the Berlin blockade, repression in the U.S.S.R. and Eastern Europe, stonewalling diplomacy and vituperative rhetoric—to lend credibility to the carefully crafted official image of the enemy. But the fear generated in the American population by national security officials, even after the outbreak of the Korean war, was not precisely the fear that galvanized the national security bureaucracy itself. Privately, officials worried about geopolitical abstractions and long-term possibilities. With the decline of British, French, and Japanese power they feared that a "power vacuum" would develop in the former colonies and dependencies of the collapsing imperial powers into which Soviet influence would inevitably flow. The only alternative would be for the United States to assume "responsibilities" for these strategic regions. Non-alignment, neutralism, or self-determination for weak nations were ruled out as a serious option. No alternative to control by one superpower or another existed. By drafting an appropriate memorandum in the National Security Council distant lands were instantly converted into "vital interests" of the United States.

But the public face put on this geopolitical analysis was different: The Soviet hordes, it was said, were about to burst out of their enormous land mass and by a variety of military and non-military efforts take over the world. Acheson likened the situation for congressional leaders to the death struggle of Carthage and Rome. Only the threat to make nuclear war, to ring the Soviet empire with military bases, and to maintain unrelenting ideological hostility to anything resembling Communism could keep the Soviets in check. Though their history, ideology, and the international climate in which they operated were quite different, Stalin and his successors were given the role of Hitler in the drama of national security.

The Lack of Debate

The geopolitical assumptions at the heart of the national security state were not subjected to political debate. The thought processes which enable sophisticated national security managers to make the stubborn facts of a disorderly world fit a Manichaean worldview border on the arcane. The public face of the national security state, on the other hand, is disarmingly simple. Preparing for war prevents war. The nation with the most weapons is the strongest. The threat of force is an effective weapon against Communism, terrorism, and other pernicious ideas.

The military research laboratories, the defense-related industries, and the labyrinthine network of national security agencies of the government understandably elicit fierce loyalty from the few million people who receive steady, sometimes handsome pay, exciting, purposeful work, and considerable prestige from these institutions. But defense workers, military contractors and subcontractors, defense intellectuals, weapons designers, and national security bureaucrats do not constitute an electoral majority. Plainly, the national security state, despite its failure to deliver either security in the commonly accepted physical sense or a feeling of security in a psychological or spiritual sense enjoys the overwhelming support of the American public. And this is so despite rising concern about huge budget deficits substantially attributable to military expenditures and a disturbing increase in secrecy and surveillance in American life all in the name of national security.

The "engineering of consent" is crucial to the national security state. Edward L. Bernays's definition of public relations accurately describes the process by which the consensus on national security is maintained. Most Americans are inhibited from having or expressing personal convictions on matters relating to national security for a number of reasons. First, the topic is amorphous and seemingly complex. The masses of numbers about weapons, budgets, "kill ratios," and other bits of jargon make it seem almost hopeless to follow the "debate." Second, the great emphasis put by government on the creation of classified information and the highly publicized, though not always successful, effort to protect secret information cause most citizens to believe that they do not know sufficient "facts" to challenge official truth. Third, the threat to the survival of the nation is invoked in support of every new weapons system.

In the Reagan administration there has been a renewed effort to use national security as a rationale for keeping tighter control over information. The Intelligence Identities Protection Act makes it a crime for a reporter to reveal what Seymour Hersh and others have disclosed about the activities of U.S. employees engaged in destabilization operations in Chile, Zaire, and elsewhere which contradicted the public declarations of the U.S. Government. The security classification system has been expanded to make more information secret. Former CIA officials and academic scientists are under increasing legal pressure to submit manuscripts and research plans for government review and approval before publication. There is no "inherent right to . . . conduct research free of government review,"

Lawrence J. Brady, Assistant Secretary of Commerce for Trade Administration, asserted. A 1983 Executive Order created a censorship system of considerable scope with a reach unprecedented in time of peace.

Ten years ago President Nixon defended the wiretaps placed on his own National Security Council employee and on well-known reporters and columnists on the grounds that freedom must sometimes be sacrificed for security. Shortly after assuming office President Reagan pardoned two former FBI officials convicted of planning and supervising warrantless break-ins of private homes in a search for members of the Weather Underground because they were acting on "high principle to bring an end to . . . terrorism." As the Judiciary Committee of the House of Representatives pointed out in the Watergate Impeachment hearings, the classic way democracies slide into dictatorship is for a democratically elected leader to assert the exclusive right to decide what the public safety requires and for the assertion to meet too weak a challenge.

While the control of relevant information by the national security establishment is a powerful device for engineering consent, the monopoly of patriotic symbols is even more effective. The one exception to the proposition that military power rarely secures a political objective for a great nation in the contemporary international system is the trivial war in which victory is glorious because the risks are small. The occupation of Grenada and the defeat of Argentina in the Falklands are examples. These victories, which briefly thrilled the public, removed no serious threat but they made a familiar point. A big nation can defeat a small nation when there is no danger that another nuclear power will intervene.

In the Grenada invasion the press was kept out lest on-the-scene reporting disturb official truth. The historic role of the press in helping to keep government honest is incompatible with the conduct of undeclared or covert wars. Since Vietnam leaders of the armed forces have expressed their concern publicly about being asked to commit American troops to military action abroad which is depicted on television, for what is shown on the screen tends to erode public support. Yet whenever the president commits American troops abroad as in Grenada or Lebanon the dignity of the nation is at stake. Few citizens feel comfortable challenging a decision of the commander in chief, at least not until it has resulted in some demonstrable catastrophe as in North Korea and in Vietnam. But by that time a heavy price in blood and treasure has already been paid, and it is politically unpalatable to suggest that it be simply written off. Citizens who may accord no weight whatever to the opinions of the man in the White House on abortion, taxation, or water conservation regard him differently when he speaks as commander in chief.

It is perhaps not surprising that during the years when the bipartisan consensus on foreign policy was robust—roughly from 1953 to 1968—there was so little challenge to the development of the national security state for in a time of unprecedented prosperity and growth most Americans had no reason to question it. The innovations of the late 1940's—security through nuclear deterrence, containment by military intervention against leftist revolutions, a global network of alliances, and a liberal economic order for which the U.S. set the rules—had indeed produced what Henry Luce had called the American Century. But by the late 1960's the consensus had unravelled and it has never been restored. The interesting question is why a new consensus with a less self-defeating approach to national security has not emerged.

The answer, in my view, is to be found in three places. First, no major institution in the society had an investment in an alternative vision of national security. The influential architects of national security policy in the Truman, Eisenhower, and Kennedy administrations crossed party lines and often worked for both parties, a practice which persists. The influential universities became part of the national security establishment rather than detached critics and still play that role. With the onset of the Cold War, professors for the first time could count on exercising great power in Washington but only if their opinions were "responsible." Hawkish views, even when they did not prevail, were no bar to advancement in the bureaucracy but those who were successfully labelled "soft" or "idealistic" or "naive" for opposing militaristic analyses and solutions found that their usefulness in government was at an end.

Nor did the religious institutions hold up an alternative vision of national security. The Catholic Church was so caught up in the ideological war with Communism that the moral issues surrounding nuclear weapons were not raised with vigor until the 1980's. Protestant churches for the most part shied away from challenging either the state or the patriotic consensus. While some Jews pondered the moral implications of basing security on the threat of a global holocaust, the threat to the survival of Israel and the plight of Jews in Russia enlisted the support of the American Jewish community for the basic assumptions undergirding the national security state. In none of the denominations did leaders ask what it now meant to be a patriot in a world in which nations threatened to defend their vital interests by blowing up the world.

The U.S. labor movement became an enthusiastic supporter of the national security consensus. For leaders of the movement the Cold War was an effective weapon to defeat communists and fellow travellers who were strong in certain unions at the end of the war. Moreover, any labor leader who wished to be treated as the representative of a major interest group rather than as an agitator had to accept the bipartisan foreign policy. For labor leaders of the last two generations endorsement of the worldview of the national security state came easily, for the Soviet Union, which claimed to be a workers' state, insisted on making labor unions instruments of state control.

In the Cold War years the control of the media became more centralized. Many newspapers disappeared, and more and more the three television networks created the image of the outside world for most American citizens. Despite a record of disclosure of shocking news, sometimes over government objection, and the presentation of reality often at odds with official truth, television by virtue of its technique and style has tended to reinforce the dominant national security consensus. Its style of cutting up the world into short, disconnected stories presents a chaos that cries out for great simplifiers, and that is a role that postwar presidents and their advisers have skillfully performed. The words of the president, the secretary of defense, and other high officials in support of the prevailing national security consensus are then carried as news. The authority of the speakers lends credibility to what they say. While peace marchers, clergy, retired generals who suddenly lash out at the arms race, or the occasional housewife who is interviewed about her anxiety concerning nuclear war also make news, the news is not in what they say so much as in the fact that they are sufficiently agitated to make a scene.

Fundamental questions about security—what are the most likely threats and how does a nation meet them—are almost never raised on national television. The commentators who appeared after the widely viewed film "The Day After" reflected the narrowness of permissible debate. The national security "generalists" such as Robert McNamara and Henry Kissinger supported the basic assumptions of the national security state. The only dissonant notes were struck by a scientist, Carl Sagan, who offered research data about the horrors of nuclear war and the writer on the Holocaust, Elie Wiesel, who pondered the moral agony. Neither was perceived as a national security expert. Newspapers regularly offer short op-ed spaces for any alternative view of national security that can be presented in 800 words. Even the occasional longer work challenging conventional wisdom that commands more than a tiny audience such as Jonathan Schell's *The Fate of the Earth* is admired for style but its substance is easily dismissed as being "utopian," particularly so since institutions for public education on alternative visions of national security are weak. Political parties in the U.S., for example, conceive their task as presenting alternative personalities, not continuing public education in alternative ideas. Thus those who may be stirred by new ideas have no institutional base either to elaborate or debate them, much less implement them. This contributes to passivity and a sense of resignation, and may explain something about low voter turnout.

The university reflects and reinforces the intellectual crosscurrents that keep thinking about national security within conventional limits. For example, the most devastating critique of an alternative idea on national security whether in a university seminar or on a TV talk show is to characterize it as "idealistic" which is a synonym for "impractical." The possibility even that human beings have the capacity to evolve their political institutions beyond the Hobbesian "realism" of the arms race is rarely taken seriously. There are few places in our society where that sort of thinking is encouraged.

A second way to keep the policy choices within narrow limits is to challenge the motives of those who put forward alternatives. In an atmosphere of permanent threat the distinction between dissent and disloyalty is often blurred in such a way as to set the limits of "responsible" debate and to discredit ideas that veer too far from the orthodox consensus. In the 1950's the term "creeping socialism" was effectively used to discredit such ideas as national health insurance. Those who wished to see social welfare programs not unlike those introduced seventy years before by Bismarck had to defend themselves against the suspicion that they were for a Soviet America. In the national security debate charges of cowardice, disloyalty, or sinister hidden motives were routinely hurled at those who dissented from the dominant national security vision. Those who advocated proposals that might be negotiable, such as Eisenhower's adviser Harold Stassen, were discredited as "soft" on the Russians. President Reagan has continued this tradition by characterizing members of the peace movement as KGB agents or dupes of KGB agents.

In the last few years there has been an organized right-wing campaign to discredit as "Soviet disinformation" ideas, proposals, or information which self-selected patriots define as excessively dissonant. On the far right there is a theory developing which could drastically reduce legitimate debate further. In 1980 the Heritage Foundation prepared a report which suggested that "clergymen, students, businessmen, entertainers, labor officials, journalists, and government workers all may engage in subversive activities without being fully aware of the extent, purpose, or control of their activities." Since "terrorists cadres" are spawned "in the splinters of dissident or extremist movements," people who are unwitting subversives must of course be watched. Since anybody espousing an idea with which, say, the Soviets might agree, is a prime suspect of being one of their tools, the Heritage Foundation theory, which fortunately is not law, simply institutionalizes paranoia and makes intelligent debate on the most basic choices facing the country even more difficult. In a highly charged intellectual and political climate it is human nature to cling to orthodox ideas even when they don't make sense. The most effective censorship operating in the United States is self-censorship.

Finally, it is easy to place the responsibility for the deteriorating international climate exclusively on forces outside the United States. It takes two to tango, as diplomats are fond of saying. International affairs are becoming increasingly anarchic. The breeding grounds of world war—the Middle East, Eastern Europe, Latin America, Persian Gulf, Sino-Soviet border—appear to be less subject to the control of either superpower than in the past. One consequence of this is that confrontations between the superpowers will grow harder to manage. Prudence dictates avoiding them altogether, but in the present poisonous atmosphere that is not a realistic expectation. Thus as the world becomes more dangerous the American people face troubling questions they have not yet confronted about the institutions that promise security but cannot deliver.

BLACK HISTORY AND THE PERILS OF EQUAL OPPORTUNITY

Vincent Harding

When faced with open eyes and open hearts, the pilgrimage of our people in this country is filled with much pain. Black history celebrations often tend either to minimize the pain and focus on the "great achievements" of our heroes and heroines, or they tend to use the pain as a club to bludgeon white America with guilt. In my opinion neither of these tendencies offers the strength and guidance we need for a new creation of our future, for a movement that will take us beyond a repetition of our past. Rather, I believe that the most mature and hopeful approach to our history must be one which faces the pain and its causes without flinching, and at the same moment seeks out the healers among us, those who point us to new possibilities for ourselves, our people and this nation.

Over the past six months I have been pressed both to reexamine and wrestle with the pain, but also to dance and celebrate with the healers. Somehow the tragedy of Grenada, the excitement over the first Black astronaut and the rescue of Lt. Robert Goodman by Jesse Jackson and his companions have all combined to send me back to Harriet Tubman, to W.E.B. Dubois, to Martin Luther King, the healers. These recent events have also conspired to fill my ears and heart with Langston Hughes' healing declaration: "America, you've never been America to me: But I swear you will be." Indeed, the events of the most recent period have driven me to explore again the fundamental difference between the life of a people who strive for "equal opportunities" in the dangerous America we know today and the life of a community committed to the struggle for the humanizing transformation of America—"I swear you will be."

The immediate focus of my wrestling with the past has been the Black experience with the military forces of the United States of America. Nowhere else do the painful ironies of our experience appear in such sharp relief. Nowhere can we see so clearly what happened when a thrust toward equal opportunities is not undergirded and informed by a swelling movement towards fundamental transformation. For if the America that does not yet exist is not brought into being soon, we will be rapidly creating a generation of poor and non-white mercenaries who will fight other poor and non-white people partly because they are deceived by the poison of anticommunism, partly because they will be given prominent and high level models of non-white "achievement" in the military and partly because the nation provides no other way for them to earn a living.

The painful symbolism and powerful realities of our situation were opened up as soon as the nation began its armed struggle for independence in the 1770's. Thousands of our enslaved people fought in that war, daring to hope not only that their own personal freedom would be won that way, but their service to this freedom-seeking new nation might mean freedom for the hundreds of thousands of their fellow Africans in chains here. At that moment the pain and the irony began. For not only were the overwhelming majority of people kept in slavery, but when the leaders of the new "democratic" nation wrote their constitution, our slavery and our degradation were written into the founding document. That was the first reward for our military service to the nation.

When the Civil War came, as white leaders from Abraham Lincoln on down tried initially to disassociate the war from the struggle against slavery, Black people saw a different vision. For most of us, there was no question that our liberating God was at work, and we sought to enlist in this "freedom war" as we insisted on calling it. Initially we were rudely refused. But when the blood of white young men began to drench the ground, when such young men rioted against the draft and often refused to renew their enlistments, when tens of thousands of Black people took their own first steps towards freedom and flooded the Union lines, when the Union commanders finally decided they could not any longer fight and win the war without enlisting Black men, the stage was set for a new irony.

Responding to the pressures of Black and white abolitionists to the initiatives taken by the slaves, and to the needs of his military commanders (as well as the wrestlings within his own spirit), Lincoln issued the Emancipation Proclamation. He called it "a war measure," and whatever else it was it was certainly that. For the proclamation ends with a presidential declaration that the newly freed Black men "of suitable condition," will be received into the armed service of the United States. "So we moved from slavery to emancipation to the armed services of the United States. And there is much evidence that while our movement into the service was certainly meant to mobilize our strength in the struggle against the Confederacy, induction into the military was also used in many places as a means of controlling large numbers of newly freed Black men who might not be otherwise controllable, and who might take their freedom more seriously than the president and his cabinet intended. (See chapters 11 and 12 of "There is a River" for a more extended treatment of this subject of the Union army serving as a means of controlling freedom-seeking Black men.)

Then, when the war ended, Black people of the South demanded the continuing presence of their Black troops among them. For this newly freed community it was obvious that if they were to exercise their citizenship rights they needed such a Black military presence to protect them against the fears, the hostility, the violence, and the refusal of the white South to deal with a new order. Instead, the federal government removed the Black troops. The men in Washington were responding largely to objections from whites in the South and the North who could not endure the thought of Black men in federal uniforms having authority over white men, even rebellious, seditious white men. The government was also responding to its own lack of will to press forward the accidental revolution that the war had opened.

Not only did they remove the Black troops, leaving the newly freed community naked to the rising violence of the resurgent white conservative forces, but in addition they compounded the pain and the irony. For after the short-term Black enlistees had been discharged, returning them to a perilous life of freedom, the long-term soldiers, the new Black professionals, were sent in all their uniformed, segregated splendor across the Mississippi River. There they were assigned the task of assisting the white forces of the U.S. army who were closing a noose of genocidal destruction around the lives and hopes of the beleaguered natives of this continent. Withdrawn from the protecting of their own people, playing the role of good soldiers, setting a pattern that would explode again in the midst of the life of our own generation. Such is the pain with which I wrestle.

Many other images arise out of that pain. At the end of the 19th century, with the onset of the Spanish-Cuban-American War, I see the same Buffalo Soldiers moved again, crammed into the lower decks of the troop ships, sent to "liberate" the African, Hispanic, and native peoples of Cuba from the domination of Spain— while brutal lynchings raged against their own people in the United States. In that same period I see Black troops carried along to help suppress the legitimate independence movement of the people of the Philippines. And I hear the voice of a wise Black leader of that time saying "the American Negro cannot become the ally of imperialism without enslaving his own race."

The pain and the search for direction continues in the memories of World War I, where tens of thousands of Black soldiers were sent across the ocean to "make the world safe for democracy," while their exposed and unsafe relatives were being attacked by mobs in this country who had not yet heard about democracy.

Nor can we forget the hundreds of thousands of Black men who went again during World War II, fighting this time for the Four Freedoms announced by Franklin Roosevelt and Winston Churchill, returning to this country without the freedom to ride on segregated trains, without the freedom to vote, with many finding themselves under attack and some murdered in their own country while still wearing their freedom-fighting uniforms of the U.S. military.

None of us can escape the pain. None of us did, whether we knew it or not. I was there as a teenager among the millions of Americans dancing in the streets in that summer of 1945. We were dancing in the streets because the war was over. We did not say it out loud very often, but we were essentially dancing in the streets because we had incinerated and radiated hundreds of thousands of Japanese children, grandparents, nuns, priests, ordinary people. But we were rejoicing we said, because the atomic bombs had "saved the lives of thousands of our boys." So not only were we being deceived by this story, but we were accepting the idea that somehow the lives of both "our boys" were more valuable to the God of life than the lives of Japanese boys and girls and men and women. So we danced in the streets, separate but equal, danced over the ovens of Hiroshima and Nagasaki.

From that time on, from Nagasaki to Grenada and Lebanon, there has been no

[97]

essential variation in the pattern. From 1945 to the present, American bombs have been dropped only on poor, non-white peoples, and American soldiers have been sent only to fight against the revolutionary struggles of poor, non-white peoples. In that setting, the Korean War deepened the pain and heightened the irony. Now the military services were being desegregated, and Black boys could kill and die with white boys, but could not really live together in America. So we were offered equality in killing and dying, fighting against Communism, we were told for the honor of a "free world" that still does not exist.

Vietnam brought it all home, and we are still living with the death it sowed within, among us. There we Black folks burst beyond the bounds of equal opportunity, and we were manning the fighting stations in numbers far beyond our proportional population in the military and in the nation. Killing poor people who had no argument against us, forgetting, as Mohammed Ali put it, "no Viet Cong ever called me nigger," we burned villages, collected our checks, and were often stoned out of our minds to help us deny what we were doing. All the while, Watts was burning, Newark was burning, Detroit was burning, Black anger, rage, and protest were burning across the face of America. The fires in Vietnam and the fires in the U.S.A. were one.

For reasons that I do not fully understand, it was the attack on Grenada that opened all of this in me again, opened me not only to the pain, but to the possibilities of healing. The criminal invasion of a tiny nation was made even worse by this country's desperate desire to believe the lies of its government, but our willingness to salivate in fear and hostility at the words "Communist revolution" or "Cuban revolution." Worst of all for me were the images of the young, Black, Hispanic, and poor white men who rode the armored military vehicles along Grenada's potholed roads. Their own pain was being cruelly manipulated by America's leaders again. Unable to find a job in civilian life, they were now being paid to intervene in the struggles of other poor, non-white people who were trying to solve the problems of poverty and colonial domination in their own country. So, our young men now had checks to send home, blood money, the blood of our brothers and sisters, our blood, the blood of America's broken hopes for a society where no one has to kill poor people in order to have a check for our families. Equal opportunity? To be all we can be? Is this what our freedom-bound foreparents had in mind? For us to be killing wherever America's leaders demanded, wherever they promise us uniforms, "security," and money for our families? No, we were meant to be more, much more, and so was our country meant to be more, much more. "I swear you will be." But how? That is the question over which we must spend the rest of our lives working to create a new answer.

Biblical Perspectives

LIMITS ON A CHRISTIAN'S OBEDIENCE TO THE STATE

Lamar Williamson, Jr.

A Personal Decision

In 1981 the United States committed itself to a massive program of armament, including the deployment of new and more deadly weapons and accompanied by the threat and use of force to achieve political and economic ends. Although these government actions were designed to preserve peace as defined by our policy makers, my wife and I were convinced that they are in fact increasing world tension and perpetuating unpeaceful situations at home and abroad. We protested this policy with our voices, votes and letters to the President of the United States and to our representatives in Congress. However, the continuing nuclear buildup, the sending of arms to other nations, and the sky-rocketing military budget led us to consider another form of protest, namely, civil disobedience in the form of refusal to pay the percentage of our federal taxes which goes to support the military. After careful reflection we redirected 41 percent of our taxes in 1981 and 46 percent in 1982 into an escrow account, pending passage of the World Peace Tax Fund Bill (H.R. 3224 and S. 2105) or equivalent legislation making it possible for us in good conscience to send our fair share of taxes to our government for peaceful, rather than military, means of settling conflict.

Our federal income tax returns were audited in the fall of 1983. We were assessed the full amount of the tax due in both years plus penalties and interest, as well as a $500 "frivolous return" fine for our 1982 return. At this point, we have paid all but the $500 "frivolous return" fine and that percentage allocated to nuclear buildup. In April of 1984 we filed a "straight" income tax return but withheld 35.5 percent of the tax due, the proportion of tax revenues actually expended for military purposes in 1983 according to the American Friends' Committee on National Legislation.

We believe that in a democracy we *are* the government, whether we like it or not. We are therefore more responsible for the actions of our country than, for example, a citizen of Russia is. We believe that to use or even to threaten to use nuclear weapons to settle a dispute is not and never can be an appropriate Christian solution to the world's problems. We believe, further, that actions speak louder than words and therefore have resorted to civil disobedience in order to make our position known loud and clear.

This decision represents a distinct shift in my thinking. When I became eighteen in 1944, I faced a decision about military service in World War II. As a candidate for the ministry, I was exempt from the draft. After careful study and consideration, however, including a weekend at a pacifist retreat, I decided I could not in conscience sit idly by while military powers swept across Europe and Asia and the Jewish people were threatened with genocide. I therefore enlisted and served briefly, until the end of the war, in the U.S. Army Air Corps.

Forty years later I am again forced to examine my stand regarding participation in my nation's military endeavors. I have come again to the conclusion that in conscience I cannot sit idly by while my own nation engages in a peacetime military buildup unprecedented in our history.

The shift in my viewpoint has been determined in part by a changed world situation. The most urgent element in this changed situation is the escalating arms race including the development of nuclear arsenals that place at risk all life on this planet. Another factor is the use our country is making of its resources as the most powerful nation on earth. Our legitimate concern about the threat of Soviet power is often distorted by a blind anticommunism which leads us to betray the principles we profess. We are diverting enormous sums of money from human services and constructive international aid to the creation of instruments of destruction. We are using our unparalleled military might to preserve American economic interests and privilege in the world and, in some cases, we are supporting oppressive governments in smaller nations to do so.

My study of the Bible as a teacher in theological institutions in Africa and the United States for the past twenty-seven years has been another major factor in the shift in my viewpoint. In particular, my work on the gospel of Mark has led me to see that to be a Christian means following Jesus, and following Jesus demands costly action in response to the rule of God in human life. Among other things it has led me to war tax resistance and has forced me to re-examine the pacifist option.

It is appropriate that the Advisory Council on Church and Society of the General Assembly (Presbyterian Church, U.S.A.) is studying the responsibilities and limits of Christian participation in a war-making society. This study has led me to develop some of the biblical and theological considerations that should, in my view, inform a Christian's decision about questions of resistance to the state in general, civil disobedience as a means of resistance, and war tax refusal as a particular form of civil disobedience.

I. The Responsibilities and Limits of the Obligation to Obey the State

A. *The primary obligation to obey God*

For Christians and for Jews, the duty to obey God takes precedence over every other loyalty.

According to the Old Testament, kings are enthroned and deposed, empires rise and fall, by the will of Yahweh. The very institution of monarchy is viewed with ambivalence in I Samuel, but the demand of obedience to Israel's sovereign God is unambiguous and pervasive.

In the New Testament the core of Jesus' message is the proclamation of the sovereign rule of God. The priority of obedience to God's authority comes to expression in Jesus' teaching that his disciples are to seek first the Kingdom of God (Matt. 6:33), and in the words of Peter and the apostles to Jewish religious authorities in terms applicable to all human authority, "We must obey God rather than men" (Acts 5:29).

B. *The presumption of duty to obey the state*

If the duty to obey God is primary, the Bible usually sees the duty to obey the state as a corollary to it since human authority is assumed in the Bible to be derived from God. In the Old Testament the Lord is king, and the king of Israel is anointed as son of God and shepherd of God's people. There is no clear distinction between civil and religious government.

In the New Testament the Roman emperor is not viewed as God's anointed, but all human authority, including that of Rome, is seen as coming from God (Rom. 13:1-2, I Pet. 2:13-14). Christians, therefore, are enjoined to be subject to governing authorities and not to resist them, but instead to show them honor and respect (I Pet. 2:17; Rom. 13:7). These texts give prudential reasons for Christians to obey civil authorities (i.e., concern for the common good, for the good name of Christians, and for self-interest), but the fundamental reason for obeying the state in the New Testament, as in the Old, is that civil authority has been instituted by God. The general rule in the Bible is that Christians should obey commands of government unless they infringe upon the sovereign rule of God.

C. *Circumstances in which the obligation to obey God overrides the obligation to obey the state*

The restrictive clause in the foregoing general rule means that occasions may arise when a Christian must resist the state because its orders infringe upon the rule of God. Criteria for determining when the obligation to obey God overrides the obligation to obey the state may be established in several ways, including the following three.

1. Conscience

Resistance to the state is sometimes based on the informed conscience, or what Immanuel Kant called "the moral law within." A good example of this humanitarian motivation based on a Transcendentalist faith is found in Henry David Thoreau's essay on civil disobedience:

> Must the citizen ever for a moment, or in the least degree, resign his conscience to the legislator? Why has every man a conscience, then? I think that we should be men first, and subjects afterward. It is not desirable to cultivate a respect for the law, so much as for the right. The only obligation which I have a right to assume is to do at any time what I think is right.[1]

Thoreau's conscience was outraged by the Mexican War of 1846-48 because it served to extend slavery into the Southwest. My own conscience is troubled by the ends actually served by U.S. military intervention in Central America today, and this has influenced my decision to resist the state through refusal to pay war taxes.

2. Church teaching

Protestant theological ethics and Catholic moral theology rely upon the convergence of several sources of guidance on this and other issues. Examples of this way of establishing norms for decisions may be seen in recent Presbyterian and Catholic studies on the issue of war and peace.

In *Peacemaking: The Believers' Calling*[2] Presbyterians draw upon an analysis of dangers in the current world situation, theological principles, and biblical texts to call believers to be peacemakers at many levels.

The Challenge of Peace, a pastoral letter of the U.S. Conference of Catholic bishops, is "based on a mix of biblical, theological, and philosophical elements which are brought to bear upon the concrete problems of the day."[3] This study focuses specifically on the threat of war and the search for peace among nations, and draws more heavily on church tradition and natural law than does the Presbyterian study paper.[4] Both represent a concurrent use of revelation and reason to establish ethical norms, and both sharply challenge present U.S. military and foreign policy at significant points.

My own decision to engage in tax resistance has been influenced or reinforced by these and related examples of Christian ethical reflection. In the present situation I believe that the natural law of respect for human life, the Biblical teachings on peace and justice, and a theology of the sovereignty of God which places distinct limits on the authority of the state converge to direct me to resist the state when it engages in policies that risk genocide and when it taxes me against my will to carry out those policies.

3. Biblical command

A third point of departure is Jesus' summary of the Law in terms of two Mosaic commandments: love of God and love of neighbor. H. Richard Niebuhr used these to define the purpose of the church. I find them appropriate as criteria for deciding when to resist the state because they rest on the authority of Jesus and Moses. They are fundamental for ethical decisions in the Old and New Testaments alike and are readily applicable to people of other faiths as well.

a. Love of God

The love of God enjoined in Scripture is an exclusive love: "You shall have no other gods before me" (Ex. 20:3). Whenever a state orders its citizens to worship a god or gods other than the one true God, faithful believers are under obligation to disobey the state. Outstanding examples of this situation are the witness of Daniel and his three friends who would not worship Nebuchadnezzar's golden image (Dan. 3) and that of Christians who resisted to the death the worship of the Roman emperor (Rev. 13). Idolatry and apostasy violate the exclusive love of God and must be resisted, even if this requires resisting the lawful order of a human state.

b. Love of neighbor

In the Old Testament, love of nieghbor is the love of God in practical form. It is spelled out in the social and ethical provisions of the various legal codes that form the stipulations of the covenant in the Pentateuch. "Thou shalt love thy neighbor as thyself" (Lev. 19:18) appears in the Holiness Code. The Decalogue treats duties to God in the first four commandments (Exod. 20:2-11) and duties to the neighbor in the six commandments of the second table (Exod. 20:12-17). The Covenant Code (Exod. 21-23) and Deuteronomic Code (Deut. 12-26) also give large attention to justice in human relationships, which is love of neighbor in practice. Not even the king was immune from resistance in the form of denunciation by a prophet when he violated the covenant rights of a neighbor (e.g., David and Uriah's wife, II Sam. 12:1-15; Ahab and Naboth's vineyard, I Kings 21:1-24).

Although "neighbor" in the Old Testament means only Israelites and resident aliens, the New Testament extends the love commandment to a community of believers ("brothers and sisters") which includes Gentiles (John 13:34; I John 3:11-18), and also people outside the church ("neighbor") (Gal. 6:10 with 5:14), particularly those in need (Luke 10:25-37). Jesus further extends the love commandment to include neighbors who are hostile: "You have heard that it was said, 'Love your neighbor and hate your enemy.' But I say to you, Love your enemies and pray for those who persecute you . . ." (Matt. 5:43-44).

The clear priority of the love commandment in the New Testament has significant implications for discerning the limits of the obligation to obey the state today when the neighborhood includes the entire planet.

When a state no longer performs its God-appointed function of maintaining an order in which the rights of neighbors are protected and conflicts between neighbors are equitably adjudicated; when a state is committed to a policy which deprives fellow Christians not only of their rights but even of their lives; or when a state is willing to contemplate committing an act that would destroy hundreds of thousands of human lives indiscriminately (as any use of strategic nuclear weapons would), then Christians must in conscience at least ask if citizenship in the Kingdom of God demands resistance to the state.

Jesus' teaching to love God and neighbor does not decide the issue, but it does provide guidance to individual Christians and representative bodies as they decide. My judgment is that in the present circumstances I must, at certain points, resist my government.

When obedience to God does require resistance to the state, that resistance may take a variety of forms ranging from verbal protest to violent revolution. Decisions about which form depends upon a number of variables, such as the gravity of the situation, the structures of the government and society in question, and the probable outcome of a given line of action. The next section of this paper will focus on civil disobedience as a means of resistance that may be appropriate in contemporary American society.

II. Civil Disobedience: The Example of Jesus Christ and Recent Presbyterian Precedent

Civil disobedience, as used here, means a public, non-violent, submissive violation of law as a form of protest.[5] As a form of resistance to the state, it corresponds to a remarkable degree to the Gospels' picture of Jesus' response to ecclesiastical and, occasionally, civil authorities when their customs, laws, and actions opposed the higher law of God.

Jesus' resistance to religious laws about sabbath, fasting, and ritual cleansing was frequent and open. He publicly attacked these laws in his teaching (e.g., Mark 7:1-23 and parallels) and flouted them in his actions (e.g., Mark 2:15-3:6 and parallels). When arraigned before the high priest and questioned about his teaching, Jesus answered that his teaching was an open record; he had said nothing secretly (John 18:20).

Jesus' resistance to human authority was also non-violent. By this I mean that Jesus never inflicted bodily harm on anyone and never used lethal force for any purpose. When his disciples sought to do so he rebuked them, saying: "You do not know what manner of spirit you are of; for the Son of man came not to destroy men's lives but to save them" (Luke 9:55, var.). Attempts to use the expulsion of money-changers from the temple to refute this assertion do not hold up under careful exegesis. This incident shows that Jesus did practice resistance to established authority and that he was aggressive in his protest, but it does not demonstrate that he took any action that would do bodily harm. Careful exegesis of Luke 22 with its various words about swords will not sustain any assertion that Jesus condoned the use of lethal force to defend himself or to advance his cause. Every strand of New Testament tradition concurs in a portrait of Jesus as one who, while quite willing to die for the cause of God's kingdom, was unwilling to kill or to have his disciples kill for this or any other cause.

Finally, when Jesus violated human laws in obedience to God, he was submissive to the rejection, suffering, and death that his actions ultimately entailed. The Fourth Gospel's picture of Jesus before the high priest and Pilate is particularly rich and nuanced in this regard. He was by no means deferential, but he did accept the judgment of these courts. His submissive demeanor before his accusers was one of the factors that led early Christians to identify Jesus as the servant of Yahweh announced in the book of Isaiah (compare Isa. 53:7 with Matt. 27:12-14; Mark 14:60-61a; Acts 8:32; I Pet. 2:23).

The Gospels insist that Jesus was not guilty of violating Roman law. His acts of disobedience were directed against the religious laws and authorities of his day. However, the modern line between religious and civil law did not characterize ancient Israel or even the Judaism of Jesus' day. The religious authorities exercised many functions we would view as civil matters. Jesus' willingness to violate the laws of duly constituted human authorities publicly, non-violently, and submissively is, I believe, at least consonant with and perhaps even a model for acts of civil disobedience when the situation is such that obedience to the state would entail disobedience to God or the violation of one's obligation to love one's neighbor.

III. War Tax Refusal and the Christian's Duty to the State

Civil disobedience to a war-making state may take many forms, such as deliberate violation of trespass laws in protest demonstrations, refusal to register for the draft or to engage in military service, and refusal to pay taxes for certain or all military purposes. This portion of the paper will focus solely upon war tax resistance in the United States.

The state has a right to tax its citizens.

This principle is established by self-evident reason and universal practice. It is sanctioned explicitly by one New Testament text: "Pay all of them their dues, taxes to whom taxes are due, revenue to whom revenue is due" (Rom. 13:7), and implicitly by several others (e.g., Mark 12:17 and parallels; Matt. 17:24-27; I Pet. 2:13-17).

The state's right to tax is limited, however, by a consideration of whether or not the state, on balance, serves the constructive purposes for which it was created by God (as in the Bible) or by the people (as in the U.S. Constitution).

Romans 13:1-7 is based on the premise that "rulers are not a terror to good conduct, but to bad" (13:3) and that the civil magistrate is "God's servant for your good . . . the servant of God to execute his wrath on the wrongdoer" (13:4). Christians are enjoined to pay taxes, "for the authorities are ministers of God, attending to this very thing" (13:6).

When the premise is not applicable, the conclusion is without force. Failing to observe this rule of logic, some interpreters through the centuries have elevated the verse about paying taxes to the status of absolute command. The result has often been church support for the status quo, no matter how sinful or oppressive it may be. The context of the verse, however, invites critical discernment of the context in life. When the government itself becomes an instrument of terror to innocent people, the injunction to support that terror by paying taxes is no longer binding.

In the present situation, I perceive my national government to be fulfilling in most of its functions the constructive role presupposed by Romans 13:1-7. I therefore willingly pay taxes to support it. In the current arms buildup and in our various military interventions around the globe, however, I perceive not "God's servant for your good" but a powerful nation intent on preserving its wealth and political advantage at whatever cost. This part of my tax I withhold, therefore, in the same way that Christians a generation after Paul refused to obey the state's command to worship the Roman emperor (Rev. 14:9-12).

For Christians the state's right to tax is also limited by a consideration of what is due to Caesar and what is due to God.

In Mark 12:13-17 and its parallels Jesus answers a trick question about paying taxes to Caesar by saying, "Render therefore to Caesar the things that are Caesar's and to God the things that are God's." This ambiguous answer escapes the trap the Pharisees had set for Jesus and forces them to decide for themselves. The "therefore" points to the explicit reference to Caesar's image and an implied reference to the image of God in which humankind was created. The duty to God comes in final, climactic position, and when the two conflict, it takes precedence over the duty to Caesar.

By paying the part of my federal tax that supports the state in all its constructive functions and refusing to pay that part which menaces all life, I am conscientiously trying to excercise the responsibility for individual decision Jesus lays upon his hearers, i.e. giving to Caesar and to God what is due to each.

American Christians, including Presbyterians, have traditionally viewed the payment of taxes as a serious civic obligation, but not as an absolute requirement. They have, on lesser grounds than obedience to God, resisted the state by refusing to pay taxes they viewed as unjust. Usually the protest was to protect their own economic interests, as in the cases of resistance to the Stamp Act[6] and the tax on tea by Great Britain before the Revolution, and to the tax on whiskey imposed by Congress shortly after the Revolution.[7]

In recent years the General Assembly has recognized "that some individual United Presbyterians will be led by conscience to make their witness against the war in Indochina in ways such as . . . refusal to pay certain federal taxes voluntarily and that some such acts may entail peaceful civil disobedience."[8] The Assembly called for support of these individuals by prayer and by legal and ecclesiastical support.

With all Presbyterians I acknowledge the right of the state to tax its citizens and the obligation of citizens to pay their taxes whether or not they approve of all the government does. Tax resistance or refusal is therefore an extreme measure to be taken only under the gravest circumstances. Today, when the issue is the preservation of life on the planet and we are taxed to support weapons capable of genocide by a government willing to contemplate using them, I believe tax resistance is not only legitimate but morally imperative. I cannot voluntarily pay taxes to support the current U.S. commitment to rearmament and military intervention which I believe to be of far greater danger to the world than was our intervention in Vietnam. I seek the support of my church in this stand to which I am led by conscience and the tenets of our faith.

ENDNOTES

1. Henry David Thoreau, "Civil Disobedience" in Charles R. Anderson, ed., *Thoreau's Vision: The Major Essays* (Englewood Cliffs, N.J.: Prentice-Hall, Inc., 1973), p. 196.
2. *Minutes of the General Assembly of the United Presbyterian Church in the United States of America*, 1980, pp. 202-212; *Minutes of the General Assembly of the Presbyterian Church in the United States*, 1981, pp. 134-136, 466-474.
3. *The Challenge of Peace: God's Promise and Our Response* (Washington, D.C.: National Conference of Catholic Bishops, 1983).
4. Charles E. Curran, "The Moral Methodology of the Bishops' Pastoral Letter" in Philip J. Murnion, ed., *Catholics and Nuclear War* (N.Y.: Crossroad, 1983), pp. 45-56.
5. James F. Childress, *Civil Disobedience and Political Obligation, A Study in Christian Social Ethics* (New Haven: Yale University Press, 1971), pp. 1-12. This definition is common to Thoreau, Gandhi, and Martin Luther King, Jr. See also the definition used in the PCUS statement on civil disobedience in 1965: ". . . the open, non-violent, and conscientious refusal to obey a law or laws, as a means of appeal to a higher law, combined with the willing acceptance of the penalty." *Minutes of the General Assembly of the Presbyterian Church in the United States*, 1965, p. 160.
6. See *Minutes of the Presbyterian Church in America, 1776-88*, pp. 393, 400, 423.
7. See *Records of the Synod of Virginia, Vol. 1, 1788-97*, pp. 125-26, 137-40, 143-45, 150.
8. *Minutes of the General Assembly of the United Presbyterian Church in the United States of America*, 1972, p. 394.

BIBLICAL AND CONTEMPORARY ASPECTS OF WAR TAX RESISTANCE

George R. Edwards

War tax resistance today is specifically addressed to the fantastic expansion of the U.S. military budget since 1981, the heightened aggressiveness of U.S. foreign policy during these same years, and the profound apprehension arising from the prospect of nuclear war between the United States and the Soviet Union. At the same time, growing numbers of people on grounds more serious than personal greed are scandalized by a tax system which favors holders of wealth and disproportionately burdens people of lower and middle income.

In May 1983 Lester Thurow, Economics Professor at the Massachusetts Institute of Technology, commented on the reduction of federal expenses by the transfer of funds from social services to the military. He pointed out that in 1981, 1982, and thus far in 1983 more than two million people in the United States each year fell below the federally established poverty level.[1] In 1983, 36 percent of all black families were included in the poverty class.[4]

While the involuntary financing of preparation for both nuclear and conventional war remains the primary concern of war tax resistance, questions of economic justice, staggering accounts of waste and fraud, and the amassing of federal debts which pass on to coming generations lifelong mortgages contracted without their voice or vote increase public discontent and sharpen the desire to act against further victimization. In the pages which follow, an effort is made to establish a profile of New Testament attitudes on taxation and tax resistance followed by a further exploration of contemporary circumstances in which these biblical guidelines must find their application.

New Testament Attitudes on Taxation and Tax Resistance

The passage most directly relevant to tax refusal is found in Mark 12:13-17 concerning tribute to Caesar, with parallels in Matthew 22:15-22 and Luke 20:20-26.[3] The episode immediately follows the parable of the wicked tenants (Mk. 12:1-12, Mt. 21:33-46, Lk. 20:9-19). Though Mark's gospel from the beginning puts the story of Jesus in a setting of conflict overshadowed by the cross,[4] the entry to Jerusalem in Mark 11 sets the final stage for confrontation and death.

Mark's story throughout is redolent with apocalyptic meanings.[5] The parable of the wicked tenants is probably a churchly construction, essentially allegorical in character and expressive of the church's conflict with the Jerusalem religious establishment.[6] The slain son (Mk. 12:6-8) depicts the passion of Jesus which controls the cruciform quality of Markan discipleship (e.g., Mk. 8:34) and tells with apocalyptic anticipation (cf. Mk. 13:9-13) the tribulations through which the believers shall pass in the final crisis. Mark 12:1-12 thus shares with Daniel, Mark 13 and other apocalypses the feature of "prophecy after the event."

While Matthew assumes over all, more than Mark, qualities of formal ecclesiastical instruction,[7] the apocalyptic setting of the tax question in Matthew is confirmed by the insertion of the marriage feast (Mt. 22:1-14/Lk. 14:16-24) based on the messianic banquet theme and conveying the eschatological coloration of the Q source from which it is taken.

The adversaries ("them" at Mk. 12:1) are presumably the chief priests, scribes, and elders of Mark 11:27. They get the point of the murder charge lodged against them (Mk. 12:12) and in Mark's narrative are prevented from immediately arresting Jesus only by the fear of the people (Mk. 12:12 par.). The section on the tax question carries over the same adversarial setting of the foregoing material, even though "some of the Herodians" at Mark 12:13 are added to the Pharisees. The motive behind the tax dialogue, therefore, is not a quest for moral enlightenment but the entrapment of a mouse in a game of cats.[8]

Mark ends the controversy story with a comment on the bafflement of the cats at the shrewdness of Jesus' answer. The trick question has been turned back upon the questioners; for it is they who must decide what is Ceasar's over against what is God's. And that is just where the contemporary reader is left in searching for moral enlightenment.

Repeated efforts have been made to find in Mark 12:17 a defense for the view that the pronouncement at the climax of the story—"Render to Caesar the things that are Caesar's and to God the things that are God's"—lines Jesus up with Zealot resistance of Roman rule in Palestine. This view has enjoyed considerable popularity in modern liberation theology with its morally justified resistance of colonialism. S.G.F. Brandon attempted to provide Biblical grounds for this.[9]

More recently, the Jesus-as-Zealot theme has been taken up by Fernando Belo. He decries the official ecclesiastical view that Jesus' command to give to Caesar what is Caesar's shows

> "Jesus' respect for 'the legality of the state' and . . . the autonomy of the political order (a class system) over against the kingdom of God that would be concerned only with the interior life of individuals."[10]

Insofar as the church asserts the autonomy of the political order as a class system and relates the rule of God only to "the interior life of individuals," Belo's stricture is deserved and welcome. But anger over religious chaplaincy to "politicians of the right" cannot be directed at all ecclesiastical circles indiscriminately and cannot, without further ado, constitute the basis for taking the text in question as a defense of the Zealots. Belo's effort to link Mark 12:13-17 with 12:1-12 is contextually sensible but not on the premise that the usurpers (the wicked tenants) in the latter passage are the Romans as the power occupying Palestine,[17] however obvious is the historical fact of Roman imperialism in the eastern Mediterranean of that day. The adversaries ("them," in Mark 12:1) seem to be the same as those who appear in 11:27—the chief priests, scribes, and elders. "They" (12:12) get the point of the parable unmistakably and send representatives (Pharisees and some Herodians, 12:13) who are the immediate opponents in 12:13-17. Belo's praise for the Zealot liberators as representatives of the proletariat and thus of Jesus himself, runs aground on its own premises by recognizing that in the final analysis, "no communist revolution was possible" for the Zealots, "any more than it had been for the Deuteronomist Levites or the Maccabees."[11]

No Zealot would touch the Roman coin demanded by Jesus in the tribute story (Mk. 12:15 par).[12] The impression of Caesar it bore was a direct violation of the commandment against images,[13] less horrifying but not qualitatively unlike the pagan sacrifice on the Temple altar ordered by the Seleucid king, Antiochus IV, in December 168 B.C.[13] This sacrifice was branded in Daniel "the desolating sacrilege,"[14] and came over into Mark 13:14 as part of the apocalyptic heritage of the earliest Gospel.

The Maccabean resistance to Seleucid rule is one of the monumental events of Jewish nationalism. The Zealots were heirs of the Maccabean religious heroism, and the modern state of Israel still commemorates the final suicidal stand of the Zealots against the Romans in 73 A.D.[15] Roman rule, asserted with power in the conquest of Jerusalem by Pompey in 63 B.C., was continuous through the lifetime of Jesus. In 6 A.D. Quirinius, governor of Syria, commanded a census (Lk. 2:2) on the basis of which Roman taxation of Palestine was to be enforced. Judas the Galilean led an uprising against this census.[16] Though written off by Acts 5:37 as a fiasco, the resistance of Judas was taken up by the Zealot movement with its refusal to acknowledge the dominion of Caesar and render to him the appointed tax.

Neither in the historical circumstance of the ministry of Jesus (encompassing the end of the procuratorship of Valerius Gratus, 15-26 A.D., and the beginning of that of Pontius Pilate, 26-36 A.D.) nor in the historical circumstance of Mark written about 70 A.D., could the statement, "render to Caesar the things that are Caesar's," have possibly meant a commendation of Zealot ideology or practice.[17] The entrapment of the tribute question, read in the light of the response of Jesus (Mark 12:17) can be understood only as an attempt to put Jesus in disfavor with the religious nationalism at the basis of the Zealot movement. Jesus' refusal to repudiate the tax completely puts an unmistakable distance between himself and the Zealots, regardless of the unpopularity such a position would provoke in some quarters.

But that is only one side of the coin. The other side is: "Render to God the things that are God's." Given Mark's apocalypticism, it is quite unlikely that the saying of Mark 12:17 expresses something like a Christian philosophy of government, a timeless truth for all generations. Martin Hengel is probably correct in saying that what is Caesar's is relativized by the imminent end which overshadows the whole of the Markan passion narrative and is conspicuously present in the eschatological judgment prophesied in 12:1-12.[18] The theology of Mark intersects at this point with the conversation between Jesus and Pilate in John 19:10-11:

> Pilate therefore said to him, "You will not speak to me? Do you not know that I have power to release you, and power to crucify you?" Jesus answered him, "You would have no power over me unless it had been given you from above; therefore he who delivered me to you has the greater sin."

The power of the executioner is indeed one which strikes terror, but in the earliest Christianity, fear of the one who can destroy both body and soul in hell is greater than the fear of the executioner (Mt. 10:28/Lk. 12:4-5). Despite the relative measure to which the fourth Gospel is theologically removed from apocalyptic emphases, these verses from John 19 clearly reflect the characteristic refrain within apocalypse, namely, that the power of civil authority, however high and mighty, stands under God and will be judged by God. But another feature of the passage also recapitulates the Markan viewpoint: the culpability (Jn. 19:11b) of the religious authorities[19] who have placed Jesus under indictment. This echoes Mark's perspective that the conspiracy against Jesus is instigated primarily by the indigenous sacerdotal leadership at Jerusalem. The Roman procurator is the direct instrument of the execution, laying upon Jesus the charge of insurrection (Mk. 15:26f), but he is presented as a secondary and somewhat unwilling agent of the primary conspirators. The importance of these observations can be underlined by glancing at Luke's editing of the Markan tribute text.[20]

Only Luke 23:2, in obviously editorial phrases, introduces into the trial before Pilate the charge that Jesus perverted the nation by forbidding tribute and calling himself a kingly messiah. Not accidentally, the accusers in Luke 23:2 are leaders of the Jerusalem religious community. This may also be seen in Luke 20:20 where Luke, again editorializing Mark, asserts that the entrapment was aimed at "delivering Jesus up to the authority and jurisdiction of the governor," i.e., Pilate. Luke 23:2 thus harks back to 20:20 in a style of complementarity or duality which has been identified as a feature of Lukan style.[21]

Kümmel and others have correctly maintained that Luke reinforces the traditional picture of Jesus' innocence before Pilate, by heightening the Jewish defamation of Jesus as an insurrectionist (Lk. 20:20, 26; 23:2, 5, 18f, 23, 25).[22] In Luke, Pilate defends the innocence of Jesus repeatedly (Lk. 23:4, 14f, 22). The same pattern is exhibited in Acts. According to Jewish accusers, Paul and the Christians are subversives (Acts 17:6-7; 24:5), but the charges are rejected by Roman officials (16:38-39; 18:12-17; 19:35-41; 23:26-30; 25:23-27; 26:30-32). It is clear from this that the political apologetic in Luke-Acts is programmatic. As Christianity moves toward Rome, Jerusalem recedes. Although the Jewish Revolt of 68-70 A.D. could not have made Judaism popular among the Romans, it is probably unwise to see in that war the single cause of Luke's political posture. It is more likely that in the Lukan account we are faced not with a contradiction of what is already found in Mark, but only an amplification of it. Already in Mark the religious establishment in Jerusalem stands under heavy indictment, and while Pilate is not as innocent as in Luke, it is presumably a Roman centurion who first confesses (Mk. 15:39) Jesus as the (or, a) son of God. On the other hand, Luke's weakening of the apocalyptic character of Mark's theology and the indefinite delay of the parousia[23] provide in Luke-Acts a somewhat triumphal view of ecclesiology more congenial to later Constantinianism.

The main points of the foregoing discussion may be summarized:

1. Mark 12:17 is two pronged: Caesar's right to the tax is acknowledged, but this obligation is relativized by the sovereignty of God looming near.

2. The qualified legitimation of the tax is a clear disavowal of the zealotic nationalism which precipitated the war of 68 A.D. against Rome.

3. Luke's accenting of the affinity of Rome and Christianity further weakens the apocalyptic tension of Mark and opens Luke to a Constantinian accommodation of Christianity.

Because Romans 13:1-7 has exercised an unbalanced influence in favor of civil obedience in the history of the church,[24] it is necessary to put this passage alongside the previous discussion as a Pauline frame of reference. V. P. Furnish has given special attention to Paul's understanding of the state and instruction on taxation in Romans 13:6-7, a parallel to Mark 12:17.[25] Furnish provides a specific historical background for the two forms of the Roman tax specified in these verses. First is the direct tax (Gk. *phoros;* Lat. *tributa*) collected by Roman officials. Then is the indirect *ad valorem* commercial tax (Gk. *telos;* Lat. *portoria*) a collection which was handed out to Roman knights on the basis of the highest bid. This second tax was subject to widespread abuse in the reign of Nero about the time Romans was written in 56 or 57 A.D. Even Nero, according to Tacitus,[26] was inclined to repeal the *telos* until his advisers warned him of the demand, sure to follow, for the repeal of the *phoros* and the consequent collapse of the imperial economy.

In writing to Rome, Paul is mindful of the tax unrest present especially among that more affluent part of the congregation engaged in commercial transaction. Paul also remembers the disturbances within the Jewish community at Rome provoked by the coming of persons who believed in Christ and resulting in the Edict of Claudius banning Jews from Rome in 49 A.D.[27] Consequently, the general injunction to "be subject" (Rom. 13:1, 5) has its specific culmination in verses 6 and 7. Because Paul plans to visit Rome at long last (1:10-13) and to receive there support for the westward mission to Spain (15:22-29), to become embroiled at Rome over the tax issue could be a direct hindrance to the successful prosecution of that mission.

These suggestions may well provide the concrete historical circumstance for the emphasis on tax compliance in Romans 13:6-7. While those verses follow upon the general recognition within both Judaism and early Christianity that the powers that be are ordained by God (13:1b) and thus possess no "intrinsic metaphysical value,"[28] they demonstrate once again how different Paul is from the attitude of Zealotism, as we have already seen in the case on Mark 12:17 in the teaching of Jesus.

In view of the appeal for subordination to civil authority in passages already mentioned and other similar expressions in 1 Peter 3:13-17 and Titus 3:1, it is not surprising that Christians who seek Biblical roots for their attitudes toward civil authority should have considered civil obedience in general and tax compliance in particular an appropriate expression of Christian conduct in the world. Christians also, in practical language (Rom. 13:4), understand that the Internal Revenue Service carries a very big stick. But the abuse of the obedience ethic as we have seen in Christian submission to Nazi rule in modern Germany, or as it occurs in any other situation where civil authority has made itself a tool of inquisitorial cruelty, torture, political imprisonment, and the violation of human rights,[29] makes it clear that an uncritical obedience to the state can only result in rendering to Caesar what is God's.

A specific historical reason has already been suggested for the emphasis on subordination in Romans 13:6-7. We must consider now further contextual reasons in this passage for remaining open to exception.[30]

The *first* reason has already been stated. Because the civil authority is subject to God (Rom. 13:1b), it cannot be the sole determinant of "the good" (13:4) it is obliged to serve. The *independence* therefore professed by Christians in the face of tyrannical government[31] is the logical corollary of the *dependence* of earthly rulers upon God. This logic, essential for the integrity of religion, human dignity, and just government underlies the Westminster axiom: "God alone is Lord of the conscience."[32]

Second, it is noteworthy that the two concluding paragraphs of Romans 12 (vss. 9-21) focus on agape and that 13:8-10 returns to this same theme. Romans 13:1-7 is thus, as Martin Hengel affirms, "framed by a renunciation of force"[33] on one side and the summary commandment to love one's neighbor on the other. Furthermore, it is difficult to deny that 12:3-8, with its appeal to the body of Christ, is already an expression of agape, just as the great agape hymn in 1 Corinthians 13 informs the body motif which occupies 1 Corinthians 12 and 14. When one considers that Romans 12:1 puts forward *nonconformity*[34] as the initial premise of Paul's great moral instruction in the final section of the Roman letter and follows this with the repudiation of vengeance and phrases reminiscent of Jesus' doctrine of love in the Sermon on the Mount, it is no less than tragic that the church should have so frequently derived from this teaching such wooden and uncritical notions of civil *conformity.*

In the *third* place, one has to look at Romans 13:11-14 also, which puts everything into a different light by virtue of the imminent eschaton. For this reason I am not as averse as Käsemann was[35] to relating dialectically the apocalyptic view of the state under Domitian as expressed in Revelation 13 with that found in Romans 13:1-7.[36] It is correct that historical exegesis—discovering what Romans *meant* in its own time—should not assert that an apocalyptic view explicitly determines the subordination enjoined in Romans 13:6-7. Nevertheless, Käsemann must also affirm in interpreting what this passage *means* today that the lordship of Christ may speak "more audibly out of prison cells and graves than out of the life of churches which congratulate themselves on their concordat with the state."[37] Seeking to clarify the kind of circumstance in which the Christian may have to resort to revolution, Käsemann cites the situation in the Third Reich after the battle of Stalingrad in February, 1943.[38]

Particularly in moral judgments, hindsight is better than foresight, but historians will not forget that Martin Niemoeller went into the concentration camp as early as 1937, six years before the battle of Stalingrad. The Barmen confessors, among whom he stood, committed themselves to a costly resistance nine years before Stalingrad. The totality of modern war underlines more than ever that if we wait until "Stalingrad" to reach a decision, the point of no return will have been passed much sooner and with infinitely greater lethal consequences.

By "revolution" Käsemann apparently means "blood and guts." So the question of non-violent resistance, which is the specific character of war tax refusal, does not come upon the horizon of his exegetical vision. It must be added to this comment that civil disobedience as exemplified in major historic figures like David Thoreau, Mohandas Gandhi, and Martin Luther King, Jr., or contemporary war tax resisters like David Kaufman,[39] William Durland,[40] Ernest Bromley and Marion Coddington, or Maurice McCrackin[41] scrupulously disavows acts of violence against the state. Such disobedience, in the moral sense, upholds the principle of subordination so clear in the teaching of Paul.

Since Käsemann must correctly relate subordination in Romans 13 to that applied to women in 1 Corinthians 11:2-16 and to slaves in 1 Corinthians 7:21 (do not strive for emancipation), historical exegesis as an end in itself can only compel us to place Paul's idea of political subordination in the museum of Christian antiquities alongside the relics of slaveholding, segregation, and patriarchy.

This discussion of Romans 13:1-7 now permits a summary not unlike what we found as a distillation of synoptic teaching on the tax question:

1. The clear espousal of civil obedience in Romans 13 is qualified by the subordination of civil authority to God; by the context of agape which precedes and follows it; by the particular Roman circumstance which gives Paul's instruction its pertinence; by the transformation urged in Romans 12:1f, and by the temporal ultimacy of Romans 13:11-14.

2. Romans 13:1-7 implicitly rebukes the armed revolution championed by zealotic nationalism without diminishing the validity of non-violent resistance to civil authority should circumstances require it.

3. The specific form of such resistance is left to the conscientious discretion of the parties involved. (Ancient and modern examples, supremely exemplified in the crucifixion of Christ, are diverse and numerous.)

It remains now to demonstrate in the concluding pages the Biblical validity of war tax resistance in the present circumstances of Christian responsibility.

The Present Case for War Tax Resistance

Earlier in this essay, reference was made to Luke's affirmative attitude toward imperial Rome. As the apocalyptic expectation of early Christianity waned and "the last hour" of 1 John 2:18 stretched out into centuries, the church as an ongoing institution in the history of the West blended its destiny with that of the Roman state. Despite the repudiation of violent nationalism in the teaching of Jesus and the apostles with the negation of the sword which was its symbol (Mt. 26:52), the

Roman centurion of Acts 10-11 already portends the church's openness to Christian soldiering. The cultural bowl of the Palestinian church was broken as Christianity made its way in the Greco-Roman world. Luke already shows how Christianity attempted to incorporate what it perceived as the benefits of Pax Romana.

The foundations of Christian pacifism lay in the radical doctrine of love and the apocalyptic expectation still vibrant in the vigorous missionary campaigns of Paul.[43] The apocalyptic hope was schooled in the tragic experience of the Hebrew monarchy and carried with it a profoundly critical view of political power.

The theory of "just war" represents the collapse of distinctive elements in the Christianity of the New Testament. Carried over from medieval Catholicism into sixteenth-century Protestantism and pressured by modern nationalism operating on the premises of Machiavelli, "just war" became a moral rationale by which Christians accommodated themselves to the slaughter of Christians of other nations appealing to the same criteria of the just war.

While not all practitioners of war tax resistance call themselves pacifists (e.g., David Thoreau), and few if any would call themselves "absolute" pacifists, they would agree in general with the conclusion that centuries of tutoring in the doctrines of just war demonstrate its inability to stop war or mitigate its horrors. On the contrary, modern war is so advanced in destructive capability that the hope of "transforming"[44] it is no longer tenable. What appealed to Luke and Paul (even earlier) in the relatively universal if not gentle submission imposed by the Roman sword is turned upon its head in the presence of today's nation states. Instead of Christian persuasion turning the nations from the bullet to the ballot box in graduated steps, we stand at the brink of "star wars" in which our military infestations are being carried into outer space. The funding for the incineration of the earth and the blasphemous invasion of the heavens is taken from the pockets of an acquiescent public and deficit manipulations of the federal treasury. Many of us believe that war tax resistance provides an immediate, concrete opportunity to say no to this acquiescence.

The ideology presently used for sustaining just war theory is that of deterrence or "balance of power."[45] Under pressure of the military industrial complex and the demonic impulses of nationalistic politics, "balance of power" translates into "arms race," while persuading the persuadable that every staggering increase in the weapons budget and every breakthrough in the science of overkill are carefully calibrated to maintain the mystical parity without which the gods will plunge us into the abyss of slavery or death. Alan Geyer has speeled out twenty-one reasons for the repudiation of deterrence ideology in our time.[46] The boast that nuclear deterrence has prevented war since 1945 arrogantly assumes that the absence of nuclear war between the United States and the Soviet Union justifies the numerous proxy wars sponsored by the nuclear powers. It also blinds us to more than sixteen million deaths[47] caused by the increasingly frequent wars since 1945. Nor can it be proved that the absence of nuclear war between the superpowers is due to the possession or balanced possession of nuclear weapons.

The Pastoral Letter of the National Conference of Catholic Bishops has once

[118]

again, despite its many edifying reflections on the problem of modern warfare, provided a continued basis for (nuclear) deterrence.[48] It is to be retained under the sole condition (sec. 188) of its contribution to progressive disarmament. Since the completion of the Pastoral in May of 1983, even the talks on strategic arms reduction have been suspended as a consequence of NATO deployment of Cruise and Pershing II missiles in western Europe.

The Pastoral's "no" to nuclear war is to be commended, but it is a direct contradiction of deterrence ideology because any weapon not intended for actual use has, by that reservation, lost its deterrent value. By hairsplitting refinements, the Pastoral still seeks through the principles of discrimination and proportionality to hand on the just war tradition. At the same time, the Pastoral discloses that the United States has sixty nuclear weapons of undisclosed megatonnage targeted on Moscow alone and forty thousand targeted elsewhere in the Soviet Union (180). Who could possibly believe that such targeting intends anything but the indiscriminate extermination of the Soviet people as well as great portions of Europe and Asia when the radioactive fallout and other consequences of nuclear war are taken into account? If the world is delivered from the atheists, who will save it from the Christians? Growing numbers of Christians, including priests and bishops, are withholding their tax dollars which finance the pending nuclear doomsday, constrained as they are by the love of God summoning human communities away from self-destruction toward a redeemed future.

An apocalyptic consciousness in both Jesus and Paul informed the peculiar ethic of the New Testament. A strange thing is now happening in the consciousness of the world. Films like "The Day After" and books like *The Fate of the Earth* (1982) by Jonathan Schell are raising consciousness everywhere that a crisis of unparalleled magnitude is upon us. Of course the Biblical literalists and peddlers of predictive prophecy seize upon this situation to tell us once again about the imminent second coming of Christ while they propagate the very attitudes which intensify the Cold War and stoke the furnaces of atomic holocaust. Gordon Kaufman has comprehended in a serious way where we actually are and has proposed that the study of religion must use the mushroom cloud as the organizing center of the theological curriculum.[49] Perhaps the first lesson of that curriculum is that Jesus is not coming back to get us off the hook of our own making.

We must face the fact that every single man and woman, and even our children must now assume, for Christ's sake, a more responsible role for the removal of the scourge of war and the omen of the mushroom cloud from the face of the earth. This is not merely an academic task, even though it is the bottom line of all intelligent education. We know what hour it is, how it is full time for us to wake from sleep (Rom. 13:11).

For too long, the decision for Christ or Caesar has been assigned to young men and women, usually jobless and bored, or too inexperienced to measure the consequences they face when military recruiters picture for them futures bright with vocational benefits and travel to exotic places. War tax resistance places the weight of decision about the human future where it belongs: upon all of us old enough and secure enough to ask what it means to pray for peace and pay for war. Saying "no" to Caesar is a tough, frightening decision, but it could be, in the grace of God, one step toward a new human future.

ENDNOTES

1. Lester Thurow, on "Nightly Business Report," Public Broadcasting Service, May 17, 1983.
2. These statistics are from the Washington office of Rep. Ron Dellums.
3. B. H. Throckmorton, ed., *Gospel Parallels,* 4th ed. (Camden, NJ: Nelson, 1979), sec. 206, p. 145.
4. Norman Perrin and C. C. Duling, *The New Testament. An Introduction,* 2nd ed. (Atlanta: Janovich, 1982), p. 238.
5. Cf. W. H. Kelber, *The Kingdom in Mark* (Philadelphia: Fortress, 1974), pp. 109-28, esp. pp. 127f.
6. Cf. E. Schweizer, *The Good News* According to Mark, trans. by D. H. Madvig (Atlanta: John Knox, 1970), pp. 238-245.
7. Perrin and Duling, *op. cit.,* pp. 111; 268-70; 288f.
8. Mark's verb "entrap" *(agreuein,* 12:13) refers to the snare or net of hunters.
9. S.G.F. Brandon, *Jesus and the Zealots* (New York: Scribner's, 1967).
10. Fernando Belo, *A Materialist Reading of the Gospel of Mark,* trans. by Matthew J. O'Connell (Maryknoll, NY: Orbis, 1981).
11. *Ibid.,* p. 85.
12. Martin Hengel, *Die Zeloten. Untersuchungen zur Jüdischen Freiheitsbewegung in der Zeit von Herodes I. bis 70 N. Chr.* (Leiden: E. J. Brill, 1961), pp. 195-201.
13. Ethelbert Stauffer, *Christ and the Caesars,* trans. by K. and R. Gregor Smith (Philadelphia: Westminster, 1955), pp. 124-132.
14. Daniel 9:27; 11:31; 12:11.
15. Yigael Yadin, *Masada: Herod's Fortress and the Zealots' Last Stand,* trans. by Moshe Pearlman (New York: Random House, 1970), pp. 201-203.
16. E. Lohse, *The New Testament Environment,* trans. by John E. Steely (Nashville: Abingdon, 1976), p. 83.
17. Against the Brandon hypothesis as a whole, the following independently conceived discussions should be weighed. Oscar Cullmann, *Jesus and the Revolutionaries,* trans. by Gareth Putnam (New York: Harper & Row, 1970); Martin Hengel, *Was Jesus a Revolutionist?,* trans. by Wm. Klassen, Facet Books (Philadelphia: Fortress, 1971); George R. Edwards, *Jesus and the Politics of Violence* (New York: Harper & Row, 1972); Helmut Merkel, "Zealot," *Interpreter's Dictionary of the Bible Supplement.* ed. by K. Crim *et al.* (Nashville: Abingdon, 1976), pp. 979-982; Ron Sider, *Christ and Violence* (Scottdale, PA: Herald, 1979).
18. M. Hengel, *Was Jesus a Revolutionist?,* pp. 33-34.
19. So R. Bultmann, *The Gospel of John,* trans. by G. R. Beasley-Murray (Philadelphia: Westminster, 1971), p. 662, n. 6.
20. Some of the ideas in the following paragraph go back to J. Duncan M. Derrett, "Luke's Perspective on Tribute to Caesar," in *Political Issues in Luke-Acts,* ed. by R. J. Cassidy and P. J. Scharper (Maryknoll, NY: Orbis, 1983), pp. 38-48.
21. Helmut Flender, *St. Luke: Theologian of Redemptive History,* trans. by R. H. & Ilse Fuller (Philadelphia: Fortress, 1967), pp. 8, n. 5; 62.
22. W. G. Kümmel, *Introduction to the New Testament,* rev. ed., trans. by H. C. Kee (Nashville: Abingdon, 1975), pp. 140f; 163.
23. Hans Conzelmann, *The Theology of St. Luke,* trans. by Geoffrey Buswell (London: Faber and Faber, 1960), pp. 95-136.
24. Martin Hengel, *Christ and Power,* trans. by E. R. Kalin (Philadelphia: Fortress, 1977), p. 35.

25. Victor Paul Furnish, *The Moral Teaching of Paul* (Nashville: Abingdon, 1979), pp. 115-141.
26. Tacitus, *Annals*, Bk. XIII, 50.
27. Suetonius, *Life of Claudius* 25; cf. Acts 18:2.
28. Hengel, *Christ and Power*, p. 35.
29. An eloquent statement of this circumstance is contained in Martin Luther King, Jr., "Letter from Birmingham City Jail," in *Nonviolence in America*, ed. by Staughton Lind (Indianapolis: Bobbs-Merrill, 1966), pp. 461-81.
30. I cannot agree with Ernst Käsemann, *New Testament Questions of Today*, trans. by W. J. Montague (Philadelphia: Fortress, 1969), p. 199, that "Romans 13:1-7 is in fact a self-contained passage . . . ." Käsemann already has linked 13:1-7 back to 12:1 at p. 198.
31. Furnish, *Moral Teaching*, p. 138.
32. *The Westminster Confession*, XX.2, in *The Book of Confessions*, Pt. I of the Constitution of the United Presbyterian Church in the U.S.A., 2nd ed. (New York: Office of the General Assembly, 1970), 6.101.
33. Hengel, *Christ and Power*, p. 35.
34. John H. Yoder, *The Politics of Jesus* (Grand Rapids: Eerdmans, 1972), pp. 197-200.
35. Käsemann, *New Testament Questions*, p. 204. I say "was" because Käsemann's "Principles of the Interpretation of Romans 13," came out in 1961, fifteen years before his daughter, Elisabeth, was killed in Argentina. (See Elaine Magalis, "Murder in Argentina," *The Christian Century* 94 (1977) 1030-33.) While his interest in liberation hermeneutics seemed to increase in later years, his *Commentary on Romans*, trans. & ed. by G. W. Bromiley (Grand Rapids: Eerdmans, 1980), pp. 350-59, still emphasizes Paul's resistance of the anarchistic tendency among the charismatics (as in 1 Cor.) and still sustains the insularity of 13:1-7 against the surrounding material.
36. This connection is a major theme of Oscar Cullmann, *The State in the New Testament* (New York: Scribner's, 1956), pp. 71-85. Adela Y. Collins, "The Political Perspective of the Revelation to John," *Journal of Biblical Literature* 96 (1977) 241-56, argues well that Rev. 13 (as the whole of the Apocalypse) rejects the Zealot option of violent revolution while supporting non-violent resistance to Roman taxation, as she interprets Rev. 13:16f (*ibid.*, 252-54).
37. Käsemann, *New Testament Questions*, p. 215.
38. *Ibid.*, p. 216.
39. See Donald D. Kaufman, *What Belongs to Caesar?* (Scottdale, PA: Herald, 1969), and *The Tax Dilemma: Praying for Peace, Paying for War* (Herald, 1978).
40. William Durland edits (with Eugenia Durland and David Stallings) *Center Peace* and works for The Center on Law and Pacifism, P.O. Box 308, Cokedale, CO 81032. He wrote *No King but Caesar?* (Scottdale, PA: Herald, 1975).
41. On Bromley, Coddington, and McCrackin, see *Guide to War Tax Resistance*, 2nd ed., by Ed Hedemann (New York: War Resisters League, 339 Lafayette St., New York, NY 10012, 1983), pp. 72-76. Stephen Wright of Solon Springs, Wisconsin, has updated the McCrackin story in an unpublished paper, "Maurice F. McCrackin: A Case of Nonconformity in the Presbyterian Chruch." His essay has been offered to *The Journal of Presbyterian History*.
42. Käsemann, *New Testament Questions*, pp. 210-13. He is fully aware that the translation of 1 Cor. 7:21 is uncertain.
43. See Roland Bainton, *Christian Attitudes Toward War and Peace* (Nashville: Abingdon, 1960), pp. 66-100.
44. Richard Niebuhr, *Christ and Culture* (New York: Harper & Row, 1951), pp. 190-229, portrays with liberal optimism Christ as "transformer of culture." This final paradigm of how Christianity is to humanize civilization fails to note that war, demanding the largest measure of devotion, resources, skills, and life blood which any institution of human culture has yet devised, now threatens us with human extermination. Most war tax resisters old enough to be faced with the issue before 1945 believed even then that the dream of

transforming rather than exterminating war was hopelessly utopian.

45. Reinhold Niebuhr, *Christianity and Power Politics* (New York: Scribner's, 1940), p. 20: "Justice is basically dependent upon a balance of power. Whenever an individual or a nation possesses undue power, and whenever this power is not checked by the possibility of criticizing and resisting it, it grows inordinate."

46. *The Idea of Disarmament!* (Elgin, IL: Brethren, 1982), pp. 34-58. My own objections to deterrence are more condensed: 1) "balance" is not the policy of our government and never has been; the actual policy is significant superiority for our side; 2) the constant proliferation of martial technology turns each temporary lull or claim of equilibrium into a castle in Spain; 3) the moral initiative in balance ideology is always surrendered to the degenerative impact of alleged or actual "betrayal" by the other side; 4) the deployment of resources required by "balance" thinking is already producing unbearable world poverty, global revolutionary unrest, and economic chaos. See Dorothy Soelle, *The Arms Race Kills Even Without War*, trans. by G. Elston (Philadelphia: Fortress, 1983).

47. Ruth Sivard, *World Military and Social Expenditures 1983* (World Priorities, Box 25140, Washington, DC 20007), pp. 20-21.

48. *The Challenge of Peace: God's Promise and Our Response* (United States Catholic Conference, 1312 Massachusetts Ave., NW, Washington, DC 20005, 1983). The World Council of Churches, meeting at Vancouver in August of 1983, spoke with more insight into our present dilemma as follows: "We believe that the time has come when the churches must unequivocally declare that the production and deployment as well as the use of nuclear weapons are a crime against humanity and that such activities must be condemned on ethical and theological grounds." *Document GR5*, par. 12.

49. "Nuclear Eschatology and the Study of Religion." *Journal of the American Academy of Religion*, 51 (1983) 2-14.

SHALOM AND EIRENE

Donald E. Gowan and Ulrich W. Mauser

Both the Hebrew word *shalom* and the Greek word *eirene* are appropriately translated "peace" in many of their uses in the Bible. For that reason the two terms, especially the former, have become favorites for the peace movement. The church has identified peacemaking as a scriptural imperative to which it is endeavoring to respond in a variety of ways. But not all of the exegetical work which is necessary to support a full theology of peacemaking has yet been done. This paper intends to offer a contribution which is the result of the individual and cooperative work of an Old Testament specialist and a New Testament specialist. It seemed appropriate for us to present some of our work as a unified account because each of us (in different ways) has been developing a kind of dialogue between the testaments on the subject of peace.

Three aspects of the dialogue will be presented here. They are: 1) The influence of the Old Testament usage of *shalom* on the meanings of *eirene* in the New Testament. 2) The different emphases of *shalom/eirene* in the two testaments. 3) The evidence for historical continuity between the testaments which is provided by Jewish apocalyptic thought.

Continuity in Old and New Testament Meanings

It has often been noted that *eirene,* which in pre-Biblical Greek simply referred to the absence of war, has been used by the translators and authors of the Bible to represent all the various meanings conveyed by *shalom* in the Old Testament. That is true, but the bare statement by itself may tend to misrepresent the relationship between the testaments as they deal with the subject of peace. One must begin with the word study, but that is only a beginning. Its results will be presented here in a compact form with a minimum of examples. Let us consider seven uses of *shalom,* together with their New Testament parallels.

1.) *Shalom denotes a harmonious relationship between people.* "When his brothers saw that their father loved him more than all his brothers, then they hated him, and they could not speak to him *shalom.*" (Gen. 37:4; cf. 44:17). "Mend your ways, heed my appeal, agree with one another, live in *eirene,* and the God of love and *eirene* will be with you." (2 Cor. 13:11)

2.) *Shalom includes personal well-being.* "Go now, see the *shalom* of your brothers and the *shalom* of the flock." (Gen. 37:14) "If a brother or sister is ill-clad and in lack of daily food, and one of you says to them, 'Go in *eirene,* be warmed and filled,' without giving them the things needed for the body, what does it profit?' (Jas. 2:15-16)

3.) *Sometimes that well-being focuses specifically on health.* "And he asked them about *shalom,* and he said, 'Is your father *shalom,* the old man of whom you spoke; is he still alive?' And they said, 'Your servant, our father, has *shalom;* he is still alive." (Gen. 43:27-28) "Daughter, your faith has made you well; go in *eirene,* and be healed of your disease." (Mark 5:34)

4.) *Often shalom is a promise of safety and security, from a stronger party to a weaker.* "*Shalom* to you; do not be afraid." (Gen. 43:23) "Only the man in whose hand the cup was found shall be my slave; but as for you, go up in *shalom* to your father." (Gen. 44:17) "When a strong man, fully armed, guards his own palace, his goods are in *eirene.*" (Luke 11:21)

5.) *Occasionally shalom means the absence of war,* as in Eccl. 3:8, but the usual term for that is "rest." *Eirene* is the opposite of war in at least one New Testament text, Rev. 6:4. *But shalom can also mean victory as the result of war,* as in Judg. 8:9: "When I come again in *shalom,* I will break down this tower." There is one possible New Testament parallel to that, in Rom. 16:20: " . . . then the God of *eirene* will soon crush Satan under your feet." That *shalom* is not by definition always the opposite of war is shown clearly by 2 Sam. 11:7: "David asked concerning the *shalom* of Joab, and the *shalom* of the people (the army), and the *shalom* of the battle."

6.) *It is possible to die "in peace,"* as in Gen. 15:15 and Luke 2:29. This probably means having completed one's life in all the fullness that could be expected.

7.) *Shalom is also closely associated with the blessing of God,* and thus with all the good things which God bestows upon God's people. The priestly benediction of Num. 6:22-27, which concludes with, "and give you peace," has clear parallels in the blessings which appear at the end of several epistles (e.g. "The God of peace be with you all," in Rom. 15:33) and also with the greeting, "Grace to you, and peace."

These are the results which a theological dictionary or a word-study article might provide: a range of meanings for *shalom* which are echoed by an almost identical range for *eirene.* If we were to add more examples from the two testaments we would see that there are sound scriptural grounds for the tendency appearing in some works on the subject to make peace comprehend almost everything Christian. The fact is that *shalom* does seem to be a kind of umbrella under which almost everything good can be found. Yet perhaps a better metaphor would be to think of it as a sort of connective tissue. As Werner Foerster remarked, ". . . *eirene* thus acquires a most profound and comprehensive significance. It indicates the eschatological salvation of the whole man which is already present as the power of God."[1] This means that the word-study approach can produce only very limited results. The remainder of this paper represents an effort to show how certain other approaches can produce additional insights.

Differences of Emphasis in
Old and New Testaments

Despite the fact that *eirene* in the New Testament has absorbed the meanings of *shalom,* there are significant differences in what the two testaments find it important to emphasize about peace. The important differences are not to be found in the familiar pictures of the Old Testament as a book filled with bloodshed and violence (although it does contain enough of that), in contrast with the New Testament as a message of love and peace. The testaments are too closely related for that kind of stark contrast to be upheld, and their differences are matters of emphasis rather than opposite points of view.

The centrality of Jesus Christ in all that the New Testament has to say about peace will be emphasized in part three of this paper. This represents a conception of peace which really does not appear in the Old Testament, despite its "messianic" passages. Certainly, it contains texts in which God's gift of peace on earth is associated with the appearance of the righteous king (e.g. Isa. 9:6; Ezek. 37:24-28), but it is God who makes peace. The New Testament has said something dramatically new when it insists that God's gift of eschatological peace is the result of the career of a single human being, the appearance of Jesus on earth.

This insistence on connecting the divine gift of peace with the work of Jesus Christ has led the New Testament authors to devote very little attention to some Old Testament emphases and to develop at great length other aspects of peace which the Old Testament does little more than suggest.

Peace in the Old Testament is described often enough as the gift of God, but the results of that gift are usually not described as affecting one's relationship with God. That is to say, there is no clear Old Testament parallel to Rom. 5:1, "Therefore, since we are justified by faith, we have peace with God through our Lord Jesus Christ." Expressions such as "the peace of God" (Phil. 4:7) and, obviously "the peace of Christ" (Col. 3:15) are also missing from the Old Testament. There is a single parallel to "he is our peace" (Eph. 2:14) in the name which Gideon gave to his alter, "Yahweh is peace" (Jud. 6:24). However, the theological potency of the two passages can scarcely be compared, and peace means two quite different things: reconciliation in Ephesians but victory in Judges.

Certainly the references in Ephesians 2 and Romans 5 are closely associated with one of the most common meanings of *shalom,* viz. the condition of harmonious relationships between two parties. In Ephesians they are still human beings, Jew and Gentile, as in the Old Testament, and in Romans God has become one of the parties. But peace with God involves aspects of the human condition which are seldom connected with *shalom.* The inner qualities of endurance, character and hope are associated with being at peace with God, and they are possible because

"God's love has been poured into our hearts through the Holy Spirit which has been given to us" (Rom. 5:5).

This inner peace is first the result of being reconciled to God. It is an almost exclusively New Testament subject because the Israelite way of thinking simply does not often say much about the inner life. That the New Testament has not turned *eirene* into a synonym for something like mere "contentment," however, is shown clearly by other passages. In Col. 3:5-17, a series of instructions on how to live together in Christian community may be found, beginning with a series of qualities which are to be avoided, then balancing them with a series of positive qualities. The key admonitions, which make that kind of life possible, are: "And let the peace of Christ rule in your hearts," followed by "Let the word of Christ dwell in you richly." It seems fair to say that for the peace of Christ to rule in your hearts means gaining that inner stability, certainty and calm which we might fairly call peace of mind yet its result is harmonious life in the church.

Other passages take the effects of having achieved inner peace beyond the doors of the church. In Heb. 12:1-17 the author considers the possibility of the persecution of his or her readers to be near and offers them an interpretation of the suffering which they may have to undergo, viz. as discipline. The passage is dominated by vigorous admonitions to be strong (vss. 1-3, 12-13), with the suffering Christ himself held up as the great example. Then at the climax of all that comes: "Strive for peace with all men, and for the holiness without which no one will see the Lord" (vs. 14). Certainly, in this context, it is impossible to think the author means some way should be found to appease one's opponents to escape persecution. This striving for peace is coupled with striving for holiness, i.e. maintaining one's full integrity as a Christian, come what may (vs. 15-17).

A similar piece of advice appears in 2 Pet. 3:14, addressed to a different problem. The readers are upset about the delay of Christ's return, but they are counseled: ". . . since you wait for these, be zealous to be found by him without spot or blemish, and at peace." This is peace which will keep Christians stable and faithful when what they had expected from God is not happening, this kind of peace also is not purely passive.

Perhaps it must be admitted that the New Testament concept of peace is just a bit "self-centered," in that it is focused in most of its occurrences on the church as the place where peace has been found and will be enjoyed until the imminent return of Christ. That he was expected to return soon seems to have been the primary reason the implications of God's work to make universal peace and the Christian task of peacemaking were not more often discussed in terms of their worldwide potential. But they had the record of such ideas and hopes in their scriptures, the Old Testament. The concluding paragraphs of this section will turn to those significant aspects of *shalom* which the New Testament does not develop at any length. Then the final section of the paper will provide additional evidence that the essential continuity was maintained, despite the shift of emphasis.

Eirene most often refers to relationships between God and the believer, and among believers within the church, with less frequent references to associations with non-believers. *Shalom* most often refers to interpersonal relationships and to political affairs with a few allusions to peace in the world of nature. These latter two uses play a very minor role in the New Testament. In order to deal with the contrast briefly, let us consider two passages from the book of Ezekiel, chosen because both use the expression "covenant of peace."

The term itself is not one which is used very often in the Old Testament (elsewhere: Num. 25:13; Isa. 54:10; Mal. 2:5). The context of its occurrences in Ezekiel (34:25 and 37:26) suggests more about its content than any of the other passages. The central promise in chapter 34 is that of restoration from exile to the Promised Land, and in chapter 37 the focus is on the reunion of the Northern and Southern Kingdoms. In both cases the covenant of peace is mentioned immediately after the promise of a new David to be prince over them, so the overtones are predominantly political. *Shalom* seems to designate primarily a state of prosperity and security for God's people who will live under a stable political system, untroubled by their old antagonists, the nations. But just after the mention of peace in chapter 34 the prophet develops the blessing of nature to a considerable extent (vss. 26-29, including additional references to the nations).

For Ezekiel, *shalom* is highly anthropocentric and Israel-centered. It means being protected from the attacks of the nations and from the dangers of nature. Positively, it means becoming evidence to the nations of God's power and grace, having a righteous king (in our terms, having good government), and being provided for abundantly by nature.

Elsewhere, the expectations are broader. In a valuable dissertation on *eirene* written by A.M. Woodruff, several Old Testament passages are identified as "peace pictures," even though they do not happen to include the word *shalom*.[2] He justified this by showing that the same ideas are elsewhere associated with *shalom*. The two most famous of them will only be mentioned here, since they are so well-known. Isa. 2:2-4 (Mic. 4:1-4) depicts peace among the nations in a way which involves perfect harmony and equality, guaranteed by the law of God, and Isa. 11:6-9 speaks of peace in nature which is so thoroughgoing that "they shall not hurt or destroy" is the watchword. Such expectations could certainly have been taken up and reaffirmed by the authors of the New Testament, but its new emphasis on peace largely overshadows them. The angels' song, "peace on earth," does not mean quite the same thing as it would if it had been written in the Old Testament.

Such differences of emphasis are clearly present and should not be overlooked, but if one goes no further the danger exists that one will fall into the familiar pattern of claiming that the message of the New Testament is entirely "spiritual," calling for a personal religion, while the Old Testament is far too worldly in its outlook. We do not want this work on *shalom* to contribute anything more to that point of view. Even in this section, which has focused on texts which highlight the difference of emphasis, the effort has been made to show that the New Testament does not deny the validity of the Old Testament's concerns for peace, and that even in its statements about "inner peace" the social implications have begun to be drawn out. The approach to the subject which will be offered in the next section of the paper will put a much stronger emphasis on the continuity between the testaments.

Jewish Apocalyptic Thought and Continuity Between the Testaments

Some important Old Testament statements about *shalom,* and their continuance in Jewish literature before the time of the emerging church, have so deeply influenced the New Testament that its view of *eirene* cannot be fully understood if this connection is disregarded. Old Testament prophetic literature contains a number of most impressive images of peace, all of which are couched in language intimating expectations of *shalom* in the future (e.g. Isa. 2:1-4; 9:2-7; 11:1-9; Ezek. 34:23-31; 37:24-28; Zech. 9:9f.). Later Jewish thought continued to develop these peace traditions and, particularly in apocalyptic writings, intensified and enriched their leading motifs arriving at a picture of peace in the world to come as the conclusion and climax of the historical drama of salvation. With a marvelous tenacity of spirit, frequently in the face of the most adverse historical circumstances, Jewish writers clung to the Old Testament's hope of an ultimate peace, giving much new color to the picture inherited through the tradition. A simplified and, by necessity, unduly systematized survey of these developments of prophetic images of the ultimate peace yields at least four major aspects.

1. The consummation of world history will lead to the establishment of universal *shalom* for all nations.

> "When indeed this fated day also reaches its consummation . . . a great judgment and dominion will come upon men . . . The cities will be full of good things and the fields will be rich. There will be no sword on earth or din of battle, and the earth will no longer be shaken, groaning deeply. There will no longer be war or drought on earth . . . but there will be great peace throughout the whole earth" (Sib. Or. III: 741-753).

The present condition is seen as a captivity in the prison of conflict and bloodshed; but the dawning of the new day of God's final deliverance will re-establish the condition of *shalom,* lost since the fall from paradise. Thus the seer Enoch is told by the angel about the coming of the Son of Man who will inaugurate the new world: "He shall proclaim peace to you in the name of the world that is to become for from hence proceeds peace since the creation of the world . . . so there shall be length of days with that Son of Man, and peace to the righteous ones" (I Enoch 71:15, 17).

2. The vision of eschatological peace is frequently accompanied by the expectation that universal *shalom* is conditioned by the cessation of idolatry and the universal obedience of the whole world to the guidance of the one God. Universal peace is imaginable only in the event of a universal eclipse of the gods and a liberation of all peoples to the service of the one and only true God.

> "They will be free from war in towns and country. No hand of evil war, but rather the Immortal himself and the hand of the Holy One will be fighting for them. And then all the islands and cities will say. . . Come, let us fall on the ground and entreat the immortal king, the great eternal God. Let us send to the

temple since he alone is sovereign and let us ponder the Law of the Most High God who is most righteous of all throughout the earth" (Sib. Or. III: 707-718).

3. Some Jewish writings of post-Old Testament time associate the ultimate establishment of peace with the coming of a single messianic figure who can be represented as the prince of peace of Isa. 9:6. The visionary Enoch sees the advent of the Messiah as the day in which "there shall be no iron for war, nor shall anyone wear a breast plate. Neither bronze nor tin shall be to any avail or be of any value; and there will be no need of lead whatsoever" (I Enoch 52:8) because all the metals previously used for warfare are now in the dominion of the prince of peace. When this messiah shall arise, then "he shall open the gates of paradise; he shall remove the sword that has threatened since Adam" (Test. Levi 18:10).

4. The blessing of an unimaginably fertile nature which is often described as a consequence of eschatological *shalom* is, on occasion, portrayed as the result of a battle of God against the powers of chaos. The old notion of Yahweh's war is not at all banished by the apocalyptic writers extolling the glory of God's final and universal peace.

"And it will happen that when all that which should come to pass in these parts has been accomplished, the Anointed One will begin to be revealed. And Behemoth will reveal itself from its place, and Leviathan will come from the sea, the two great monsters which I created on the fifth day of creation and which I shall have kept until that time. And they will be nourishment for all who are left. The earth will also yield fruits ten thousandfold. And on one vine will be a thousand branches, and one branch will produce a thousand clusters, and one cluster will produce a thousand grapes, and one grape will produce a cor of wine. . . And it will happen at that time that the treasury of manna will come down again from on high, and they will eat of it in those years because these are they who will have arrived at the consummation of time" (II Baruch 29:3-5, 8).

In sum: the image of *shalom* in Jewish thought around New Testament times, based on adaptations of prophetic passages in the Old Testament, is embedded in eschatological expectations awaiting the restoration of a warring world to the peace of creation. It holds on to this expectation as a universal blessing in which, in some texts, all nations on earth will have their part; it remains inseparable from the validity of the first commandment insisting on the end of the worship of all false gods; it connects the coming of one single human being as the prince of peace with the introduction into a new creation of peace; and it views the establishment of a *shalom*-filled world as the triumph of God over historical and meta-historical enemies in an ultimate holy war.

In all of these characteristics, *shalom* is freedom from war connected to the death of the gods, the harmony and justice of human relationships, the security of life, the health of body and mind, and the enjoyment of a beneficial and non-destructive realm of nature. Seldom, if ever, are these characteristic elements united into one comprehensive passage. Rather, the motifs appear here in isolation and there in differing mixtures with each other, sometimes standing in some tension to one another in details. While it is not possible to fashion a consistent "drama of eschatological peace" out of its single motifs, the motifs are richly developed and are ready for reception and adaptation in many possible forms.

The New Testament's message of *eirene* is largely dependent on the store of Jewish apocalyptic hope for the *shalom* to come, and its proclamation of peace is in large part a process of the actualization of the apocalyptic hope. In support of this view, we add a few observations on the New Testament concept of peace.

Christ our peace. The sentence "Christ is our peace" means in Ephesians (2:14) something quite specific. But it is still no falsification to say that the statement "Christ is our peace" can stand as the summary of all that the entire New Testament has to say about peace. The Gospels present him as the bringer of peace, and the Epistles see him as the Lord of peace. The characteristic element of late Jewish writings which attributes such outstanding and unique significance to the coming of the messianic prince of peace comes to a head in the New Testament concentration on Jesus Christ as the one and sole purveyor of peace. Of course, this New Testament praise of Christ as the only real mediator of peace is much more concrete and detailed than any of its antecedents in Jewish eschatology, simply because it draws on the actual memory of a lived human life and the actual experience of his concrete Lordship. But this memory and experience are still planted in the soil of an eschatological expectation of the messianic bringer of peace whose accomplishments are the work of God in the final re-creation of an old decaying world. This messianic mediator of peace is often presented in Gospels and Epistles alike, as the single human being who did not ever bow to false gods and who thus rids the world of the curse of idolatry which is the root-cause of all destructions of *shalom.*

Therefore, Jesus Christ is in the New Testament not only an, nor even *the,* agent of peace, but peace itself in person. Christ as "our peace" is not a temporary stopgap operation, a timebound maneuver which succeeds in bringing a momentary measure of safety and happiness to some sufferers amidst a flood of unabated warfare. Christ is the definition, the reality and the promise of all peace truly worthy of its name.

Peace and Holy War. Very old New Testament texts appear to indicate that some early Christian confessions spoke of the risen Christ as the agent of God's kingdom of peace. The pre-Pauline tradition used in Rom. 16:20 combines in typically apocalyptic manner God's peacemaking with the war against Satan: "The God of peace will soon crush Satan under your feet." Similarly pre-Pauline may be the substance of the sentence in Rom. 14:17 which links the kingdom of God with righteousness, peace and joy.

The peace envisaged in these extremely old fragments of tradition is the final and unalterable triumph of *shalom* in a new world. It corresponds to the remains of a Palestinian confession in Rom. 1:3f. where Jesus is called the son of David after the flesh and the Son of God in the power of the resurrection. In and through his resurrection Jesus is the royal (i.e. messianic) Son of God and by this the agent of the eschatological *shalom.* Therefore, "since we are justified by God by faith, we have peace with God through our Lord Jesus Christ" (Rom. 5:1). This peace means neither a state of mental contentment, nor any peaceful condition in the world as Rom. 5:3-5 clearly shows when it speaks of sufferings, endurance, patience and hope. The *shalom* here in view is the status of reconciliation with God in which human hostility to God is overcome by God's act in Christ which inaugurates the reality of peace. This peace is the destruction of "every rule and every authority and power" reaching to the destruction of death as the last enemy through Christ's resurrection (I Cor. 15:24, 26).

What surfaces only in small bits and pieces in Paul's letters as remains of an old apocalyptic concept of Christ as the mediator of God's eschatological peacemaking is preserved in fuller compass in the Book of Revelation. There the picture of the peace of the new world is painted entirely in Old Testament colors:

> "Then I saw a new heaven and a new earth; for the first heaven and the first earth had passed away, and the sea was no more . . . and God himself will be with them; he will wipe away every tear from their eyes, and death shall be no more, neither shall there be mourning nor crying nor pain any more, for the former things have passed away" (Rev. 21:1-4).

Although the word *eirene* is not used in this passage, it is manifest that the image is a description of the ultimate *shalom* of the world to come. This is preceded, in the Book of Revelation, by an elaborate description of the wars of God and his Christ against the forces and empires of the world, wars which are fought simultaneously in heaven and on earth. It is not possible here even to sketch this description. But it may be added that the Synoptic tradition preserves sayings of Jesus in which he implies his involvement in the war of God against the chaotic enemy of peace. "Do not think that I have come to bring peace on earth; I have not come to bring peace, but the sword" (Matt. 10:34). In its context, this is a call to endurance in the situation of persecution against those who, as messengers of the kingdom, impart the *shalom* of the kingdom to every house they enter (10:13). Or again, "the kingdom of heaven has suffered violence (through the killing of John the Baptist) and men of violence take it by force (probably zealotic leaders)" (Matt. 11:12). Finally, "when a strong man, fully armed, guards his own palace, his goods are in peace; but when one stronger than he assails him, he takes away his armor in which he trusted, and divides his spoil. He who is not with me is against me, and he who does not gather with me scatters" (Luke 11:21-23).

The establishment of God's peace in the world is understood, in important passages in Gospels and Epistles alike, as the victory achieved in warfare against God's enemies through the leadership of a warring Messiah. Lest this be misunderstood, it must be added at once that nowhere is this eschatological warfare conceived as a military triumph of a Messiah wielding the sword, or as a call to crusade on the part of Christian people against secular powers. On the contrary, the sword is eliminated in this contest (Matt. 26:52f.). The seemingly contradictory passage Luke 22:35-38 may well be a confirmation of the condemnation of the sword.[3] The principle of power politics which dominates the "Pax Romana" is met by its very antithesis in the sacrificial service of the Son of Man (Mark 10:42-45).

The exhortation to the Christian to put on the armor of God "not contending against flesh and blood, but against the principalities, against the powers, against the world rulers of this present age, against the spiritual hosts of wickedness in the heavenly places" (Eph. 6:12) may well be understood—*mutatis mutandis*—as an apt description of the messianic war fought and won by Jesus in the Gospels. This much is certain: the gaining of peace in the New Testament is not the result of a passive attitude to the evils of the world, rather it is the costly prize of a conquest which can be won only in marshalling all energies for the defeat of evil.

Peace and the Messiah. The old apocalyptic picture of Jesus as the messianic prince of peace who conducts the ultimate war of God to achieve everlasting *shalom* is drawn in the Synoptic tradition into the life of Jesus. The prince of peace is at once a historical and meta-historical figure. Luke has announced the birth in the city of David (2:11) of the son of a man from the lineage of David (2:4) (i.e. the child of the messianic line) by the angelic pronouncement "glory to God in the highest, and on earth peace" (2:14). He concludes his report of the activity of this messiah by the retrospect of his own disciples "blessed is the king who comes in the name of the Lord. Peace in heaven and glory in the highest" (19:38). These cross-allusions are a redactional arrangement which makes the point that from birth to death this man's life has brought peace to heaven and to earth, as the whole story of this Jesus Christ is the "gospel of peace" (Acts 19:36).

The entire Synoptic tradition is filled with accounts of Jesus as the agent of God's *shalom.* The woman healed of a flow of blood is sent away with the words "go in peace, and be healed of your disease" (Mark 5:34). In this narrative *shalom* is the restoration to full health, as well as in numerous other healing stories in which the word *eirene* does not appear. The notorious woman who washes Jesus' feet with her tears is released with the words "your faith has saved you, go in peace" (Luke 7:50). Here, *shalom* is the restoration to a condition of forgiveness, and also in a great deal of Jesus traditions concerned with the pardoning of the guilty without the use of *eirene.*

The feeding stories in the Gospels unmistakably echo the giving of the manna in the accounts of Moses and are, in post-canonical Jewish tradition, a consequence of the dawning of the messianic kingdom of peace (see Barach 29:3-5, 8).

The fight against the chaos monsters, a prelude to the coming of the messianic reign of peace, is mirrored in many of the Markan exorcism stories and in the accounts of Jesus' power over water and sea. We have mentioned these instances very briefly; they are in need of a great deal more precise and detailed exposition. But the general impression of this sketch may suffice. Its sum total is this: the earthly Jesus of Nazareth is the powerful agent of God through whom the *shalom* of the human condition and of the condition of nature are marvellously restored.

Peace in Anticipation of the End. One final point may be added in greatest brevity. In Eph. 2:11-22 the word peace is used with greater frequency than anywhere else in the New Testament. It signifies there the creation of a new humanity out of the separated and hostile groups of Jews and non-Jews, and thus provides the justification of a world-embracing mission which swept in a few decades over the entire Roman empire. In view of the fact that Jewish thought and practice alike reserved the incorporation of all nations into God's world of peace for the world to come in which idolatry has ceased and one law of one God is universally acknowledged, there can hardly be any doubt that the Pauline mission (whether Eph. was written by Paul or not) regarded the powers of the eschaton as driving forces which call forth historical realization. The prince of peace is in the Pauline mission not only the historically identifiable person Jesus of Nazareth, nor only the meta-historical redeemer, but also the continuous presence of God's ultimate peace in the stream of time. The peace of the world to come is reality not only in heaven but also on earth; and the light of the eternal *shalom* sends out its rays even now into the very core of darkness. In all this, the New Testament proclamation of peace is fulfillment of the prophetic hope.

ENDNOTES

1. Weiner Foerster, "Eirene" in Gerhard Kittel, *Theological Dictionary of the New Testament* (Grand Rapids: Wm. B. Eerdmans Publishing Company, 1964), p. 415.
2. A.M. Woodruff, *Eirene in the Pauline Corpus* (Ann Arbor: Xerox University Microfilms, 1976).
3. Paul S. Minear, "A note on Luke xxii 36," *Novum Testamentum* VII (1964-65), pp. 129-134.

Acts of Resistance

1984: ORWELL AND BARMEN

Robert McAfee Brown

When George Orwell published a novel about totalitarianism in 1948, he arrived at a title simply by reversing the last two digits of that year, so that the date became 1984. Ever since, 1984 has been more than just a date, it has been a symbol. Orwell's book describes a hideous universe of thought control, torture and informers, along with the essential governmental propaganda industries of Newspeak and Doublespeak, which exist to make syntactical and logical sense out of three slogans that dominate the book and the world it describes: WAR IS PEACE, FREEDOM IS SLAVERY, IGNORANCE IS STRENGTH.

Many people believe that *1984* describes life in the Soviet Union, and Big Brother does bear a resemblance to Uncle Joe Stalin. Others see it as a description of the German Third Reich, defeated by the Allied armies even as the book was germinating in the author's mind. A few others, myself included, view it apprehensively as an exaggerated version of tendencies that, in more subtle fashion, are further advanced in our own society than we want to believe.

But if the year 1984 is a symbol in the Orwellian sense, for those of us within the Christian family it is a symbol in another sense as well. For, as we have recently been reminded in a variety of commemorative celebrations, it is also the fiftieth anniversary of the "Barmen Declaration" of the Confessing Church in Germany. Issued in May 1934, well into Hitler's second year of power, the Barmen Declaration was one of the very few corporate challenges to Hitler and what was being done in Germany by the Nazis.

The juxtaposition of Orwell's book title and the anniversary of Barmen is an important juxtaposition, for if we are to stand against those evidences of the Orwellian world that we already see in our midst, important resources for doing so will be found in the stance and conviction, and courage of the creators of the Barmen Declaration. For the worlds of Orwell and Barmen are incompatible. If we really want Orwell's 1984, we will take all Barmen types into custody, and if we affirm Barmen we will be forced to challenge almost every aspect of the Orwellian universe.

Perhaps more important, if we are concerned about the *possibility* today of drifting into a 1984 world without quite realizing what is happening, then Barmen provides a timely point of view from which to seek to stem the tide. For the tragedy of Barmen, along with all the courage that prompted it, was that *it came too late.* Hitler had by that time so consolidated his power that the only real witness left against him within Germany was the witness of martyrdom. The telltale signs in Germany were not taken seriously enough soon enough. So the fact that we are not yet today living within the crudities of Orwell's world, but are aware of the presence of some of its subtleties, is an even more important reason to reflect on the meaning of Barmen, in order to learn to speak and act while there is still time. This means that we cannot put the Barmen Declaration back in mothballs, waiting only to dust it off for the big seventy-fifth celebration reminiscence in 2009 A.D., but must see its ongoing importance on the contemporary scene.

A Brief Historical Excursion

To those for whom "Barmen" is not exactly a household word, a brief historical word will suffice. By 1934, Hitler's increasing control had made Germany look very much like Orwell's world. And in the face of that control, most of Germany had capitulated—the business community, the universities, the cultural groups and the churches had almost without exception bought into the Nazi vision. A few Christians continued to resist—Franz Jaegerstetter, Martin Niemoeller, Dietrich Bonhoeffer, Bishop Lichtenberg, Fr. Delp to name a few—but the church itself was increasingly taken over by the "German Christians," a group that affirmed Hitler as a new Messiah, accepted the anti-Semitism of Nazism, and was willing to be dictated to by the Nazi party. And it was largely in reaction to the excesses of the "German Christians" that another group, called the *Bekentiss Kirche* (the Confessing Church), was formed chiefly out of the Lutheran and Reformed churches. The "Barmen Declaration" was the work of this group, written at its initial Synod in Barmen in May 1934. The fine hand of Karl Barth, a Swiss theologian who was still teaching in Bonn at the time, is evident throughout the document, and the document is a good case-study in Barth's ongoing contention that theology and politics go hand in hand.

The Declaration Itself

On first reading, however, the document hardly seems political, let alone "dangerous." It is strongly theological, massively Biblical, and centered in concern for the church. Such a reading, however, is wide of the mark. For there was no way, in the Germany of 1934, to make the kind of theological affirmations contained in Barmen without being extremely political. We can see this clearly by considering the two sides of the initial proposition, the affirmation and the consequent negation. The affirmation reads:

Jesus Christ, as he is attested for us in Holy Scripture, is the one Word of God which we have to hear and which we have to trust and obey in life and in death.

This is good solid, even Barthian, Christian doctrine, that most people in the

Christian family could affirm without much trouble or without thinking it would get them into trouble. But we must notice the strength of the verbs, and their cumulative force. It is one thing to *hear,* and a good many people can do that. But the thrust is to move beyond hearing to *trust,* and to trust is to take what is heard with sufficient seriousness to bank one's life upon it. Trusting means remaining faithful even when the evidence goes the other way. And that already has us most of the way to the need to *obey,* which involves not only an inner commitment but an outer deportment. To obey is to follow through on trust, to be open to taking the consequences. That the costs might be high is recognized by the signatories, who, realizing this was not a fair weather agreement they were endorsing, went on to acknowledge the need to hear, trust and obey "in life and in death." To "hear, trust and obey" is to put one's life on the line.

How so? Because to affirm certain things means to deny certain other things. The negation, following immediately upon the affirmation, makes this clear:

> We reject the false doctrine, as though the Church could and would have to acknowledge as a source of its proclamation, apart from and beside the one Word of God, still other events and powers, figures and truths, as God's revelation.

That still doesn't sound very "dangerous." The word "Hitler" occurs nowhere in the statement, nor in the entire Barmen Declaration, for that matter. But nobody living in Germany in 1934 could fail to get the point that the reality of Hitler had called forth the entire document. For precisely what Hitler had claimed and gotten from the German people was an acknowledgement that the truth for them *was* found "apart from and beside the one Word of God," i.e. in the Nazi party, and that it *was* in "other events and powers, figures and truths," i.e. in the Nazi ideology, the Nazi rise to power, the Nazi leaders, that Germany's salvation was located. "Blood and soil," racial purity, anti-Semitism, and the people who propounded such ideologies, were to be accepted as truth. So to say "yes" to Jesus Christ (as the affirmation does) meant to say "no" to Adolf Hitler and all that he represented (as the negation does).

The same point is succinctly made in the title that Martin Niemoeller gave to a book of sermons published during this period. He called it *Christus ist Mein Fuehrer,* Christ is my "Fuehrer" or leader, and we may be sure that the use of the word "Fuehrer" was not inadvertent, since everybody in Germany referred to Hitler as the Fuehrer. To be saying "Christ is my Fuehrer" was *also* to be saying "Hitler is not my Fuehrer." And that meant Dachau—for seven years—as Niemoeller discovered.

There are five other propositions in the Barmen Declaration, which spell out in more detail the overall theme of the first proposition.

A *status confessionis*

Theologians frequently resort to foreign phrases to make a point (a sin to which I am about to succumb) and in the kind of moment Barmen represents, they talk about a *status confessionis,* a "confessional situation," in which the church, in order to be true to itself and its message, must distinguish *as clearly as possible* between truth and error. There are often situations, particularly when public policy is concerned, in which Christians can disagree without anyone having to call the integrity of the other's position into account. But sometimes there are situations in which the issues are so fateful that no dissimulation, no compromise, is possible. The signatories of Barmen clearly felt that they were in such a time, a time when no one and no church could any longer say, "We affirm both Christ and Hitler," but rather "Either Christ or Hitler, but not both." They were saying in effect, "The discussion about supporting or not supporting Hitler is now closed. We have rendered our verdict. There is no longer a basis for negotiation." Either/or, not both/and.

Situations of such clarity, it can be argued, are rare, and should not be prematurely or artificially invoked for they can lead to terrible acts of spiritual judgment and pride. But there has been another *status confessionis* in the church since the time of Hitler, and it is worth brief examination. In this case the issue has not been Hitler but *apartheid,* the forced separation of the races, and the location has been not Germany but South Africa. Until 1982 members of the various Reformed Churches in South Africa had managed to occupy all sides of the issue. Many affirmed that *apartheid* was consistent with the Christian gospel; others affirmed that it was not; some were saying that the matter wasn't clear, and the rest were saying that the debate was inconsequential since it wasn't the church's business anyhow. But the issue of the injustice and destructiveness of *apartheid* finally became so clear that, at the urging of churches of South Africa who are members of the World Alliance of Reformed Churches, the latter body, meeting in Ottawa in August 1982, formally declared that *"apartheid* is a heresy." It was no longer possible to affirm the Christian faith as proclaimed by the Reformed Churches and affirm *apartheid* as well. It was another instance of a *status confessionis,* in which a clear either/or had been reached: either Christ or *apartheid,* but not both.

Is There a *status confessionis* for Us Today?

Before dealing with this question on the American scene, there is an important interpolation that must be made. Barmen talk is very much in-house Christian talk, for the obvious reason that those at Barmen were very in-house Christians. It works well for those of us within the Christian community. But as we face our own nation today, we need to be conscious of a religiously pluralistic situation that is quite different from the Germany of fifty years ago. During the Vietnam years a number of us gathered to explore the possibility of creating a kind of "Confessing Church" in our own land and of issuing our own counterpart to the Barmen Declaration, this one aimed at our own government and the need for us to say an unequivocal "no" to its foreign policy. We decided against it largely on the grounds that we were already working closely with many people in the Jewish community. To render our witness in the Christological terms of Barmen would cut us off from them. That was a price we were not willing to pay.

Today, as we explore the possibility that a *status confessionis* may be approaching for us, in which a "yes" to Jesus Christ means a "no" to many policies of our government, we must find ways to do this in concert with Jews who share the same concerns, rather than apart from them. When Christians say that "Jesus Christ is Lord," meaning that nothing else can command our total allegiance, and that therefore the state is *not* Lord, this is our way of saying what Jews say when they give assent to the first commandment, in which God says, "You shall have no other gods before me." Whatever we may say within our church assemblies, we must find ways in the public forum to close ranks with Jews—and indeed with all other persons of good will—to speak unitedly about our common concerns. It is one of the shortcomings of the Barmen Declaration that it did not see clearly what was already happening to Jews in Germany, and thus failed to address the most obscene of all of Hitler's policies.

Is there a *status confessionis* for us today? Probably a lot of support could be mustered for the notion that in extremely perilous times—such as the times we have just examined in Orwell's *1984*, the Germany of the 1930's and the South Africa of the 1980's—when issues of right and wrong emerge with stunning clarity—there is a place for unequivocal stands.

But a lot less support would be forthcoming for the notion that we are even remotely close to times of such extremity in the United States today. Christians disagree about our domestic and foreign policies. The notion that we could take any one position along a spectrum of points of view and either baptize it—or anathematize it—would strike most folk as theological imperialism of the worst sort. I might privately believe that my position was the "only" true Christian position, and I might publicly do all I could to persuade people of its truth, but I would be unjustified in seeking to deny the name of "Christian" to those who disagreed with me. That, after all, is the American way of doing things, especially in a time when issues are too ambiguous to justify or demand a *status confessionis* in relation to them.

Or is that too benign a scenario? *Are* there issues where such a judgment is now demanded, or at least close to being demanded? I believe there are at least two kinds of issues concerning which we are being forced closer and closer to the decision that faced our German counterparts, when a "yes" to the God we worship forces a "no" to certain policies and demands our nation and its leaders espouse.

The first of these is the issue of *nuclear weapons*. I sometimes fear that just as Germans today look back on the early 1930's and say, "How could we have been so blind as not to have seen the peril of Hitler," so people of a later generation (if, indeed, there is one) will look back on us and say, "How could they have been so blind as not to have seen the peril of nuclear weapons?"

The Roman Catholic bishops have given us a starting point in their recent pastoral letter, which contains an implicit logic that all of us together need to push even further. As I understand their position, they argue that there is no situation in which the *use* of nuclear weapons could be morally permissible as something consonant with the will of God. But if *use* is wrong, it must also be wrong to *possess* such weapons, since possession tempts powerfully toward use—whether by deliberate decision, technological accident or human error. And if one power has possession, other powers will also feel the need for possession, thus compounding the likelihood of use. And if it is wrong to *use* weapons and wrong to *possess* them, it must also be wrong to *manufacture* them, since manufacture inevitably means possession and possession almost inevitably means use. The bishops' letter does not push that argument to its conclusion, arguing that for the moment possession may be *provisionally* justified if it is used as a basis for sincere negotiations to reduce and finally eliminate all nuclear weapons. If such acts of good faith are not forthcoming, however, the bishops might in the near future be forced to press the argument all the way. That would comprise a *status confessionis,* since one would have to say an unequivocal "no" to nuclear weapons in light of one's faith.

The World Council of Churches, at its assembly in Vancouver in August 1983, approved a report on "Confronting Threats to Peace and Survival" that does seem to push the logic all the way and declare a *status confessionis.* We must be clear, however, that the report is "commended to the churches for study and appropriate action" without in any sense binding the member churches. But the very structure of the section on "Nuclear arms, doctrines and disarmament" recapitulates the structure of Barmen: first an affirmation of Jesus Christ and then a consequent negation. The first lines of the section follow:

> It would be an intolerably evil contradiction of the Sixth Assembly's theme, "Jesus Christ—the Life of the World," to support the nuclear weapons and doctrines which threaten the survival of the world. . .
>
> We believe that the time has come when the churches must unequivocally declare that the production and deployment as well as the use of nuclear weapons are a crime against humanity and that such activities must be condemned on ethical and theological grounds. . .
>
> Nuclear deterrence, as the strategic doctrine which has justified nuclear weapons in the name of security and war prevention, must now be categorically rejected as contrary to our faith in Jesus Christ who is our life and peace. Nuclear deterrence is morally unacceptable because it relies on the credibility of the *intention to use* nuclear weapons: we believe that any intention to use weapons of mass destruction is an utterly inhuman violation of the mind and spirit of Christ which should be in us. . .
>
> (for the full report see Gill, ed., *Gathered for Life.* Eerdmans, 1984, pp. 72-82. The above quotation is on p. 75)

Such an unequivocal stance is a risky stance. But the Confessing Church's stance in 1934 was a risky stance also. Risk is part of the authentic Christian vocabulary and lifestyle.

But we have not yet disposed of Barmen's challenge to us. For there are other things happening in our life today about which Barmen calls us to respond. They have not yet brought us to Orwell's 1984, but they are signs and portents on the scene that if not checked, could slowly but inexorably lead us into that world. Here the important thing to remember is that Barmen came too late, and we must not replicate that tardiness.

The issue under which the signs and portents can be gathered can be called the doctrine of *national security.* This is a position well advanced in many other parts of the world where, in the name of "national security," all acts of challenge are summarily dealt with and perpetrators are tortured, imprisoned or killed. Let us use the Orwellian slogans cited above as a way of indicating items on the horizon that, if not checked, could gradually assume center stage. What will prevent their assuming center stage will be the most open and unequivocal discussion of their penchant for doing so.

Take the Orwellian doctrine that *War is Peace*. The United States recently engaged in the military invasion of another country—Grenada. But we were repeatedly told by our president that it was *not* a military invasion but a "rescue mission." He emphatically insisted on this distinction at a news conference, chastising reporters who had been so short-sighted as to call it a "military invasion," an act of war. No, he insisted, it was a "rescue mission" of medical students, an act of peace and charity (even though, as we subsequently discovered once the governmentally imposed censorship was lifted, the medical students had in fact been in no danger.)

Similarly we are constantly told that we are *not* engaging in war in Central America, and that the only fighting is being done by the people in the countries themselves, even though it turns out that our own C.I.A. has mined harbors in international waters, which is an act of war (and a violation of international law) if there ever was one. The government's rhetoric is no more convincing in this case than is its dubbing missiles of first-strike nuclear capability "Peacekeepers." All this is Orwellian Doublespeak. It is our nation beginning to tell us that War is Peace.

Take the Orwellian doctrine that *Freedom is Slavery*. We are told that if we speak too much, debate too much, question too much, those very expressions of freedom will make us vulnerable to the enemy and this will lead to our enslavement. Consequently, such freedoms must be held in check. A good example of seeking to hold them in check is a fall 1983 piece of White House-initiated legislation mandating that all public officials who have had access to classified material and who want to comment on public affairs, either now or in the future, must obtain governmental clearance for their remarks ahead of time. The provision applies not only while they are in office but *for the rest of their lives*. This provides a powerful new weapon to those in public office who want to forestall criticism of their acts— criticism which, as Floyd Abrams of the *New York Times* has pointed out, would come from those most knowledgeable of all to voice it.

What could be more threatening to the healthy discussion and critique that should characterize a democracy than such a law? Even though, because of public outcry, enforcement of the legislation was recently put on hold, it was not rescinded, and thousands of public officials have already agreed to abide by it, it illustrates the mind-set of those in power in our nation and their desire in the interests of "national security" to forestall criticism.

Take the Orwellian doctrine that *Ignorance is Strength*, that a government must not let its people know too much or they will be in danger of losing their dominance in the world. One of the most disturbing examples of this attitude in recent years has been the unprecedented refusal of the Reagan administration to let the press cover the invasion of Grenada. There was total news management and governmental censorship for four days. Only after a free press was finally admitted to Grenada did we learn that many of the statements issued by the White House during those four days were factually incorrect. News favorable to the administration's position was shared; news unfavorable was either not reported or falsely reported. Because of the censorship, there was no way for citizens to engage in an assessment of critique—or support—from an informed standpoint. During those four days we had a preview of 1984 Orwell style, and I am still amazed at the relative lack of public outcry in the face of such manipulation. Furthermore, the tactic portends a scary future: since it "worked" so well this time, the administration may well reason, why not four *weeks* censorship next time if we decide to engage in a "rescue mission" in, say, Nicaragua?

As I was drawing the above parallels together, I stopped at one point to reflect: isn't this all rather paranoid? aren't these parallels overdrawn and even slightly hysterical? And at the moment when I was almost persuaded that some blue-pencilling was in order, another sequence of events took place that persuaded me that the tone, rather than being more muted, should indeed become more bold.

The events began with an address by the President at Georgetown University in which he complained about the way Congress was meddling in his attempts to carry out foreign policy by challenging his decisions publicly and even by withholding funds from activities he thought were essential. While he conceded that there should be debate before decisions were made, he felt everyone should close ranks behind him once the administration embarked on a policy. No more criticism, in other words.

The seriousness of this perspective was emphasized shortly afterwards by proposal of Mr. McFarlane, a high-ranking State Department official, that if members of Congress disagreed with the administration's policy, they could send private letters to the White House or State Department but should not voice the criticism publicly.

It was only shortly after this that it became public knowledge that our government was directly involved in the mining of the harbors of Nicaragua, that the President had personally endorsed the project, and that it had been carried out without proper notification to the congressional committees who are entitled to be informed. All this was known to Mr. Reagan and Mr. McFarlane *at the time they were insisting that there should be no public disagreement* with administration policy. The actions being undertaken were illegal, but no one was to object.

Finally, when the facts were known and Nicaragua quite appropriately filed a brief with the World Court, where there could be a judicial hearing under international auspices, the administration responded by announcing that for a period of two years it would refuse to recognize the jurisdiction of the World Court in any matters pertaining to Central America.

Such a posture, I insist, is the beginning of what can grow, and appears to be growing rapidly into a totalitarian mentality that says, "We are above the law. We are not beholden to accountability by our own government or a world court. We need not tell people what we do, and if people challenge us, even in Congress, we will simply reply that they make us weak and destroy our ability to stand tall. Give us a blank check.''

War is peace. Slavery is freedom, Ignorance is strength.

And so, in the face of all that, we return to Barmen. It is the claim of Barmen that there is only ''one Word of God which we have to hear, and which we have to trust and obey in life and in death.'' For Christians, that one Word of God is Jesus Christ. For Jews it is the God of Sinai, the God of the prophets, the God of the Hebrew Scriptures. Jews and Christians can affirm that they are calling upon the name of the same God. And in the name of that God, we must protest today in the same fashion that Barmen protested yesterday when a government even begins to say, ''Hear, trust and obey *us*. We'll tell you what to think. We'll decide what information you should have. If we withhold information it is for your own good. If our public arguments don't make sense, be assured that there are reasons behind them that we can't really share with you.'' When a government begins to say such things, as ours clearly has, then *that* is the time for challenge, because when a government does that, it is beginning to play God over our lives, and the taste of such identification is a very heady thing. It is becoming identified with what Barmen calls the ''other events and powers, figures and truths'' that are trying to elicit unquestioning and docile loyalty.

As that begins to happen in our time, our response, like the Barmen response, must be ''no,'' because we have already said ''yes'' to the one Word of God whom we have to hear, trust and obey, in life and in death.

CHRISTIAN COMPLICITY AT A CROSSROADS: THE LEGACY OF THE 1934 BARMEN DECLARATION FOR AMERICAN CHRISTIANS

Nancy Lukens

Just over fifty years ago the Protestant Churches in Nazi Germany were confronted with a question many North American Christians are facing today in a new context. The central issue at the Barmen Synod of May 29-31, 1934, out of which grew the oppositional Confessing Church now associated with names like Karl Barth, Dietrich Bonhoeffer and Martin Niemöller, was this: At what point in the public interaction of church and state, of individual Christian citizens and their government, does it become necessary in light of the Christian gospel to enter into resistance to state authority? In short, what happens when national political interests and one's commitment to Biblical faith stand in direct conflict?

In the following pages I shall focus first on the issues at stake in Barmen, 1934. While Barmen is just one example of Christian public opposition to government, it serves well to address what I see as the basic dilemma of faith and national identity in America today, namely that of passive complicity of Christians in the structures and practices that make evil and injustice not only a way of life, but a false religion. The Barmen Declaration, though beset with ambiguities and failures we will examine below, is one example of Christians taking responsibility by their faith to define the limits of state authority under God, and to confront the churches when they allow themselves to become organs of unjust state policy.

Secondly, I will summarize how the issues of Barmen have been interpreted by the official church in West Germany since 1945, and more recently by leaders in the West German peace movement. Recently, in view of the nuclear threat and the arms race the churches in both Germanies began to address the crucial question of their own complicity in the Holocaust of 1933-1945. They ask how such blindness was possible, and warn against similar error in today's even more threatened world. A number of contemporary voices I will cite from the peace movements in both Germanies go farther than the official churches in drawing conclusions from the failure of Christians in the so-called Third Reich to speak out and resist evil. They now proclaim not only the right, but the duty of Christians and justice-minded citizens to enter into civil disobedience in certain contexts.

Finally I shall suggest that despite substantial differences of political and historical situation between Nazi Germany and the America of the 1980's, there are important parallels, and that by implication there are positive models for Christian resistance as a means of calling the state back to its own responsibility for justice and peace. One model with which I will conclude is that of the Sanctuary movement in the U.S. today, its theological and historical roots and its premises, as one area of Christian resistance in which churches are moving beyond the paralysis of passive complicity into a dynamic witness to the peace and justice of the Kingdom of God.

Barmen, 1934

One thing was clear among the delegates at the Synod of Barmen, despite many political and theological differences: Hitler's power was becoming more and more consolidated. The Nazi ideology of supremacy, militant nationalism and racism was laying more and more total claims to the allegiance of every patriotic German. This entire way of life was being superimposed upon both the organizational order and the message of the now Nazi-aligned "German Christian" movement of the Protestant Churches. This is what led to the formation of the Confessing Church, in opposition to this alignment. In fact, the majority of church leaders and laity among the "German Christians" did not perceive the blatant identification of National Socialist values with values of Christian unity, patriotism and renewal to be a problem at all. In face of the general collapse of economic and political stability, the positive impulses of a new youth movement, a new language of unity and strength built on virtues of family and national heritage, and a collective mission to restore morality seemed like the answer to all of Germany's problems. That the churches should be a part of this national renewal was taken for granted. One did not have to be a Nazi to find some of the Nazi accomplishments and values welcome. The middle-class Professional majority among the Protestant Churches in Germany adhered to the "German-National" party values, which Hitler very cleverly channeled into his National Socialist policies.

One of the major forces Hitler knew he could count on among the mainstream of the German population, and churchgoing Christians were no exception, was the fear of Communism. Hence any church policy which served to buoy up the nation's morale for service to God and country against godless Bolshevism was understandably appealing to middle-class Protestants. What came into the bargain, however, was a whole ideology and practice of anti-communism and anti-Semitism nourished by suspicion and hatred of everything non-German. The basis of this ideology and practice was an image of 'The Enemy' which pervaded public life on every level. It began with propaganda against Jews and Communists and Social Democrats, continued with more and more euphemisms for ridding German culture of its "alien elements," and culminated in the so-called "Final Solution." Let it not be forgotten that the churches in Germany bought into this mentality and practice for the duration of Nazi rule, welcoming or at least condoning foreign policy moves that seemed necessary to guarantee security at home.

Two concrete developments were among those leading to the formation of an oppositional or Confessing Church. One was the endorsement and adoption by the Prussian General Synod of the infamous "Aryan Paragraph" in the fall of 1933. This was a provision of Nazi law that excluded Jews and others of non-Aryan origin from public service, from intermarriage with Germans, and eventually from all the benefits of citizenship. The adoption of this provision by the Protestant Church meant the exclusion of non-Aryans from the ministry. This affected hundreds of assimilated Jews who had converted to Christianity and their descendants of non-Jewish blood, not to mention any other minorities. A second development in November, 1933, was a mass rally staged by the "German Christians" in the *Sportpalast* of Berlin. There prominent church leaders proclaimed the gospel of National Socialism, with a trimphant Jesus Christ as its hero, a Bible "purified of its alien elements" (i.e. the Old Testament) as its Scripture, and Adolph Hitler as its Führer.

It was in response to this series of developments that Martin Niemöller and others formed the "Pastors' Emergency League" and scores of Protestant pastors left the "German Christian" movement, protesting publicly from their pulpits on November 19, 1933, the false gospel represented by the Nazi-aligned church policies.

The delegates to the Barmen Synod of May, 1934, based their statement on the Constitution of the Protestant Churches in Germany recognized by the Reich government on July 14, 1933, which states that "the inviolable foundation of the German Protestant Church is the gospel of Jesus Christ as it is attested for us in Holy Scripture."[1]

The delegates to Barmen concluded that they could no longer tolerate the demands of National Socialism for the ultimate trust of Christian citizens in the Führer as source of all good for the German nation and still claim to be the Church. Confessing faith in the God of compassion for the weak and living the gospel of love for one's enemies had to lead eventually to a head-on collision with the presuppositions and requirements of Nazi culture. For in its espousal of the so-called "positive Christianity" proclaimed in the Nazi Party Program, the state was in effect creating a new civil religion of racism, militarism, and nationalism and forcing its practice on the German people, at the high price of eliminating its Jewish citizenry and other minorities.[3] The time had come to refuse to be used in this way in the name of "national security," above all in the name of a racially superior, Nazified Christ.

In its six paragraphs, the Barmen Declaration states essential truths of Scripture which conflict with the teaching and practice of the Nazified "German Christians." Each of the six statements not only contains an affirmation of faith, but concludes with the rejection of specific areas of Nazi policy. In effect, the Declaration paved the way for the formation of a new Confessional Church, in rejection of the idolatry of the German Christians. Such a public stand in opposition to Nazism would have political consequences for those involved, More difficult was the conscious act of declaring other professed Christians to be in defiance of the true Church, thus inevitably causing bitter division. This claim of Barmen struck at the heart of European Protestantism as it then existed in Germany.

The Meaning of Barmen Today

In an April, 1984, address at New York's Union Seminary commemorating the fiftieth anniversary of Barmen, Professor John Godsey of Wesley Theological Seminary spoke to the question of how a Christian could theologically justify participation in active resistance to one's own government. Godsey quoted Dietrich Bonhoeffer's statement that "if a madman is driving down the street hitting people, it is the duty of the Church not just to bind the wounds of those injured, but to fall between the spokes of the wheel to stop him."[4] Professor Eberhard Bethge, close friend and biographer of Bonhoeffer, went further in his reply to a similar question regarding how Bonhoeffer the pacifist could later justify his own involvement in the violent overthrow attempts of 1938-1945. "People who never pass the threshhold [to active resistance]," said Bethge, "ask this question, but the question is macabre and obsolete. The question should actually be worded the other way around: 'How can Christian people as accomplices of crimes theologically justify their non-action?' "[5] Bethge's insight into the problem of passive complicity is the fruit of four decades of critical struggle over the meaning of the experience of the Third Reich and the church's failure to act responsibly in that situation.

In fact, this seems to be the key issue in discussions of recent years regarding what can be learned anew today from the era of the Barmen Declaration. For there must be no illusions: That public statement, and other statements and actions of faith arising out of the Confessing Church, were a far cry from active political resistance in Bonhoeffer's sense of "falling between the spokes of the wheel to stop him." All witnesses to Barmen and scholars of the church struggle agree that there was in fact a concerted effort by the majority at Barmen to avoid any explicit political overtones in the Declaration. What was opposed in 1934 and after by the Confessing Church was not social injustice or preparation for war, but only the intrusion of Nazism into the church, and the idolatry of Nazism's demands on personal faith. If we commemorate the heroism of Barmen, therefore, we must also be honest and sober enough as we consider the implications for America today to acknowledge that most of the same pastors who gathered to utter that word of dissent were more than eager to enlist to fight Hitler's war, and for the most part remained passive complicitors in the elimination of the Jews of Europe.

In the immediate postwar years, in fact, there were public declarations of guilt to this effect coming from the Protestant Churches in Germany (at that time East and West were still one in church organization). The Stuttgart Confession of Guilt (1945) merely stated that the churches had not "prayed enough" for their brothers and sisters in distress. The Darmstadt Declaration of 1947 took the next step, naming the churches' error of complicity with absolute power, as that power was manifested in Nazi Germany's militarized society. Professor Bertold Klappert of the *Kirchliche Hochschule* in Barmen-Wuppertal, in a recent lecture on "Barmen and the Totalitarian State—Justice and Limits of Governmental Power,"[6] referred to this as well as three other failures of the Confessing Church. Besides the "error of complicity with absolute power," Klappert points out, the Darmstadt statement asserts that there is "a lawful power of resistance from below" which the churches failed to acknowledge or draw upon. Thirdly, they had fallen into the simplistic

Nazi "enemy mentality" of anticommunism which attributed all evil to communist subversion. Finally, the churches had failed to act in solidarity with the victims of oppression in those years.

Both of these early postwar statements were soon forgotten, however, in the ensuing Cold War years amidst Adenauer's program of rearmament. As we will see below, few were the voices that kept such warnings in the public ear, and they were quickly denounced as "communist-inspired," or at best "endangering national security." In the past five years, however, there has been much broader-based discussion of peace and security issues among Christians in both German states which has shown just how little the problem of passive complicity of Christians in the war-making society of 1933-45 and beyond has really been acknowledged as a continuing problem. In 1980, after years of study, the Rhineland Synod passed a resolution deploring the failure of Barmen 1934 and of Darmstadt 1947 to recognize the churches' complicity in the destruction of the Jews. Not only had they become co-responsible for the absolute power of evil of the Nazi regime by not resisting it actively, the Rhineland Synod maintained, but their passivity also condoned "the disenfranchisement of the powerless."

But how can such insights into past failures be made fruitful in the present, and appropriately translated into different contexts without oversimplifying history? How should Christians today translate the ethical imperatives implicit in the positive experiences as well as the failures of Barmen into today's context of an ever-increasing spiral of militarism, an escalation of enemy-images both within our respective societies and across superpower frontiers?

One source of convincing conceptual models as well as political practice, which I believe are based on a proper understanding of the passive complicity of the Nazi years and a commitment to overcome the church's failures, is a non-partisan German peace group known as the "Gustav Heinemann Initiative," comprising leading individuals from church, political and social circles. Among the founding members in 1978 were Berlin theologian and former Confessing Church pastor Helmut Gollwitzer and his wife Brigitte Gollwitzer; Tübingen professor Walter Jens, former parliamentarian Erhard Eppler, Bishop Emeritus and Confessing Church pastor Kurt Scharf, Constitutional Court Judge Helmut Simon, and historian Carola Stern. Their mentor, Gustav Heinemann, had been one of the few insistent voices of dissent over the rearmament of Germany and the development of nuclear weaponry as early as 1951-52, and a major spokesman of the "Ban the Bomb" movement of the fifties and sixties. He left his cabinet post under Adenauer out of protest against Adenauer's insistence on re-arming Germany; later, Heinemann became a Social Democratic member of parliament, and in 1970, President of the Federal Republic. His significance for our purpose here lies in the fact that, as Carola Stern points out at the group's 1982 annual conference ("Peace—The Germans' Task"), it was in the Confessing Church that Heinemann "made the long overdue clean break between Church and State."[7] First, he distanced himself from the violence of Hitler's terrorist state. Later, in the fifties, in view of the complicity of Christians in two world wars and in view of new weapons of mass destruction, Heinemann preached and worked politically out of "a peace ethic whose emphasis was no longer a just war doctrine, but concern for a secure peace."[8] Heinemann argues: "To plead that we are 'forced' to match Soviet arms with our own is to use an atheist concept. Only those who deny God's sovereignty in history can talk that way."[9] Carola Stern poses the pressing question for Germans today, which I think obtains for Americans as well: "Who is challenging the Christian Democratic government of West Germany today as Heinemann did, with the question: 'Can Christians justify, i.e. tolerate, the existence and deployment of nuclear weapons of mass destruction, and still claim to be the Church, whose mission is to proclaim and minister to life?' "

One answer to Stern's question comes from the other side of the 'Iron Curtain' and leads us to consider voices of Church leaders from the German Democratic Republic on this issue. Retired Lutheran Bishop Albrecht Schönherr, student of Dietrich Bonhoeffer and Confessing Church pastor, voiced his own and the GDR Federation of Churches' position on nuclear weaponry and the outdated "just war" and "national security" concepts before the same Heinemann Initiative conference in 1982. Schönherr stated that Germans in both East and West, Christians above all, have a special responsibility to prevent any future war from beginning or spreading "from German territory," and that since the advent of nuclear weapons, the concepts of "nation" and "national security" have become highly problematic, since "we all know that no nation would survive a war in Europe today."[10] Schönherr, speaking explicitly out of the experience of the Third Reich, which leaves surviving adults today with a deeply disturbed relationship to the concepts of "nation" and "evil enemy," proclaims with many of his West German colleagues a "theology of the enemy" as the only politically viable stance for Christians and others concerned for peace:

> I am convinced that security today in the nuclear age can be achieved only in the form of *mutual* security of enemy camps. Either we think together, cooperatively, and are equally concerned for the security of the other side, or we will never get around to such thinking because we will die together.[11]

Schönherr sees the German churches' task to be one of calling the state to accountability in view of its failure in the Nazi period to resist and stop the war machine. He can also point with some pride to concerted efforts by the GDR churches to support draft resisters, to confront its state leaders with the necessity to break down rigid "enemy images" and work toward building trust and knowledge of those seen as opponents. He affirms the minority status of the church in the GDR as one which, in contrast to the easy alliance of church and state power in capitalist societies, perhaps offers less temptation to Christians to forget the cost of their vocation.

Dorothee Sölle makes the intricate connectedness of German and American reflections on issues of peace and civil disobedience today become apparent. She reflects on the American tradition of civil disobedience to her German compatriots, and on the experience of the Third Reich and current German fears of U.S. arms escalation to her American friends. In her book, *Beyond Mere Obedience*, Sölle addresses both the perennially German question of blind obedience to state authority, and the universal religious, social and political issue of what obedience means for Christians today in light of the German experience and in light of the the the village of My Lai in the Vietnam war.[12] Her conclusions form a basis, I believe, for an ethic of Christian resistance—defined as imaginative and responsible disobedience to unjust authority out of obedience to God's law of love.[13] Sölle says of the Barmen Declaration that "to celebrate it is to call for active resistance to the idolatries of today," namely the bomb, the myth of national security as the highest value, for which increasing proportions of civilian energies must work, and if necessary, die.[14] In 1980, Sölle points out, 40% of all scientific effort in the U.S. was devoted to developing and producing instruments of mass destruction, whether the participants were aware of the final use of their work or not. Sölle proposes that the Christian response to the "new state religion of nuclearism," in light of Barmen, should be to refuse to condone an allegedly neutral stance by the churches toward practices of our technocratic society (not only of our government) which deny life and deny the sovereignty of a just and life-giving God of all humanity. "The consequence of confession," Sölle concludes, "is resistance."

Toward a Theology and Praxis of Christian Resistance

I believe that as Americans, we have a special responsibility to learn appropriate lessons from Barmen, not merely to emulate or heroize that moment. What does it mean to American Christians today who are witnessing mass murder with U.S. military assistance in Central America, to be reminded that at the Nazi War Criminal trials at Nuremberg barely forty years ago, ordinary German bureaucrats were prosecuted by American justice officials for failing to resist the power of the state they had been under oath to obey?

The temptation for American Christians today, as William Stringfellow pointed out ten years ago in an article on the question, "Does America Need a Barmen Declaration?,"[15] is to make facile comparisons of Nixon (or Reagan) with Hitler, of Watergate (or Grenada) with the Reichstag fire which Hitler used as an excuse to assume total power in the name of national security. Instead, Stringfellow convincingly argues, we have the responsibility to understand that history is not static and recurring, but dynamic and full of paradox and ambiguity. Rather than reducing the historical events surrounding Barmen to parallel figures today, we must see through these to the "perennial issues embodied in changing circumstances" of the present. By merely commemorating Barmen as Christian heroism without struggling through its ambiguities and failures, we contribute to our own blind complicity in U.S. crimes today. To be sure, these take place not in the blatantly totalitarian setting of Nazi Germany, but in a technologically refined system which, Stringfellow asserts, requires much less manipulation by propaganda and information control than was necessary in the Third Reich. What suppresses initiative and dissent in this country, besides state secrecy and intimidation common to Nazi Germany, is the sheer volume of partial information which often leads more to confusion than to critical response; secondly, our reverence for property has legitimized state secrecy regarding the nuclear arms industry. When the "Ploughshares Eight" attempted to demonstrate by civil disobedience in 1980 at the King of Prussia, Pa., General Electric plant that it is not proper for nuclear warheads to be deemed the property of the U.S. Government, the idolatrous notion of security through protection by weaponry was exposed.

What we need to learn is the task of the churches to mark the limits of proper state authority by asserting God's sovereignty and justice in face of the state's "assault on sanity and conscience," as Stringfellow put it in 1973. What the churches hold in common, it would appear to me, is no less "grievously imperiled" by the burgeoning electronic and civil religion of facile patriotism and anti-communism than it was at the May, 1934 juncture when a new confession was called for at Barmen.

For "what the churches hold in common" is trust in the God of truth, justice, compassion and peace as our source of security, even of national security. As it was in the German context, that is indeed threatened today when churches and Christian citizens condone God's being taken hostage to prop up a myth of national virtue, strength and right against an "evil empire." If the churches proclaim the God of personal salvation for all, but then do nothing to stop the idolatry of war-making in God's name, they are complicitors in that war-making, and the triumphalism of personal religion becomes an insult, if not a death blow, to those we help oppress by our passivity. In the age when militarism rules the world and a conflict in the Third World could touch off nuclear war, those we oppress by ignoring our complicity in their destruction are the majority now living on earth. This, I believe, is the crucial lesson of Barmen today.

U.S. war-making in Central America and the U.S. treatment of refugees from those wars who seek safe haven within our borders pose issues which Barmen illuminates. The issue of the estimated 700,000 refugees from El Salvador and Guatemala has presented itself directly to our churches.

This is a situation in which many Americans see national political interests and Christian responsibility to be in direct conflict. What, then, should our response be, if not the neutralism Sölle rejects, the cynicism that denies God's redeeming power, or the paralysis of passive complicity? I believe there are diverse examples of Christian resistance being lived out by Americans today, where resistance is understood not as escape or defiance, but as an affirmation of faith and of Christian responsibility to break the chain of injustice perpetrated by one's own governing authorities. With specific regard to Central American involvement, many are refusing to pay that portion of taxes that fuels that war. Other studies in this series have dealt with this form of resistance. The Witness for Peace in Nicaragua is another expression of refusal, coming ultimately out of the affirmation that we are called to defend life, and that we will do all within our power, by non-violent physical presence, to prevent an immoral and illegal incursion in our name. The third response, and the one on which I will focus here, is to provide public sanctuary for refugees of the wars in El Salvador and Guatemala, whom our government regards as "illegal aliens" coming primarily for economic reasons and therefore representing a threat to Americans' jobs and other resources.

There are several aspects to the conflict between the task of the churches and governmental interests in the Central American refugee issue. First, there is the conflict over the definition of a 'refugee.' The United Nations Refugee Act of 1980, which was taken into U.S. law as the U.S. Refugee Act of 1980, states that a refugee is "a person outside his/her country of nationality . . . who is persecuted or has a well-founded fear of persecution on the grounds of race, religion, nationality, membership in a particular social group or political opinion. . ."[16] It also specifies that "the Attorney General cannot deport any alien to a country in which the alien's life or feedom would be threatened on account of race, religion, nationality, membership in a particular social group or political opinion," with the exception of Nazi war criminals and those who have committed crimes constituting a danger to U.S. security.[17] The first conflict, therefore, consists in the presence of over half a million refugees from a terribly brutal war, who bring more than convincing evidence that they have reason to fear persecution or death. Having turned back countless Jews who had risked their lives to escape Nazi Germany to our shores, and having prosecuted Germans for not resisting the regime that made their escape necessary, it would seem not only a matter for Christian concern and action, but a matter of simple accountability to International Law to recognize these refugees. However, over the past five years we have deported from 500 to 1000 Salvadorans and Guatemalans per month to almost certain torture or death when they are received at home as "subversives."[18]

The second direct conflict is between the letter of Immigration Law and the accompanying attitudes of civil authorities toward the refugees on the one hand, and God's law of hospitality and compassion on the other. The Immigration and Nationality Act, Section 274A, makes it a federal felony to harbor, transport, or in any other way assist an "illegal alien," i.e. a person who has no legal papers qualifying him or her as a citizen or a refugee. Concretely, then, although this is not and should not be the central issue for churches considering offering sanctuary, it has become a crime to take in a Central American refugee escaping terror. Again, it would seem not only a Christian responsibility, but the only human thing to do, to disobey this law, while at the same time doing everything within our power to change it. This is what the Sanctuary movement is attempting to do.

The tradition of Sanctuary goes back to the Old Testament cities of refuge, which were given the special task of offering asylum to fugitives otherwise subject to vengeful acts of violence due to blood guilt. The church altar had the function of "marking a limit to violence," as Bill Kellerman notes in an article on "The Hospitality of God."[19] Kellerman also points to eleventh century France, where the church took in people victimized by violent squabbles over turf and debts, as a form of active resistance to buy time for negotiated settlements. In medieval England, fugitives were depicted as sitting on a *frith stool* (peace stool), protected by the clergy from armed invaders. In all these instances there was in fact no distinction made between legally innocent and guilty fugitives, significantly. It is the church's job not to play God, but to do God's work of protecting life against forces of death. Kellerman appropriately calls sanctuary a "circle of refusal and rebuke" which marks the limits of civil authority and celebrates the sovereignty of God. He compares the creation of sanctuaries for Central American refugees with the creation of Nuclear Free Zones, which proclaim: The Killing Stops Here.

The first sanctuary as such in the U.S. took shape in April of 1982 when the Southside Presbyterian Church in Tucson, Arizona, opened its doors to the first of some 3,000 refugees it has now assisted to safe havens across the country. By now there are over 120 sanctuary sites in churches and improvised spaces in all areas of the U.S., connected by an "underground railroad" of individuals and groups who offer transportation and overnight shelter along the way to one of the sponsoring groups. The rediscovery of the "underground railroad" tradition from the American Civil War is surely not insignificant, as it serves to remind us that history is indeed dynamic. If the churches then had not taken heart to break an unjust law and harbor fugitive slaves, slavery might have remained legal much longer and much more violence been done in the name of freedom for the few. Just as the first underground railroad was the conscience of people seeking an end to injustice under the law, the sanctuary movement seeks an end to illegal as well as legal, but inhumane, actions by our government. Some 36,000 Salvadorans were murdered by the government forces we support between 1981 and November of 1983 alone.[20]

Lest there be a new false heroism or romanticism of resistance, let it be emphasized that the number of refugees actually assisted by Sanctuary is minute in comparison with the need. The great majority are truly underground, subject to detention, interrogation and deportation. Hence the other emphasis of the Sanctuary movement is that of calling the government to account: to stop the deportations and above all to stop fueling these civil wars in the name of national security and in our names.

Dietrich Bonhoeffer wrote a short reflection on civil courage shortly before he was taken to Tegel Prison in 1943, ten years after Hitler assumed power. In it, he defines civil courage not only for Christians in America today, but for humans in any place where faith and conscience conflict with the interests and practice of state:

> Through our long history, we Germans have had to learn the necessity and the power of obedience. . . [We] did not realize that submissiveness and the willingness to sacrifice oneself in the name of duty could be exploited for evil ends. . . It turned out that the Germans had failed to learn one crucial lesson: the necessity of free, responsible action, even when it is contrary to one's work and one's duty. Instead we had irresponsible unscrupulousness on the one hand, and on the other hand agonizing scrupulousness that never led to action.
>
> But civil courage can only grow out of free human beings freely assuming responsibility for their actions. Only now are the Germans beginning to discover what this free responsibility means. It rests in a God who demands the leap of faith that leads to responsible action, and who promises forgiveness and comfort to those who become sinners in the process.[21]

The risk of such free, responsible action by Christians today in offering sanctuary is truly minimal compared to the risks taken by those struggling for justice in Central America itself or fleeing for their lives. Much larger than the risk of a $2,000 fine or up to five years in prison, it seems to me, is the risk of "agonizing scrupulousness that never leads to action."

ENDNOTES

1. The text of the *Theological Declaration of Barmen* as cited throughout Part I on this paper can be found in the Presbyterian *Book of Confessions,* available from the Materials Distribution Service, 341 Ponce de Leon Ave. NE, Atlanta, GA 30308.
2. Nazi Party Program, Article 24, as quoted by Arthur Cochrane in "Barmen Revisited," *Christianity and Crisis* XXXIII, 22 (December 24, 1973), 268.
3. Recent scholarship and discussion has shown that the Barmen Declaration failed to make public outcry about this "high price" by never explicitly mentioning the evil of the anti-Jewish laws. See p. 9f below.
4. An account of the papers and discussion held at Union can be found in the *New York Times* of Sunday, April 15, 1984, in an article by Kenneth Briggs.
5. Eberhard Bethge made this statement as part of a paper given in slightly varied forms at the Union Seminary event reported in the *New York Times* of April 15, and again at an International Symposium of Scholars and Church Leaders in Seattle, April 25-28, 1984, "A Half-Century After Barmen: Religion, Totalitariansim and Human Freedom in the Modern World."
6. The following summary of Klappert's comments is based on notes taken at the lecture given at the Seattle Symposium mentioned in Note 5.
7. Carola Stern, "Gustav Heinemann und die Friedensbewegung heute," in *Frieden— Aufgabe der Deutschen,* published by the Gustav Heinemann Initiative (Stuttgart: Radius, 1982), p. 23.
8. Stern, p. 23.
9. Stern, p. 25.
10. Albrecht Schönherr, "Kein Krieg mehr von deutschem Boden," in *Friden—Aufgabe der Deutschen,* p. 29.
11. Schönherr, p. 35.
12. Dorothee Sölle, *Beyond Mere Obedience,* translated from the original German *Phantasie und Gehorsam: Überlegungen einer künftigen christlichen Ethik,* 1968). The American version appeared in 1982 with a new Introduction by Sölle (Pilgrim Press).
13. I am not quoting Sölle, but summarizing and interpolating from both *Beyond Mere Obedience* and more recent public statements.
14. This and the following arguments were made by Sölle in her address to the above-mentioned Seattle symposium of April 24-29, 1984, entitled "Justice is the True Name of Peace."
15. The entire issue of *Christianity and Crisis* in which Stringfellow's article appeared is a very useful resource on this topic. It is Vol. 33, No. 22 of December 24, 1973, and also includes articles by Roger Shinn ("Barmen and Ourselves") and Arthur Cochrane, author of *The Church's Confession under Hitler* ("Barmen Revisited").
16. Section 201 of the Refugee Act of 1980, Part (a), Paragraph 42.
17. Section 203, part (e) of the Refugee Act of 1980.
18. INS Statistic reported by Renny Golden in "Sanctuary—Churches Take Part in a New Underground Railroad," *Sojourners* Magazine, December, 1982.
19. Bill Kellerman, "The Hospitality of God—The Theological and Historical Meaning of Christian Sanctuary," *Sojourners,* April, 1983.
20. Chicago Religious Task Force on Central American Refugees, "Sanctuary: A Justice Ministry." This booklet plus several others are most helpful resources for groups considering offering sanctuary. They are available at the Task Force office, 407 So. Dearborn Ave., Suite 370, Chicago, IL 60603.
21. Dietrich Bonhoeffer, "Civil Courage?" in After Ten Years," *Letters and Papers from Prison* (New York: Macmillan), 1972, p. 5-6. I am quoting not this published version, but my own translation from Bonhoeffer's German.

JESUS CHRIST THE LIFE
OF THE WORLD

Allan A. Boesak

Jesus Christ the life of the world! These are words that speak of joy, of meaning, of hope. For some, they may even speak of triumph and victory. These are words that have a ring of certainty in them. Yet, in the uncertain world of suffering, oppression and death, what do they mean? The realities of the world in which we live suggest the cold grip of death rather than the freedom of life.

Violence, greed and the demonic distortion of human values continue to destory God's world and God's people. Economic exploitation is escalating rather than abating and economic injustice is still the dominant reality in the relationships between rich and poor countries. Racism is as rampant as ever, not only in South Africa, but also in other parts of the world. In its alliances with national security ideologies it has required a new cloak of respectability and has become even more pervasive. In South Africa apartheid and injustice still reign supreme. Inequality is still sanctified by law and racial superiority is still justified by theology. Today, with the blatant support of so many Western governments, apartheid seems stronger than ever and the dream of justice and human dignity for South Africa's black people more remote than ever.

In our world, it is not the joyful, hopeful sound of the Word of life that is being heard. No, that Word is drowned by the ugly sound of gunfire, by the screams of our children and the endless cry of the powerless: "How long, Lord?"

In too many places too many children die of hunger and too many people just disappear because they dare to stand up for justice and human rights. Too many are swept away by the tides of war and too many are tortured in dungeons of death. In too many eyes the years of endless struggle have extinguished the fires of hope and joy and too many bodies are bowed down by the weight of that peculiarly repugnant death called despair. Too many young people believe that their youth and their future are already powdered to dust by the threat of nuclear destruction. And even in the face of all of this, too many in the Christian church remain silent. We have not yet understood that every act of inhumanity, every unjust law, every untimely death, every utterance of faith in weapons of mass destruction, every justification of violence and oppression is a sacrifice on the alter of the false gods of death; it is a denial of the Lord of life.

No, for millions of people it is true: we are not uplifted by the Word of life, we are crushed by the litany of death.

Yet the gospel affirms: Jesus Christ is the life of the world. (John 6:35, 48; 10:10; 11:25; 14:6; Rev. 1:17, 18; etc.). That means He is the source of life, He is the giver of the sacred gift of life. That He intends for us a life filled with abundance, joy and meaning. He is the Messiah in whose eyes our lives are precious.

But this is precisely the problem. Dare we believe this? Can we believe this without making of our faith a narrow, spiritual escapism? Can we avoid the cynicism of "reality"? Can we find a way to live with that painful dilemma: "Lord, I believe, please help my unbelief!" And even more painful: can we accept the reality of hope and the call to battle that lie in this affirmation? In other words, is the joyous affirmation, this confession that Jesus Christ is the life of the world, really meant for the millions who suffer and die, who are oppressed and who live without hope in the world today? While discussing this theme with a group in my congregation, a woman said quietly, almost despairingly: "It seems you have to be white and rich to believe this."

But there are two things we must remember when talking about this. First, in the gospel this affirmation is never a triumphalistic war cry. It is never a slogan built on might and power. It is a confession in the midst of weakness, suffering and death. It is the quiet, subversive piety which the Christian church cannot do without. Second, we must be reminded that in the Bible this affirmation is given to people who in their situation *were* the poor, oppressed and the weak. They were the people who lived on the underside of history. And it is they who are called upon to confirm this truth: Jesus Christ is the life of the world.

In the gospel of John, chapter 4, the story of Jesus and the Samaritan woman is a good illustration of this truth. She is the paradigm *par excellence* of the despised, the weak and the oppressed, just like the children are that elsewhere in the gospel. She becomes the very example of the dejected people of this world. First of all, she is a woman, with all that that means in the society of her day. Notice how John makes a point of stating the disciples' astonishment that Jesus was in discussion with a woman. She is also a Samaritan, and therefore despised and rejected by the Jews. Her religion is considered inferior and in her own community she is an outcast because of her way of life. (This is probably the reason why she goes to that well alone, at a most unusual hour of the day.) But it is precisely to her that Jesus speaks of these unfathomable things: the life-giving waters, and the waters of life.

Likewise, the Apocalypse of John is written to a weak, scattered underground church, suffering severely under the persecution of a ruthless tyrant. They were people who had no recourse, no protection under the law, no "connections" in high and powerful places, no political or economic power. Their lives were cheap. They were completely and utterly surrendered to the mercy of a man who did not know the meaning of the word, whom John could only describe with the telling title: "beast". From a purely human point of view, they had not a chance in the world, there was preciously little upon which they could build their hopes for the future. But like the Samaritan woman, *they* are the ones who hear the message and to whom this is proclaimed: "I am the first and the last and the living One. . ." They knew with a certainty not born of earthly power: Jesus Christ, not the Caesar, (in spite of all *his* power!) is the life of the world. The claims of divinity, of immortality, of omniscience and power are the lies, the half-truths, the propaganda without which no tyrant can survive. But the truth stands: Jesus Christ is the life of the world, and He is indeed Lord of life.

The church understood this confession not only as comfort in times of trial and darkness, but as an essential part of that basic, subversive confession: Jesus Christ is Lord. In this way it became not only comfort to the persecuted, oppressed Church, but also a ringing protest against the arrogance of earthly potentates who wanted so desperately to create the impression that *they* decided over the life and death of the people of God. And the church knew this to be the truth, not only for the life hereafter, but the truth for the very life and the very world in which they struggled to believe, to be faithful, to be obedient. To understand that is to understand the power, nay more, to experience the power of the life-giving Word. It is to drink of the life-giving and living waters even while facing suffering, destruction and death. It is to understand and experience what it means to worship that is not confined to certain moments only. This is a worship which encompasses all of our life, so that every prayer for liberation, every act for the sake of human dignity, every commitment in the struggle for true human freedom, every protest against the sinful realities of this world, becomes an offering to the living One for the sake of his Kingdom.

Jesus says: "The hour comes, and it is now. . ." Here the present and the future coincide. The moment of the hesitant, yet faithful human response and the moment of the favor of the Lord come together.

This is the source of the acts of sublime courage sometimes displayed in the witness and the life of the Christian church. This is what led to the witness of the Christian church at the martyrdom of St Polycarp:

"The blessed Polycarp died a martyr's death on the 23rd of February, on the Great Sabbath, the eighth hour. Herod imprisoned him when Phillip of Tralles was the High Priest, and Statius Quartus was the Proconsul, whilst for ever is King our Lord Jesus Christ. His be the glory, honor, majesty and an everlasting throne from generation to generation. Amen."

And indeed, it may seem as if for the moment the dictators of this world, the powerful and the mighty have full control over this world. Their arrogance seems to have no bounds. Their power seems unchecked. But the church knows: Jesus Christ is Lord of history, He is Lord of life, and his truth shall have the final word.

In the same way Christians in South Africa begin to understand that for us God's moment is brought together with our present reality.

In discerning that, the church is called to an extraordinary, courageous witness for the sake of the gospel. So we hear Bishop Desmond Tutu, the General Secretary of the South African Council of Churches saying to the Minister of Law and Order: "Mr. Minister, we must remind you that you are not God. You are just a man. And one day your name shall merely be a faint scribble on the pages of history, while

[161]

the name of Jesus Christ, the Lord of the Church, shall live forever. . ."

The Christian church can take this stand, not because it possesses earthly power, nor because it has "control" over the situation. Over against the structures of political, economic and military power who seek to rule this world the church remains weak and in a sense defenseless. But it takes this stand because it refuses to believe that the powers of oppression, death and destruction have the last word. Even while facing these powers the church continues to believe that Jesus Christ is Lord and therefore the life of the world. And it is this faith in the living One, this refusal to bow down to the false gods of death, that is the strength of the church.

But this affirmation has another ramification. Jesus Christ is the life of the *world*. His concern is not only for the church but for the world. In his life, death and resurrection lies not only the future of the church, but the future of the world. In the letter to the Ephesians, Paul is persistent in proclaiming Jesus Christ as Lord of the church and of the cosmos. Therefore, his being our peace, has consequences not only for the church, but also for the world. Therefore the church must proclaim, clearly and unequivocally, that Jesus Christ came to give meaningful life to the world, so that all of human history, all human activity can be renewed and liberated from death and destruction.

The life of the world, the destruction of this world, the future of this world, is therefore the concern of the church. We have a responsibility for this world, for it is God's world. And if this world is threatened by the evils of militarism, materialism, greed, racism, it is very much the concern of the church. It is the church who has heard the words: "Today I am giving you a choice between good and evil, between life and death . . . choose life!" It is the church who has heard the words: "I have come so that they may have life, and that abundantly . . ." And because we have heard this, and because we confess Jesus Christ as the life of the world, we dare not be silent.

This Assembly must speak out. We must confess, humbly but without any hesitation, our faith in Jesus Christ, the life of the world. We must, humbly but without any hesitation, renew our commitment to Jesus Christ, the life of the world. And this faith, this commitment, must be the basis of our action on the issues of peace, justice and human liberation. We must not hesitate to address ourselves to the question of peace and to the possibility of total nuclear destruction. We must be clear: the nuclear arms race, the employment of God-given human talents and possibilities for the creation of ever more refined weapons of mass destruction, and the call to put our faith in these weapons so as to secure our peace, is not simply a temporary madness, it is essentially sinful and contrary to the purposes of God for this world and for the people of God's heart.

I am not persuaded that the issue of peace is simply one of fashion, a fad that will go away tomorrow. I do not agree with those who believe that this issue is simply one of political and military calculations, so that the church should withdraw from the debate and let the problems be solved by the politicians and the military strategists. I remain convinced that the issue of peace as it faces us today, lies at the very heart of the gospel.

But there is something else I must say about this. When the World Alliance of

Reformed Churches met in Ottawa last August, we spent considerable time discussing a statement on peace. During the debate, a delegate from Africa made a remark that very poignantly raised some of the tensions surrounding this issue in the ecumenical movement today. He said: "In this document, the world 'nuclear' is used a number of times, but I don't even see the word 'hunger.' In my village, the people will not understand the word 'nuclear,' but they know everything about hunger and poverty."

What he was really talking about was the concern of many Christians in the Third World that the issue of peace will be separated from the issue of justice, making of "peace" primarily a North Atlantic concern. This should not happen. First of all because ideologies of militarism and national security are international in character and cause deprivation and the continiation of injustice everywhere, but especially in the so-called Third World countries. But secondly, and more importantly, in the Bible peace and justice are never separated. Peace is never simply the absence of war, it is the active presence of justice. It has to do with human fulfillment, with liberation, with wholeness, with a meaningful life and well-being, not only for the individual, but for the community as a whole. And the prophet Isaiah speaks of peace as the offspring of justice.

So it may be true that the issues of justice, racism, hunger and poverty are largely unresolved issues for the ecumenical movement. It may be true that these issues presented the churches with painful dilemmas, but it cannot be true that we will be willing to use the issue of peace to avoid those dilemmas. One cannot use the gospel to escape from the demands of the gospel. And one cannot use the issue of peace to escape from the unresolved issues of injustice, poverty, hunger and racism. If we do this we will make of our concern for peace an ideology of oppression which in the end will be used to justify injustice.

But there is one last point we have to make. Jesus Christ is the life of the world because He reveals the truth about Himself, the Church, humankind and the world. He is the Messiah, the chosen One of God who proclaims the acceptable year of the Lord. In Him is the fulfillment of the promises of Yahweh. He is the Servant of the Lord who shall not cease his struggle until justice shall triumph on the earth. (Is. 42:1-3; Mt. 12:17-21). In Him shall the nations place their hope.

Jesus, in his life, death and resurrection, is Himself the guarantee of life, peace and human dignity. He is the Messiah who struggles and suffers with his people. And yet, He is the Victor. He is King in his suffering, not in spite of it. There is therefore an inseparable link between Pontius Pilate's "Ecce homo!" and his "There is your King!" (John 19:4, 19). So it is that the Apocalypse speaks of Jesus both as the Lamb that was slaughtered and as the Rider on the white horse. The One who died is the One who lives forever. The suffering Servant of the Word is the Ruler of the kings of the earth. The One who was willing to give up his life is Jesus the Messiah, the life of the world.

This is the truth that is revealed to the church even as we speak the words: Jesus Christ is the life of the world. The Revelation of John reminds us of the victory of the saints. But again, it is not a victory brought about by earthly powers. "They won the victory over (Satan) by the blood of the Lamb, and by the truth they proclaimed, and because they did not love their life unto death" (Rev. 12:11). This truth is the basis upon which the church stands. It is the essence of the witness of the church in the world. It is the essence of the confession: Jesus Christ is the life of the world. The church can only say this, if we are willing to give our life for the sake of the world. We can only say this if we truly believe that there are some things so dear, some things so precious, some things so eternally true that they are worth dying for. And the truth that Jesus Christ is the life of the world, is worth giving our life for.

The truth that the Messiah reveals is contrary to the lies, the propaganda, the idolatrous, the untrustworthy in the world. His truth is the truth that holds the freedom and the life of the world. And this we are called to proclaim. And so as we begin these two weeks together as the assembled churches of the world, let us affirm this truth, and let us believe:

It is not true that this world and its people are doomed to die and be lost—
This is true: For God so loved the world that He gave his only begotten Son, that whosoever believes in Him, shall not perish, but have everlasting life;
It is not true that we must accept inhumanity and discimination, hunger and poverty, death and destruction—
This is true: I have come that they may have life, and that abundantly;
It is not true that violence and hatred should have the last word, and that war and destruction have come to stay forever—
This is true: For unto us a child is born, and unto us a Son is given, and the government shall be upon his shoulder, and his name shall be called wonderful councilor, mighty God, the Everlasting Father, the Prince of peace.
It is not true that we are simply victims of the powers of evil who seek to rule the world—
This is true: To me is given all authority in heaven and on earth, and lo I am with you, even unto the end of the world.
It is not true that we have to wait for those who are specially gifted, who are the prophets of the church, before we can do anything:
This is true: I will pour out my Spirit on all flesh, and your sons and your daughters shall prophesy, your young men shall see visions, and your old men shall have dreams. . .
It is not true that our dreams for liberation of humankind, of justice, of human dignity, of peace are not meant for this earth and for this history—
This is true: The hour comes, and it is now, that the true worshippers shall worship the Father in spirit and in truth . . .

So let us use these two weeks to dream, let us use these two weeks to prophesy; let us use these two weeks to see visions of love, and peace and justice. Let us use these two weeks to affirm with humility, with joy, with faith, with courage:
Jesus Christ—the life of the world.

Divine Obedience

The Honourable A. Schlebusch
Minister of Justice
Union Buildings
Pretoria

Dear Sir,

A short while ago you thought it your duty to address the South African Council of Churches, as well as church leaders, very sharply and seriously over radio and television and in the press in connection with the SACC resolution on civil disobedience. Although the resolution was not taken as a direct result of my address, I did express my point of view openly on that occasion, and I am one of those who support the SACC in this respect.

You are the minister of justice, and it is in this capacity that you have issued your serious warning. I take your words seriously. Hence my reaction, which I express to you respectfully and which I ask you to read as a personal declaration of faith.

Your warning has become almost routine in South Africa: the government continually says to pastors and churches that they must keep themselves "out of politics" and confine themselves to their "proper task": the preaching of the gospel.

However, on this very point an extremely important question emerges: What is the gospel of Jesus Christ that the churches have been called to preach? Surely it is the message of the salvation of God that has come to all peoples in Jesus Christ. It is the proclamation of the kingdom of God and of the lordship of Jesus Christ. But this salvation is the liberation, the making whole, of the *whole person*. It is not something meant for the "inner life," the soul, only. It is meant for the whole of human existence. This Jesus who is proclaimed by the church was certainly not a spiritual being with spiritual qualities estranged from the realities of our human existence. No, he was the Word become flesh, who took on complete human form, and his message of liberation is meant for persons in their *full humanity.*

Besides, the fact that the term "kingdom" is such a political term must already say a great deal to us. For example, this fact brought Reformed Christians to believe (and rightly so) and profess with conviction throughout the centuries that this lordship of Jesus Christ applies to all spheres of life. There is not one inch of life that is not claimed by the lordship of Jesus Christ. This includes the political, social, and economic spheres. The Lord rules over all these spheres, and the church and the Christian proclaim his sovereignty in all these spheres. Surely it is the holy duty and the calling of every Christian to participate in politics so that there also God's law and justice may prevail, and there also obedience to God and God's word can be shown.

The Dutch Reformed Church professes this in its report "Race Relations in the South African Situation in the Light of Scripture." The report states plainly that in its proclamation the church must appeal to its members to apply the principles of the kingdom of God in the social and political sphere. When the word of God

[165]

demands it, the church is compelled to fulfill its prophetic function vis-à-vis the state *even in spite of popular opinion.* The witness of the church with regard to the government is a part of its essential being in the world, says the report. This is sound Reformed thinking, and the Dutch Reformed Church accepts this because it wants to be Reformed. Why, then, are you refusing to grant other churches and Christians (also other Reformed Christians!) this witness and participation?

But there is still another problem. Through its spokesmen your government has often warned that those of us who serve in the church must "keep out of politics." Yet at the same time it is your own colleagues in the cabinet who want to involve the clergy in political dialogue!

The only conclusion that I can come to is that you do not really object in principle to the participation of the clergy in politics—as long as it happens on *your* terms and within the framework of *your* policy. This seems to me to be neither tenable nor honest. In addition, are you not denying your own history by holding to this viewpoint? Did not the Afrikaner clergy speak as leaders of their people, and did they not inspire their people in what you saw as a just struggle? Did not the churches of the Afrikaner, even in the Anglo-Boer War, stand right in the midst of the struggle? Why, then, do you reject today with a sort of political pietism that which yesterday and the day before you accepted and embraced with thankfulness to God?

But, Mr. Minister, there is even more in your warning which I cannot ignore. It has to do with the exceptionally difficult and sensitive issue of the Christian's obedience to the government.

It is important that you understand clearly that I have made my call for civil disobedience as a Christian, and that I was addressing the church. The context and basis of my call may thus not be alienated from my convictions as a Christian addressing other Christians upon that same basis.

It surprises me that some have tried to interpret this as a call for wanton violence. It is precisely an *alternative* to violence! And I turn to this alternative because I still find it difficult to accept violence as an unobjectionable solution. Or perhaps there are some who fear that should Christians in South Africa perform their duty in being more obedient to God than to humans, the idolized nature of this state will be exposed. Surely a state that accepts the supreme rule of Christ should not have to be afraid of this?

I believe I have done nothing more than to place myself squarely within the Reformed tradition as that tradition has always understood sacred Scripture on these matters.

Essential to this is the following: It is my conviction that, for a Christian, obedience to the state or any earthly authority is always linked to our obedience to God. That is to say, obedience to human institutions (and to human beings) is always relative. The human institution can never have the same authority as God, and human laws must always be subordinate to the word of God. This is how the Christian understands it. Even God does not expect blind servility; Christians cannot even think of giving unconditional obedience to a government.

Our past experience has taught us that this is exactly the kind of obedience, blind and unquestioning, that your government expects. I want, however, to be honest with you: this I cannot give you. The believer in Christ not only has the right, but also the responsibility, should a government deviate from God's law, to be more obedient to God than to the government. The question is not really whether Christians have the courage to disobey the government, but whether we have the courage to set aside God's word and not obey *God*.

Over the years, nearly all the Christian churches in this country have condemned the policies of your government as wrong and sinful. My own church, the Dutch Reformed Mission Church, last year at its synod condemned apartheid as being "in conflict with the gospel of Jesus Christ," a policy that cannot stand up to the demands of the gospel. I heartily endorse this stand my church has taken. Your policy is unjust; it denies persons their basic human rights, and it undermines their God-given human dignity. Too many of the laws you make are blatantly in conflict with the word of God.

I have no doubt that your policies, and their execution, are a tremendous obstacle to reconciliation between the peoples of South Africa. There are laws that are most hurtful, or more draconian than others, and these especially have been condemned by the churches. Now the churches have reached a point where we have to say: If we condemn laws on the grounds of the word of God, how can we obey those laws?

In my view, Christians in South Africa today do not stand alone in this decision. Scripture knows of disobedience to earthly powers when these powers disregard the Word of the living God. Daniel disobeyed the king's law when he refused to bow down before the graven image of Nebuchadnezzar (Daniel 3:17-18), because he regarded the king's law as being in conflict with the demands of his God. Peter's refusal to obey the commands of the Sanhedrin not to give witness to Jesus has always been the classic example of disobedience to a worldly authority. To this day his answer still resounds like a bell in the church of Christ: "We must obey God rather than men" (Acts 5:29). There are other examples. Paul displayed nothing of a servile obedience when the magistrates of Philippi wanted to release him from prison after having confined him unlawfully (without a trial!): "They gave us a public flogging, though we are Roman citizens and have not been found guilty; they threw us into prison, and are they now to smuggle us out privately? No, indeed!" (Acts 16:37).

In the case of Peter and John, the Sanhedrin was the highest authority, not only in religious matters, but in everything that did not lie directly in the sphere of the Roman procurator. In the case of Paul, the magistrates were the highest officials in the Roman colony of Philippi. For both Peter and Paul it was clear that occasions could arise where disobedience to unjust authority was the only honorable way for the Christian.

Furthermore, Luke 23:6-12, Mark 15:1-5, and John 18:8-11 teach us that Jesus himself did not always demonstrate obedience to state authority. Before Herod, on one occasion, "he answered him not a word." Also before Pilate there were those moments when he chose to give reply neither to the questions of Pilate, nor to the charges of the high priests and scribes. John tells us something else of great significance. He tells us that Jesus reminded Pilate of something that every bearer of authority must remember or be reminded of: " 'You would have no authority over me at all,' Jesus replied, 'if it had not been granted you from above' " (John 29:11).

I am not arguing that there is "proof" from these actions of Jesus, Peter, and Paul that violent, revolutionary overthrow of a government is justifiable. That is a completely different issue. I am saying, rather, that blind obedience to civil authorities is alien to the Bible; and that, for the Christian, loyalty and obedience to God are first and foremost. May I also point out, parenthetically, that the issue on which everything hinges, and the lesson that South Africa has to learn, is that what is needed is *not* servile submissiveness of citizens to the state, but *rightful co-responsibility* for the affairs of the state? And this is precisely what your policy denies millions of South Africans.

This is not the place to present a full treatment of Romans 13. However, I would simply point out that the first verse of Romans 13, which is often taken as unconditional legitimization of a government's contention that its authority can never be challenged by Christians, is in fact a very serious criticism of that very authority. A government wields authority because, and as long as, it reflects the authority of God. And the power of God is a liberating, creative, serving power. Thus Paul can refer to civil authority as "a servant of God *[diakonos!]* for your good." Thus, throughout the years, it has been taken for granted in Reformed thinking that a government has authority as long as there is evidence that it accepts responsibility for justice, for what is right.

Put another way, the definition of government in Romans 13 does not simply point out that civil authority exists. It also suggests that there is proper authority only where there is a clear distinction between good and evil, so that it is not only important whether a government is "Christian" or not, but really whether it is still truly *government*—that is, understands the difference between good and evil. Where there is no justice and no understanding, the authority of the government is no longer derived from God, but is in conflict with God. Resistance to such a government is both demanded and justified.

Even Augustine, one of the respected fathers of the church, who was concerned particularly with protecting the state and who defended political authority with extraordinary energy, had this to say: "Justice is the only thing that can give worth to a worldly power. What is wordly government if justice is lacking? It is nothing other than a bunch of plunderers."

Calvin echoed this sentiment when he wrote to King Francis in the letter published as the prologue to his *Institutes:* "For where the glory of God is not made the end of the government, it is not a legitimate sovereignty, but a usurpation." And Calvin added, "Where there is no vision, the people perish." Calvin also stated clearly that "worldly princes" lose all their power when they rise up against God. Christians should resist such a power, not obey it.

When, precisely, do the actions of a government collide with the demands of the word of God? In deciding this, the church should be led by the word itself, knowing the demands for justice and peace, and also by the actual experience of the people. It is in the concrete situations of actual human experience that the word of God shows itself alive and more powerful and sharper than any two-edged sword.

In making this decision, the church should look for criteria not among those who make the laws and who have political and economic power, or among those who are favored by unjust laws, but rather among those who are disadvantaged by these laws, who are hurt at the deepest level of their being: those who suffer, those who have no voice—the oppressed, the "least of these my brethren." And in the eyes of the least of the brethren in our country, your government and your policies stand condemned. I need not repeat these accusations; I simply want to draw your attention to them, and to the truth that is in them.

The untold suffering of men, women, and children, the bitterness of too many, the wounds caused by your policy through the years can never be forgotten, nor compensated for by the "concessions" your government is apparently willing to make. The superficial adjustments to apartheid already initiated do not touch the root of the matter. It is as one of your colleagues has said, "The fact that a black man is allowed to wear a *Springbok* emblem (as he participates in multiracial sports) does not give him political rights." Indeed, and we may add: it does not give him his God-given humanity either.

You complain that the churches are "against the government." But it is because of your policies that so many churches and so many Christians find themselves against you. In this, we really have no choice, because the church of Christ in South Africa *must* obey God rather than you. I plead with you: stop your disastrous policies.

May I end with a personal word? I am not writing this letter in order to be brave or arrogant. I must honestly confess that I am afraid of you. You are the minister of justice. As such, you have at your disposal awesome powers such as only a fool would underestimate. The victims of these powers are sown across the path of the past and recent history of South Africa.

I, like any other South African, want to live a normal life with my wife and children. I want to serve the church without fear. I want a country where freedom is seen as the right of every citizen and not as a gift to be given or withheld by the government. I want, along with millions of our people, to have co-responsibility for government in our native land, with everything you want for yourself and your children. I, too, want peace, but authentic peace, which is the fruit of active justice for all. However, my longing for a "normal" life must not undermine the service to which God has called me. That would be intolerable. And my service is also to you. That is why I write this letter. I shall surely stand guilty before God if I do not witness against this government.

I think the time has come for your government to make a choice: you are either the "servant of God" of Romans 13, or you are the "beast from the abyss" of Revelation 13. Unless and until the right choice becomes *evident* (through the wholehearted and fundamental change of your policy), Christians in South Africa shall be called upon, *for the sake of their faith,* to resist you as we would the beast of Revelation 13. For the Christian, obedience to God and God's word must be the first priority.

I am aware that the decision to resist the forces of government cannot be an easy one. That is why the synod of the D.R. Mission Church made this so clear last year: "If a Christian is bound by his conscience to follow the way of criticism, which brings him into conflict with the state, then he should obey God more than humans. In this case, however, he must be prepared to accept suffering in the spirit of Christ and his apostles."

Once again, this is not a matter of being brave. Rather, I should like to use this occasion to urge you to realize that peace and salvation, indeed the future of South Africa, do not lie in more "security laws," in more threats, or in an ever-growing defense budget. They lie, rather, in the recognition of the human dignity of all South Africans, in the pursuit of justice, and in respect for the God-given rights of all.

You as whites are not in a position to achieve this on your own. That is why the churches have pleaded for a national convention where the people could be represented by authentic, chosen leadership. We demand the right to have the vote, so that our citizenship in South Africa may become meaningful. Give us the right to express ourselves and our political will. We need to have the opportunity to participate fully and meaningfully in the political processes in South Africa. Is this not the fundamental thing you grant yourself?

I plead that you make use of the offer and the opportunity to have discussions. Honest negotiations with the intention genuinely to share together in South Africa is always better than to stand against each other as enemies.

I am using this letter as an open witness, and thus will make it available to the press.

I thank you for giving me your time.

May God give you wisdom in everything.

Sincerely,
Allan Boesak

Ethics and Nuclear Weapons

THINKING ETHICALLY ABOUT THE UNTHINKABLE: THE JUST WAR THEORY AND NUCLEAR WAR

Cynthia M. Campbell

Are moral judgments about nuclear war possible? Considering the potential destruction of masses of people, perhaps of human civilization, moral judgments seem impossible or superficial. Further, such judgments imply real choices; but do we have any such choices, or is our only alternative to rely on vast nuclear arsenals as a deterrent to nuclear war?

Debate about the nuclear arms race has escalated in the last five years. It is a moral issue which has come into the homes of more Americans with greater force than almost any since the Vietnam War and civil rights. And yet one of the most difficult aspects of the issue of nuclear war, given the complexity of weapons systems and the almost unimaginable potential for destruction, is that of making moral judgments which have relevance for the formulation of strategies and public policy.

There is a common aphorism "all's fair in love and war." The Harvard Nuclear Study Group points out that very few people actually *mean* that phrase to suggest that ". . . any dishonesty is fair in romance and any kind of violence is justified in warfare. What is really meant is that moral standards are made more difficult—and therefore are followed less often and often less strictly when extreme competition rules."[1] But they go on to argue that even when one says "all's fair", there is still a sense of moral outrage when one's moral standards or society's conventions are violated. Judgments about military conduct are in fact made in our society all the time; they were part of the debates during World War II, Korea and Vietnam. The existence of these debates suggests that moral standards need not be abandoned in the nuclear age. Indeed, the case can be made that the nuclear situation makes such standards even more necessary.

It is the intention of this paper to examine the applicability of the so-called 'just war' theory to the issue of nuclear war. The issue is whether criteria therein traditionally used to justify war and govern its conduct are valid in the current situation. It is the thesis of this paper that ways can be found to make ethical judgments about nuclear armaments and warfare just as we have made judgments about what are now called "conventional" armaments and warfare. Further, it will be argued that the criteria of the 'just war' theory provide the basis for just such judgments and for the formulation and critique of military and political policies.

The Just War Theory

The discussion of when war is justified and what means are acceptable has its roots in the writings of Augustine of Hippo. Particularly as Christians could be numbered not only among soldiers but also among political leaders and policy makers, the question of moral behavior in war became an issue. The work of Augustine was taken up and elaborated during the Middle Ages when the Christian Church wielded significant political and military power as well as moral suasion. The theory reached its fullest expression in the work of Thomas Aquinas and was intended to provide a framework by which warfare might be limited and controlled in Christian Europe.

The just war theory begins with the premise that to engage in warfare is *de facto* to do something which is wrong, namely to take the lives of other human beings. Therefore, warfare can be morally acceptable only when conditions exist such that greater harm results from avoiding war than from engaging in it. The just war theory sets out to specify in the first instance the conditions under which resorting to warfare may be judged morally acceptable. These conditions include such considerations as the protection of innocent or defenseless persons, self-defense, the exhaustion of all other means of settling the dispute, action instigated by the lawful authority (the government), reasonable hope of success, and a response which is commensurate with the evil to be offset or avoided.

In addition to criteria which specify the conditions for engaging in warfare, the just war theory also specifies conditions for the conduct of war. Not only must one justify the *why* of war but also the *how*. The theory suggests two criteria: first, the means used must be in reasonable *proportion* to the end that is to be achieved. This criterion is intended to limit (among other things) massive retaliation for initial attack: because one shot is fired, the enemy nation should not therefore be wiped out. The second criterion is that of *discrimination:* in the conduct of war, soldiers and weapons should be able to discriminate between combatants and noncombatants. This provision of civilian immunity is designed again to limit so-called 'total war' and to limit vulnerability to those actually bearing arms in combat. Such provisions have indeed been used in setting strategy during warfare. They have also provided the bases upon which treaties banning germ and chemical warfare have been drawn up and enforced.[2]

Numerous arguments have been made against the just war theory. Obviously those from a pacifist tradition argue that the theory makes a specious argument. It attempts to find ways to approve actions which can never be justified, and thus makes a mockery of moral discourse. Others argue that the just war theory requires a universal moral community and a reasonable system of sanctions and enforcement. What might have made sense in Europe during the Middle Ages when armies (and populations and armaments) were limited and when the church could provide some enforcement through the power of excommunication may make little or no sense in a world where there is no international authority and little moral consensus. Many who found just war theory applicable to "conventional" warfare now find themselves unable to make sense of it in a nuclear world. The criteria seem to many to have become obsolete in the face of new and immensely powerful weapons which do not disciminate in their destructive consequences.

A Reformed Perspective

Such opinions invite a number of responses from those who approach moral and theological issues from the Reformed perspective. Obviously, if one approaches the matter of war from a pacifist position, the just war argument is not only senseless; it is offensive. But most Reformed Christians have traditionally not been pacifists, and this may be related to the seriousness with which the doctrine of human sinfulness has been taken in that tradition. If one believes that sin and its destructive consequences for human life are endemic to the human condition and not to be avoided completely this side of the end of history, then one believes that the incidents of oppression, violence, greed and anger which lead to armed conflict are likely to be with us always.

But Reformed Christians also tend to believe that sin is not the last word with respect to the human condition, that God does not abandon human beings in the midst of violence and oppression, and that in fact God is active in the world working against sin and its consequences as the creation move towards its fulfillment. Therefore, Reformed Christians have often argued that it may be necessary if regrettable to take arms to redress a wrong or prevent harm. While the Reformed tradition has not used all of the language of the just war tradition, it has certainly employed many of its categories. In so doing, the Reformed tradition has attempted to avoid fatalism which often accompanies a strong doctrine of human sinfulness ("it's so bad there's nothing that can be done, so anything goes"). But the Reformed tradition, especially through the voice of Reinhold Niebuhr, has attempted as well to avoid a utopian view that enough agreements and negotiation will bring an end to both warfare and its causes. The Reformed tradition, like the just war theory, attempts to find a way to live with and in the world as it is without submitting either to the notion that the way it is, is the way it ought to be or that human effort can bring in the promised kingdom.

The View of Paul Ramsey

One of the most prominent applications of just war theory to modern, and in particular to nuclear, warfare come from Protestant ethicist, Paul Ramsey. Ramsey's basic ethical program is an intricate balance of Protestant or evangelical principle with Catholic method. He begins with *agape* or love as the essential value of his ethical system. But he argues that love alone is not very helpful unless one has some way of saying what love means in a particular situation. Ramsey then sets forth a means of determining various regulating principles such that it becomes possible to determine what love requires under different circumstances. This procedure enables one, among other things, to determine when it might be right to sacrifice the good of some persons in favor of others.

In the traditional just war argument, Ramsey finds such a set of principles

[177]

which enable him to determine how to act in loving ways while not shying away from violence in the modern world. With this theory, Ramsey is able to determine when the killing of combatants is not illegal murder but rather when it constitutes the loving thing to do. He believes that there are situations where the consequences which such killing may prevent (e.g. killing innocent victims) or the results which it may achieve (e.g. self-protection) outweigh the evil of killing itself.

Ramsey's views have been most controversial, however, when he has applied them with respect to the nuclear situation. Ramsey thinks that there are situations in which engaging in nuclear combat may be justified. Beginning with the principle that one should always do the loving thing, Ramsey applies the "principle of double intention" which asserts that a given (evil) action may be justified if its *ultimate* intention is to do good. Applied to nuclear weapons this means that use of them can be justifiable when the intention in the first instance is *not* to destroy but rather to prevent destruction. Therefore the "loving thing" to do in a world of nuclear weapons is both to produce and improve them and to deploy them such that they can be a reasonable deterrent, thus preventing their use.

Obviously, if Ramsey is to employ the just war criteria he must show how it is that nuclear weapons do not constitute a disproportionate response to any threat or danger and how the matter of non-combatant immunity can be resolved. He accomplishes the first by arguing that the use of nuclear weapons should not be compared with respect to proportionality to the action of an aggressor but in proportion to the threat which the escalation of nuclear war has on world peace. Nuclear deterrence and the threat to destroy the enemy is proportionate, he argues, to the importance of maintaining global stability. With respect to the matter of non-combatant immunity, Ramsey argues that deterrence depends on the threat of "collateral civilian casualities." He claims that only this fear can really prevent the use of nuclear weapons, which is for him the highest value in this situation. Ramsey admits that a direct threat to kill an "innocent party" is morally indefensible. But he argues that simply targeting military installations will cause enough "collateral damage" so that the population remains in jeopardy without involving us in a *directly* immoral threat.

Such use of the just war principles and of ethical reasoning has left many persons dissatisfied. It appears that Ramsey has constructed an argument in which certain moral principles are used to justify an end which the principles themselves make impermissible. In the first place, he uses the principle of intention in such a way as to make that notion almost meaningless. He virtually argues that as long as one *intends* an ultimate good, then that intention not only mitigates the evil which is done, but it also removes any suggestion that one has intended the evil which may transpire. In the case of nuclear weapons and the targeting of military installations, the language of intention becomes a smokescreen. Even if significant numbers of both Soviet and American military installations were not (as in fact they are) located in or near major metropolitan areas, the fallout of even tactical weapons is such that civilian casualties will number in the thousands or millions. In such a situation to argue that one did not *intend* those casualties without making a judgment about the consequences makes a mockery of ethical reasoning.

Perhaps the most troublesome aspect of Ramsey's arguments is his contention that the *threat* of nuclear destruction is in fact justifiable and not disproportional. Threatening to wipe out another nation (or to wipe out non-combatant nations, e.g. most of Europe in a nuclear exchange between the United States and Soviet Union) is justifiable because of the proportionate good of the peace which could be secured by the act of making the threat. But, as we shall see as we turn to the pastoral letter written by the U.S. Catholic bishops, the notion of threat itself depends on the intent to carry through with the threat. A threat makes no substantial difference if a nation is not prepared to state at least some conditions under which the threat would in fact be carried out. A commitment to a threat is a commitment to an action. Therefore, one must be able to justify the ultimate *action* and not just the threat which itself may accomplish a good end. If that is the case, then Ramsey is *de facto* in the position of arguing that the destruction of large numbers of persons in a nuclear holocaust is a legitimate action.

On the Bishops' Pastoral Letter

While Paul Ramsey's use of the just war theory with respect to the nuclear arms situation presents some difficulties, a much more adequate use is found in the recent pastoral letter of the Roman Catholic Bishops, "The Challenge of Peace: God's Promise and Our Response." In this lengthy and carefully written document, the American bishops move into territory in which the Roman Catholic Church has either not taken a stand or in which it has traditionally supported U.S. military and defense policy. The letter opens with a discussion of the Biblical and theological foundations of the subject. Peace, they argue, is God's *gift* and God's intention for all creation. While the final realization of God's peace is eschatological, nevertheless we are called to *respond* to God by doing those things which not only inhibit war but which create the political and social climate which will build peace on earth.

With this Biblical and theological vision in hand, the bishops then turn to the traditional just war argument as a way of determining how we think about both entry into armed conflict as well as the conduct of it. The most substantial difference in the bishops' application of just war theory to the nuclear situation from that of Paul Ramsey lies in the discussion of the *means* of warfare. At the center of the debate, the bishops raise the following questions:

> Do the exorbitant costs, the general climate of insecurity generated, the possibility of accidental detonation of highly destructive weapons, the danger of error and miscalculation that could provoke retaliation and war—do such evils or others attendant upon and indirectly deriving from the arms race make the arms race itself a disproportionate response to aggressions?
> . . . how many deaths of non-combatants are 'tolerable' as a result of indirect attacks—attacks directed against combat forces and military targets which nevertheless kill non-combatants at the same time?[3]

The fundamental position of this letter is that nuclear weapons must be evaluated on their own terms as *means* of warfare apart from the question of the *ends* towards which they are directed. Implicit in the just war theory is the conviction that ends do not in all cases justify the means; rather, the means themselves have independent moral considerations. The first of their questions concerns the matter of proportionality. Whereas Ramsey argues that nuclear means are indeed proportional to the good obtained by preventing (a major) war, the bishops contend that even the threat to use nuclear weapons is disproportionate to any good envisioned. It is significant to note here that they point beyond the massive destruction which would result from the *use* of nuclear weapons to the negative effect which they believe the possession of nuclear weapons has on all of us here and now. The threat of use and therefore the threat of destruction constitutes a morally indefensible action because of the climate of fear which it produces, thereby damaging the quality of life for all humanity.

The second question concerns the criterion of non-combatant immunity. While recognizing that, in modern technological societies, specifying who is and who is not directly related to the 'war effort' is difficult in ways not envisioned by medieval theologians, nevertheless the bishops argue that non-combatant immunity is a value to be defended. They conclude from their research that even in a limited nuclear exchange the number of dead are likely to number in thousands and millions, particularly if such a war is fought in Europe. In their judgment this amounts to destruction in both the short- and long-range which is an unacceptable price for a civilian population to pay for the benefits of peace.

Based on these considerations, the bishops argue that nuclear weapons are in and of themselves immoral as means of war. This obviously leads them to what becomes the serious problem: namely, the morality of nuclear deterrence. As they themselves state it, the question becomes: "may a nation threaten what it may never do? May it possess what it may never use?" In distinction to Ramsey, the bishops argue that possession and threat are as immoral as use because threat (and possession) depends on a commitment to use. Does this not mean, then, that the current strategy of nuclear deterrence is impermissible? Is one led inexorably to immediate, unilateral nuclear freeze and disarmament?

Here the bishops make their most interesting, and most controversial case. Deterrence *is* an acceptable policy, they argue, *for the interim*. They agree with most strategists that a unilateral freeze or unilateral disarmament would destabilize the international situation and would thus invite military and political chaos. Disarmament can only proceed by mutual negotiation. And deterrence seems to be a necessary factor in creating incentives for serious negotiation. But nuclear deterrence must never be seen, at least by Christians and persons of moral conscience, as anything other than a means to the end of reduction and removal of nuclear weapons. Because nuclear war is morally unacceptable, the goal must be not simply to prevent one from beginning or to "win" one if started, but to make such warfare impossible. In concrete terms this means that development of weapons which would encourage a repeated exchange of weapons is unacceptable. It means that the goal of weapons production must be "sufficiency" to deter but not superiority. It means that the criterion for each new development must be the impact which it will have on the goal of reduction and disarmament.

Obviously the bishops have moved from abstract moral argument to questions of strategy. But that is precisely to the point: namely, that moral considerations can be utilized in the development of public policy and strategic decisions. The pastoral letter admits that these are matters about which persons of good conscience can (and perhaps should) disagree. But as they apply their moral judgment about the nature of nuclear weapons and warfare to the current situation, they maintain that the goal of 'sufficiency' has several implications. Working towards sufficient deterrent means a mutual, bilateral and verifiable freeze on production, deployment and testing of nuclear weapons, bilateral cuts in nuclear arsenals, and a new comprehensive test ban treaty.

The strength of this arugment is that it embraces both hope and realism. While urging abstinence from nuclear stockpiling, the bishops recognize that nuclear weapons *do* exist, and second, that they cannot be eliminated overnight. Some policymakers seem to argue that nuclear weapons are to be taken for granted as aspects of the modern political situation. That is to say, they seem to suggest that nuclear weapons are simply another stage in military development and must be accepted as such. As theologian Jacques Ellul has suggested, there is a notion in the modern consciousness that once something *exists,* once it is a *fact,* it cannot be questioned or criticized. That something is the case becomes tantamount to accepting it as inevitable.

To put it another way, much of the contemporary reliance on nuclear weapons suggests an argument which might be characterized as "can implies ought." We *can* develop, test, deploy and develop strategies for the use of nuclear weapons, therefore either we *ought* to or we cannot be prevented from doing so. Such arguments, although rarely stated explicitly, are dangerous because they suggest an abdication of moral judgment with respect to the work of science and technology. It is true that new developments in various scientific fields present us with moral questions for which there are often very few precedents and precious few guidelines. Advancements in medicine which effect the generation and prolongation of life are clear examples of this. Such capabilities as *in vitro* fertilization and the freezing of embryos for later implantation suggest only a few of the difficult issues which confront medical ethics and social mores. But in the medical field it has been clear that the scientific and general communities have rendered judgments about the morality of certain procedures. Once doctors know what they *can* do, they know that they must decide, indeed the broader society must decide, what they *may* do.

Such debates and subsequent moral and legal decisions suggest an important parallel to the nuclear debate. Once it is clear what can be done it remains to be determined what ought to be done. Scientific advancements need not hold citizens hostage or create a climate of inevitability. The bishops have provided us with a clear and hopeful position when they insist that nuclear weapons need not be taken for granted. Rather, they argue that such weapons can and must be evaluated and decisions rendered with respect to their impact on the quality of human life. The bishops refuse to abandon the question of nuclear weapons and warfare to the arena of military strategy and political consideration as though moral issues should not be addressed.

The bishops' pastoral letter is helpful as well because it does not imagine that the solution to the nuclear issue is as simple as immediate destruction of all nuclear weapons and a return to a pre-nuclear world. It would seem to be an easy step from the moral judgment which they make with respect to nuclear weapons, namely that they are *de facto* immoral as means of war, to the conclusions that "ban the bomb" is the immediate and only strategy. The letter suggests, as seems to be the case, that peace *does* depend to a large extent on an international balance of power and therefore to nuclear armament. As the Harvard Study Group suggests, treaty negotiations require a climate of trust, assurances that there is something to be gained from agreement, and recognition that there is much to be lost from failure to agree. For this reason, limits on production and deployment and eventual destruction of weapons must proceed in climates where such actions can be perceived as mutually beneficial and as improvements on the alternatives which currently exist. The pastoral letter presents a reasonable approach to a difficult problem: it is reasonable because it recognizes the impossibility of the nuclear situation and because it refuses to accept the *status quo* as the only option. Paul Ramsey's position appeals to another type of reasonableness: if you have a weapon, the reasonable thing is to be able to use it under certain specified conditions. The bishops declare that the weapons themselves are *unreasonable:* it is not rational for human beings to destroy their habitat and themselves. Therefore the reasonable thing to do is precisely to find a way out of the dilemma and to do as much as possible to prevent humanity from destroying itself.

Concluding Observations

It has been argued by many that the nuclear situation has rendered the old categories of the just war argument obsolete, that you simply cannot think about war today the way you could in another age. As the analogy with medical ethics suggests, new developments do indeed stretch old ways of thinking about various situations. Often the question which must be asked is whether on the one hand, the situation is so new that the very subject matter must be redefined or whether on the other hand, that it is a matter of adaptation of values which are essentially sound. The fundamental value contained in the just war theory is the presumption that killing is wrong, and that therefore it must be *justified* as aiding some greater good or preventing some greater harm. The Catholic bishops are persuasive in their conviction that this is a universal moral principle binding on all persons of conscience regardless of religious conviction or lack thereof. The other ethical values implicit in the just war theory follow directly from the first. The theory prescribes conditions for the engagement in and conduct of war which require an assessment of the *consequences* which that warfare is likely to have for both combatants and noncombatants alike. The just war theory makes the very obvious point that if a military conflict is designed to protect either one's own or another's nation from harm, then it is irrational to engage in a type of warfare which would destroy the very society which the war is designed to protect. The just war theory has always prohibited the mass destruction of the enemy (soldiers or civilians); nuclear warfare is only the latest and most completely devastating of the means of total war. If it is to be argued that nuclear war makes these criteria obsolete, then it is incumbent on the proponents of nuclear weapons to show how and why the mass destruction of human life could ever be justified.[4]

One of the great dangers of the current military and political situation is despair and a lapse into a modern-day determinism: that's the way it is, and nothing I can do will change it. Indeed, many military and political leaders feed such notions when they argue that the average citizen cannot understand the complexity of either the weapons systems or the geopolitical situation. As the Harvard Study Group points out, few of the leaders of at least the United States government who determine policy can be classified as "experts" on these matters: few are nuclear scientists, engineers, ballistics experts, etc. All of us are dependent on the available data in order to make the best decisions possible. Historically public opinion has had a significant and often determinative impact on United States foreign policy. This fact, perhaps the most puzzling to many other nation states, is and has always been our greatest strength. But the exercise of public opinion depends not only on access to information but on a public which is motivated to analyze, judge and make determinations with respect to that information.

It is the responsibility of the public to form opinions, and it is precisely at this point that the just war theory and the values which it contains are of invaluable assistance. The value of just war theory is that it gives concerned and responsible people a framework and a set of considerations which must be addressed in making moral judgments. Far from becoming obsolete with the advent of the nuclear age, the just war theory continues and is perhaps strengthened in its ability to assist people in thinking through a difficult moral situation. Obviously all who employ the criteria of the just war argument do not agree as to its implications or applications. This threat of nuclear war is a matter of ultimate importance for the future of the planet, but there are several strategic responses possible. For the time being, it is more important that men and women are using the criteria than that they have deduced from them only one solution. As the bishops remind us, strategies will vary. Particular judgments are matters of debate and subject to change. The matter of most importance is the acceptance of fundamental values, of "binding" moral principles upon which disagreements about policies can be based. *Living* with nuclear weapons means finding ways in which to prevent their use. Ultimately this means as well finding ways to prohibit their existence. Obviously there is a long road to be traveled in this process. But the moral values contained in the just war theory provide an excellent way to move forward so as to maintain sight of the goal and to determine appropriate stations along the way.

ENDNOTES

1. The Harvard Nuclear Study Group (Albert Carnesale, Paul Doty, Stanley Hoffmann, Samuel P. Huntington, Joseph S. Nye, Jr., and Scott D. Sagan), *Living With Nuclear Weapons,* Cambridge, Massachusetts: Harvard University Press, 1983, p. 243.
2. For an excellent study of the history, development and implementation of the just war argument, see Michael Walzer, *Just and Unjust Wars: A Moral Argument with Historical Illustrations* (New York: Basic Books, 1977).
3. United States Catholic Conference, "The Pastoral Letter of the U.S. Bishops on War and

Peace, The Challenge of Peace: God's Promise and Our Response,'' May 3, 1983, pp. 33 and 34.

4. This argument avoids mention of the notion of ''limited'' nuclear war or the tactical use of nuclear weapons in a limited military exchange. Any notion of such limited use depends on something like the argument that was used with respect to the first nuclear weapon: first use will end the conflict. That argument worked in a situation where there was no possibility of retaliation. Since 1945, even tactical nuclear weapons are far more powerful and far more dangerous than those first bombs. Even if tactical use would not escalate to all-out warfare, the devastation for those immediately involved would be of such magnitude as to be, at least by this reading, unjustifiable as a means to an end.

THE JUSTIFIABLE WAR TRADITION

Ronald H. Stone

The perspective taken on the tradition of the justifiable war is crucial. It is of central concern that the tradition be examined in light of an ethic of the just peace. For the Christian life, the ethic of the just peace ought to predominate. Consideration of questions of the justice of particular wars or justified participation in a particular war is a secondary part of any adequate Christian ethic. Even after all that has been possible to do for peace has been undertaken, the morally sensitive Christian will be confronted by the question of whether a particular struggle involving armed forces can be entered. The justifiable war tradition itself has this requirement: for a war to be accepted it must be a matter of last resort. We live in a world besieged by war and rumors of war, a world predisposed to war. The most peaceful nation will be confronted by the question of engaging or refusing to engage in wars in which issues vital to its well being are involved. The Christian individual cannot escape reasoning about the morality of particular conflicts which impinge upon life, family and community. Even if we were to achieve an international order which would reduce the current international anarchy, decisions about threats to that order would still have to utilize moral criteria about the just or unjust use of military force.

Those who are seeking the peace of God still live in a world in which war is to be expected, through particular wars can be avoided and international conflicts are often resolved without war. The twentieth century is characterized by war and even the most peaceful have to think about the reality of war. Those who try to achieve peace after the style of the Romans and who mix the use of force with diplomacy also have to think about justifying war. Christians who want to be politically responsible, while seeking to make war less likely, also have to be able to reason about each potential conflict while holding that reason within a Christian theological perspective.

The justifiable war tradition is not primarily an issue of Biblical ethics. The wars of Israel are seen in the perspective of God controlling the affairs of humanity, and they seldom rise to the perception of human beings reasoning about the appropriateness of war. The hunger for peace is a major motif of Biblical faith, but the role of humans acting as agents to achieve that peace or to prevent war isn't often acknowledged. Jesus resisted the appeals to force and did not adopt the Zealot option of resisting Rome by force. His early followers sought to participate in God's peace, but they did not try to formulate state policy actively. Despite the blessing of the peacemakers, the avoidance of Zealotry, the ethic of non-resistance, Jesus does not unequivocally provide advice as to how his followers are to live regarding conflict between states. He was realistic in expecting violence, but he did not provide guidance for how his followers would direct a state. The historical probability is that he anticipated the end of history and God's complete victory as more imminent than the possibility of his followers succeeding to power in Rome. Those earlier followers of Jesus addressed in the New Testament were a relatively separatist, sectarian movement without political power.

The first three centuries of the Christian era found Christians opposing war, though some soldiers were converted to Christianity. Disarmament was not a requirement of conversion. By the end of the second century Christians are in the armies and many Christians are witnessing that the Christian way is that of non-violence. From the end of the second century until the time of Constantine in the beginning of the fourth century, the evidence of Christian presence in the armies increases while the voices of the major theologians oppose Christians taking human life in war.

Augustine of Hippo

The situation changed with Constantine's victory over his foes. Constantine favored Christianity and used it as a civil religion to cement the torn fabric of the empire together. On his death bed he was baptized and in his life he turned the empire toward the faith he adopted. Given its growing civil status, Christianity began to adjust to its imperial perogatives. Ambrose, the spiritual father of Augustine, used the just war teaching of Cicero to justify the Christian use of force in defensive wars. Augustine himself was to give to Christian thought the outlines of a position justifying the use of armed force. His reflections shaped Christian morals on the issue and laid the groundwork for both the Roman Catholic theory in Thomas Aquinas and in Protestantism in the thought of John Calvin and Martin Luther.

Augustine (354-430) lived in an age of war and plunder and none of his writing glorifies war. He had a great aversion to war and scorn for those who gloried in it. War originated in sin and it was not to be praised. His major work, *The City of God,* elaborated the search for peace and the peace of God. Peace was the aim of all peoples, but few found it and the peace achieved in the earthly realm was usually only an armed truce. The Roman Empire's peace, even in its successful years of the past, had led to civil and social wars.

In a letter to Boniface, the Count of Africa, he censured the personal morals of Boniface and reminded him of his spiritual destiny. He instructed him to "Love the Lord thy God with all thy strength; and love thy neighbor as thyself." He reminded Boniface that in a personal conversation he had urged Boniface not to retire to a monastary, but to fulfill his earthly responsibilities. He praised his earlier work as a military commander when he had defended Africa against the invaders. He urged him, now, to secure the peace so that Africa could live in harmony. He urged upon him the necessity of ordering his commanders so that the aggressors could be defeated and peace be secured. As he wrote elsewhere he advised him in the spirit of:

"Therefore even in waging war, cherish the spirit of a peacemaker, that by conquering those whom you attack, you may lead them back to the advantages of peace; for our Lord says: 'Blessed are the peacemakers; for they shall be called children of God' "[1]

The urgings of Augustine on his friend to stem the "African barbarians" did not bring an end to the wars, or peace to Africa. Shortly after Augustine's death his own city of Hippo was devastated. His testimony to Boniface reflects the insight of Augustine that wars in defense of people and the order of the state could be morally defended.

The goal of any justifiable war is still peace. Peace is the great goal of humanity and the inner desire to achieve peace must be the aim of any war. This is the appropriate context for all Christian thinking about war. Peace—not just a Roman peace or a truce—reflecting the deep Old Testament longing for fullness of life and the New Testament sense of peace as a blessing is the goal. Peace as the harmony among people is the theme of Augustine's great philosophy of history in *The City of God* and it points to a fullness of the meaning of peace similar to the definition of justice in Plato's *The Republic*.

A war—to be rightly engaged in—must vindicate justice. This is not to imply perfection in history, but certainly it excludes wars of selfish conquest or illegal wars. In Augustine's thought it is close to the first requirement that the intention is peace. It must accomplish peace or harmony among people rather than contribute to disharmony, discord and further wars.

The disposition of those engaged in the war must be love. Augustine's neo-platonism could permit him to devalue the body and be a little casual about the possibility of loving the one whom one slays. Yet the requirement of love in disposition stands as a testimony against the hatred that usually accompanies war. It distinguishes thought about a justifiable war from fanatical crusades in which love of the enemy is rejected. The love ethic which dominates Augustine's thought enjoins him in the direction of responsibility for those who cannot protect themselves. Boniface would have retired from public life, but in this world Christians are obligated to fulfill their roles as public citizens to protect order—even though disorder is contained within the public institutions. The love is also obligatory towards those opposed in war.

It is this requirement to protect the innocent through the agencies of public order that underlies the further requirements of a justified war. It must be carried out by those responsible for public order. Love is expressed though the ambiguous institutions of the state as they properly fulfill their responsibility to protect the citizens. Only much later in Christian history, after ideas of the sovereignty of the people had been accepted, could the idea of a justified war be transmitted into a justified revolution.

Roland H. Bainton in drawing upon the studies of Gustave Combès[2] understands Augustine also to require the conduct of war be subject to moral rules. The rules were drawn from classical sources and prohibited massacre, looting, looting of temples, atrocities, etc., and required that dealings with the enemy be honest. He saw the very barbarians who were invading Rome as demonstrating the influence of Christianity in their conduct of warfare.

For Augustine, Christians would only participate in war in their official capacities in government or in the army. The private citizen had no right to take the sword even in self-defense. Clergy and monks because of their religious vocation were excluded from war. The monks were to seek perfection and their obligations forbade participation in war as it excluded them from marriage or ownership of property.

Augustine's ethic clearly excluded most wars from the recognition of justified warfare. War was a horrible evil and the Christian was more to be praised for avoiding war through negotiation than for engaging in a war—even if it *were* justifiable.[3] Basically, only wars of defense or to right an objective wrong could be justified. Even when justified the Christian could engage in war *only* with a sorrowful mind. He expressed a great repugnance to war and only wars which punished wrong or defended the innocent could be justified.

His position, in summary, was that of an ethic of love thinking about difficult choices in a sinful warring world. He could use insights from Scripture, classical philosophy, the history of the world, but he transformed these insights through the ethic of love to promote peace. The openness to some participation in war combined, however, with political responsibility could lead others less rigorous in their commitment to peace to rationalize participation in wars that Augustine would have regarded as unjustified.

Augustine's influence continued in church circles, but the influence of his just war tradition was minimal.[4] Popes used his political ideas in their own way, and the major center of Christian civilization of Byzantium was relatively free of Augustine's influence. The church tried to restrain war through the Truce of God and the Peace of God. Gradually some merging of the spirit of the conquerors and the teaching of the church emerged in the rules of chivalry. The wars of the Crusades were of a spirit quite contrary to just war tradition and the Crusading Religious War emerged as a third option in the Christian ethic of war.

In the twelfth century Roman law was revived by Gratian's canon law. Augustine was the major source on the ethics of war for his codification of law—the *Decretum*. James T. Johnson locates the origin of the medieval theory of just war with Gratian and his successors in canon law.[5]

Thomas Aquinas

Augustine had written at a time of the destruction of civilization. Thomas Aquinas (1225-1274) wrote at a time of the rebuilding of civilization. He is portrayed as calm with a book in his hands. The Crusades were not yet defeated; religious extremism, papal schisms and the Black Death were in the future. Political institutions, law, universities, cathedrals, business were being developed. It was a mediating time, and Thomas' great work was to mediate the newly discovered Aristotelian philosophy into Augustinian theology.

He did not criticize the Crusades, in fact inasmuch as they had been to defend rights of Christians in pagan lands, he approved of them. His own noble family, the Aquino, suffered under war. He himself chose the contemplative life and did not become in his writing a party to the struggles of his day. He turned down the preferred bishopric of Naples which his family wanted for him and continued his teaching and writing.

His writing on war is brief. He draws upon Augustine to support the conclusions about war drawn from natural law. The natural law is the inclination to good which corresponds to human rational nature. The teaching on justifiable war is in his treatise on political philosophy within the *Summa Theologica*. The natural law participates in the eternal law of God's mind; it is the way rational creatures reflect God's law.

He presupposed some unity in Western Europe, even though Christian Spain was fighting to drive out the Moslems, internal wars among Christian princes continued, and neither the Emperor nor the Pope could effectively govern. City states were emerging and in England and France the foundations of the nation states were slowly taking shape. The tendency from his beloved Aristole's pupil Alexander toward empire was beginning to come undone, but still there was sufficient unity to articulate a universal ethic based on rational principles. His thought still undergirds Roman Catholic thought on war and is foundational to the pastoral letter of the U.S. bishops. Protestant theologians have recently used his thought to reinforce their rejection of the American participation in the Vietnam War. Aquinas listed the principles in a systematic way, but such a listing cannot obscure his own sense of a universe full of people conjoined both to evil and good. Through the agency of ordered life the good in humanity could order and contain the evil, expressing more fully God's intention. Part of the good ordering of the human community was the need for the defense of the common good against assaults by the enemy, even through the resort to war.

In the *Summa Theologica*, Thomas put his views succinctly:

1. The war must be declared by the competent ruler who has the duty to defend the state.
2. There must be a just cause for the war. (He quotes from St. Augustine to the point that the war is to correct a wrong.)
3. There must be a right intention on the part of the belligerents. The desire to hurt, the thirst for power, the cruel vendetta are all condemned.[6]

This thought of Aquinas has been expanded in various ways by other moral theorists. Joseph C. McKenna[7] has summarized Roman Catholic just war thought in seven principles:

1. Legitimate authority declares and executes the war.
2. The injury which the war is intended to prevent must be a real injury (not a fiction).

3. The seriousness of the injury to be prevented must be proportionate to the destructiveness of the war.
4. There must be a reasonable hope of success. (McKenna: "Defensive war may be hopeless, but offensive war must contain element of success.") Pope Pius XII ruled out offensive war as an instrument of policy. No movement across boundaries can be justified.
5. War must be engaged in only as a last resort.
6. The intention of entering into the war must be just.
7. The measures used in conducting war must be defensible. Preservation of non-combatants has always been a factor in questions of just war.

John Calvin

John Calvin (1509-1564) continued in the Augustinian tradition. In his exposition of the sixth commandment "You shall not kill", killing means murder. He deepens the commandment to exclude hatred. The neighbor is to be held sacred. "If you wish or plan anything contrary to the safety of a neighbor, you are considered guilty of murder." Intent to do harm is condemned, even murder of the least is forbidden, for God looks upon the intention as well as actions. However this strong teaching also enjoins responsibility:

> We are accordingly commanded, if we find anything of use to us in saving our neighbors' lives faithfully to employ it; if there is anything that makes for their peace to see to it; if anything harmful to ward it off, if they are in any danger to lend a helping hand.[8]

This responsibility to prevent harm means that the magistrates must defend their people. The responsibilities of the rulers to punish wrongdoers for the public's protection extended to the ruler's responsibility to protect their territory from invasion. His reference to the rule of natural justice is to defensive war *only*. He believed that the Old Testament declared such defensive wars to be lawful, and the New Testament contained no rules against the lawfulness of such wars to Christians. He urged all the rulers to be very cautious in regard to war. All other means should be tried first. Wars were not to become excuses for the fulfillment of one's own passions. Following Plato he argued that the object of war must be peace.[9] On this right of defensive war followed the appropriateness of garrisons, alliances, and the possession of civil munitions, i.e., the means to defend the territory. The needs of Geneva, a small city state, were well served by the factors Calvin mentioned. His ministry would include the strengthening of the city's defenses and defensive alliances.

Contemporary Use of the Tradition

Obviously, the defense of the American empire is a long way from the defense of Geneva. The Presbyterian Church, however, as recently as 1969 affirmed the just war tradition as a way of thinking about issues of Christian participation in war. The tradition was affirmed as a way for individuals to think about war and to decide upon their individual participation or refusal to participate in war. The General Assembly quoted from a Presbyterian ethicist's book, affirming six principles as representative criteria:

1. All other means to the morally just solution of a conflict must be exhausted before resort to arms can be regarded as legitimate.
2. War can be just only if employed to defend a stable order or morally preferable cause against threats of destruction or the rise of injustice.
3. Such a war must be carried out with the right attitudes.
4. A just war must be explicitly declared by a legitimate authority.
5. A just war may be conducted only by military means that promise a reasonable attainment of the moral and political objectives being sought.
6. The just war theory has also entailed selective immunity for certain parts of the population, particularly for non-combatants.[9]

Such guidelines—whether regarded as rational reflection upon the natural order as Augustine taught or as principles of a natural law as Thomas thought or as a distillation of the moral tradition of the Western World as Michael Walzer uses them—are guidelines for our thinking.

The guidelines do permit some limited uses of military force in defensive wars. They clearly prohibit massive bombing of population centers as exercised in World War II and the Vietnam conflict. They rule out wars of aggression and wars to gain political influence over another country or for Cold War advantage. They can, if amended, be used to justify some wars of revolution against governments which oppress their population. For Christians who regard the defense of the innocent from loss of their lives or liberties as an action to be taken sorrowfully out of responsibility, they provide a means of moral reasoning.

These criteria clearly regard as illegitimate any wars conducted for selfish national interest calculations. Most wars that characterize our warring planet should be regarded as immoral by Christians using these criteria. Weapons of mass destruction, whether biological or chemical or nuclear, are clearly unable to be used under the requirement of protecting the lives of non-combatants. These weapons cannot be limited in their destruction to legitimate military targets except for a few highly unlikely uses of the weapons. The targeting of these weapons on available military targets, at the present time, involves intending to murder millions of citizens—including millions of children and other non-combatants. Such weapons mean that the war cannot be a responsible act of self-protection. The available evidence regarding nuclear war points to unacceptable levels of ecological destruction, and the possible end of human history.

Christian ethics permits limited use of deadly force to officers defending themselves and others in society. It does not permit police officers to destroy an apartment house full of people to stop the illegal activity of a criminal. The analogy applies to war: some use of deadly force by the appropriate officers of a state is permitted, but Christian ethics does not permit the destruction of an enemy nation's population, even in the defense of others.

Christian ethics is not only an ethic of means and ends, it is also an ethic of intention. Jesus was concerned about the immorality of the person's mind, as well as the immorality of the person's actions. It is immoral to intend to do evil. Therefore, we cannot morally tolerate a policy which threatens the children of a rival power. Deterrence fails not because it may not work, but because it is itself evil in intention. Thus, under modern conditions of some wars, Christians arguing in terms of the ethics of responsible love in just war reasoning will be led to nuclear pacifism. When they focus on the intention of deterrent policy which will under certain conditions destroy the other nation's population, they will reject it. To reject the deterrence of nuclear holocaust is not to reject deterrence by means of legitimate deployment of armed forces. The policy of deterrence and intended use of nuclear weapons fails by several other criteria of the justified use of military force. Reference to the criteria of the 1969 General Assembly makes this clear.

1. It has led to actions which thwart the search for just solutions to the conflict between the superpowers. Our diplomacy is characterized by a lack of imaginative solutions to the issues dividing the superpowers. The installation of the new missile systems for the sake of the capacity to increase our war-fighting capacity has resulted in the suspension of arms negotiations and the increased bellicosity between the superpowers.
2. The second criteria could conceivably be fulfilled.
3. Nuclear war cannot be carried out with right attitudes. Present plans for a limited counterforce exchange identify sixty military targets in or near Moscow. The U.S.S.R. repeatedly has stated that a nuclear war will not be limited, but that it will result in the total destruction of both societies.
4. No authority has the legitimate right to practice genocide or omnicide. Such warfare is a crime against humanity and against God's authority.
5. Nuclear war is not carried out by military means appropriate to the moral and political objectives being sought. Nuclear war is an act of madness.
6. Selective immunity for non-combatants is violated in the planning for nuclear war.

The Pastoral Letter of the U.S. bishops on war and peace, *The Challenge of Peace: God's Promise and Our Response,* using just war criteria, arrived at a slightly different position. They were led to ". . . *a strictly conditional moral acceptance of nuclear deterrence. We cannot consider it adequate as a long term basis for peace.* " They then moved on with several suggestions for moving beyond deterrence. They also said that they could not approve of every system of weapons or policy designed to strengthen deterrence. Our judgment is different: we cannot approve of the present system of deterrence or of the projected plans for space weapons, Pershings, cruise missiles, MX missiles, B-1 bombers, stealth bombers or the matching of Russian systems, expansion of the Chinese deterrent or the increasing development of the British and French deterrent. The intention of nuclear war is wrong—even if it is a response to the failure of deterrence.

The French bishops meeting at Lourdes issued a statement on "Winning Peace" on November 8, 1983. It is a rigorous, imaginative statement by the bishops of a country with its own nuclear deterrent. The bishops admit their deterrent, one of the strong being deterred by the weak, is an anti-city strategy. Still they insist that the threat to use nuclear weapons must not be treated morally the same as the actual use of the weapons. "Threat is not use." With the German bishops they argue that "Charity cannot replace right." They recognize two evils: capitulation or counterthreat. They think counter threat is morally acceptable if it meets certain conditions.

—It must concern defense exclusively;
—Overarmament is avoided: deterrence is attained the moment the formulated threat renders aggression by a third party;
—Every precaution is taken to avoid "an error" or the intervention of a demented person, a terrorist, etc.;
—The nation taking the risk of nuclear deterrence adheres to a constructive policy in favor of peace.[11]

The French bishops' statement fails logically as they put the options as capitulation or counterthreat. They are led by the position of their church and government to have to grudgingly support counterthreat, and to distinguish threat from use. The willingness to use however is necessary to threat. One cannot intend to do evil. There are other options; diplomacy, negotiation and the building of mutual interdependence between the Soviet Union and Europe are the most obvious examples of other options. The bishops want diplomacy, and negotiation; our judgment is that firm church opposition to the intention to use these weapons is a central Christian action to encourage the nations to act reasonably.

As followers of John Calvin and the tradition in Protestant ethics of distinguishing between a spiritual realm and a worldly realm we might argue that the intention to do evil is characteristic of the worldly realm. In the tradition of Christian realism we might argue that there is no absolute justice in the political world. We might argue that the evil intention is acceptable if the results of the intention are to produce a good: the avoidance of nuclear war. However, by working within the framework of just war thinking, we have already made our concession to thinking about the real world of power and sinful governments. Sinful governments which realize some justice very imperfectly are still accountable to God. The targeting policies of all of the nuclear powers are necessarily, given the weapons, too indiscriminate to be moral. Deterrence, because of its intention to do unjust acts under certain conditions, fails to meet the worldly criteria of the just use of military force. Christian ethics, in our understanding, using the traditions of just war thinking says *no* to nuclear deterrence as it is now practiced and as it is projected by the nuclear powers.

From this *unequivocal no* to nuclear deterrence comes the moral obligation to translate peacemaking concerns into an ethic of a just peace and into politics of peacemaking. Peacemaking, according to just war theory, must precede any war— war using weapons of mass population destruction is immoral; therefore, the political means of dismantling those weapons along with those of our allies and projected enemies is of utmost urgency. *Peacemaking: The Believers' Calling* led Presbyterians in 1980 into peacemaking. *The U.S.-Soviet Relations: A Call to Reexamination and Reconciliation,* a resolution of the United Presbyterian Church, U.S.A. (1982), stressed the type of work necessary to begin to lay the groundwork for improved U.S.A.-U.S.S.R. relations which is the *sine qua non* of arms control agreements leading to the control of weapons of mass destruction. Because nuclear deterrence is unacceptable, Presbyterians must find ways to pressure their governments into changing policy toward mutual arms reduction as part of a policy of cooperation with the U.S.S.R. in reducing the danger. The choice for humanity is not one of "dead or red." The choice is one of reconciliation and cooperation for the health of the world. There is no foreseeable policy of the U.S.S.R. which can be countered only by nuclear weapons. An ethic of a just peace and politics of peacemaking can lead us forward into a day when two ideological systems can compete without threatening each other's children while most of the nations of the world find their own way in a world characterized by a rich diversity of religions. philosophies, values, economics, and social systems.

This study concludes that the just war criteria which are a way of thinking about permissible Christian use of violence for defense are helpful guidelines for many of the wars that occur in the modern world.[12] The modern weapons of mass destruction fall outside of the permissible use of violence by Christians. Biological and chemical weapons carry inherently within themselves grave risks to noncombatant populations which just war thinking protects. Nuclear weapons have taken on the characteristics of suicide for the human race. Jonathan Schell's *The Fate of the Earth* summarized and synthesized the scientific evidence to show that nuclear exchanges among the nuclear powers could destroy human life. The research reported by Carl Sagan[13] establishes the high probability that even a controlled nuclear war of 500 to 2,000 explosions of strategic war heads would create a worldwide climatic catastrophe which would destroy humanity. Sagan refers to his groups' findings in the science fiction terminology of the doomsday machine. We have created, unrestrained by just war criteria, means of war which if used will kill us all. Also relevant to the argument that nuclear wars cannot be made rational is the existence of plans and communication equipment to fire all U.S. nuclear weapons in a final last gasp of national revenge against an enemy. We are living in the shadow of doomsday potential and the intention to use it. All of this stands outside the permissible use of violence under the just war tradition.

Obviously we know it is wrong to intend actions which threaten to destroy all of humanity. This conclusion can be reached without the just war traditon. No Christian ethics can rightly argue for nuclear war. Calvinist Christian ethics must also consider the intentions of our planning. We must cherish the neighbor as made in the image of God and in our same flesh, as Calvin said:

> He who has merely refrained from shedding blood has not therefore avoided the crime of murder. If you perpetrate anything by deed, if you plot anything by attempt, if you wish or plan anything contrary to the safety of a neighbor, you are considered guilty of murder.[14]

So Christian ethics when it permits the killing of another human being, does so only under highly restricted conditions. Wars of defense and wars of revolution may occasionally meet these restrictions, nuclear war cannot.

We have the just war tradition and its insight in terms of what it is sometimes permissible to do to protect our neighbor. This tradition regarding weapons of mass destruction is clear: they are morally intolerable. If a government over a long period of time is threatening the survival of humanity on the planet, it begins to lose its legitimacy. Governments are constituted to restrain sin, to promote order, to secure for their people life and liberty. If their constituted regular policies are to plan to destroy all human life under certain circumstances, they need to be changed. Some of the means for changing these governments will be discussed in other parts of this study.

ENDNOTES

1. Henry Paolucci, ed., *The Political Writings of St. Augustine* (Chicago: Henry Regnery Company, 1962), p. 182.
2. Roland H. Bainton, *Christian Attitudes Toward War and Peace* (New York: Abingdon Press, 1960), p. 97. This article's exposition of Augustine on the just war follows Bainton except on one point. Paul Ramsey has the better of the argument when he argues that no requirement for the absolute justice residing with one side in a war was suggested by Augustine. Paul Ramsey, *War and the Christian Conscience* (Durham: Duke University Press, 1961), pp. 15-33.
3. Herbert A. Deane, *The Political and Social Ideas of St. Augustine* (New York: Columbia University Press, 1963).
4. Donald L. Davidson, *Nuclear Weapons and the American Churches* (Boulder: Westview Press, Strategic Studies Institute, U.S. Army War College, Carlisle Barracks, Penna., 1983), p. 5.
5. *Ibid.*
6. A.P.D. Entreves, ed., *Aquinas Selected Political Writings* (Oxford: Basil Blackwell, 1965), p. 159, 161.
7. Joseph C. McKenna "Ethics and War: A Catholic View," *American Political Science Review* (September, 1960).
8. John Calvin, *Institutes of the Christian Religion* (1559) ed. John T. McNeill, trans. Ford Lewis Battles (Philadelphia: Westminster, 1960) II. viii. 39.
9. *Ibid.,* IV. xx. 12.
10. Edward Leroy Long, Jr., *War and Conscience in America* (Philadelphia: The Westminister Press, 1968), pp. 24-29.
11. "Winning Peace," Text of the Statement Issued by the French Bishops, Lourdes, November 8, 1983. Translated by the Press and Information Service of the French Embassy, Washington, D.C.
12. The author is indebted in his reflection to the excellent resources in "The Promise of Peace," *Church and Society* (September/October, 1983).
13. Carl Sagan, "Nuclear War and Climatic Catastrophe: Some Policy Implications," *Foreign Affairs* (Winter, 1983/84), pp. 257-292.
14. Calvin, *Institutes,* II. viii. 39.

JUST WAR AND NUCLEAR DETERRENCE

Kermit D. Johnson

Just war theory is a legacy to Western civilization from Roman Catholic and Protestant thought going all the way back to St. Augustine in the fifth century A.D. It attempts to resolve the conflict of duty "between the prohibition to inflict harm and the obligation to prevent harm" toward one's neighbor.[1] Like pacifism, it is rooted in the commandment: "Thou shalt not kill." It is a presumption against violence, "the presumption *in favor of peace* and *against* war."[2] War is an evil.

On the other hand, in cases of "tragic necessity," if the innocent are to be protected from aggressors, war can be seen as a "lesser evil." But when force is employed in the cause of justice, it must be strictly regulated. Certain criteria must prevail, those related to going to war (jus ad bellum) and others governing the conduct of war (jus in bello). It is legitimate to use force only when it is declared by proper authority, as a last resort, for a justifiable cause, with just intentions, in which the total good is expected to outweigh the evil, and with the reasonable hope of success.

In the conduct of war, violence must be both discriminate (immunity for non-combatants) and proportional (means appropriate to ends). For centuries Christians have resorted to these criteria, both for conscientious participation in war and for concientious objection against war. And for a century nations have appealed to these criteria directly or indirectly through the secular Geneva Conventions and Rules of Land Warfare to either justify war or to declare it a violation of human rights or decency.

Thus, just war theory has occupied the center stage of Western civilization and the 'mainline' churches up until the present time. Pacifism has exercised a continuing but minority witness and the crusade or "holy war" has been intermittent in its influence. However, just war theory has recently fallen on hard times. Defectors and cynics abound. There are at least three central reasons for just war theory's fall from grace.

First, there is the persistent tendency of nations to justify their actions and be supported in these actions by the loyalty and patriotism of their people. Reinhold Niebuhr noted that "self-deception and hypocrisy is an unvarying element in the moral life of all human beings" and "the most significant moral characteristic of a nation." Easily the "means of defense" can be "transmitted into means of aggression." "The will-to-live becomes the will-to-power." "In other words, it is just in the moments when the nation is engaged in aggression or defense (and it is always able to interpret the former in terms of the latter) that the reality of the nation's existence becomes so sharply outlined as to arouse the citizen to the most passionate and uncritical devotion toward it."[3]

Thus the individual's unselfishness is easily transformed into what Niebuhr called "national egoism." This recurring feature in the life of citizens and nations led Arthur Koestler to conclude that aggressiveness is not the main trouble with the human species, but rather "an excess capacity for fanatical devotion."[4] All of this spells a deep cynicism regarding "just war," because nations and their peoples so easily justify their actions—whatever they may be.

Second, just war theory is held to be of little real-world use because of the nature of war itself. It is not simply that "good wars" are hard to find. The difficulty is spelled out by bumper stickers which read: "Just War is just war." This position is held in common not only by those who stand against war, but also by those who may approve of a particular war, but chafe under any restraint. This view of the intrinsic nature of war was expressed by Lord John Fisher, when he exclaimed:

The humanizing of War! You might as well talk of the humanizing of Hell! When a silly ass at the Hague got up and talked about the amenities of civilized warfare and putting your prisoners' feet in hot water and giving them gruel, my reply, I regret to say, was considered totally unfit for publication. As if war could be civilized! If I'm in command when war breaks out I shall issue my order:—
'The essence of war is violence.
Moderation in war is imbecility.
Hit first, hit hard, and hit everywhere.'[5]

Third, doubters and defectors from just war theory often consider it irrelevant in the light of historical change. Most obvious in this respect is the advent of the bomb, as Lloyd Averill indicates:

That quantum leap in terror transmogrifies everything we knew about justice and warfare, and renders established moral and tactical consideration obsolete. That is why Catholic bishops can no longer appeal to traditional teaching about a "just war." Given its ultimacy and indiscriminacy, nuclear warfare is inherently, irredeemably unjust, regardless of who uses it for what purposes.[6]

Just war theory is said to be of "no help" since all categories for moral and military measurement have been shattered.

More subtly, many believe just war theory is an anachronism in a world where the "real action" is in the explosive power of revolutions, not in the unusable power of nuclear conflicts. Just war theory is seen to represent the elastic and formal rules of engagement for first world powers at war with one another, but to be increasingly obsolete because those wars have become too dangerous and costly to fight. (Only five of the forty-two wars being fought in the world today are classic across-border wars. The others are revolutionary and separatist guerilla conflicts.)[7] Even worse, those rules are now regarded by many as the rules of repression, when applied to the Third World. To many, the high-sounding talk of defense of freedom, values, and Western civilization really mean the opposite: repression and suppression of freedom. They view just war theory as obsolescent because they feel the verdict of history favors revolutionaries who use violence in the cause of freedom over against reactionary counterrevolutionary force. Hannah Arendt once wrote:

> In the contest that divides the world today, those will probably win who understand revolution, while those who still put their faith in power politics in the traditional sense of the term and, therefore, in war as the last resort of all foreign policy may well discover in a not too distant future that they have become masters in a rather useless and obsolete trade.[8]

The underside of the world's peoples, who see revolution as the only means to secure justice, are likely to view first world criteria for a "just war" against them as neither just nor relevant.

All of this may spell the disuse, if not the demise of just war theory. Certainly it raises questions as to its utility. At the very least, chastened just warriors who recognize the logic of these arguments will be forced to a more circumscribed application of just war theory. That is where I wind up. Yet the limited utility of just war theory may signal its importance at a time when we least expect it. Dr. Ralph B. Potter, Jr., used just war criteria "to separate rationalizing pretexts from justifiable causes of war," and in so doing, established a powerful indictment against the Vietnam War.[9]

On the positive side, it is impossible to predict those situations in which war may indeed be justified. Perhaps this is hard for us now to realize because our nation has adopted a counterrevolutionary stance in a revolutionary world. But under enlightened leadership, it would not be difficult to envision a time when the United States would intervene militarily in South Africa, if not to do so would mean the virtual extermination of 21 million blacks at the hands of 4.5 million whites. I am not referring to present conditions of incipient genocide, but to that imaginable time when fear-crazed whites might go about a program of actual genocide in the interests of "security." It would seem that such an intervention by our nation on behalf of black South Africans would satisfy all three of the just causes of war: "to protect the innocent from unjust attack, to restore rights wrongfully denied, and to reestablish an order necessary for human existence."[10]

If such future scenarios seem ill-founded or theoretical to some, then the present utility of just war theory needs to be demonstrated. That demonstration is needed for all persons and church bodies who are unable, for whatever reason, to embrace pacifism as operative theory for all questions concerning war and peace. It is hard to imagine a revolution of such seismic order that would add, say, the Presbyterian, Roman Catholic, and Lutheran Churches to the list of historic "peace churches." Yet many of their clergy and laypersons are "at sea" because they are unable to see a place for just war theory. My purpose is not to "bring them back" by engaging in the intramural struggle between merits of pacifism versus the just war, nor even to assuage doubts about just war theory, but simply to provide the basis for a somewhat diminished claim of validity for the just war. That opportunity exists in relation to the strategy of nuclear deterrence.

In 1960 an editorial in *Worldview* stated that nuclear weapons had made the norms of just war obsolete. To this, the just war ethicist Paul Ramsey responded:

> The just war theory cannot be repealed; it can only be violated. It states the limits beyond which war as such becomes in itself a wholly non-human and non-political activity, and the point beyond which military force becomes senseless violence, and our weapons no longer weapons of "war." This is not because war has an "essence" or "nature" but because man has; and because political society has a nature to which military means must be kept subordinate.[11]

This is the essence of the case for the just war, even in the nuclear age. If indeed the criteria of the just war have been shattered by the characteristics of nuclear weapons and nuclear war, as was stated earlier, it does not make those criteria invalid, but rather establishes them. The reason one can conclude that "nuclear warfare is inherently, irredeemably unjust, regardless of who uses it for what purposes" is precisely because it violates just war principles. It is understandable that defectors from just war theory want to insure that just war criteria can never be used to positively justify nuclear weapons of war. What they overlook is the value of just war theory in determining the immorality of nuclear war as well as a negative judgment upon the strategy of nuclear deterrence.

Making negative judgments on nuclear weapons, deterrence and warfare is not nearly as obvious a task as might be supposed. This requires using just war criteria against just war proponents who "neglect the weightier matters of the law" in justifying nuclear deterrence and use. On the secular front, it is the task of confronting those who engage in what Theodore Draper calls "nuclear scholasticism," conceptual ways of rationalizing the threat and actuality of nuclear war.[12] On the religious front, it is the task of confronting those who seemingly automatically identify self-interest or national interest with a high moral purpose. This confrontational work is not easy. It is difficult to achieve a measure of transcendence, the ability to rise above the assumptions and presumptions of a society or culture. It takes a peculiar brand of courage and patriotism to be able to challenge something so sacred as "national security."[13] In this pantheon, nuclear deterrence is given special reverence. In a not-for-attribution session, I once heard a White House official call it "the keystone of the keystone of national security."

Nuclear deterrence is enshrined as the epitome of national interest. It is not surprising, then, to find just war theory employed in its support. One of the leading Roman Catholic just war theorists, Professor William V. O'Brien, speaks of his desire "to overcome the skepticism about just and limited war" because of "the perennial need for war as an instrument of policy and the dangers of nuclear war or of reversion to conventional total war."[14] Judging all-out nuclear war to be immoral, he employs just war theory to substantiate a limited and "moral" nuclear war. He assures us that "a flexible response counterforce posture could strengthen deterrence precisely because it could be employed morally." Then, in what must be music in the ears of U.S. nuclear planners, he says "the United States has, in fact, the will and the capability to threaten and, if necessary wage a very limited war"[15] and "all trends in U.S. policy are toward war-fighting strategies that would increasingly respect just-war standards of proportionality and discrimination."[16] It is not strange that nuclear strategists and military journals so often cite Professor O'Brien as a moral authority on nuclear deterrence and war!

Thomas Merton warned us that:
'the theoretician who splits hairs about "just war" and makes nice distinctions in journals for experts is actually supporting the military mind and military policies, which imply no such fine distinctions at all. . . The state of affairs is this: men with nuclear weapons will use them when they think the situation is sufficiently critical. And they will not use them with any regard for restraints demanded by moral theologians.'[17]

Professor O'Brien's acceptance of a counterforce or war-fighting strategy can hardly be seen as a "fine distinction." But his unquestioned support for present U.S. nuclear strategy alerts us to Merton's warning.

The same warning should be considered in the case of Protestantism's most erudite just war scholar, Paul Ramsey. He too inveighs against the immorality of counterpopulation warfare. In its place, Ramsey says that "counterforce nuclear war is the upper limit of rational, politically purposive military action."[18] What is this distinction worth however, when we hear Ramsey's undisguised approval of the "bonus effect" of "collateral damage" (i.e., the killing of innocent civilians)? He insists "it is moral to mount a deterrent whose effects flow from shared fear of the 'collateral' (unintended civil) damage unavoidably connected with targeting modern weapons of war, especially nuclear weapons upon legitimate military objectives."[19]

This fits to a "T" Merton's warnings about just war theoreticians who make "nice distinctions . . .for experts" in support of "military policies, which imply no such fine distinctions at all." "Double effect" or "unintended effect" may allow Ramsey moral tranquility, but the real-world collateral damage effect will be civilian casualties by the millions. But more on this later. Suffice it to say for the present that both Ramsey and O'Brien genuflect to the horrors of nuclear war in its total form, but then are rather sanguine about the nuclear deterrent and even nuclear war if it is prosecuted on a counterforce basis.

Not so, say the U.S. Roman Catholic bishops. Their Pastoral Letter reflects the struggle and anguish of men who take a clear stand against nuclear war in all its forms, counterforce included. They are also very critical of nuclear deterrence. But for the very reason that the Pastoral Letter is perhaps the most prophetic statement yet issued by any church body, it is all the more troubling that its unequivocal "no" to nuclear war in our present "moment of supreme crisis," should end in a bottom line which confers "a strictly conditioned moral acceptance of nuclear deterrence."[20] Of course the boundary statement within which the bishops did their work was provided by Pope John Paul II: "In current conditions 'deterrence', based on balance, certainly not as an end in itself but as a step on the way toward a progressive disarmament, may still be judged morally acceptable."[21] Whether Pope John Paul II meant his statement to be definitive and limiting under changing historical conditions is a moot question. These words were originally spoken in French at the United Nations in a speech in which he was not explicit about deterrence—"une dissuasion" refers to *a* deterrent. Even if this definitely meant *nuclear* deterrence, the words "may still be judged morally acceptable" hardly sound like endorsement.[22]

Apart from whether the American bishops felt bound either by substance or strategy to the Pope's words, the Pastoral Letter's strong critique of nuclear weapons, war and deterrence are in sharp contrast with its conditioned moral acceptance of nuclear deterrence. I maintain that the bishops could do this only because of a "fine distinction," namely, their acceptance of the "bluff," even though this is not stated in the letter. Their understanding of a deterrent which can be possessed morally but not used morally is certainly not the understanding which government leaders have of nuclear deterrence. The state guardians of nuclear deterrence believe that possession of nuclear weapons, threatening their use and willingness to use, if need be, are all essential elements of deterrence and *this* understanding of deterrence is what they deem "moral."[23]

It is ironic indeed that the "nice distinctions" which allow agonizing bishops to deem nuclear deterrence temporarily "morally acceptable" support "military policies, which imply no such fine distinctions at all."[24] The bishops carefully utilize just war criteria to reach very negative conclusions about nuclear deterrence and the strategies used to maintain it, only to weaken at the finish line. After a short breather, the bishops need to continue the race by considering the words of Jonathan Schell: "Thus, unlike the bishops, I cannot support deterrence conditionally, because I think it is as wrong conditionally as it is eternally."[25] This can be demonstrated by showing the incongruity between just war principles and nuclear deterrence.

Before we apply just war criteria, we must first understand that when we speak of nuclear deterrence, we are speaking of a constantly changing and evolutionary concept. Granted, nuclear deterrence has always meant the willingness to possess nuclear weapons for the purpose of threatening a potential enemy with use, if need be. It is a hope that nuclear war can be avoided by discouraging a rational opponent from initiating war, when faced by a credible deterrent which promises to do more damage than he would be willing to accept. Beyond this, any coherence of meaning stops. This is so because nuclear deterrence is rooted in technology and perceptions.

Because nuclear deterrence is linked to technology, it has fueled a quantitative and qualitative arms race. Simple deterrence, as Bernard Brodie, America's earliest nuclear strategist conceived it, existed to avert war, not to win wars. It was a defensive posture based on a "stable balance" and "retaliation in kind." For this purpose 200 nuclear weapons were sufficient, with an upper limit of 2000. Today the United States and the Soviet Union each have approximately five times that upper limit, not to mention tens of thousands of tactical nuclear weapons. The potential target list has grown from 70 to 1949 to over 40,000 at the present time. Secretary of Defense Schlesinger said during his watch that the "built-in surplus of warheads" made an expanded target list possible.[26] The original moral appeal of nuclear deterrence, solely to avert war, has been lost as nuclear weapons have been employed in "levels of redundancy of such grotesque dimensions as to defy rational understanding."[27] In other words, what started as nuclear deterrence based on "balance" is now an arms race to achieve superiority.

Nowhere is this more clear than in the adoption by the U.S. under Presidential Directive 59 in July 1980 of a counterforce or war-fighting strategy. This is the ability and intention to use nuclear weapons against Soviet nuclear forces, conventional military forces, military and political leadership, and economic and industrial targets.[28] Much has been said about the moral superiority of a counterforce strategy over a countervalue or counterpopulation strategy. Henry Kissinger spoke before a conference on the future of NATO in Brussels in September of 1979 of "bloodthirsty strategies" and that we needed to "move away from the senseless and demoralizing strategy of massive civilian extermination."[29] But it was not moral development, but technological development which made it possible to adopt a war-fighting strategy. A whole family of super-accurate, hard-target-kill-capable weapons is coming into being: the MX, Trident II, Pershing II and cruise missiles. Now Secretary of Defense Weinberger speaks of the necessity to "hit a hard target (such as a Soviet missile silo) and do it with a degree of accuracy . . . If you have developed the ability to take out their missiles, you have achieved a degree of deterrence."[30]

This, however, is what a less aggressive "retaliation in kind" was meant to avoid. Colin Gray, a nuclear strategist who is a strong advocate of counterforce is more forthright: "The principal intellectual culprit in our pantheon of false strategic gods is the concept of stability."[31] He is also perfectly up-front in admitting that if the U.S. ever used a counterforce strategy, since so many targets are in or around Soviet cities, it would mean that the U.S. had "done its worst."[32] In fact, as Colin Gray looks at American strategic policy in the light of just war guidelines he concludes what moral theologians ought to conclude: "In short, U.S. nuclear strategy is immoral."[33] Gray apparently realizes that nuclear weapons have always been in search of a strategy and a morality, not the other way around.[34] The shift from a counterpopulation to a counterforce strategy was a shift from one immoral strategy to another occasioned by "the continuous inventiveness of the scientific community, and I am afraid primarily the Western scientific community, that has made the pursuit of a stable nuclear balance, of mutually assured *deterrence* . . .seem to be the chase for an *ignis fatuus,* a will o' the wisp."[35]

In other words, the world of "stable nuclear balance" upon which the U.S. bishops base a conditioned moral acceptance of deterrence, simply does not exist. The history of the arms race shows that the U.S. and U.S.S.R. have never accepted "parity." A major reason for this is that military analysis always takes into account the "worst case" which fosters what Alan Geyer calls "arms proliferation through infinite anticipation."[36] We are now into a hair-trigger world where the unmistakable emphasis is on war-fighting and war-winning which in the leaked words of the 1982 *Defense Guidance* call for nuclear forces which can "prevail and be able to force the Soviet Union to seek earliest termination of hostilities on terms favorable to the United States . . . even under the condition of a prolonged war."[37] Nuclear deterrence is then a moving target, determined by advancing technology. In an Oxford debate this year, Secretary Weinberger said that nuclear deterrence is "a dynamic effort, not a static one." In other words, the capability or technology determines the strategy.

Nuclear deterrence is also elastic because it is linked to changing perceptions. The Scowcroft Commission Report defines nuclear deterrence as "the set of beliefs in the minds of the Soviet leaders, given their own values and attitudes, about our capabilities and our will. It requires us to determine, as best we can, what would deter them from considering aggression, even in a crisis—not to determine what would deter us."[38] By lodging nuclear deterrence "in the minds of the Soviet leaders," it can mean anything we wish it to mean. It is wholly subjective. We should not be surprised, then, if the blank check of deterrence is written on the high side. That is exactly how General Bennie L. Davis, the Strategic Air Command chief understands it:

> We cannot permit the Soviets either an actual or perceived edge in force capability or national determination that they could turn into a military calculation (or miscalculation) of acceptable risk. So we have adopted and planned for more flexible strategic options, all without sacrifice of our ultimate capability for all-out retaliatory attacks."[39]

That about covers it—every actual or perceived possibility for nuclear use up to and including *"our ultimate capability for all-out retaliatory attacks."* The arms race is guaranteed. And lest just war theoreticians who like to make "fine distinctions" think as Professor O'Brien does that "the United States is bending every effort to plan only wars with limits,"[40] they had best look again.

Nuclear deterrence is referred to as "the bedrock of our security." But advancing technology and changing perceptions have made it the foundation of an arms race without limits. Any examination of nuclear deterrence in the light of just war criteria must take this into account. The limits described and hoped for by America's earliest nuclear strategist, Bernard Brodie, are gone. Yet that is what just war theory is all about—limits and restraints.

We are now prepared to explore the relationship of just war criteria to nuclear deterrence. Both the "going to war" criteria and the "fighting the war" criteria must be taken into account. Precisely because nuclear deterrence depends on the possible or actual use of nuclear weapons in war, it is essential to examine it on both of these bases.

The two essential elements in examining nuclear deterrence in the light of just war criteria are the political factor and the control factor. The political factor applies mainly to going to war, in the questions of just cause, legitimate authority, last resort, reasonable hope of success and right intent. The control or limiting factor applies mainly to fighting the war, in the issues of discrimination and proportionality. If nuclear deterrence can pass the political test and the limitation test, then, by just war criteria, it can be said to be "moral" or "just" in the relative sense in which just war criteria address conflict. Another way of putting this twofold task we are about was expressed by the Prussian General Carl Maria von Clausewitz: "No one starts a war—or rather, no one in his senses ought to do so—without first being clear in his mind what he intends to achieve by that war and how he intends to conduct it."[41]

Clausewitz held that "war is only a part of political intercourse, therefore by no means an independent thing in itself." If war were ever to become separated from the political factor, it would then become "a senseless thing without an object." Thus, "The subordination of the political point of view to the military would be contrary to common sense, for policy has declared the war; it is the intelligent faculty, war only the instrument and not the reverse."[42] Clausewitz' thinking is critical in assisting us to focus on the political factor of just war criteria in relation to nuclear deterrence. Only as nuclear weapons are deployed and employed for some valid political purpose can they be said to possess any military utility whatever.

To the contrary, nuclear deterrence represents the subordination of the political view to the military. Before any nuclear weapons are ever launched, nuclear deterrence locks us into a permanent state of war, albeit a Cold War, with the Soviet Union. They are regarded as an enemy, imminently deserving of being threatened moment by moment with nuclear destruction. The overall political relationship between the U.S. and the Soviet Union is fixed by this military reality. Nuclear deterrence is the subordination and surrender of the political point of view to the military. (This is why wise Clausewitzian soldiers have said nuclear weapons have no military utility.)[43]

At all times, in only a matter of minutes, the Cold War could become a hot one. Once having turned hot, then the question is whether political authorities could have any meaningful control, either over forces, weapons or results. Without human control, nuclear war would be "senseless." It is generally agreed that any nuclear war would leave millions killed on both sides, certainly enough to refer to as "mutual destruction." The just war questions would then be: What injury or what cause could possibly justify mutual destruction? What political goal could be achieved through mutual destruction? Survival? Justice? Peace? Or would the intent be extermination, vengeance or revenge? In catastrophic destruction, how can the total good possibly outweigh the evil? What is a reasonable possibility of success in a nuclear war? Would there be any winners? Would or could a political leader who decided to press the button be exercising legitimate authority?

The answer to these questions is found in the context of nuclear deterrence strategy itself. Nuclear deterrence is based on the rationality of a potential enemy. That is, the enemy, understanding what would befall him if he initiated a nuclear war, *could never rationally define a political goal that would be worth such destruction.* Rational persons conclude that there are *no* political goals worth the cost of a nuclear war, and are deterred: "It is precisely the fact," Bernard Brodie explained, "that one finds it difficult if not impossible to find a valid political objective that would justifiy the destruction inevitable in a strategic nuclear exchange that makes the whole concept of nuclear deterrence credible."[44] Yet, deterrence is also based on *willingness* to take that irrational step—to use nuclear weapons without any achievable and sensible political goal. At that point, nuclear deterrence and war will have become "an independent thing in itself" and therefore "a senseless thing without an object." By the very definition of deterrence, then, there could be no just cause, justifiable goal, just intent, overall good, or success if deterrence failed. And therefore, no leader could legitimately decide to "push the button." That is not a rational political decision.

Yet, if a wave of irrationality did not exist, the strategy of nuclear deterrence could not exist. From time to time, even the historical guardians of such policy cannot refrain from remarking on this flaw. Robert McNamara indicated that "There is less and less deterrent value to threatening to commit suicide."[45] And Henry Kissinger, in a moment of lucidity said, "It simply does not make much sense to defend one's way of life with a strategy which guarantees its destruction."[46] Despite such lapses, the shocking truth related to deterrence is the continued willingness of leaders and enough of our people to "think the unthinkable" and willingness to "do the undoable," if need be.

Of course, the official documents use distancing language which cushions us from the reality. Nevertheless the truth is there: "Deterrence depends on the assured capability and manifest will to inflict damage on the Soviet Union."[47] Undergirding official deterrence policy is the commitment of individual citizens both in and out of government, each with varying perceptions. Michael Novak goes so far as to say, "Deterrence is a form of nonviolence, a legitimate use of force, based upon legitimate authority."[48] One of the top officials in the Defense Department assured me that if a nuclear war occurred "it wouldn't be much worse than in World War II when 50 million were killed." Still counting, Roger Molander tells of meeting a Navy captain in the Pentagon who complained that people were "talking as if nuclear war would be the end of the world when, in fact, only 500 million people would be killed."[49]Advancing further, William F. Buckley, Jr. takes us to the other end of the scale, saying that "if the Soviet Union opted for massive nuclear war, our option must be to return that hell in kind. And that option we would need to choose for so simple a reason as that we would not then have died for nothing, because it is better than nothing to rid the world of such monsters as would unleash such a war."[50]

Whether nuclear deterrence is supported as a "form of nonviolence" or seen to have a modest body count anywhere from 50 to 500 million or even near total annihilation, the point of all this is that every person supporting nuclear deterrence must do a cost-benefit analysis involving the lives of human beings. Even lower estimates of people killed mean that the words "genocide" and "suicide" can be used without hyperbole. We would be both executioner and victim. Surely, as Adam Roberts said, "a policy which could involve us in the roles of Nazi and Jew at the same time has unique moral defects."[51] Nuclear deterrence is said to be essential to the defense of our freedom and values. But Jonathan Schell properly points out: "It's when *we* annihilate *them* that our 'values' are destroyed."[52] A nuclear deterrence which commits our leaders and people to the constant willingness to commit genocide and suicide is antithetical to the defense of freedom and its values. What this adds up to is this: there is *no* just cause, *no* valid political goal, *no* possibility for reasonable success and *no* benefit or good that is proportional to the evil incurred through nuclear war. As Archbishop of Canterbury Robert Runcie put it, "There is no such thing as just mutual obliteration."[53]

Since nuclear deterrence does not protect a people and their values, for such purposes a government cannot be regarded as a legitimate authority. In our democracy, the government derives its just powers from the consent of the governed. It is inconceivable that our people or any people would consent to their own destruction. Perhaps this accounts, in part, for the fact that nuclear weapons development and strategy has been a technical operation conducted in secret by experts, unimpeded by the opinions of ordinary people. Niebuhr was both accurate and prescient in the spring of 1950 when he remarked with respect to the development of the H-bomb: "The fact that this was done without public debate represents a real threat to the democractic substance of our life."[54] In each instance, nuclear deterrence violates the criteria which makes it permissible to go to war: legitimate authority, just cause, justifiable goal, proportionality and reasonable possibility for success.

Finally, there is the control factor relating to fighting the war in the principles of discrimination and proportionality of means.[55] The freedom of a people falls victim not only to the political factor of going to war, but also to the control factor of fighting the war. Francis X. Winters put it succinctly: "Literally no one might be in control of the war. Exit free choice."[56] So much has been written on the highly dubious possibility that nuclear war can be controlled or limited,[57] that I will simply draw attention to these factors:

1. Soviet doctrine calls for mass employment of nuclear weapons, not limited nuclear war.

2. Escalation is highly likely. In fact, the deployment of Pershing II missiles and cruise missiles to Europe is for the very purpose of "coupling" tactical and intermediate range nuclear forces with strategic nuclear forces to assure the people of Europe that war would not be limited to Europe alone.

3. There is no reason to believe the "American way of war" involving maximum firepower and annihilation with conventional weapons can or will be changed when annihilative nuclear weapons are used.[58]

4. It will be exceedingly difficult for an enemy to perceive *any* use of nuclear weapons against him as a *limited* intention, since the willingness to use nuclear weapons is such a radical act and the effects are so destructive. Whether attacks on either side are limited or massive, it will be very difficult to avoid an extermination response in revenge or vengeance—a clear violation of just means or attitude.

5. Since U.S. strategy stresses destruction of Soviet political and military leadership targets, to the degree the strategy is successful, there will not be Soviet leadership to negotiate with or to exercise control over their forces.

6. If tactical and/or strategic nuclear weapons are used, the chances for a

limited war will be in inverse proportion to the destruction wrought upon the command, control and communications instruments and facilities which are necessary to keep war limited.

7. A limited war is contingent upon the rationality of all political and military decision makers and obedience to release authority.

8. With the deployment of devastating multiple warhead weapons such as the MX in vulnerable silos, there will be incentive for the Soviets to take out these lucrative targets pre-emptively and by the same token, for our nation to launch them pre-emptively before they can be destroyed in place.

9. It is doubtful that the passions and momentum which could not be controlled *before* the start of a nuclear war can be controlled or diminished *in* a nuclear war. By definition, the start of a nuclear war signals the total failure of political rationality and negotiation.

10. Because of the unprecedented destructiveness of nuclear war over a compressed time frame, the "fog of war"—unforeseen and unpredictable circumstances making control less possible—is apt to increase in proportion to the shortened time frame.

11. Counterforce strategy cannot prevent massive collateral damage because most military and leadership targets are located in and around cities. Since it is certain that collateral damage will be catastrophic, resorting to the idea of "unintended effects" is sheer sophistry.[59] Also, if plans to prevail even in a prolonged war are carried out, the collateral damage will be even more catastrophic.

12. Already, from Hiroshima and Nagasaki, we know from an exhaustive study that nuclear destruction

> is so complex and extensive that it cannot be reduced to any single characteristic or problem. It must be seen overall, as an interrelated array—massive physical and human loss, social disintegration, and psychological and spiritual shock—that affects all life and society. . . The essence of atomic destruction lies in the totality of its impact on man and society and on all the systems that affect their mutual continuation.[60]

Nations whose economies, transportation systems, medical facilities, farms, industries, schools, and cultural centers were decimated would place in doubt the mutual continuation of these essential life systems. The effects of a nuclear winter would decrease further the likelihood of survival. There is no conceivable end which could justify such destructive means.

In sum, nuclear war would obliterate any moral understanding of discrimination or proportion. By applying just war criteria to the strategy of nuclear deterrence, both in the reasons for going to war and in the conduct of fighting the war, we reach a negative verdict. Nuclear deterrence is immoral. That judgment may not seem to be particularly profound or useful. However, it is in direct contradiction to the views of our government. It is an important judgment because it seems highly unlikely that the permanent war which nuclear deterrence fosters will cease, until and unless the people and leaders of the United States become convinced it is *wrong*.

This does not mean there is some purely moral direction we can go. The "nuclear fall" closed off that possibility. But it does mean we have to realize that a deterrence-sponsored arms race has killed all imagination and incentive for moving in a safer direction. It is not that countless concrete proposals have not been put forward. We simply have not had the political and moral will and imagination to carry them out. By accepting nuclear deterrence as moral, even provisionally, we have accepted the permanence of war and the abolishment of peace. Nuclear deterrence means very simply that we choose war over peace. Not until we break this log jam can we begin to apply strategies for peace. The modest service we can render by using just war theory is to demonstrate that nuclear deterrence can never be a moral choice, thereby opening the way to theologies and ethics of peace.

So, "we labor on—not toward a strategy of annihilation but toward a strategy of peace."[61]

ENDNOTES

1. Gaspar B. Langella, paper entitled "Limited War in the Nuclear Age," January 1983, p. 8.
2. *The Pastoral Letter on War and Peace, The Challenge of Peace: God's Promise and Our Response*. Origins, NC Documentary Service, May 19, 1983, p. 10.
3. Reinhold Niebuhr, *Moral Man and Immoral Society*, New York: Charles Scribner's Sons, 1932, pp. 95, 42, 18 and 96.
4. Arthur Koestler, *Janus*, New York: Random, 1979, p. 14.
5. Quoted in Roland H. Bainton, *Christian Attitudes Toward War and Peace*, New York: Abingdon Press, 1960, p. 247 from Reginald Hugh Bacon, *Lord Fisher*, London, 1929, I, pp. 120-121.
6. Lloyd J. Averill, *The Christian Century*, April 14, 1982, p. 437.
7. See "A World At War—1983," *The Defense Monitor*, Washington, Volume XII, Number 1, 1983, pp. 1-2. Since publication, two more wars have begun, now totalling 42.
8. Hannah Arendt, *On Revolution*, New York: Viking Press, 1965, p. 8.
9. Ralph B. Potter, "The Moral Logic of War," *Occasional Papers on The Church and Conflict 5*, Department of Church and Society, The United Presbyterian Church, U.S.A., p. 17. See also Potter's book *War and Moral Discourse*, Richmond, 1969.
10. Potter, "The Moral Logic of War," p. 10.
11. See Donald L. Davidson, *Nuclear Weapons and the American Churches*, Boulder: Westview Press, 1983, p. 42, quoting from Paul Ramsey, *The Just War*, New York: Charles Scribner's Sons, 1968, p. 164.
12. Theodore Draper, "Nuclear Temptations," *The New York Review*, January 19, 1984, p. 49.
13. In 1947 Albert Einstein said, "The fact that men have become accustomed to war preparations has so corrupted their mentality that objective and humane thinking becomes a virtual impossibility; such thinking will even be regarded as suspect and will be suppressed as unpatriotic." *Einstein On Peace*, edited by Otto Nathan and Heinz Norden, New York: Schocken Books, 1960, p. 427. "To be against nuclear weapons is not anti-American, it is not anti-defense, and it is not dangerous. In my judgment, under the present circumstances, it is profoundly patriotic," Admiral Noel Gaylor, "Opposition to Nuclear Armament", *Annals*, AAPSS, September 1983, p. 21.
14. William V. O'Brien, *The Conduct of Just and Limited War*, New York: Praeger, 1981, p. 8.
15. William V. O'Brien, *The Washington Quarterly*, January 20, 1983, p. 140.
16. William V. O'Brien, *Commentary*, December 1983, p. 10.
17. Thomas Merton, *The Non-Violent Alternative*, New York: Farrar, Straus, and Giroux, 1980, p. 92.

18. See Davidson, *op. cit.*, p. 46 quoting from Paul Ramsey, *The Just War*, p. 214.
19. Ramsey, *op. cit.*, p. 315. See also pp. 252 and 320.
20. *The Pastoral Letter on War and Peace*, p. 18.
21. *Ibid.*, p. 17.
22. Bruce M. Russett, "Ethical Dilemmas of Nuclear Deterrence," *International Security*, Spring 1984, p. 42. Russett, principal consultant to the bishops who wrote the Pastoral Letter, stresses the ambiguous and open nature of the Pope's words.
23. For a more extended discussion of the differences between the bishop's "bluff" position and the nuclear deterrence which is in place, see my article "Will the Bishops Spar with Shadows?," *Christianity and Crisis*, March 19, 1984, pp. 81-82. See also Elliot Abrams, "Nuclear Weapons: What is the Moral Response?," *Department of State Bulletin*, December 1982. Abrams, Assistant Secretary of State for Human Rights and Humanitarian Affairs, speaking in his " . . . responsibility . . . to insure that American values are adequately weighed in our foreign policy" (p. 38) says that "Deterrence is moral." (p. 41).
24. The bishops are not unaware of this possibility: "Moreover, these voices rightly raise the concern that even the conditional acceptance of nuclear deterrence . . . might be inappropriately used by some to reinforce the policy of arms buildup." *The Pastoral Letter on War and Peace*, p. 19. The strategies and weapons systems now in place or coming into place, which the bishops find it necessary to reject or question, is a tacit admission that the deterrence which the bishops conditionally justify *does not exist*.
25. Jonathan Schell, "The Abolition, Defining the Great Predicament," *The New Yorker*, January 2, 1984, p. 69.
26. James Schlesinger, *Report of the Secretary of Defense to the Congress on the FY 1975 Defense Budget and FY 1975-1979 Defense Program*, p. 35.
27. George F. Kennan, *The Nuclear Delusion*, New York: Pantheon, 1982, p. 176.
28. See Desmond Ball, "Counterforce Targeting: How New? How Viable?" *Arms Control Today*, February 1981, p. 6 and Thomas Powers, "Choosing a Strategy for World War III," *The Atlantic Monthly*, November 1982, p. 86.
29. Henry Kissinger, "NATO: The Next Thirty Years," *Survival*, Nov/Dec 1979, pp. 266-267.
30. *United States Military Posture Statement for Fiscal Year 1983*, Washington, p. 19. The characteristics of "first strike" nuclear weapons to which Mr. Weinberger refers make dubious the possibility of adherence to the just war criterion that war should be *declared* as a *last resort*.
31. Colin S. Gray, "Nuclear Strategy: The Case for a Theory of Victory," *International Security*, Summer 1979, p. 15.
32. Colin S. Gray, "Targeting Problems for Central War," *Naval War College Review*, p. 13. Also, "Many Soviet political control targets are in or fairly close to major cities. U.S. strikes on almost any scale against the political control structure could well be indistinguishable, in Soviet eyes, from a countercity attack." (pp. 13-14).
33. Colin S. Gray and Keith Payne, "Victory is Possible," *Foreign Policy*, Summer 1980, p. 17.
34. See E.P. Thompson, *Beyond the Cold War*, New York: Pantheon, 1982, pp. 4-5. Also: "As the scale of military force becomes unhinged from political objectives, strategy becomes merely a rationalization of weapons capability." p. 33. (Daniel Deudney, "Whole Earth Security: A Geopolitics of Peace," *Worldwatch Paper* 55, p. 33).
35. Michael E. Howard, "On Fighting a Nuclear War," *International Security*, Spring 1981, p. 5.
36. Alan Geyer, *The Idea of Disarmament*, Elgin: Brethren Press, 1982, p. 92.
37. Quoted in Fred Kaplan, *The Wizards of Armageddon*, New York: Simon and Schuster, 1983, p. 387.
38. *Report of the President's Commission on Strategic Forces*, April 1983, p. 3.
39. Address to Air Force Association symposium in Chicago, "Deterrence is More Than Just Hardware," as reported in *Aerospace Daily*, April 13, 1982, p. 254.

40. O'Brien, *op. cit.*, *The Washington Quarterly*, p. 140.
41. Carl von Clausewitz, *On War*, edited and translated by Michael Howard and Peter Paret, Princeton: Princeton University Press, 1976, p. 579.
42. Carl von Clausewitz, *A Short Guide to Clausewitz On War*, Edited by Roger Ashley Leonard, New York, 1967, pp. 215, 216 and 217.
43. "As a military man who has given half a century of active service I say in all sincerity that the nuclear arms race has no military purpose. Wars cannot be fought with nuclear weapons," Earl Louis Mountbatten speech in 1979, quoted in *The Defense Monitor*, Vol. IX, No. 4, 1980. " . . . as a soldier, I have never considered nuclear war to be a rational instrument of policy," Lieutenant General Arthur S. Collins, Jr., "Strategy for Survival," *The Washington Quarterly*, Summer 1983, p. 68. "I see no military usefulness for nuclear weapons," Admiral Noel Gaylor *op. cit.*, p. 12.
44. Bernard Brodie, "The Development of Nuclear Strategy," *International Security*, Spring 1978, p. 73.
45. *Newsweek*, December 5, 1983.
46. Henry Kissinger, *The Necessity of Choice*, New York: Greenwood Press, 1961, p. 56.
47. *United States Military Posture Statement* for Fiscal Year 1983, Washington, p. 19.
48. Michael Novak, "Moral Clarity in the Nuclear Age," *National Review*, April 1, 1983, p. 362.
49. Roger Molander, "How I Learned to Start Worrying and Hate the Bomb," *Washington Post*, March 21, 1982, p. D5.
50. William F. Buckley, Jr., *Wall Street Journal*, May 21, 1982.
51. Adam Roberts, "The Critique of Nuclear Deterrence," *Adelphi Paper* no. 183, part II, IISS, London, p. 14.
52. Schell, *op. cit.*, p. 64. Also, Reinhold Niebuhr remarked on the advent of the hydrogen bomb: "Thus we have come into the tragic position of developing a form of destruction which, if used by our enemies against us, would mean our physical annihilation; and if used by us against our enemies, would mean our moral annihilation." "The Hydrogen Bomb," *Love and Justice*, edited by D.B. Robertson, Philadelphia: Westminster Press, 1957, p. 235.
53. *Washington Post*, January 29, 1983, p. C12.
54. Niebuhr, "The Hydrogen Bomb," *Love and Justice*, p. 235.
55. The control factor is also an issue *before* war takes place. President Eisenhower registered alarm when his science adviser, George Kistiakowsky reported gross overkill after a visit in 1960 to Strategic Air Command: "The sheer number of targets, the redundant targeting, and the enormous overkill surprised and horrified him. Kistiakowsky, a scientist who represented no parochial service interest, had made the President realize that the SIOP [Single Integrated Operational Plan] might not be a rational instrument for controlling nuclear planning, but rather an engine generating escalating force requirements." (David Alan Rosenberg, "The Origins of Overkill," *International Security*, Spring 1983, p. 8.
56. Francis X. Winters, "To the Editor of Commentary," *Commentary*, December 1983, p. 5.
57. See especially LTG Collins, *op. cit.*, and Desmond Ball, *op. cit.*
58. See Russell F. Weigley, *The American Way of War: A History of United States Military Strategy and Policy*, New York: Indiana University Press, 1973.
59. "In our consultations, administration officials readily admitted that while they hoped any nuclear exchange could be kept limited, they were prepared to retaliate in a massive way if necessary. They also agreed . . . that even with attacks limited to 'military' targets the number of deaths in a substantial exchange would be almost indistinguishable from what might occur if civilian centers had been deliberately and directly struck." *The Pastoral Letter*, p. 18.
60. *Hiroshima and Nagasaki: The Physical, Medical and Social Effects of the Atomic Bombings,* the Committee for the Compilation of Materials on Damage Caused by the Atomic

Bombs in Hiroshima and Nagasaki, translated by Eisei Ishikawa and David L. Swain, New York: Basic Books, 1981, pp. 337-339.

61. John F. Kennedy, address at American University, June 10, 1963, *Documents on Disarmaments*, 1963, p. 222.

FROM DETERRENCE TO DISARMAMENT

Dana W. Wilbanks

Deterrence as Doctrine and Strategy

It is of great significance that questions of nuclear weapons policy are becoming matters of public debate. During most of the period in which fateful steps have been taken to develop reliance on nuclear weapons for security, policies have largely been entrusted to scientific experts and public officials with little political struggle. There have always been a minority of dissenters, but until recently they have not been able to generate a wide enough public response to make nuclear arms policy a vital political issue. Certainly, part of the reason is that nuclear weapons policies have seemed to most people to be too complicated to understand and too remote to do anything about anyway. However, a deeper reason is that such policies have been developed in an environment in which an astonishingly unified perception of the world rendered any other course unthinkable.

This taken-for-granted perception of the world arises out of the doctrine of deterrence. Deterrence is the belief that the most effective way to prevent war and to protect national security is through the capacity to retaliate against aggression with an unacceptably devastating response. This doctrine was raised to political orthodoxy after World War II. The appeasement of Chamberlain at Munich and the eventual military success of the Allies provided the paradigmatic historical experience for proving the truth of the deterrence doctrine. Military weakness and efforts at conciliation invite aggression and war, whereas military strength and readiness to utilize it, paradoxically, are more likely to preserve a rough but reasonably stable peace.

Not only foreign policy officials but also most post-World War II religious ethicists have accepted the truth of deterrence doctrine. Reasoning has intertwined both political and moral considerations. One argument is that preventing a major war between the Soviet Union and the United States is a moral good, especially preventing the use of nuclear weapons; and, pragmatically, the most effective means to prevent war is through nuclear deterrence. Producing and deploying nuclear weapons is morally troublesome but unfortunately necessary in a world where national interest and aggressive power are dominant realities. A second argument is that nuclear deterrence serves justice as well as peace because without a powerful military capacity by the United States the U.S.S.R. would engage in unjust aggression against weaker countries, including perhaps the U.S. itself.

An influential representative of the moral reasoning employed by religious ethicists is Reinhold Niebuhr. Soon after the development of the hydrogen bomb, Niebuhr spoke of "the tragic position of developing a form of destruction which, if used by our enemies against us, would mean our physical annihilation; and if used by us against our enemies, would mean our moral annihilation."[1] He counseled the maintenance of a nuclear deterrent while arguing that we should "make a solemn covenant never to use it first." Yet, to continue to produce nuclear weapons "may serve to guarantee that it will never be used."

In those relatively early days there was a measure of hope in the possibility of stabilizing the arms race when the U.S. and the U.S.S.R. had reached roughly equivalent nuclear capability. Since the weapons are so devastating, holding them as a credible deterrent makes war between the superpowers less likely than in a non-nuclear world. As the nuclear era unfolded, this doctrine of deterrence attained the status of orthodoxy, nearly unassailable truth. Any alternative to deterrence as a way to provide for national security and to prevent war has been "unthinkable," not only naive but even dangerous. This orthodoxy of deterrence has held the U.S. in a grip as tight as any religious dogmas of previous historical eras.

The most significant feature of the contemporary debate about nuclear weapons is broadened and deepened critical attention to the assumptions of deterrence doctrine. It is, of course, late to be considering deterrence critically now when so much of American and international life has already been shaped by this doctrine; but it is not too late to consider alternatives and to seek to move the historical course in a different direction. The most striking evidence of a shift in thinking among religious ethicists is the Pastoral Letter on War and Peace by the National Conference of Catholic Bishops.

The bishops identify the present moment as one of crisis because of the danger to planetary survival posed by nuclear weapons. Rejecting the determinism of deterrence doctrine, the bishops argue that "it is neither tolerable nor necessary that human beings live under this threat."[2] The prospect for a human future depends on our capacity to make a fundamental historical shift. The shift is from the presumption of nuclear deterrence as the preferred way to prevent war to a presumption for nuclear disarmament as the only morally defensible long-range strategy for pursuing a more just and peaceful world.

This letter, therefore, challenges the long-prevailing notion that nuclear deterrence is the only practicable way to prevent the use of nuclear weapons. Disarmament is not proposed as a politically irrelevant ideal or as a prophetic witness against the madness of nuclear weapons but as the basic orientation toward peace and international security which should function as the basis for evaluating policy options. The method of reasoning is teleological. Disarmament is the long-range good which humans are required to seek. The choice of means will involve prudent calculations consisting of both moral and political considerations.

While it is true the bishops do not reject deterrence entirely, they do reject deterrence as the governing doctrine for nuclear weapons. Their acceptance of deterrence is at the level of means rather than end, and it is clearly subordinated to the primary political and moral end which is disarmament. Nuclear deterrence is accepted morally in only a "strictly conditioned" sense. "We cannot consider it adequate as a long-term basis for peace."[3] What, then, are the moral objections to deterrence?

The responses to this question depend on the level of meaning which is given to deterrence. One level is doctrinal, the sense in which deterrence is a perspective on and orientation to the world requiring credible retaliatory capacity to prevent war and to provide security. It is this level of meaning which the bishops reject and replace with disarmament because of the dangers inherent in the nuclear arms race and the persistent threat of nuclear war so long as nations produce and deploy them.

The second level of meaning is strategic. Deterrence in this sense involves the strategies employed to implement deterrence doctrine. A great deal of the discussion about deterrence in ethics and politics has been at this strategic level of meaning, without necessarily examining critically the doctrinal assumptions used to justify the development of deterrence strategy. Because of the varied strategies of deterrence and debates about them, there has been plenty at this level to keep persons busy. Yet preoccupation with strategies of deterrence has often proceeded with a tacit acceptance of a perspective which is the level which most needs attention.

Strategies of Deterrence

Particular questions of deterrence strategy have received a great deal of attention by ethicists. "Countervalue" targeting has been critiqued because it aims nuclear weapons at civilians and cannot be discriminate in its destructiveness. The bishops argue: "It is not morally acceptable to intend to kill the innocent as part of a strategy of deterring nuclear war."[4] Countervalue targeting has also been charged with holding vast populations hostage to the machinations of East/West struggles and with requiring such populations to bear the overwhelmingly disproportionate cost of any accidental or intentional use. George Kennan has written with indignation: "Was there ever a better example of the corruption worked on people's minds and assumptions by this habit of thinking about war in terms of nuclear weaponry—this concept of holding populations hostage with a view to extorting advantage from their governments?"[5]

Countervalue deterrence has been defended ethically as preferable to strategies which seem to make the use of nuclear weapons more likely and acceptable. Countervalue strategy involves such potentially horrifying destructiveness that it functions as an effective deterrent. In this point of view countervalue is pragmatically the most effective way to ensure that nuclear weapons will never be used. Although almost no ethicist would justify actual massive retaliation, the capacity and threat are regarded as justifiable to deter the use of nuclear weapons by an adversary.

Similar differences are found in arguments about counterforce targeting. Some argue that counterforce is morally preferable to countervalue because it is theoretically feasible to discriminate between military targets and civilian centers. Ethical approval of counterforce depends on the assumption that rational and moral limits could be placed on the use of nuclear weapons so that the destructiveness would not be disproportionate to the cause for going to war. The most common example of counterforce strategy is to deter the Soviet Union from moving militarily against Western Europe. If deterrence fails and such aggression occurs, those who advocate counterforce strategy argue that nuclear weapons potentially could be used in a limited and militarily effective way to stop the Soviet Union.

Ethical critiques of counterforce are numerous. The most common one is that this strategy is too linked with war-fighting plans, weakening the abhorrence of nuclear war by giving the dangerous impression that such weapons could be used effectively in armed conflict. Counterforce represents the delusion that war could be fought with nuclear weapons in a way that limits destructiveness and avoids escalation to more destructive levels of use. For critics, to base deterrence on counterforce moves policymakers across the critical threshold of preventing nuclear war to the psychological and military readiness to fight a nuclear war. The risks involved in believing that nuclear weapons could be used in a restrained way and without unacceptable levels of collateral damage are far beyond any value counterforce might be presumed to have.

Ethical critiques of deterrence strategies have also considered a tangle of questions surrounding the relation of possessing nuclear weapons and the intention to use them or not. Even if it might be possible to justify possessing nuclear weapons, is it justified to intend to use them, giving the unlikelihood that their actual use could be justified? Some would argue that possessing nuclear weapons is an ethically acceptable deterrent but planning that actually represents the intention to use them is ethically unacceptable. Others argue that this posture would undermine the credibility of the deterrent so that at least the appearance of the intention to use the weapons is necessary. Then is bluff or threat justified for the sake of deterrence, though intentionally misleading? A great deal of literature in ethics dealing with deterrence revolves around puzzles like these.[6]

Often such discussions of deterrence strategies miss the ways these theoretical options are already operational in planning and how they function in relation to U.S. foreign policy more generally. Strategic deterrence in its most limited and justifiable sense "exists only to prevent the *use* of nuclear weapons by others."[7] Yet this has not been nor is it now the U.S. strategy of deterrence. The bishops report: "In our consultations, administration officials readily admitted that, while they hoped any nuclear exchange could be kept limited, they were prepared to retaliate in a massive way if necessary."[8] U.S. policy is clearly characterized by plans to use nuclear weapons as a retaliatory measure, regardless of the genuine possibility of planetary catastrophe. Furthermore, it is clear that the U.S. strategy includes first use of nuclear weapons under certain circumstances, chiefly Soviet aggression in Europe. Thus the U.S. is not prepared to reach a mutual agreement with the Soviet Union that neither side will first use nuclear weapons.

U.S. deterrence strategy goes far beyond the limited purpose of preventing the use of nuclear weapons. Randall Forsberg has recently argued that the function of nuclear deterrence is "to deter conventional warfare."[9] She continues: ". . . the initial goal of U.S. nuclear policy was not to protect U.S. cities by threatening retaliation against Soviet cities, but to deter conventional war by threatening Soviet cities as a target of last resort."[10] Moreover, Farraro and FitzGerald contend that deterrence for the U.S. has always included war-fighting capability. They believe the Reagan administration is in continuity with previous nuclear weapons policy. "By its proponents' own admission [Reagan administration], the war-fighting strategy is designed not merely to deter war, but to create the conditions in which the United States can use military power as it deems appropriate to pursue its general foreign policy objectives."[11] From the first, nuclear weapons have been integrated into an overall approach to foreign policy designed to contain the Soviet Union and to secure U.S. interests.[12]

In an ethical assessment of deterrence strategies, therefore, it is crucial to go beyond public rationalizations and narrow argumentation to actual plans and policies governing nuclear weapons and their function within the framework of broader U.S. foreign policy objectives. Deterrence strategies function under the broad umbrella of deterrence doctrine that justifies U.S. hegemonic orientation to international affairs.[13] Any attempt to critique deterrence ethically at the strategic level that does not push to the presuppositions of deterrence doctrine remains too superficial. Whereas most of the attention has been given to the level of strategy, the greater need is to critique the very doctrine that legitimates the arms race and renders any alternative unthinkable. One of the many virtues of the Bishops' Pastoral Letter is that it critiques deterrence at both levels.

Within the framework of disarmament, the bishops apply three criteria to nuclear weapons policy. Each of the criteria is so far removed from existing U.S. nuclear arms policy that the letter should have been more explicit in its moral repudiation of the meaning and function of deterrence. *First,* nuclear deterrence can be approved only if it serves to prevent the use of nuclear weapons. Any purposes that go beyond this are to be rejected. *Second,* nuclear deterrence strategies are to be evaluated on the basis of what is sufficient to deter, not on arithmetical equivalence nor superiority. Presumably, sufficiency here could mean a credible second-strike capability which would reduce considerably the number of weapons necessary for deterrence. *Third,* nuclear deterrence strategies are to be evaluated on the basis of whether they contribute to or make more unlikely progress toward disarmament. On the basis of these criteria, the bishops evaluate certain specific options within deterrence strategies. Although it is clear they heard and considered very seriously the call to reject deterrence entirely on moral grounds, they adopted instead the above "strictly conditioned moral acceptance of nuclear deterrence."[14] Such deterrence can provide a "peace of a sort" while the U.S. moves with urgency, intelligence and prudence to the objective of mutual progressive disarmament.[15]

The bishops have adopted a strictly conditioned view of nuclear deterrence as prudentially necessary in the movement from the threat of nuclear war to an authentic peace served by nuclear disarmament. A similar conclusion is reached by David Hollenbach, S.J., who argues that deterrence strategies should not be entirely repudiated but should be evaluated on the basis of "whether a concrete policy option will change the current situation in a way that decreases the probability of war and increases the possibility of arms reduction."[16] According to these views, the most likely way to achieve disarmament is through a provisional and limited acceptance of nuclear deterrence.

Even without rejecting strategic deterrence entirely, it is difficult to avoid the conclusion that U.S. policy has been and continues to be at such variance with the criteria enunciated by the U.S. bishops as to require specific repudiation. This will be even more evident if, as seems likely, the U.S. continues a deterrence strategy that has little relation to the fundamental moral priority of disarmament. Then, it will be a question of how long the bishops will wait before they speak out that progress toward disarmament is being delayed, that U.S. deterrence strategies violate the criteria of strictly conditioned acceptability, and that Roman Catholics are to be in clear opposition to U.S. nuclear weapons policy.

While it is not unimportant to analyze critically strategies of deterrence, preoccupation with the logic of reasoning behind strategic options and issues has meant that the doctrine of nuclear deterrence has not been sufficiently scrutinized. While persons debate counterforce and countervalue strategies, it is assumed that one or the other is necessary. Options outside the framework of conventional deterrence strategies are not considered. Moreover, attention is given to particular weapons such as the MX or the Pershing II without attending to the overall orientation to nuclear weapons and U.S./Soviet relations. Arms control talks are governed by the intricacies of deterrence strategies and have not been contexts in which serious efforts at arms reduction and disarmament have even been attempted. So long as analysis and evaluation remain at the strategic level, the doctrine of deterrence itself determines the issues and options which are to be considered realistic.

More important, then, than ethical analysis of deterrence strategies is analysis and evaluation of the doctrine of deterrence and not solely on the basis of internal logic but also political experience. As Seymour Melman has counseled peace activists against focusing on particular questions of arms control: "[They] should not get snarled up in a coast-to-coast debate and discussion about no first use while the factories continue turning out material . . ."[17] In the current debate in the U.S. the most important level is perspectival, and the two chief alternatives are the continuation of the deterrence doctrine or its replacement with disarmament doctrine.

Deterrence Doctrine

Most frequently ethical critiques of deterrence doctrine have pointed to the catastrophic consequences of either accidental or intentional use of nuclear weapons. Even though such weapons have not been used since 1945, this can be no assurance against their use in the future. So long as superpowers possess and continue to increase the number of these weapons, the long-range prospect for human survival is at tremendous risk. Therefore there is a moral imperative to seek to provide security in a fundamentally different way. This is the ethical perspective of the Catholic Bishops and of Jonathan Schell as well. A great deal of recent literature is devoted to vivid depictions of what would happen in a nuclear war in order to demonstrate the dangers of continuing to rely on nuclear deterrence for security. In the face of such awesome destructiveness other considerations are relativized and diminished in import. George Kennan speaks of our duty not just to ourselves but also "to the continuity of the generations, our duty to the great experiment of civilized life on this rare and rich and marvelous planet . . ."[18] For him there are only two basic options: a disarmament course in which there are dangers yet a faint hope, or a deterrence course in which there can be no hope at all. In calculating risks of the two courses, the risks of continuing the arms race are much greater than the risks of taking steps to reverse the arms race.

Although the argument based on risks and dangers is central to ethical critiques of deterrence, there are additional assumptions and dynamics in deterrence doctrine that also need to be critiqued.

The *first* is anticipated in the quotation from Kennan above. Deterrence doctrine is characterized by a fatalism or a silence about the future. Deterrence advocates assume we live in a world which will presumably always involve nuclear deterrence. We have established a structure for national security which is basically in place. It is unrealistic to think that anything other than revisions of this structure can be accomplished. Hence, the implicit if not stated conception of the future is one characterized by ever more sophisticated weaponry targeted at real or imagined enemies as the price that must be paid to deter aggression. Alternative futures are rejected because deterrence doctrine will not permit persons to imagine that national and international security could be established on any other basis. Is it possible to shape a future that is not dominated by nuclear terror? In deterrence doctrine, the answer is "no." History is perceived to be on a basically unalterable course which we can only seek to manage and shape in a prudent way.

Disarmament advocates challenge this assumption, arguing that human beings are not fated to live out the logic of deterrence but have the capacity to move history on a different course. Humans have the moral responsibility to make decisions which shape the future rather than passively to acquiesce in deterministic forces. It is a particularly rich human characteristic to imagine a different way to deal with intractable problems than conventional ways, to imagine a different future than predominant features of the present would seem to dictate. Disarmament advocates are not sanguine about the ease with which imagination could shape a different future, but they are committed to the intellectual and political tasks involved in such a project. At minimum, there is an ethical responsibility to test out vigorously and persistently alternatives to deterrence rather than merely to assume that this is the only way realistically, however precarious, to provide for security.

Second, deterrence doctrine has failed to provide the stability and security its advocates promised. The nuclear arms race continues and even timid efforts at arms control do not halt the nuclear escalation. Deterrence does not lead to a relatively stable and fixed balance of nuclear arsenals. It has led to a never-ending spiral of competitiveness between the U.S. and the U.S.S.R. in the magnitude and number of nuclear weapons and to the prospect of widespread proliferation among other nations. Superiority and inferiority in nuclear strength are endlessly debated and never resolved. Arithmetical advantages and disadvantages are used as trump cards in seeking concessions or increased budgets in an esoteric game of deterrence scholasticism. Instead of providing security and stability in relations between the U.S. and the U.S.S.R., each side feels anxiously compelled to catch up or to remain a step ahead lest the other gain an advantage. Heightened anxiety and insecurity, if not inherent in the doctrine of deterrence, represent the political experience of having lived under its reign.

Recent deployment of Pershing II missiles in Europe is a clear example of the insecurity that emerges out of deterrence doctrine. Because the Pershing IIs can reach Moscow in five or six minutes from Europe, the Soviets are considering a "launch on warning" policy for their missiles. "Launch on warning" would mean that decisions about the use of nuclear weapons will not be made by responsible officials but will be built into computer systems. The danger of nuclear war by accident is clearly heightened by such a development. Additional examples of destabilization can be provided as well. New weapons systems such as the cruise missile present great difficulties for verification. Others such as the MX are tied to war-fighting strategies which render nuclear war more thinkable. Still other technological possibilities for weaponry are continually being developed, such as the utilization of satellites and orbital space stations. Political experience gives us no grounds for hope that reasonable stability and security can be provided under the governing doctrine of deterrence. This then lends strong support for the need to pursue disarmament as an alternative way to approach such objectives.

Third, deterrence doctrine has not proved capable of generating discriminating judgments about which weapons are necessary to deter and which are not. Although some proponents of a narrow or strict interpretation of strategic deterrence (only to prevent the use of nuclear weapons) do so precisely in hope that discriminating judgments can and will be made, our experience to date should make us very skeptical about this possibility. Michael Novak has written: "A deterrent system must be reasoned and thorough; it must cover every major contingency."[19] When this is the prevailing interpretation of deterrence in shaping nuclear weapons policies, it is understandable why deterrence is used to justify every new arms proposal that comes through the military technological system. Technical possibilities easily become translated into national security necessities through the use of deterrence justification. Everything technologically feasible becomes strategically necessary in order to cover an endless range of contingencies.

No matter how vigorously persons may want to redeem deterrence from its promiscuous applications to a more rigorous one, their hope seems idealistic indeed. So long as deterrence doctrine remains pre-eminent in arms policy it is far more likely that it will function to legitimate a continuation of the arms race as it has in the past than to keep the arms race under a tight rein. As the bishops have shown, it is possible to change the paradigm from deterrence to disarmament while still maintaining on pragmatic grounds a limited place for deterrence strategies. It is far more likely that this far more narrow view of deterrence can be maintained under the doctrine of disarmament than under deterrence doctrine.

Fourth, and perhaps most important, deterrence doctrine has fostered a militarization of U.S. approaches to national security and foreign policy, devaluing diplomatic, political and economic efforts. George Kennan speaks passionately and eloquently about this development:

". . . this anxious competition in the development of new armaments; this blind dehumanization of the prospective adversary; this systematic distortion of that adversary's motivation and intentions; this steady displacement of political considerations by military ones in the calculation of statesmanship: in short, this dreadful militarization of the entire East-West relationship in concept, in rhetoric, and in assumption, which is the commanding feature— endlessly dangerous, endlessly discouraging—of this present unhappy day."[20]

Nuclear deterrence arose in tandem with increasing tension between the U.S. and the U.S.S.R. following World War II. An evaluation of deterrence cannot take place without careful attention to assumptions about the Soviet Union and U.S./U.S.S.R. relations. In significant part U.S. policy toward the Soviet Union has been militarized because the primary threat is perceived to be military aggression and the primary way to deal with it is perceived to be through military containment. Deterrence arises out of and continues to feed the assumption that the central way for the U.S. to deal with the U.S.S.R. is militarily, specifically the threat of force. Consequently, deterrence advocates have generally argued that it is only in the context of U.S. military credibility that the Soviet Union will be moved to negotiate seriously on such matters as arms control and reduction. Yet, again our political experience has given us little reason to hope that deterrence will ever lead to effective negotiation over nuclear weapons. The few agreements that have been negotiated do not alter the basic dynamics of the arms race itself.

George Kennan regards U.S. views of the Soviet Union as gross exaggerations that render it impossible to engage in a reasonable assessment of Soviet policy and possibilities for reaching agreement. Since deterrence rests on hostility, threats and fear, one could hardly expect this doctrine to contribute to the cultivation of an environment of civility in which negotiation is possible. In Kennan's view the militarization of U.S./Soviet relations rests on dangerous rather than sober and realistic views both of ourselves and of the Soviet Union. If we could demilitarize our attitudes and approaches, it would be possible to improve relations significantly through greater attention to political, economic, diplomatic and cultural initiatives. Although there is little likelihood for a genuinely friendly relation between the two superpowers, the possibility for significant agreements is available.[21] Since deterrence and militarization of Soviet/U.S. relations are so thoroughly interrelated, the only realistic way to achieve demilitarization is through replacing deterrence assumptions with disarmament objectives.

Fifth, and similarly, deterrence has led to the increasing militarization of American society. Even if it could be proven that nuclear deterrence has prevented the use of nuclear weapons, this alone would not provide adequate justification. First, this would not prove that other policies could not also provide such protection. Second, the costs of the arms race on the U.S. economy and, more broadly, on our society and the world are tremendously high. Huge amounts of human and material resources are invested in the arms race rather than in other kinds of endeavor potentially more beneficial. The Catholic bishops write: "If the arms race in all its dimensions is not reversed, resources will not be available for the human needs so evident in many parts of the globe and in our own country as well."[22] An ethical evaluation of deterrence requires an assessment of its impact on national economies, structures of international relations, and especially on those peoples who suffer from militarization, poverty and injustice. It is not enough to question the impact of deterrence on nuclear weapons policies alone. It is also essential to ask about the character of societies and international relations that are being fashioned out of this doctrinal framework.

The U.S. has developed an economy that is vitally dependent on military priorities with damaging consequences to other economic sectors and functions. Many persons, organizations and institutions are integrated into the network of a militarized society. This leads to widespread dependence on, even addiction to, weapons technology quite apart from requirements of international security. Deterrence has provided the justification for such militarization. Because of the many ways citizens' self-interest is woven into the fabric of the arms race, deterrence is seen as necessary to protect the kinds of positions, jobs, and corporate enterprises persons have come to depend on for their livelihood as well as to prevent Soviet aggression.

The needs for militarization are systematized in American life. The Soviet threat is required to perpetuate the system created by deterrence. Perceptions of the Soviet Union are shaped as much or more by those who have a vested interest in portraying them as our deadly enemy as by those who have studied the Soviet Union carefully. If the Soviets were not in fact a serious military threat, there would still be tremendous pressure to exaggerate the danger or to transfer our fears to another couuntry in order to maintain the military industrial orde that has been spawned by deterrence doctrine. There seems to be no way out of this fatal symbiosis of militarism and deterrence without shifting to the entirely different orientation of disarmament. As this will call for thoroughgoing changes in nuclear arms policies, it will also involve similarly sweeping changes in the structures of our society and of international relations.

Conclusion

In conclusion, it is essential that deterrence be evaluated ethically not only at strategic levels but even more important at the doctrinal level. The heart of the critique is not only the dangers of nuclear war but also the failure of deterrence at the level of lived historical experience to provide a credible hope for security, peace and justice in international relations. U.S. life is consumed by the necessities of the nuclear arms race which has been justified by the doctrine of deterrence. It is implausible that an alternative interpretation of deterrence could affect the fundamental changes that will be necessary to change our historical course. Disarmament best captures the alternative framework within which to develop the kinds of changes that will be needed.

In this analysis nuclear disarmament is proposed as a framework, perspective or long-range objective for national and international security. After decades of being regarded as foolishly idealistic, disarmament is becoming genuinely thinkable as a practicable alternative necessary to consider. The primary change needed is the paradigm shift from deterrence to disarmament. Within the disarmament paradigm, there are numerous and varying strategic proposals. President Kennedy presented the last serious and thorough disarmament proposal by the U.S. government in 1962. About the same time Charles Osgood argued in his GRIT proposal that the U.S. could reverse the arms race by taking unilateral initiatives and invite the Soviets to reciprocate. Unilateral initiatives would be significant in reversing the momentum without rendering the U.S. vulnerable to Soviet aggression. More recently, George Kennan has made several suggestions, making it clear that there are any number of ways to break decisively with the arms race mentality. His best known proposal is for the U.S. president to propose a 50 percent across the board reduction of nuclear arsenals to the Soviet Union and, if this were successful, to press for further reductions.[23]

Each of the various strategies for disarmament will need scrutiny and widespread discussion. Many are variations of a similar strategy: First there is a need for a decisive and bold step by the U.S. to break out of the vicious spiral of the arms race and to initiate the movement toward disarmament. This then would be followed by negotiations, probably outside the public glare, to reach agreement about mutual reductions in carefully designed step-by-step processes. The bishops' proposal is somewhat more cautious, supporting such efforts as "immediate, bilateral, verifiable agreements to halt the testing, production, and deployment of new nuclear weapons systems;" "negotiated bilateral deep cuts" in the nuclear arsenals of both the U.S. and the U.S.S.R., and a negotiated comprehensive test ban treaty.[24]

There is not an absence of strategies for pursuing disarmament, from more cautious to more bold. Most include something of the bishops' "strictly conditional moral acceptance" of deterrence as the movement toward nuclear disarmament proceeds, and their emphasis on "sufficiency" in the meantime. In the interim, a "sufficient" deterrent is adequate to serve the only justification for deterrence, i.e., to prevent the use of nuclear weapons.

The chief objection to moving from deterrence to disarmament is that we do not know if disarmament can be achieved. But it is clear that disarmament has never been pressed with seriousness. Alan Geyer writes: "In almost every government, the basic reality is the same: *defense* is a top-level, high priority, high-prestige, well-financed, well-propagandized operation of senior cabinet rank, while *disarmament* is a low-level, underbudgeted, under-staffed, invisible and anonymous subdivision in the policy hierarchy."[25] The U.S. has been no more serious about disarmament than the Soviets. Both countries have been interlocked in the deterrence dance. It is not until disarmament has been persistently attempted that its practicality or impracticality can be established. Most proposals for disarmament involve a progression of steps and mutual agreement, thus not putting international security at risk while disarmament is pursued. Security is at much greater risk if the nuclear arms race continues under the deterrence doctrine.

Clearly the major element in the movement from deterrence to disarmament is U.S. perceptions about the Soviet Union. If conventional perceptions of the Soviet Union are heavily flawed, as George Kennan believes they are, then the primary justification for almost forty years of nuclear deterrence has collapsed. One does not have to "trust the Russians" nor regard Soviet power as benign to develop the case that disarmament is in the interest of both the Soviet Union and the United States.

As the Catholic bishops have maintained, there can be no morally convincing basis for regarding deterrence as the long-range strategy for pursuing a more just and peaceful world. Disarmament is the historical alternative which we must pursue with the creativity, imaginativeness and boldness of which humans are capable.

ENDNOTES

1. Reinhold Niebuhr, *Love and Justice*, edited by D. B. Robertson (Cleveland: World Publishing Co., 1957), pp. 235-237.
2. National Conference of Catholic Bishops, *The Challenge of Peace: God's Promise and Our Response* (Washington: United States Catholic Conference, 1983), #3.
3. *Ibid.*, #186.
4. *Ibid.*, #178.
5. George Kennan, *The Nuclear Delusion* (New York: Pantheon Books, 1983), p. 107.
6. See J. E. Hare and Carey B. Joynt, *Ethics and International Affairs* (New York: St. Martin's Press, 1982), pp. 101-124.
7. National Conference of Catholic Bishops, *op. cit.*, #188; also Theodore Draper, "Nuclear Temptations," *The New York Review of Books* (January 19, 1984), pp. 42-48.
8. National Conference of Catholic Bishops, *op. cit.*, #180.
9. Randall Forsberg, "Confining the Military to Defense as a Route to Disarmament," *World Policy Journal* (Winter, 1984), pp. 285-318.
10. *Ibid.*, p. 299.
11. Vincent Ferraro and Kathleen FitzGerald, "The End of a Strategic Era: A Proposal for Minimal Deterrence," *World Policy Journal* (Winter, 1984), pp. 339-360.
12. *Ibid.*, pp. 339-340.
13. George Shepherd, "Non-Dominance and Self-Reliance: New Basis for American Foreign Policy," Occasional Paper of the Colorado Consortium on International Policy, Denver, Colorado (1984).
14. National Conference of Catholic Bishops, *op. cit.*, #!86.
15. *Ibid.*, #189.
16. David Hollenbach, S. J., *Nuclear Ethics* (New York: Paulist Press, 1983), p. 76.
17. Seymour Melman, "Disarmament Out of the Dustbin," *Sojourners* (September, 1983), p. 30.
18. Kennan, *op. cit.*, p. 182.
19. Quoted in Hollenbach, *op. cit.*, p. 72.
20. Kennan, *op. cit.*, p. 141.
21. *Ibid.*, pp. 102-126.
22. National Conference of Catholic Bishops, *op. cit.*, #271.
23. Kennan, *op. cit.*, pp. 180-181.
24. National Conference of Catholic Bishops, *op. cit.*, #191.
25. Alan Geyer, *The Idea of Disarmament* (Elgin, Illinois: The Brethren Press, 1982), p. 144.

Ethics and Tactics of Resistance

A CHRISTIAN ETHIC
OF RESISTANCE IN
A WAR-MAKING SOCIETY

Walter E. Wiest

What are the ethics of peace*making*? Specifically, what *means* are ethically approvable in working for policies that make for peace? There are ethical problems here, for the available means are both legal and illegal, violent and non-violent. Which of them are ethically justifiable? In the name of peace, is it ethical to enter a munitions plant (trespass) and hammer the nose cone of a missile (violence against property)? Is it morally right or wrong to attempt to obstruct operations of a military installation? Is it ever right to break the law, even in a good cause? Is lobbying in legislative halls an unfair effort to impose the views of a minority upon the majority of other citizens? Should employees in weapons-making industries resign as a moral protest? These and other such questions are the subject of this essay.

We assume in this essay that peacemaking is an ethical goal for Christians. Our concern is with the ethics of means rather than of the end or objective. We should be aware, however, that an end or goal may be embraced by different persons for different reasons, and that these reasons may make for different judgments about some of the means to be used. Some who work for peace are absolute pacifists or devotees of absolute non-violence. Some are nuclear pacifists. Some perhaps hold that there might have been justifiable wars in the past, but modern war—even of the so-called conventional kind—is unconscionable. Some still argue for the justifiability of conventional warfare under certain conditions, but hold that many current policies of our government make more for war than for peace, and increase the risk of escalation toward nuclear war. Of those who agree that nuclear war cannot be justified, some argue for unilateral nuclear disarmament; others, for retaining the weapons as deterrents until we can reduce or remove them by negotiation.

It is important to recognize such differences just so that we can join forces as much as possible in the interests of peace. If we are aware of the differences we shall be better able to define the things on which we can agree and be sensitive to points at which disagreements might arise. Many, if not all, of those in the above categories can agree on something like the following:

1. There is nothing that can justify a nuclear war. It would be both immoral and futile.

2. A "limited nuclear war" is either a fantasy or at least would present too much of a risk of escalation to full-scale nuclear conflict.

3. Therefore, every effort must be made to control and reduce nuclear armaments, and to avoid military responses to international conflicts and tensions.

4. It is a serious mistake to suppose that we can force Russia into accepting our terms for arms control by our becoming so superior in armaments that they will have no other option. The attempt to do this simply escalates the arms race.

5. While the danger of nuclear war is of paramount concern, it is also wrong to rely primarily on conventional military force and the threat of force as we are doing in too many situations now. Current policies in Central America and recent ones in Lebanon are instances. Conflicts which arise from long-standing economic and political injustices or cultural and religious differences cannot be resolved simply by sending in military advisers and equipment into Honduras or firing naval guns into Lebanese hills. While there may be disagreements among us as to how the U.S. might justifiably use its power to protect its legitimate interests in such situations, we can surely agree that we need less bellicosity and more statesmanship, and more sympathy with those who struggle for liberty and justice in which we profess also to believe.[1]

If we are united on these things, we then have a responsibility to work for policies consistent with them. As Christians, our primary motivation and the basic criteria by which we judge what is right to do are theological; that is, they are to be derived from the content of Christian faith. The extent and nature of our responsibilities is also determined in part by the social context in which we find ourselves. There are negative limits; there are some things we cannot do. (We cannot worship an emperor.) What we can and should do depends partly on the opportunities available to us in our social environment.[2] The early Christians lived in an undemocratic empire and had no significant political power. We live in a constitutional democracy, however imperfect. A democratic order has at least two features: it attempts to provide protection of certain basic rights and it attempts to provide opportunities for all to participate in political processes. We shall have occasion to speak of rights in certain connections, but shall be primarily concerned with political participation. When Christian ethics calls for approval of some policies against others on matters of great ethical importance, Christians in a democracy have an obligation to take political action for or against particular policies.

Our commitment to peace is positive and we are committed first to supporting and promoting positively peaceful attitudes and policies. The present widespread concern about peace is based on a deeply felt misgiving about present policies which seem too war-prone or militaristic; however, our immediate focus is upon means of protest or resistance. This is the more so because of the realization that in the dangerous world in which we live, unsound policies may result in catastrophe at any moment. Time presses. Governments on the other hand are not always responsive to citizens' opinions, even when they are strongly held by large numbers or even by a large majority. To bring about change often requires building substantial political pressures, and the less time there is, the more pressure is needed. Thus the immediate emphasis is on the negative, on opposition to policies and programs which we believe need changing. At the same time it should be said that all the measures to be considered here, however forceful some may be, also have the aim of communication and persuasion and of provoking and contributing to public debate on the issues.

We shall be paying particular attention to the tactics of withdrawal from war related vocations, to the "Watch for Peace" in Nicaragua, the Sanctuary movement for El Salvadoran refugees, resistance to military draft, and other civil disobedience tactics including tax withholding (which is discussed more thoroughly in other essays). It has already been mentioned that the means of protest or resistance fall into the categories of legal and illegal, violent and non-violent. None being considered here involves violence against persons, only against property (vandalism). Classifications are not exclusive; some actions are non-violent but illegal, some are both legal and non-violent. Job resignation and the Nicaragua Watch, e.g., are both legal and non-violent. Sanctuary and tax-withholding are illegal but non-violent. All acts of civil disobedience are (by definition) law-breaking, but some involve no violence, while others involve damage done to property. In Christian ethics, illegality and violence require special justification.

There is another item, that of force or coercion, which reveals the fact that it is not always easy to distinguish between violence and non-violence. (A similar difficulty arises sometimes between legal and illegal, as we shall see later.) Black persons have pointed out that racial injustice does psychological and social, as well as physical, violence to persons. In the political area, pressure tactics in a sense force or coerce political decisions[3] or attempt to do so, even if they do not make use of physical violence. The tactics which perhaps come closest to violence are those which attempt to obstruct or impede some activity. For instance, if a protest demonstration includes occupying a place of business not only to communicate a message effectively and dramatically but also in order to halt operations, that is obstruction. While admitting some ambiguity, we shall take it that as long as the protesters do not fight back when others attempt to remove them (though they may go limp to make it more difficult), they are still being non-violent.

Legal and Non-Violent Actions

Tactics which are non-violent and within the law are ethically most readily justifiable. Except for those who would separate Christian faith from politics altogether, there would seem to be no objection to working for political ends by attempting to persuade or educate. Producing and disseminating printed materials (from leaflets to books), seeking access to media where possible (at least writing letters to editors), issuing public statements, using audio-visual materials, conducting educational programs, study groups, teach-ins—all seem unobjectionable per se. To be ethically responsible, we need only ask which actions are likely to be most effective in any situation, and now to do them well.

[231]

Other options are more directly political *action*. There are protest marches and demonstrations and picketing, which can be done quite within the law and have become recognized means of participation in political processes and public debate on important issues. There are also lobbying efforts with legislators, and testimony before legislative committees when opportunity affords. There are objections to certain kinds of lobbying, but as long as it is done within legal rules and for ethical ends, we take it as a legitimate part of the democratic process. It is a way of bringing constituents' views directly to their legislators. Then there are activities within partisan politics such as working within party organizations or in election campaigns for positions and candidates favorable to peacemaking. The only serious question for us about these things is which ways of speaking and acting are appropriate for *churches*, and which ones are partisan enough so that they should be undertaken by Christians who group together for such purposes and who do not attempt to represent the church as a whole. We shall not try to resolve that question but only analyze the issues ethically for those of us who are ready and able to act.[4]

To this category also belongs the act of *resigning from a job*, where the job seems too closely connected with morally unacceptable armaments or with policies that seem to make for war rather than peace. This could affect persons working in private industry (munitions plants, most obviously) or in government (Departments of Defense or of State, e.g.). The act is an especially individual one, though it may well have political effects and motives. Individuals may reach a point where they feel they must act strictly for conscience' sake: "Here I stand, I can do no other." Since our interest is in political action we are concerned with cases in which the intent is also to communicate, to witness for peace. It is important to say, however, that as Christians we act out of this same sort of conscientiousness even when we are being most political. We act for the right, "as God gives us to see the right," in Lincoln's words. Some things we should or should not do, regardless of consequences. But we also must have an eye to effects or consequences if we are to be fully responsible, and this is especially true in political action. We are committed to what might affect policies and programs.

Resignation from a job represents such loss for an individual—and for the individual's family, if there is one—that one is tempted to say that only another who faces the same sacrifice has a right to urge it. Still, to state the arguments pro and con might be helpful.

Against such a move, it might be argued that while it might satisfy one's conscience, it won't have much practical effect. It is too individual an act, not many will do it, and it will not get much notice. Someone else will step into the job, and it will not impede production as can, for instance, the refusal of a union to do certain work. Without concern for practical effects, satisfying conscience or assuaging personal guilt can become a rather selfish motive. Also, other jobs not so obviously connected with armaments or warlike policies are still part of the system and we all share responsibility. A seminary professor is just as involved as a munitions worker. Therefore, not only is there no special reason for some to quit their jobs, there is no escaping responsibility in another job. The one who resigns will still be in the system. Finally, if a family is affected, this is another and more immediate responsibility to which some would give priority and greater weight, perhaps even if the family agreed to the resignation.

In response, it can be argued, first, that while concern for effects or consequences for doing something politically effective is essential; there are some things we cannot do, regardless of consequences. Although we may differ on what some of these things are, we can honor those who differ and share their motivation. The fact that someone else will do the job cannot override the conviction, "But I cannot do it!" It is never a sound ethical argument to say that one might as well do something one is convinced is wrong just because someone else will do it. But this act is not for the admittedly sometimes selfish motive of keeping one's own skirts clean and reinforcing one's own sense of righteousness. The person who does this is concerned about others, about the effects of policies and armaments on people, here and abroad. The aim is also to make a public statement and provoke further thought and public debate, and some others will hear about it, especially one's fellow-workers. Some others might even be persuaded to do likewise.[5] It is true that we all share responsibility for these things in our society, but it is wrong not to recognize different kinds and degrees of responsibility. On the one hand, the German manufacturers who contracted to produce ovens to cremate Jews should not be permitted to claim that they were only doing business and had no share in the moral guilt of the concentration camp commandant. On the other hand, Dietrich Bonhoeffer, who acknowledged his sense of sharing in the guilt of his nation, class, and church, nevertheless gave his life as a member of the resistance to the Nazi regime, and surely no reasonable person would insist that he was equally guilty with the others. It is crucial that we see the parallels to our own present situation.[6]

We should not talk of "responsibility" only in an abstract sense. When we are involved in activities which are hurting people and have the potentiality of doing further harm, we have a way of becoming insensitive to the persons being hurt. We have become familiar with one of the ethical problems about modern warfare, that its mechanization often removes military persons from the effects of what they do and thus deadens or fails to arouse their feelings. Bomber crews, e.g., do not *see* persons dismembered by their bombs, and thus tend not to *feel* what is happening. In a less dramatic version, government officials who deal with things at the policy level must be at least sorely tempted to forget or repress their feelings about what policies often do to persons. We do not point the finger of blame self-righteously; this is a general human failing. The point is that those who resign from certain war-related jobs seem not to have lost this sensitivity to the effects of what they are helping to make. They should be honored for this.

As for the family situation, obviously this is something for the individual to decide together with spouse and children, and the rest of us must honor the decision. It would be wrong, of course, for the jobholder to act without reference to the family. On the other hand, families can be supportive of the decision to resign. The rest of us can only provoke the issues, offer counsel when asked, and support and help when someone makes the move. There is no question, however, that the move itself is ethically justifiable.

Also falling into the category of legal and non-violent actions is the Watch for

Peace movement in Nicaragua. This grew out of the experience of twenty-eight religious leaders from North Carolina who went to Nicaragua in April, 1983, to try to find out what was happening under the Sandinista regime and what U.S. policies and agencies were doing there. They discovered, among other things, that when they visited an area on the border between Nicaragua and Honduras, in which attacks had been occurring by the Contras (backed and organized by the C.I.A. and the U.S. military in Honduras), an expected attack did not occur. From this it was deduced that the presence of U.S. citizens in the area might serve to inhibit such attacks and contribute to a search for non-military solutions to the problems in Central America generally. To this was added the group's conclusions that the U.S. government's characterizations of the Sandinista regime as "totalitarian" or "terrorist" were untrue and unfair (though they recognized that the regime is criticizable as undemocratic in some ways) and that the U.S. role in Nicaragua and Central America overall has been in essential respects contradictory to our own professed standards of freedom and justice.[7] The result was the Watch for Peace movement, which enlists volunteers who go into a border area in Nicaragua to share in the life of the people and in worship services and demonstrations which exhibit a Christian "presence" there. The means are entirely non-violent and, while opposed to official U.S. policy, are not illegal. The purpose of the movement has been stated by Dr. Arnold Snyder, Managua Coordinator of WFP:

> We are not "anti-U.S. government." To the contrary, as Christians who are also U.S. citizens, we are calling our government to return to the high and worthy principles of justice on which this nation was founded. We are convinced that our government's funding of terrorism is immoral and a betrayal of this country's stated principles . . . in protest, repentance and contrition, we have resolved to stand with the victims.[8]

There can and will be differences about judgments of fact in such situations, even among persons who agree as to principles. If some Christians believe honestly that U.S. policies in Central America are contrary to our country's own ideals and principles, and if (as we maintain is the case) a large body of evidence and analysis supports this view, then these Christians justifiably involve themselves in projects like Watch for Peace. They have it in their favor ethically that they have no discernible selfish motivation, that they do this at some considerable self-sacrifice, that they expose themselves to risk of bodily injury and politically inspired reprisals. Even those who disagree might be moved by their sincerity.

From Nicagaragua we could move readily to the Sanctuary movement in which churches or church groups are sheltering Salvadoran refugees from U.S. government authorities who would send them back to El Salvador. Since this activity is illegal on the face of it—that is, it goes against policy of duly constituted authorities who claim to be acting in accordance with existing law—it comes under the heading of civil disobedience. But this is a rather complicated subject to which some attention must now be given before addressing the sanctuary issue in particular.

Civil Disobedience

Acts of civil disobedience involve law-breaking but are ethically motivated[9] and are directed against a law or policy[10] thought to be seriously immoral. A common definition is that such acts must be (1) non-violent, (2) public (not clandestine) and (3) submissive (with readiness to submit to legal penalties). The definition clearly fits Martin Luther King's sort of protest. We shall not be quite so fastidious, but shall include some acts which involve violence against property.[11]

The most commonly occurring kind of civil disobedience is connected with protest marches, demonstrations and picketing. These things can be done within the law but demonstrators may also do something illegal. Perhaps the most familiar instance is that of the anti-segregation demonstrations of the 1950's and early 1960's, which involved defiance of local segregation laws. Sometimes demonstrators will add an illegal act to an otherwise lawful protest. For instance, in May, 1983, the "Ground Zero" group who were picketing the Trident submarine base in Bangor, Washington, decided to go inside the fence and walk down some railroad tracks on the base property, thus committing trespass.[12] On another occasion, some of the group used rowboats to try to block the channels used by submarines entering or leaving the base, an act of attempted obstruction which was also illegal. Part of a group demonstrating at the Seneca Army Depot in New York from which Pershing II missiles were to be shipped to Europe went under the fence and were arrested in October, 1983. In December, some tried to blockade the airstrip with their bodies, an illegal act of obstruction.[13] The "Ploughshares Eight" added property destruction to trespass by invading the plant of the General Electric Company in King of Prussia, Pennsylvania, and hammering the nose cones of nuclear missiles.[14] During the Vietnam era several groups damaged draft files. Others sat in at draft offices in protest against both the Vietnam war and the military draft, some of them with intent to obstruct as well as to register protest. Refusal to sign up for the draft may also have the aim of obstruction as well as protest and individual resistance.

Acts of civil disobedience can be located roughly on an ascending scale of difficulty as regards ethical justification. This does not mean that the more difficult justifications are necessarily any less valid or compelling. "Difficulty" simply means greater complexity due to certain factors having been added. The least complex are those which consist of *direct* disobedience of a law which is considered both immoral and unconstitutional (i.e., wrong legally in view of a higher law). Such were the anti-segregationist protests of the fifties and sixties. They involved disobedience of local or state laws in the confidence that such laws violated constitutional rights. When the protest is against broader policies, however, there may be no particular laws available as immediate targets. One may then have to choose a target which is *indirect,* but *related* (e.g., a draft board or a military installation munitions factory).[15] Next, when an illegal act (e.g., trespass) is *added* to an otherwise lawful action, additional justification is needed. Attempts to *obstruct* an operation raise further questions. Finally, *damage to property* involves the issue of violence.

The first ethical problem is posed by our obligation to the laws of the state. God is God of order, not anarchy, and some political ordering of life is necessary (the message of Rom. 13 and I Pet. 2). Ordinarily, Christians are to be law-abiding. But law is not absolute. Christians have from the first resisted when the state's demands ran counter to faith (cf. Rev. 13). "We must obey God and not men;" "God alone is Lord of the conscience." Especially in the Calvinist tradition, the view developed that resistance is justified to laws or regimes which are egregiously unjust and tyrannical. There is also that Puritan concept of political covenant which envisioned political authority as not being bestowed upon a monarch and exercised upon subjects, but as being first established between God and people, with governmental officials subject to the covenant's moral requirements. This has similarities to secular "social contract" theories of government, which influenced the founders of the U.S.A. along with Puritan ideas. One implication is that a law or government policy which is inconsistent with the "values" (including moral principles) for which the state is supposed to stand has forfeited its claim to obedience. Reinforcing this conclusion is the conviction that obligation is owed first to one's fellow-citizens and secondarily to the state.[16] This does not mean that we are entitled to disobey every law which displeases us. It applies only to those which raise very serious problems of conscience and which are particularly threatening to peace, justice of freedom.[17] Douglas Sturm has recently put the matter well:

> Law is not merely what a constitution ordains or a legislature commands. Law is an instrument for realizing fundamental rights and securing the common good. . . . Paradoxical though it may seem, current movements engaged in civil disobedience throughout the country demonstrate a deeper devotion to rule of law than those whose high office was designed to uphold the constitution.[18]

Ethical justification of civil disobedience, then, appeals to moral principles for which we believe the law should stand. It assumes that the system still exhibits enough justice and common good to merit continued loyalty and overall obedience.[19] In fact, some of the moral principles are already in law, especially in the federal constitution and Supreme Court interpretations, often reinforced by legislation such as civil rights laws. These provide the most ready justification of obedience to particular laws, for they at least mitigate the factor of law-breaking. There is some argument whether acts covered by such principles are really illegal at all, since they are obedient to a higher law within the system.

It is not always certain, of course, which principles may apply and how. This is a reason for trying out some actions, for only court rulings in test cases can determine such questions. Test cases may also be the occasion for adding to the moral elements in the law. H. L. A. Hart speaks of the "penumbra" of uncertainty which surrounds the possible applications of some laws. Justice Cardozo spoke of "gaps" or "interstices" where the law does not explicitly cover certain cases.[20] At such points, judges must make use of other materials, including moral principles which express something of our sense of what constitutes justice and the common good. R. M. Dworkin has criticized Hart for looking upon such principles as being introduced into the law at the discretion of judges instead of seeing them as already part of the law.[21] At any rate, they certainly become law when incorporated in majority opinions. Thus through test cases the law may be morally amplified as well as further justification given for civilly disobedient acts. This also means that we do not have to be sure that our action will be covered by higher law, only that we have a reasonable belief that it should be.

Sanctuary

Turning back to the sanctuary movement, we find a situation in which those involved are convinced they are resisting an illegal policy imposed by the present administration. As one spokesperson has said:

> We ask only that the Reagan Administration obey the law. The 1980 Refugee Act, passed by Congress, guarantees that victims of political persecution be granted this "Temporary Extended Departure Status." It says that anyone who has a reasonable fear of persecution is eligible for this treatment. The Reagan Administration says we are violating the law, but it is the INS (Immigration and Naturalization Service) that is refusing to enforce the Refugee Act. There's never any problem getting asylum if you're from a Communist country. But somehow, those fleeing persecution at the hands of governments we support are generally denied. It's that inconsistency we protest.[22]

The administration's position is that these Salvadorans are not refugees but are only seeking economic opportunities in this country. Enough has been published about the oppressiveness of conditions in El Salvador to make it clear that large numbers of people can and have been jailed, tortured and killed for political reasons. The administration has obviously been embarrassed by these facts, and while maintaining in regard to the refugees that there is no problem, has at the same time argued in Congress (where aid to El Salvador has been tied to human rights stipulations) that there has been improvement in this non-existent situation. It finally proposed and jockeyed through Congress an aid proposal detached from any requirement of progress in human rights. Administration figures like Jeane Kirkpatrick have expressed the view that we should not hold our allies or friendly regimes to the same standards of human rights as we should unfriendly ones. Recent events seem to show that the present administration has been trying to get around the human rights requirement of Congress. One tactic has been to deny that those who flee El Salvador can be refugees from political oppression.

Church people trying to protect these refugees have made use of the concept of sanctuary. This is a concept which has had an impressive and long-standing place in the history of the church and of Western civilization.[23] The difficulty is that it seems to have no place in U.S. law. There is always the chance that in a test case, it might be given some recognition. Regardless of this, it is a fitting concept for Christians to use. During the Roman era, Christian churches were officially recognized as places of sanctuary for refugees and law-breakers at the end of the fourth century A.D. Sanctuary was an expression of the church's commitment to compassion, mercy and the protection of human life. It also represented the Christian belief that there are obligations which transcend the claims of the state. While the protection offered to criminals varied a good deal from one place or time to another, it is interesting that in the Germanic kingdoms of the early Middle Ages a felon would be surrendered to authorities only when an oath had been given that the offender's life would be spared. Protection of those who fled personal or political enemies was a consistent expression of Christianity's special concern for the oppressed and afflicted.

Sanctuary as a legal institution disappeared from Western countries by the end of the eighteenth century, as a result of the secularization of Western society. It was, of course, part of the establishment of Christianity in Roman and medieval times. Americans are committed to the disestablishment of religion. Yet we are counted among the most religious of the "Christian" Western nations. In Robert Bellah's account of American civil religion there is included a belief in a moral/ spiritual order, a set of principles which transcend the state. These are the principles for which the state is supposed to stand and are the basis on which actions of governments may be criticized or opposed. The appeal to sanctuary might well fit into this sort of framework. Churches can appropriately speak for a transcending moral order.

Like the Nicaraguan Watch, the sanctuary movement has two other virtues: it calls upon U.S. Christians to take some risks and perhaps make sacrifices in taking a stand against injustice and oppression, and it enables them to take this stand in unity with fellow Christians from Central America. In discourses on civil disobedience it is often said that willingness to suffer the penalties of the law in the interests of a moral cause is honorable and impressive, and possibly persuasive, to others. While there are possible legal grounds for defense, there is no guarantee that fines or jail sentences will not be imposed. Willingness to run this risk is testimony to the genuineness and depth of one's convictions and can be honored even by some who disagree with the action itself. It can make an important contribution to public debate on the issues. Perhaps even more important, it provides protection and support for the refugees in their tragic and dangerous situation. It is the one effective thing which has been done so far for at least some of these unfortunate persons. Whatever the legal outcome, can there really be doubt that it is consistent with the moral principles which underlie and legitimate our legal system?

In Central America the cause of freedom and justice is clearly tied to the peace issue because of the fighting now involving Nicaragua, El Salvador and Honduras, and the role of the U.S. in it. This dimension of the problem also raises another question of legality, i.e., as to whether the U.S. Government is violating items of international law in Central America. International law is found in or deduced from such things as the Hague Conventions, the United Nations Charter and Declaration on Human Rights, principles of the Nuremberg trials, deliverances of the World Court. To these we might add the various treaties and pacts to which the U.S. is signatory, such as the Organization of American States. International law is a complicated affair and there is a serious question whether it has any recognizable authority in U.S. courts. Americans have nevertheless assumed that our government honors these things and we are quick to criticize other nations for violations of them. On both nuclear and Central American policies, protestors have claimed that our government has been breaking international laws and agreements. The recent refusal of the administration to submit to World Court adjudication in the matter of the mining of the harbor in Nicaragua reinforces such claims. Despite the uncertain status of international law, it does represent the same moral principles as our own national system and is something to which the U.S. has obligations. Where breaches of it can be shown, those who are disobedient to the policies concerned have another ground for justifying their actions.

Acts of Obstruction

The sanctuary movement also involves obstructing the work of a government agency. Obstruction is a tactic to which ethical objections have been raised. Childress, who approves some forms of civil disobedience, has argued that this one "is not consistent with democratic commitment and process."[24] He says further,

> It is difficult to see how clogging the war machine (which is being oper-
> ated by duly elected representatives) can be construed as a valid . . . form of
> *democratic* dialogue. When a minority acts to thwart the results of an untram-
> meled democratic process, its action cannot easily be reconciled with a demo-
> cratic commitment. . . . Such disobedience can be justified, but only if revo-
> lution (non-violent and perhaps violent) is justified.[25]

The objection, then, is that obstruction attempts to short-circuit democratic process by interfering with elected representatives, who are assumed to represent majority opinion and thus to impose the view of a minority upon the majority of citizens.

Most acts of obstruction are really symbolic and are meant more to dramatize the issue, calling attention to it and making a statement about it than actually trying to halt an operation for very long. Sanctuary does seriously impede part of an operation but is tied to efforts to change opinion. It is also recognized as temporary and partial; getting policy changed must be the long-range goal. Meanwhile, it reduces the damage done to some persons. Can it be justified ethically?

The answer depends on one's view of democratic process. Is it really as neat and effective as theory often presents it? Do representatives always "represent" us? Do policies always enjoy positive majority backing? Childress acknowledges that the channels of democratic process often become clogged. There may be a "refusal more or less deliberate to correct" a serious injustice.[26] The wheels of government may grind too slowly, and "rights can be as effectively destroyed by restraining their exercise . . . as by prohibiting their exercise altogether."[27] There may be "temporary cloture of other channels" of redress or "the impossibility of securing funds for promulgating ideas." A large part of the electorate may be uninformed and apathetic, much inclined to go along with what their leaders do or tell them. "Democracy may need an occasional 'prophetic shock minority'—in Jacques Maritain's phrase—to awaken its dormant conscience." We might add that substantial minorities often combine with a middle-ground swing group of persons who are open to persuasion, thus constituting an effectual majority.

Childress accepts such considerations as providing the basis for justification of some acts of civil disobedience. He sees that such acts will not necessarily undermine a democratic order, if they have limited and justifiable objectives, if they are done publicly with a view to contributing to public debate on significant issues, and if they involve "submission."[28] He also allows that the tactics used may include the use of coercion, especially the sort of economic coercion which was part of the sit-ins, boycotts and other protests of the fifties and sixties.[29] But why isn't the use of such coercion as much an interference with democratic processes, through the imposition of the will of a minority, as are obstructive tactics? Why is obstruction so much less acceptable? There might well be practical considerations against these tactics—for instance, the danger of backlash from those who think such actions are going too far—but Childress insists that this is not the main point. Rather, the major argument is that obstruction is inconsistent with democratic processes.[30]

The democratic process seems less tidy and rather tougher than this. As one moves from courts of law through legislatures to the hurly-burly of partisan politics and public debate, one comes to see a good deal that does not conform to more abstract statements about democratic process. With it all, the Republic survives. There is minority obstructionism within the structures themselves: powerful chairpersons of congressional committees bottling up proposed legislation, small groups of senators filibustering, special interests exerting influence in legal ways (lobbying, campaigning, financing). These are, of course, part of democratic due process since they are within the law, but are they so much different from or better than acts of disobedience to law done in the interests of justice and common good? Furthermore, in the larger area of public political action and debate much happens that would not be appropriate in law courts or even Congress. It is not clear why limited and partly symbolic acts of obstruction should be so much harder to justify than, say, protest acts involving both trespass and the use of economic coercion.

On the contrary, certain limited acts of obstruction might be justified on some combination of the following conditions:

1. They are intended to provoke concern and public debate about matters of basic importance to justice or the common good, as well as making a statement about them.
2. The government is slow to act and not really responsive to opinion or has indulged in cover-ups, misinformation or ideologically slanted interpretations of situations, and perhaps even acted illegally.
3. The public is significantly misinformed or uninformed, is largely apathetic and should be awakened at least to the importance of the issues.
4. Time presses and serious damage to human beings threatens.

There are many persons who sincerely believe that some version of all four conditions pertain to peace/war issues and to the Salvadoran situation.

Childress is right in one respect. Obstruction is rather a more drastic measure than others considered here. The case for it is strengthened if other more moderate measures have been tried and found wanting, lives are threatened or disaster could result from a mistaken policy, and delay could be fatal. There will be different judgments about such things. All we can ask ethically is that honest people be honestly convinced and that they have reasonable bases for their conviction. In the case of the sanctuary movement, the threat to Salvadoran persons seems immediate and clear. In addition, those North Americans who commit themselves to this project have no perceivable selfish motive and are prepared to submit to legal consequences. This testifies to their sincere moral motives.

We must say again that most obstructionist tactics are meant to raise up an issue and publicize opposition to it, and demonstrate sincerity by willingness to submit to penalties. The intention is not to suppress or override other views but to promote and contribute to public consideration of an issue. The same ethical justifications apply *a fortiori* to demonstrators who add trespass or other minor offenses to picketing and leafleting. When money and time are short, there is a limited number of other means available which might be politically effective. These moves are really speech-acts which are within the area of public debate. Certain acts such as picketing by labor unions and anti-segregation sit-ins have been counted by the Supreme Court to be protected by the First Amendment right of free speech. While it is not clear that other such acts will be thus protected,[31] they can be viewed as free speech ethically. Sanctuary does obstruct but is open, submissive to legal penalty and meant to provoke debate. Further, the fact that denominations have given support to the movement suggests strongly that there is substantial public disagreement with present policies to which the administration has not been adequately responsive. It is hard to see how most obstructive acts of protest could override government policy and short-circuit the democratic process.

Violence to Property

Non-violence is commonly given as part of the definition of civil disobedience, but we revise this to include certain acts of vandalism which are sometimes done by protestors. There is a vast difference between violence to persons and violence to property, and the acts in view—such as thumping the nose cones of a couple of missiles—involve such limited destruction that they are obviously intended as symbolic speech-acts, with the actors ready to accept arrest and prosecution. The ethical judgments pertaining to the illegality of acts of trespass and obstruction are also applicable here. But why add destruction to these other items? One motive has been to dramatize the fact that, where war is concerned, property is less valuable than lives, and a society which is more solicitous of property than of human beings has something wrong with its values. The economic cost of such acts is relatively inconsequential and the protestors "pay" for it. The advisability of such acts really depends upon practical or "teleological" considerations of political effect. On the one hand, they are dramatic and may reinforce the message proclaimed verbally. They might conceivably get more publicity and publicity is important to political action. There is good reason why we believe in freedom of the press, and media coverage seems more important than ever today. These acts also emphasize the urgency protestors feel about the matter. On the other hand, the destruction may seem unnecessary and offensive to many, and negative reactions could offset any positive gains. But even those who do not agree in particular cases might sympathize with the motives of the actors and see such acts as justifiable under certain circumstances. Persons really are more important than property, though property rights have their place.

Draft Resistance

Resistance to military draft, whether a full-fledged draft or the preliminary registration now in effect, is another act of civil disobedience, which might be committed either by an absolute pacifist or by one who accepts a "just war" view and objects to a particular war or kind of warfare. Absolute pacifists, as conscientious objectors, can accept exemption. They would still be indicating protest and resistance to all war, but would not be disobedient. Many have chosen rather to refuse to register. This means that they want to make an added political statement, through the act itself and through being willing to accept legal penalties. They may believe that the draft is an undemocratic and unjust militaristic measure which fosters further militaristic attitudes and policies. They may feel that accepting an exemption simply co-opts a person into the system and nullifies protest.[32] They may see militarism as part and parcel of a set of social wrongs which are interconnected and which pervade the whole society—racism, economic injustice, destruction of the natural environment—and feel impelled to protest and resist the whole network of evil by resisting draft registration.[33]

It is good that provision is made for conscientious objectors in our draft laws. It is also understandable that some CO's are concerned not to be coopted. The number of CO's has never been large enough to affect military programs seriously and an exempted CO is carried along with the rest of the society on its way to war, seemingly non-resistant. Militarism is a problem. The vastly increased role of the military in the U.S. since World War II represents a profound change to which we have grown so accustomed that we tend to forget how profound it is and to ask whether it is really desirable or necessary, although we are reminded of the dangers of the military-industrial complex from time to time. Surely we can respect those who feel honor-bound to protest and resist, at severe cost to themselves. For persons of pacifist convictions to find their beliefs leading them to acts of protest and resistance is understandable and justifiable. How effective such acts may be in changing attitudes and policies is difficult to judge. Some of the public are impressed. Others no doubt cannot understand why those for whose scruples a provision has been made in the law should still decide to break the law.

The view that militarism is part of a vast web of evil in our society may not be convincing to everyone but it is important to see connections between various social issues and ethical principles. We have seen in the Central American situation how issues of justice and freedom are linked with those of peace. It is crucial to keep the peace movement related to these other concerns. Millions of people abroad are threatened with poverty and hunger, and with arbitrary imprisonment, torture and death at the hands of unscrupulous and tyrannical rulers. These people are inclined to see the current peace campaign as one in which Western white people are involved because their own welfare is at stake. Those who may be murdered by death squads or see their children starve to death tomorrow may not be quite so immediately concerned about the threat of nuclear war. Members of our own minority groups ask why whites are not equally concerned about racism and the deplorable conditions of life in our slums and ghettos. Many of our social ills are part of a pervasive pattern. Peace and justice, freedom and humanity are related and interdependent in their meanings and in their practical applications. At the least, a nation that devotes so much to armaments while some of its children starve may deserve to have a letter or two of its draft laws broken in efforts to revive its spirit of justice and humanity.

Selective conscientious objectors (SCO's)—i.e., those who object to particular wars or armaments (nuclear, biochemical)—of course have no legal provision made for them. If they cannot compromise, they must either refuse to register or, in the case of an active draft, refuse to serve. Many objections have been raised to the proposal that we make provision for SCO's in our draft laws. Childress has taken these into account in a recent book and made an excellent ethical case in favor of legalized SCO.[34] His more thorough analysis should be consulted, but we summarize these points:

1. The view that some wars are just and others unjust, and that participation must be selective is therefore just as authentically moral as absolute pacifism, even though it is not as simple and requires additional judgments about the facts of a given case.
2. In fact, the selective view has been that of many more churches and individual Christians (and non-Christians) than has absolute pacifism. In the interests of fairness and equal respect for persons, the two points of view should be given equal treatment.
3. There would be some added practical problems in administering an SCO exemption but the presumed difficulties have been much exaggerated. The program could be managed. At any rate, out of fairness it should be tried.

Of course, an SCO with possible exemption might still choose, like some other CO's, to resist. The motive would be to make a more public statement of opposition and to avoid seeming to be co-opted. SCO's, on the other hand, might not oppose the principle of a draft; they might see it as the fairest, most democratic way to select personnel for the armed forces. Related issues of justice, freedom, and humanity would be decisive in their decisions about which wars or means or warfare they could conscientiously support.

Decisions of this sort will be made by some on a deontological basis: "I can do no other." Insofar as the aim is also to make public statements and affect politics and policies, judgments must be made about possible effectiveness, admittedly difficult and inexact judgments. Certainly draft resistance must be combined with educative efforts, demonstrations and the rest. One of the practical difficulties foreseen with SCO exemptions is that an unmanageable number of persons might qualify for exemption. One could say rather that widespread disagreement among the citizenry would register effectively if very many persons resisted registration or claimed exemption. In such a case, as Childress remarks,[35] reconsideration of a war or a warlike policy would be indicated, due to lack of public support. We repeat, however, that if no provision is made in law for SCO's, they have no moral recourse where conscience is involved except that of refusal.

Tax Resistance

Finally, a brief comment about tax resistance. Among acts of civil disobedience, this is in one sense relatively easy to justify. Assuming that it is meant as public protest and includes a note on the tax return stating reasons, it is simple for the IRS to handle with individual returns. It therefore poses no great threat to law and order. Such an act does not lead logically to a justification for withholding tax payments in relation to any issue on which one has negative feelings. Those who engage in tax resistance are committed to paying taxes generally, and thus helping to support many programs to which they may be opposed. It is only when a principle is involved (peace) which is fundamental and overrides another (taxpaying) that the act is ethically defensible. Principles do sometimes conflict. Some acts, normally wrong, can sometimes be justified as means to a moral end. Ethics has to weigh principles and evaluate ends and means. Since a major part of the federal budget goes to defense, tax payments seem an appropriate target of protest and peace a sufficient principle and goal, if one is honestly convinced that current policies are unnecessarily and unethically warlike.

The chief questions about this are practical. Will it have any appreciable effect? The tax money one does pay can still be used for military purposes. The IRS can easily recover the balance by attachment of one's salary or bank account. A fine may be assessed, usually small,[36] which simply gives the government more money to be used at its own discretion. To be politically effective, tax resistance would have to assume substantial proportions. Millions of tax returns would present difficulties, and even a minority of the public, if sizable and dedicated, could make waves. It would be interesting to watch what would happen when the seismic shock reached Capitol Hill.

ENDNOTES

1. There are important connections between peace and other issues of social justice, a subject to which we shall return later.
2. This is a very abbreviated version of the approach taken by James Childress, who has proposed that we cannot get all the material needed for ethical judgment from theology alone, that theology gives us a particular perspective and framework from which to interpret Christianly the institutions, activities and moral points of view in society (as Karl Barth has said, Christian ethics is an interpretation of *human* morality from a Christian standpoint), and that political ethics of issues such as ours should be done with specific reference to particular political contexts, democratic or otherwise. Cf. *Civil Disobedience and Political Obligation* (New Haven and London, Yale University Press, 1971), pp. 47-50.
3. Childress *(op. cit.)* has maintained that there is an element of coercion in all tactics other than educating or persuading.
4. There are those who question whether churches have a right, through their councils or judicatories, to pronounce or act on any controversial issues where members may and have a right to disagree. Paul Ramsey has pressed this question in his book, *Who Speaks for the Church?* Presbyterians are no doubt aware that statements of the General Assem-

bly are not binding upon members. At the same time, it is part of our theology that the Spirit of God may and at least sometimes does speak through such bodies. Councils can err, but they are not to be despised; God puts divine treasure in earthen vessels. John C. Bennett has suggested helpfully that statements on social issues by denominational or ecumenical bodies may be taken as speaking *to,* rather than *for,* the church. Such statements should be taken seriously enough to give pause, at least, to those who disagree.

5. Jim Douglass testifies that as a result of demonstrations at the Trident submarine base in Bangor, Washington, five workers have resigned from their jobs. Cf. "Civil Disobedience: A Forum," in *Sojourners* (May, 1983).

6. Cf. L. L. Rasmussen, *Dietrich Bonhoeffer: Reality and Resistance* (Nashville: Abingdon Press, 1972), pp. 54-58.

7. There is much literature which provides substantiation of these assessments, but for a brief summary of the facts, cf. Richard Taylor, "For Penance and for Peace," *Sojourners* (September, 1983). For essays arguing both sides of the issues, cf. P. Rosset and J. Vandermeer, eds., *The Nicaragua Reader: Documents of a Revolution Under Fire* (Grove Press, 1984), and the review by Gary Prevost in *Worldview* (July, 1984).

8. From *Network News,* publication of The Witherspoon Society of the Presbyterian Church (March/April, 1984).

9. This distinguishes them from merely criminal acts.

10. This distinguishes them from revolutionary acts directed against the government as a whole. "Seriously" immoral means that those who disobey do not expect perfection and are prepared to obey many laws and policies which they do not approve. It is only in the most serious cases that they feel impelled to disobey.

11. The issue is only one of definition. Childress, e.g., *(op. cit.)* proposes the strict definition given in these three points, but does not intend that only such actions can ever be justified ethically. The underground railroad of slavery days was justified but was neither public nor submissive.

12. Cf. "Civil Disobedience: A Forum," articles by Jim Douglass and Shelley Douglass, in *Sojourners* (May, 1983). Members of the group have also been threatened with charges of obstructing traffic, pedestrian in roadway, and soliciting.

13. Cf. the accounts in *CALC Report,* published by Clergy and Laity Concerned (January/February 29, 1983).

14. In 1981, the group was convicted; in 1984, the conviction was overturned by the State Superior Court on technical legal grounds. The group is still subject to further prosecution.

15. On this, cf. Childress *(op. cit.),* pp. 33f., 219-221.

16. Childress takes essentially this position, saying that our primary obligation is to our fellow-citizens according to a concept of justice as "fair play," which he takes pains to define and explain *(op. cit.,* Ch. III), and to the values we share. From the point of view of a lawyer, Burton Zwiebach arrives at a similar position; cf. *Civility and Disobedience* (Cambridge: Cambridge University Press, 1975).

17. Childress includes in his concept of fair play a *prima facie* obligation to obey the law. This means that we should expect to obey many laws with which we disagree, and that when we confront one too offensive to conscience, we may disobey but should have special justification for doing so.

18. *Christianity and Crisis* (July 9, 1984), p. 269.

19. Submission to legal penalties expresses this attitude. If such basic loyalty is not present, then there is an at least potentially revolutionary situation. Childress also notes, however, that minority groups who do not share fully in rights and benefits have thereby less reason for loyalty and obligation to the system.

20. Cf. Hart, *The Concept of Law* (Oxford: Oxford University Press, 1961), and Cardozo, *The Nature of the Judicial Process,* 1921 (thirteenth printing, 1971).

21. *The Philosophy of Law,* ed. Dworkin, Ch. II.

22. Sister Kay Hauer, in *Christianity and Crisis* (July 9, 1984), p. 275.

23. The concept of sanctuary has little place in contemporary ethical literature. The few facts

given here are drawn from the article in the *Encyclopedia Brittanica*, vol. 19 (1951), pp. 930-931.
24. Childress *(op. cit.)*, p. 218.
25. *Ibid.*, pp. 211-212.
26. *Ibid.*, p. 191, quoting John Rawls.
27. *Ibid.*, p. 219.
28. He notes particularly that such disobedience does not provide a justification for a generalized principle of law-breaking; cf. *ibid.*, pp. 194-200. Cf. also his reference to Howard Zinn's observation about the counter-balance of society's tendency to maintain traditional order (p. 234) and to Ernest Barker's judgment that where a society is basically stable, there tradition, custom, and habit will likely preserve the basic order of things so that "the electric disturbance of a new idea, pressed to the point of resistance, may serve to correct [the human] tendency to settle down on the lees of custom" (p. 241).
29. *Ibid.*, pp. 210, 218.
30. *Ibid.*, p. 213.
31. Cf. Carl Cohen's essay, "Law, Speech and Disobedience," in H. A. Bedau, ed., *Civil Disobedience* (Pegasus, 1969).
32. Cf. the article by A. J. Muste in H. A. Bedau, ed., *Civil Disobedience* (Pegasus, 1969), pp. 135-145.
33. Cf. the statement of this view in the article by Elizabeth McAlister in the aforementioned "Forum" on Civil Disobedience, *Sojourners* (May, 1983).
34. Cf. *Moral Responsibility in Conflicts* (Louisiana State University Press, 1982), Ch. Six.
35. Childress *(op. cit.)* adds that if the survival of the nation were really at stake, officials could limit the total number of exemptions and choose/decide by lottery who would receive them.
36. One case mentioned in Civil Liberties Record (ACLU of Penna., March, 1984) involves a fine of $500 for a "frivolous" tax return.

RESISTANCE TO TAXES FOR MILITARY PURPOSES

W. Dean Hopkins

As defense spending continues to escalate and the terror of nuclear weaponry becomes ever more evident, increasing numbers of persons are considering military-tax refusal as an act of resistance against United States' military policies. Many others are already engaged in one form or another of tax refusal. Clearly there are legal as well as moral and religious questions that are raised by such actions. This essay gives special attention to the legal issues in military-tax refusal while also exploring the responsibilities of churches for those members who cannot in conscience contribute money for military purposes.

The Legal Status of Military-Tax Refusal in the United States

Although United States law provides statutory exemption from military service for conscientious objectors, there is no statutory exemption for those whose consciences lead them to refuse to pay the part of their income taxes used for military purposes.

Various court decisions have dealt with military-tax refusal. In 1961, the U.S. Tax Court decided the case of *Abraham J. Muste.*[1] A well-known peace activist and long-time executive secretary of the Fellowship of Reconciliation, he had refused to file income tax returns because he objected to the use of federal funds for military purposes, and he had informed the government in writing at filing times of his reasons of conscience for not filing. The court held him liable for the tax and for penalties for failure to file; but it rejected the government's claim for a fraud penalty, such rejection being based on the fact that he had acted openly.

The *Muste* case has been followed and cited with approval in 91 cases.[2] There appears to be no court case relieving a person from paying his or her full income tax on the basis of conscientious objection.

No military-tax protest case has been decided by the U.S. Supreme Court. In 1982, however, it decided the case of *Lee v. U.S.*[3] This case involved an Amish employer who claimed that he should be exempt from Social Security taxes on his Amish employees, because accepting support from the government violates Amish religious convictions. (A specific statute exempts self-employed Amish persons

A shorter version of this material was published under the title, "The Legal Status of War-Tax Resistance" in *The Christian Century*, February 15, 1984.

from Social Security taxes.) The lower federal court held the tax unconstitutional as to the Amish employees of an Amish employer. The Supreme Court reversed and held the Amish employer and his employees subject to the tax, all nine justices concurring in the decision and all but one concurring in the opinion of Chief Justice Burger. In denying the taxpayer's claim, the court said:

> If, for example, a religious adherent believes war is a sin, and if a certain percentage of the federal budget can be identified as devoted to war-related activities, such individuals would have a similarly valid claim to be exempt from paying that percentage of the income tax. The tax system could not function if denominations were allowed to challenge the tax system because tax payments were spent in a manner that violates their religious belief . . . Because the broad public interest in maintaining a sound tax system is of such a high order, religious belief in conflict with the payment of taxes affords no basis for resisting the tax.

The quoted language is what lawyers call "obiter dictum" because it is not essential to the decision of the case before the court. It is, therefore, not binding precedent. It is extremely unlikely, however, that the Supreme Court would decide differently in a case involving the refusal to pay taxes used for military or war-fighting purposes.

In its opinion, the Court referred with approval to two Court of Appeals cases which it had declined to review. Both cases involved conscientious objection to "war-taxes." In one case, the Court said:

> If every citizen could refuse to pay all or part of his taxes because he disapproved of the government's use of the money on religious grounds, the ability of the government to function could be impaired or even destroyed.[4]

In the other case, the Court of Appeals summarily approved the action of the Tax Court, which had denied the military-tax deduction and had assessed a negligence penalty for claiming it.[5] The Tax Court said:

> We understand petitioner's desire to champion his cause but pointed out to petitioner that he had chosen the wrong forum, as had so many war-tax protesters; the Courts cannot allow the deduction unless Congress provides for it. We think the already overcrowded courts are not the place for such individuals to repeatedly attempt to publicize their cause.[6]

Arguments Against and Arguments for Military-Tax Refusal

Biblical

The Biblical approach cannot be ignored even by a lay person with no theological training and with no bent for theological thinking. Each Christian will give at least some attention to his or her understanding of the Bible in determining the rightness of tax refusal.

Probably the texts most often cited against tax resistance are Matt. 22:21, Mark 12:16, Luke 20:25, and Romans 13. Each of the gospels reports the answer of Jesus, "pay Casear what is due to Caesar, and pay God what is due to God." (NEB). Paul's instruction to Roman Christians was, "Let every person be subject to the governing authorities." (Romans 13:1).

The "render to Caesar" incident is reported in the three gospels in almost identical language. Scholars support what seems clear from the context, that the response was a clever rebuke to questioners who were seeking to entrap Jesus.

Those who cite Romans 13 as requiring the payment of all taxes seldom refer to the immediately preceding verse, "Do not be overcome by evil, but overcome evil with good," or the earlier part of chapter 12, "Do not be conformed to this world." They seem inclined to assume that Paul was speaking to the citizens of Rome and of the United States but not to those of Nazi Germany, or the Soviet Union, or Cuba, or even Nicaragua. Of course, there is also Peter's declaration, "We must obey God rather than men." (Acts 5:29).

Although the Old Testament is not usually cited for or against tax resistance, Old Testament scholar G. Ernest Wright has written:

> The greatest figures of Scripture were all objectors in one way or another, on the grounds of conscience or the will of God, to some established order, so as to lead them to leave it. Abraham left home and kindred. Moses vs. Pharaoh was a conscientious objector. Joshua vs. the established order of the Canaanite civilization. Jotham in his wonderful parable vs. his brother's first attempt at monarchy in Israel. Samuel vs. Eli and then vs. Saul. David vs. Saul. Nathan vs. David. And every prophet until Ezekiel, and after Ezekiel there is Malachi, who delivered the word of God vs. the corrupt clergy of the time.[7]

Christian conscientious objectors seem to arrive at their convictions with little reference to isolated verses of Scripture but rather on the basis of their understanding of Christ's mission. They are likely to state their conclusion in terms of opposing the idolatry of reliance on military force, or as a matter of faith in the gospel of love preached by Jesus and by Paul.

The tax resisters who presented testimony at hearings at the 1984 meeting of the General Assembly of the Presbyterian Church (U.S.A.) had served as volunteers in the armed forces. Their consciences had pushed them to decisions they did not claim to be "pure," decisions that resulted from real struggle with the tension between being a loyal American and being a Christian.[8]

Law Versus Anarchy

The argument for being law-abiding is attractive because it opposes order to anarchy. Most Christians in most situations strongly prefer not to violate laws.

The problem for some persons is that the anarchy of tax resistance seems preferable to the annihilation of large parts of the world's population, a danger that is increasing with our nation's military expenditures and policies.

Anarchy is not the necessary result of selective disobedience to law if the disobedience is done openly with a stated purpose. Such action is usually called civil disobedience, and in the United States it has a long history of generally recognized usefulness. Actions that were at one time illegal were instrumental in ending slavery, securing the vote for women, giving legal recognition to conscientious objectors to combatant service, and gaining rights for minority persons. It is easy to forget our pride that our forebears were part of the underground railroad and that they were subject to severe penalties under the Fugitive Slave Law for such resistance.

The historian Page Smith writes of Thoreau's opposition to the Mexican war, " 'There is a higher law,' Thoreau said, 'and I have discerned it and placed myself in obedience to it' . . . We may call Thoreau's scandalous doctrine 'romantic individualism' or 'philosophical anarchism' or whatever other name pleases us, but it remains the rock on which the mightiest ships of state must break themselves if unjustly captained."[9]

The United States Supreme Court has made a similiar point in this language:

> All of our history gives confirmation to the view that liberty of conscience has moral and social value which makes it worthy of preservation at the hands of the state . . . nothing short of the self-preservation of the state should warrant its violation; and it may well be questioned whether the state which preserves its life by a settled policy of violation of the conscience of the individual will not in fact ultimately lose it by the process.[10]

Is Tax Resistance a Logical Or Appropriate Expression of Conscience?

Perhaps the best negative answer to this question is: In our nation, Congress has the power and the obligation to levy taxes and to determine how they shall be expended; taxes are used for many different purposes, some of which are salutary by any standard, and there is no way to separate one part of the tax from the whole. A taxpayer can and should exert his or her influence on Congress on the allocation of tax spending, and there are various legal ways to exert such influence. Moreover, even if the taxpayer withholds 52 percent of the tax because that is the military portion of the budget, 52 percent of the 48 percent paid will still go for the military portion of the government's expenditures.

The response of the objector may be something like: "My conscience requires me to protest against being forced to pay for killing others against my religious convictions, and the fact that our present tax system does not lend itself neatly to the exercise of my conscience does not relieve me from action."

It is almost certain that one reason for increased military-tax resistance lies in the progressive escalation in the nature of the preparation for war to a kind in which killing may occur by sophisticated and costly weapons aimed at millions of unseen persons. This has led a person of sensitivity (perhaps sentimentality, depending upon the point of view) to write: "I killed a man today. . . The IRS insisted that I kill against my will . . . I killed a man today. Or was it a woman or a child?"[11]

It has been argued that our tax system could not withstand special treatment for everyone who objects on religious grounds to having tax money used for such things as contraception, abortion, welfare benefits, or farm subsidies. One answer is that the amount of tax money and the percentage of the budget involved in any of the other categories is minuscule in contrast with the military portion of the budget. One legal scholar has also responded to this argument by claiming that in contrast to the others the category of citizens who object to all wars is "a centuries-old, well-defined classification.'' [12] A more fundamental response to the argument that because the law allows A it must also allow B is this: A legislature or a court has the power and the duty to make judgments, and if allowing A is more important than allowing B, the legislature or the court should allow A even though it does not allow B, which bears similarity to A. This argument is strongest when applied to legislation.

What Are the Results for the Tax Resister?

There is no alternative available to the conscientious objector to *military taxes* parallel to that available to the conscientious objector to *military service*. For this reason, the result for the objector is either (1) being ignored or overlooked by the Internal Revenue Service (probably less and less likely), or (2) being required to pay the tax with interest and probably with penalties. It is assumed that the resistance has been open rather than hidden, and the courts have consistently held in such cases that no fraud penalty is incurred. Since 1982, however, there has been provision in the Internal Revenue Code for a $500 penalty for filing a ''frivolous'' tax return, and this is being applied to conscientious military-tax resisters.

If resistance leads to payment of the tax with interest and penalties, the government may have benefited more financially than if there had been no protest. The procedure, therefore, appears ''impractical.'' From the resister's point of view, however, conscience has been honored.

What Are the Results for the Cause of Peace?

If the resister has been ignored, there is no impact except to the extent that the action is known to others who are influenced by it, and to the extent that the withheld money has been directed to peacemaking purposes. The taxpayer's resistance to collection may be making a public witness for peace. This appears to have little effect on the Internal Revenue Service. It is difficult, however, to judge the cumulative effect on Congress or on other citizens of persons' acting to their financial disadvantage for the sake of conscience.

A Case Study of Tax Refusal by a Pastor

Charles Hurst is co-pastor of Bethany Presbyterian Church, a congregation of approximately one hundred members located on the near west side of Cleveland, Ohio. For five years he has been withholding what he considers the military portion of his income taxes. His formal statement in part is:

> I have instead given that portion of my taxes to church organizations engaged in activities to bring life and wholeness to people. . . .
>
> In withholding this amount of my taxes, I have many times communicated with the IRS what I am doing and why. I enclose such an explanatory letter with my 1040 each year, as well as letters to the IRS with my quarterly payments. I have also often met with IRS officials.
>
> I made the decision to begin withholding the military portion of my taxes only after much prayer, reflection, and discussion with close friends. It was not a decision entered into lightly. This is an action I feel I must take to be consistent with my conscience. My understanding of my faith, how I experience God in

Jesus Christ calling me to live out the gospel in my life, makes it too uncomfortable for me to contribute my money to the arms race and to our nation's trust in weapons of mass death. I believe we have come close to making idols of our weapons systems. . . . .

I struggle, as we all do, with what living as a part of the body of Christ in the world means. My actions with my taxes are not *the* answer, only what I feel God is calling *me* to do. . . .

The IRS found Hurst's bank account and took it to apply against his deficiency. After finding that insufficient to cover the balance due for the tax year 1981, the IRS issued a levy against Bethany Presbyterian Church, ordering it to make monthly payments from the amounts it would owe its pastor less the statutory exemption allowed an individual free from levy. This led to meetings of the session. At one of these meetings, an attorney who had researched tax law explained to the session members: (1) The Internal Revenue Code provides that if a person (individual or organization) owes money to a delinquent taxpayer, the IRS may levy against that person as the taxpayer's debtor. (2) The law applies to any person who owes money to a delinquent taxpayer. Because its application is not affected by the taxpayer's employment status, it is not relevant that for Social Security purposes a minister is considered self-employed. (3) If the debtor unreasonably fails to pay the IRS the amount owed to the taxpayer (up to the amount of the deficiency), the debtor may be assessed a penalty of 50 percent of the amount of the delinquent tax. (4) If a debtor organization fails to pay, all of the provisions may be applied to any officer of the debtor organization. (5) There is no exception for a church in any of these provisions. (6) Bethany has the unicameral system, so that each session member is also a trustee of the Ohio corporation which is the church, and trustees could be individually liable.[13]

Mr. Hurst urged the session members not to feel any obligation to take any stand that would jeopardize them individually. They were sympathetic to his point of view and had no question of his good faith. They reluctantly agreed that the church would begin paying the deficiency from the monthly amounts owed to Mr. Hurst, but they took the first payment to the federal building where they held a short prayer meeting and made public protest. Their action was reported on the first page of the Cleveland daily paper.

Bethany Presbyterian Church is a part of the Presbytery of the Western Reserve, which is centered in Cleveland and covers northeastern Ohio. Mr. Hurst promptly informed the executive of presbytery when the levy was filed against the church. The matter was referred to Swords into Plowshares, a committee of presbytery. It proposed that resolutions to presbytery be discussed at its meeting of February 28, 1983, and then be voted on at the subsequent meeting. At its April, 1983, meeting, presbytery adopted the resolutions after further discussion and several minor changes in wording were made for clarification. The adopted resolutions were:

(1) The Presbytery of the Western Reserve is aware that the large majority of the members of its churches pay the full amount of their federal income taxes

and that many of them find methods to protest the way the taxes are spent. The Presbytery recognizes that Charles Hurst has found that his Christian conscience has required him to take a different action as a protest against our nation's military expenditures—the withholding of what he considers to be the military portion of his taxes and giving it to organizations to "bring life and wholeness to people." This action has been taken openly and with acceptance of the consequences of this decision. The Presbytery recognizes one of the basic historic principles of the Presbyterian Church is that "God alone is Lord of the conscience." The Presbytery records its support of Charles Hurst's right to follow his conscience in his decision. The Presbytery commends the Session and members of Bethany Church for their understanding and support of Charles Hurst in his witness.

(2) The Presbytery of the Western Reserve urges members of Congress to give careful consideration to enacting law that would permit a conscientious objector to military expenditures to direct part of his or her income taxes to a fund for non-military purposes.

(3) The Presbytery of the Western Reserve urges members of Congress to amend the Internal Revenue Code so that churches will be exempt from levy for the collection of income tax deficiencies of any person, thus giving appropriate recognition to the separation of church and state under the First Amendment to the United States Constitution.

Several ministers of other churches expressed concern, if not outrage, that a church could be forced to collect taxes from a person who had withheld them as a matter of conscience. One minister made a formal request to the Mission Council of presbytery that it (1) consider asking presbytery to adopt the stand of the Philadelphia Yearly Meeting of Friends that it would not recognize any levy against it for an employee's taxes withheld as a matter of conscience, and (2) urge individual churches to take that position and support them in such a stand.

When this request came before the Mission Council, in May, 1983, it was learned for the first time by those considering the matter that in September, 1982, Congress had enacted a new section of the Internal Revenue Code under which a $500 penalty was being assessed for "frivolous" returns, and that protest against military tax was being treated as frivolous. Mission Council then assigned the matter for further study, and at the October meeting of the presbytery it presented resolutions for discussion to be voted on at its November meeting. At the October meeting, Rev. Victoria Curtiss, co-pastor of Bethany Church, announced that at the November meeting she would offer an additional resolution as an amendment as follows:

We encourage our church members and employees to explore their own consciences regarding payment of the military portion of their federal income tax and to seek support from the church body at the time they respond to a call to witness for peace.

This motion was offered at the November meeting and was defeated by a vote of 49 to 78. The other resolutions were then before the meeting. By motion, action was delayed until the March, 1984, meeting with the stipulation that material be made available to the session of each church so that the issues could be studied before the vote. The moderator and the stated clerk of Presbytery sent a packet of materials to every session, including a set of arguments for and against tax resistance and an explanation of the World Peace Tax Fund and the Peace Academy. The forwarding letter asked each session to allocate at least forty minutes of a session meeting time to consideration of the issues.

At the March meeting of Presbytery, two short formal presentations were made, designed to be for and against. These were followed by extended debate resulting in a few changes in wording, but all of the resolutions were finally adopted as follows:

1. That Presbytery take no action on the recommendation to adopt the position of the Philadelphia Yearly Meeting of Friends. Our perception is that Presbytery has at this point no consensus of conscience on the issue. We note that a process of study and reflection is under way in the church; the Advisory Council on Church and Society has been asked to bring recommendations to the next General Assembly, and this Presbytery has set aside the November pre-presbytery seminar for consideration of the issue.

2. That Presbytery reaffirm the right of conscience of our sisters and brothers who understand themselves to be called in Christian conscience to the witness of military tax refusal.

3. That Presbytery endorse legislation to create a World Peace Tax Fund, and to legalize the payment to the fund, by individuals qualifying as conscientious objectors, of the portion of federal income taxes determined by the U.S. Comptroller General to represent the portion that would be used for military purposes; and that the Presbytery communicate this endorsement to members of Congress serving the area of the Presbytery, and to the President of the United States.

4. That Presbytery endorse legislation to create a National Academy of Peace and Conflict Resolution, and communicate this endorsement to members of Congress serving the area of the Presbytery, and to the President of the United States.

5. That the Moderator of the Presbytery appoint a special committee of five persons, to include the Stated Clerk and Presbytery's legal counsel, to study the recent actions of the Internal Revenue Service in treating as "frivolous" income tax returns in which a portion of the taxes is withheld as a matter of conscience, and to report its findings to the Mission Council not later than at its June, 1984, meeting. (Time for reporting was later extended to September.)

6. That Presbytery commend to its churches and sessions study of the issues involved in conscientious nonpayment of military-related taxes as appropriate to our continuing quest for the mind of Christ in a violent and militarized world.

Promptly after filing his tax return for 1982, Charles Hurst received a notice from IRS stating: "You have been assessed a penalty under Section 6702 of the Internal Revenue Code for filing a frivolous income tax return." IRS made no effort to collect either the unpaid tax or the penalty from Hurst, but soon thereafter it levied against Bethany Presbyterian Church for the $500 penalty. The session met to consider whether to make payments from the amounts it will owe its pastor from time to time. The session members decided that because this levy was to collect a fine for the expression of conscience, it required different treatment from that of the previous levy which had been for taxes and interest only. The session appointed a committee to draft a letter of refusal to the IRS. The following letter was approved by the session, signed by its clerk, and mailed to the IRS:

> This is in response to your notice of Levy (Form 668W) dated 2/16/84 mailed to Bethany Presbyterian Church requesting it to make payment toward the penalty assessed against its pastor the Rev. Charles Hurst for filing an Income Tax return, which the Internal Revenue has claimed to be "frivolous."
> This Levy is not an attempt to collect taxes. It is an attempt to collect a penalty or fine sought to be levied against Charles Hurst solely because of his expression of conscience with reference to payment of taxes for military purposes. We know our pastor; we know his deeply held conviction based upon his religious faith. It would border on blasphemy for us to cooperate in treating his action as frivolous.
> We are saddened to have an agency of our government treat as frivolous an expression of religiously based conscience. We cannot believe that it is a correct interpretation of a law of the United States. We cannot believe that such action is permissible under our constitution which guarantees freedom of speech and the free exercise of religion.
> The members of the Session (the governing body) of Bethany Presbyterian Church have considered this matter with great care at a regular meeting held on March 14, 1984. On the basis of the foregoing, we must respectfully decline to comply with your request.

On April 18, 1984, an IRS agent found the treasurer of the church at his place of work (much to the treasurer's surprise) and handed him a "Final Demand" which states that if compliance is not made within five days, "we will consider it your final refusal and may then start proceedings under Code Section 6332." A copy of that section is printed on the back of the demand; it is the one that provides for personal liability of officers and the penalty of 50 percent. The Cleveland *Plain Dealer* reported the church's action on the front page of its issue of April 26. The article quoted an IRS spokesman who said "6,639 taxpayers had received the penalty from September, 1982 to September, 1983, the last figures available."

Later the IRS made demand on Hurst for the unpaid tax and also immediately made demand on the church for payment of the tax from the obligations of the church to Hurst. This time the session of the church after careful consideration decided to refuse to make any payment on account of the tax, and so informed the

IRS. On July 31, 1984, the Church received notice that the matter had been referred to the Justice Department.

Soon thereafter the Justice Department sent a letter to Bethany Church stating that it would file suit against the church if the taxes, interest, and penalties were not paid promptly. Conversation with the Justice Department representative indicated that there would not be the usual delay in action, but that priority was being given to this type of case. The session of the Church reconsidered the situation, including the fact that the employment of one of the session members was being jeopardized by the continuing resistance of the church. The session voted on August 13, 1984, to pay the levies from amounts becoming due Mr. Hurst, including the one for the "frivolous" penalty.

Methods of Tax Resistance and Legal Consequences

Reduction in tax by use of legally recognized exemptions and deductions

1. *Simplifying Lifestyle.* An obviously legal method is that of reducing income below the taxable level. For most Americans, simplifying lifestyle is probably a commendable goal; but it will be an acceptable method of avoiding all income taxes for very few, especially those with family obligations.

2. *Investing in Tax-Exempt Bonds.* The income from state and municipal bonds is exempt from federal income tax. For those who have savings, this method can be an effective way to minimize federal income taxes. For a retired person without substantial taxable pension income it could be used to avoid all federal income taxes.

3. *Contributions to Charity.* Charitable contributions are deductible from taxable income up to 50 percent of adjusted gross income. If the taxpayer's highest bracket is 30 percent, contributions of $1,000 will reduce tax by $300.

Tax refusal

Refusal to pay income taxes may take different forms. Most of them may be described under the following headings:

1. failing to file return;
2. filing a blank return with a note of explanation;
3. filing a correct return but refusing to pay a token amount with explanation of reason;
4. filing a return but refusing to pay a percentage of the tax such as the part for military spending or the part for nuclear weapons;
5. filing a correct return and paying the full amount, but with written protest;
6. filing a correct return and paying the full amount, and then filing a claim for refund based upon a deduction of the military portion.

The first two methods above are subject to penalty for failure to file a return (under the old law, 5 percent per month up to 25 percent of the tax; and under the new law, if the delay exceeds 60 days a minumum of $100 plus 100 percent of the tax). In addition, there is a penalty of $1/2$ percent per month up to 25 percent of the tax for failure to pay tax. In all cases, reasonable cause will excuse the penalty; but it should not be anticipated that protest will be reasonable cause.[14]

The third and fourth methods will result in the collection of the deficiency with interest and penalties. If the return attempts to compute the tax by use of a "war-tax" deduction or exemption, it will now draw the $500 penalty for a frivolous return under Section 6702 IRC. It has also been held subject to the negligence penalty which has been 5 percent of the tax, and is now also 50 percent of the interest on the tax under Section 6653 IRC.[15] These methods are not available to employees whose withholding has covered all of the tax owed. Some of such refusers in the past have claimed extra exemptions to reduce withholding; but this raises a question of openness and the possibility of fraud with its civil penalty of 50 percent of the tax. One taxpayer who claimed three billion dependents because of his stated feeling of responsibility for all human beings was prosecuted for criminal fraud and sentenced to eight months in prison. The decision was reversed by the Court of Appeals on the ground that although the statement was false, it was not deceptive.[16]

Although the fifth method appears safe from the $500 penalty, some of the pending cases indicate that there may be attempts to assess the penalty even here. In any event, interest and the negligence penalty are likely to result.

A claim for refund can always be filed within three years from the due date of a timely filed return. A claim based on the right to an allowance by reason of conscience, method 6, will be routinely denied. The form for claiming a refund of taxes is now 1040X rather than the general Form 843. Form 1040X is titled "Amended U.S. Individual Income Tax Return." It may, therefore, come within the language of the frivolous penalty section which refers to filing "what purports to be a return." If the refund form is used, it is most likely to be safe from the penalty by showing the correct tax and attaching a statement of protest with a request for refund. Of course, the refund will not be granted.

The Penalty for Frivolous Tax Returns

Section 6702 of the Internal Revenue Code is titled "Frivolous Income Tax Return." It is part of the so-called Tax Equity and Fiscal Responsibility Act of 1982 (TEFRA). This section provides that an individual who files an income tax return that "contains information that on its face indicates" that the computed tax "is substantially incorrect," and this is due to "a position which is frivolous" or "a desire (which appears on the return) to delay or impede the administration of Federal income tax law, then such individual shall pay a penalty of $500." The section provides that this penalty is in addition to any other penalty.

The explanation of this section in the Senate Committee report states that the penalty could be imposed if the return shows an incorrect amount of tax because of a "claim of a clearly unallowable deducton such as . . . a 'war tax deduction' under which the taxpayer reduces his taxable income or shows a reduced tax by that individual's estimate of the amount of his tax going to the Defense Department budget, etc. In contrast, the penalty will not apply if the taxpayer shows the correct

[257]

THE PEACEMAKING STRUGGLE

tax due but refuses to pay the tax. In such case, of course, the Secretary [of the Treasury] can assess and collect the tax immediately." This section is part of an act that amended more than a hundred sections of the Internal Revenue Code, including many of the most technical dealing with pensions. It is likely that few legislators saw the Senate Committee report or even read the penalty section before voting for the whole bill.

Page two of the instructions with Form 1040 for 1982 lists nine items under the boldface title, "Important Tax Law Changes," and features an "Important Reminder" that the government will accept separate contributions to reduce the public debt; there is, however, no mention of the new penalty provisions.

It is understandable that church people are concerned that the word "frivolous" is used to describe a position based upon conscience. The primary meaning of the word is "trivial" or "silly." It is, therefore, a serious matter for our government to treat an act of conscience as trivial and to levy a fine for it. Part of the problem is that "frivolous" has acquired a special meaning of "unallowable" or "groundless" as applied to actions in court. Black's Law Dictionary quotes several court opinions so defining it.

Section 6673 of the Internal Revenue Code was amended in 1982 as part of the same act (TEFRA) to permit the Tax Court to award damages to the government if an action brought by a taxpayer is based upon a position that is "frivolous or groundless." In the *Abrams* case,[17] decided in 1984, the Tax Court on its own motion assessed $5,000 of damages (the new maximum increased from $500 under the previous section which referred only to delay) against a taxpayer who claimed that wages could not constitutionally be taxed. Oddly, the court referring to that statute emphasizes that it says "frivolous *or* groundless," and finds that the taxpayer's position "is frivolous and groundless." Principles of statutory construction would lead to the conclusion that Congress meant something different by "frivolous" in Section 6702 from "frivolous and groundless" in Section 6673, both enacted as part of the same act. It appears, however, that the courts will not give Congress credit for meaning something different by the two different provisions adopted at the same time. The *Abrams* opinion cites other cases in which the courts have assessed damages for what they designate as frivolous appeals, including one by the U.S. Supreme Court. One of the opinions cited complains that: "Meritless appeals of this nature are becoming increasingly burdensome on the Federal court system. We find this appeal frivolous."[18]

A 1984 opinion quotes Webster's Third International Dictionary for a meaning of "frivolous" as having "no basis in law or fact." That opinion dealt with eight cases consolidated for decision; in all of them the $500 penalty was approved.[19]

Another judge in a recent case, in approving the penalty, says "Whatever else may be meant by this term, it is beyond cavil that a claim is frivolous when there is no argument on either the law or the facts to support the claims . . . or where the law has been long settled against the claimant."[20] One possible problem with this is that "long-settled law" does change. At one time, the U.S. Supreme Court held child labor laws to be unconstitutional. In 1940, the Supreme Court approved laws that required children to salute the flag as a condition of attending public schools even though it was violation of their religious beliefs. In 1943, the Court overruled that decision with only one dissent.[21]

We are confronted with a paradox of the English language—an action is frivolous (unallowable) even though its motivation is the direct opposite of frivolous (trivial or silly).

Another concern with the frivolous penalty is that it is really being used to penalize free speech. The penalty has been asserted in cases in which the IRS admits that a refund is due the taxpayer, and in cases in which the determination of the correct tax due is obvious from the return even though a military-tax deduction has been claimed. One Federal District Court has held for the taxpayers in this kind of case; but the taxpayers were forced to litigate.[22]

Other cases are pending in which the validity of the penalty tax is being attacked on various grounds; several have been briefed exhaustively by the American Civil Liberties Union.

Summary

I shall review the main points of this essay by responding to seven questions.

1. What is the case against and what is the case for military-tax refusal? I have tried to state arguments pro and con in the second section. Each person must make his or her own decision on whether to resist. If the choice is in the affirmative, the explanations in the fourth section could be helpful in choosing the method.[23]

2. Should the Presbyterian Church (U.S.A.) offer spiritual guidance to members who are seeking to determine whether they should on the basis of conscience refuse to pay the part of their taxes used for military purposes? It would seem to be a primary function of the church to support a person who has taken a position based upon his or her religiously guided conscience. The church should make clear that it is available for such guidance.

3. To what extent should the church support persons who have conscientiously refused to pay the part of their taxes used for military purposes? There is no consensus on the kind of support the church should give to those who have made the decision to resist taxes based upon conscience. The minimum should be an affirmation of the right to make such a decision based upon conscience, expecting to accept the consequences.

4. Should the church urge individual members to examine their consciences on this issue? As indicated in the third section, this issue was placed before the Presbytery of the Western Reserve, and it lost by a vote of 49 to 78. Of course, that does not foreclose the issue. The UPCUSA General Assembly of 1969 stated: "Faced with the agonizing choices of war, each Christian must satisfy his own conscience under God and with his fellow men, that any war is 'just and necessary.' We call upon each church member facing these choices, to inform and enliven his conscience. . ."[24] This statement was dealing with military service, but it is urging a positive examination of the issue that has become military service by substitution of tax dollars.

The Rev. Richard Clewell, a Chaplain at a Veterans Hospital, testified at hearings held at the 1984 General Assembly of the Presbyterian Church (U.S.A.) at the request of eleven Vietnam veterans. They wanted him to report that they believe that when they were eighteen and nineteen years of age they were sold a bill of goods and then dumped, and that their churches did not help them distinguish between loyalty to God and loyalty to nation. This should motivate the churches to give more consideration to this fourth question.

5. Should the church recommend that each of its governing bodies take a position upholding its employees who are conscientious military-tax resisters? It was the consensus of the Presbytery of the Western Reserve that our churches are not ready for this stand. Later, Bethany Church took this stand without the support of Presbytery, yet still abandoned it later under pressure.

6. What position should the church take with reference to federal law which treats as "frivolous" any tax return claiming a deduction of the military portion of the tax, and levies $500 penalty for such filing? From the point of view of the church, it is obvious that Congress has chosen an unfortunate word in "frivolous" to express the meaning of "unallowable." It is unlikely that there will be any court relief on the basis of the standard meaning of "frivolous," and Congress is notably slow in correcting tax legislation. The existence of the problem provides strong argument for the conclusion in the next paragraph.

7. Should the church support proposed legislation that would recognize conscientious objection to military taxes by permitting the objector to direct the military portion of his or her taxes to non-military purposes? The Presbytery of the Western Reserve has gone on record urging the enactment of the World Peace Tax Fund, and its clerk has been corresponding about this proposal with Ohio Senators and the Representatives whose districts include any part of the Presbytery.

Senator Mark Hatfield has stated the case for the proposal: "Requiring taxes for current military outlay from people whose moral and spiritual background and framework forbid them participation in violent means of conflict resolution is a dark blot upon our national human rights policy."[25]

It is clear that the courts will not recognize conscience as a basis for failing to pay taxes. The advantage of the World Peace Tax Fund bill is that it would recognize conscience in the same way that the military service exemption does, and the conscientious objector could pay his or her full share of taxes without violation of conscience. The World Peace Tax Fund Act offers an appropriate alternative for one whose conscience equates paying for killing with the act of killing. It should be supported.[26]

We must recognize, however, that the proposed bill in its present form does not provide for the person who cannot affirm that he or she is "opposed to war in any form." There are those who would refuse to support the use of nuclear weapons, or who would refuse to participate in or support an invasion of Nicaragua, but who cannot say that they are opposed to war in any form. They are not covered by the present law exempting conscientious objectors from military service; and they would not be covered under the World Peace Tax Fund Act as now proposed, because its eligibility provisions are the same as for exemption from service. The statement of the General Assembly quoted under Question 4 clearly contemplates the possibility of selective conscientious objection to some wars. This is an issue that will not go away.[27]

ENDNOTES

1. *Abraham J. Muste*, 35 TC 913 (1961).
2. This is the number of cases listed in the Prentice-Hall Citator as following the *Muste* case. The case may be cited for the holding that the tax must be paid, and it may also be cited for the holding that there is no fraud when the taxpayer acts openly.
3. *U. S. v. Lee*, 455 U.S. 252, 49 AFTR 2d 82-802 (1982).
4. *Autenrieth v. Cullen*, 418 F.2d 586, 24 AFTR 2d 69-5970 (CA 9 1969).
5. *Lull v. Commissioner*, 602 F.2d 1166, 44 AFTR 2d 79-5278 (CA 4 1979).
6. *Howard W. Lull*, TC Memo 1978-74.
7. Quoted from a letter of Dr. Wright to Rev. Richard E. Moore, and included in his paper "A History of Civil Disobedience," submitted by him as counsel for Rev. Maurice McCrackin in a hearing before the Permanent Judicial Commission of the United Presbyterian Church in the U.S.A, May 1962.
8. See essays by Edwards and Williamson for more thorough treatment of Biblical texts related to questions of tax refusal.
9. Page Smith, *The Nation Comes of Age, a People's History of the Ante-Bellum Years* (McGraw-Hill Book Co., 1981), pp. 228, 229.
10. *United States v. Seeger*, 380 U.S. 163, 170 (1965).
11. Peter J. Ediger, "Obituary," *People Pay for Peace*, by William Durland. (Colorado Springs: Center Peace Publishers, 1982), 14.
12. Charles R. DiSalvo, "Saying 'No' To War in the Technological Age-Conscientious Objection and the World Peace Tax Fund Act," *DePaul Law Review*, 31 (Spring, 1982), 497-531.
13. The advice was based upon Section 6332 of the Internal Revenue Code (IRC).
14. Section 6651 IRC.
15. *Howard W. Lull*. See Note 6.
16. *U.S. v. Snider*, 502 F.2d 645, 34 AFTR 2d 74-5388 (CA 4 1974).
17. *Gale C. Abrams*, 82 TC No. 29.
18. *Edwards v. Commissioner*, 680 F.2d 1268, 1271, 50 AFTR 2d 82-5390 (CA 9 1982).
19. *Sharon Franklet et al v. U.S.A.*, 578 F.Supp 1552, 53 AFTR 2d 84-555. Opinion by Judge William W. Schwarzer, U.S. District Judge for Northern District of California, decided January 9, 1984.
20. *William D. Hummon v. U.S.A.* Opinion by Judge Robert M. Duncan, U.S. District Judge for the Southern District of Ohio, Eastern Division, decided May 9, 1984 (not yet officially reported).
21. *Board of Education v. Barnette*, 519 U.S. 624 (1943).
22. *Richard H. Jenney v. U.S.A.* Opinion by Judge A. Wallace Tashima, District Judge for the Central District of California, decided March 19, 1984 (not yet offically reported).
23. For current information on military-tax resistance, the following organizations can be helpful:

    Center on Law and Pacifism
    P.O. Box 1584
    Colorado Springs, CO 80901

    War Resisters League/War Tax Resistance
    339 LaFayette Street
    New York, NY 10012

    Conscience and Military Tax Campaign
    44 Bellhaven Road
    Bellport, NY 11713

24. *Minutes of The General Assembly of The United Presbyterian Church in The United States of America*, 1969, p. 670.
25. *Congressional Record*, April 4, 1979.
26. Current information on the status of the World Peace Tax Fund can be obtained from:
    National Campaign for a World Peace Tax Fund
    2121 Decatur Place NW
    Washington, DC 20008
27. Those having interest in this problem can obtain further information from:
    National Interreligious Service Board
       for Conscientious Objectors
    Suite 600
    800 18th Street NW
    Washington, DC 20006

NON-VIOLENT DEFENSE

Liane Ellison Norman

The Elizabethans had a dramatic form known as the "revenger's tragedy." Its best examples are *Romeo and Juliet* and *Hamlet*. These tragedies are based on a code of honor which demanded that an injury be revenged. An act of revenge, however, always inflicted new injury, also requiring revenge. Remedial revenge constituted new injury and so on. In the last scene of these death-dealing plays, the stage is all casualties, the leading characters nearly all dead. "See what a scourge is laid upon your hate," the Prince of Verona rebukes the heads of warring houses, "That Heaven finds means to kill your joys with love!" Capulet and Montague finally embrace and raise monuments to their children, but the children and "a brace of kinsmen" are dead. Even "The sun for sorrow will not show his head," mourns the Prince. Hamlet's friend, Horatio, surveying what's left of Danish government, speaks "Of carnal, bloody, and unnatural acts,/ Of accidental judgments, casual slaughters,/ Of deaths put on by cunning and forced cause,/ And, in this upshot, purposes mistook/ Fall'n on the inventors' heads."

War has always been revengers' tragedy, never more in the present time. Modern weapons, incapable of achieving rational objectives, can do nothing *but* inflict massive, indiscriminate and long-lived revenge on combatants, non-combatants, battlefields and homes alike as well as insure that the sun, for sorrow, will not show its head. Modern Montagues and Capulets, modern kings and princes, stand menacing one another, weapons poised. Each insists that only his bellicosity deters the other's wickedness: each dares the other to acts of defiance. Modern princes call this period of bated breath "security" and fear any kind of change that might interrupt the pause before the final scene. That pause is all we have between us and the possible end of our kind. Each local skirmish, each new weapon developed threatens the revenge tragedy to end revenge tragedies.

We contemplate theatrical bloodshed knowing its pretense. The actors will rise, join hands, take the applause and live to kill one another tomorrow night. They but rehearse reality. But the drama we find ourselves caught in is no rehearsal. The real thing stymies us. It's easier to see the beams in Capulet and Montague eyes, to judge the folly of court intrigues in made-up Denmark, than to call off our own revengers' tragedy, to interrupt our history of carnal, bloody and unnatural acts, accidental judgments, casual slaughters, deaths by cunning and forced cause, which—purposes mistook—fall on the inventors' heads.

Weapons and Defense

Our problem is that we want a safer play without changing the revengers' code of honor. And so we live, skewered by both horns of a dilemma. While weapons have rendered war illegitimate and obsolete, the need for defense is both legitimate and present. Some things have, historically, required defending: territory, home, institutions, values. Similarly, some things must be fought for, usually having to do with justice. But on the other hand, the weapons we now possess cannot achieve military or political advantage. Further, they may be used by accident or misjudgment as well as by malevolent intent. However secure such weapons make some *feel*,[1] they constitute a threat merely by existing. Their ever-increasing numbers and their sophistication as instruments of first-strike capability (number, accuracy, co-ordination, unanswerability) increase the anxiety of adversaries and hence the possibility of worst case misinterpretation and accident. They threaten the escalation of any conflict anywhere in the world. They furthermore make terrible, massive and indiscriminate non-nuclear destruction seem less terrible because it is *not* nuclear. Such weapons, if used, will injure belligerents and non-belligerents alike. They pose incalculable but real risks to the natural environment upon which all life depends. They impoverish human society materially and spiritually, for we all live in fear, jumping at the slightest explosion in dreadful anticipation, trying to grow up without the prospect of a future. The destructiveness of these weapons is so great that even those who advocate their stockpiling believe their purpose is never to be used. But the presence of such weapons tempts us *not* to find other ways to conduct international and domestic affairs than by relying on them. Richard Falk and Robert Jay Lifton have written about "nuclearism," the logic-proof worship of these engines of death and despoliation, which because they are not rejected, are instead embraced.[2]

Caught in an intellectual bind, we talk past one another. Hawks equate the legitimate *need* for defense with illegitimate *means*: doves dismiss the *need* for defense because they too equate defense with the traditional *means* thereof. This state of affairs *seems* hopeless. We must defend ourselves: therefore we must all die. Most shrug and business continues as usual, some of that business-as-usual being the daily sophistication and production of new weapons and accompanying strategies. Robert Jay Lifton calls this state of mind "psychic numbing." It includes sometimes nearly hysterical manifestations of tough-minded "cool;" apathy; despair; hectic hedonism; inappropriately focused rage, fear. Just when we most need our cunning, creativity and courage, we find ourselves stewing in conformity, convention and cowardice. Most thought on the subject takes forms George Orwell warned about, inexact imagery, pretentious diction, "an accumulation of stale phrases [which choke] like tea leaves blocking a sink."

The equation of *defense* with *violence* and *violence* with *power* brings us to this pass. Some recent thinkers, pressing up against the prospect of nuclear extinction, have struggled with this problem. Jonathan Schell, in his painstaking examination of the consequences of our reliance on nuclear weapons declared war already abolished and recommended the "re-invention of politics." Though he didn't specify what shape the re-invented politics should take, he intimated that it would have to take account of "Gandhi's law of love."[3] (He subsequently seems to have retreated from this position.) Freeman Dyson, reflecting on nuclear weapons in *The New Yorker*, coupled the idea of unilateral disarmament with non-violent resistance. "Gandhi and Andre Trocme proved that the concept sometimes works—that it can be practical as well as noble." But, he concluded, "There are three main obstacles to Non-violent Resistance as a practical concept for the United States . . . . vicarious pacifism, lack of robustness, and original sin."[4]

Robert Holmes' splendid essay in *Harvard Magazine*[5], examines indications that war is no longer consistent with human survival. He argues that "the alternative to war's renunciation isn't passive acceptance of evil. It's resistance and defense, but of a non-violent sort. This requires not only conversion to a peace-oriented economy, but also the development of alternative means of national defense."

Power and Non-Violence

Gene Sharp, the foremost student of non-violent alternatives to military violence, considers power as separate from violence. It's a crucial distinction for finding ways out of our present impasse. Power, says Sharp, "is inherent in practically all social and political relationships. . . ."[6] Holmes also makes this distinction.

Power, from a social standpoint, is the ability to achieve one's objectives. And although capacity to use violence is one measure of power and may be effective in some contexts, it's demonstrably ineffective in others. That virtually every war has at least one loser attests to this. Destructive force doesn't automatically add up to social power.

Consider this proposition: that every person has political power and its corollary, that no person is a-political. By "political," I mean having an influence on the policies whereby public life is ordered. Most of us *feel* powerless, including, as Gerald and Patricia Mische point out, those presidents, prime ministers, bosses, etc., we credit with possessing power.[7] One reason we feel powerless is that we've been taught to think we exercise political power only when we vote or, sometimes, when we lobby our representatives. We've also been taught not to notice all the evidence there is of our power. If we don't know we have power, we're unlikely to make constructive use of it.

But if we refuse the customary notions, that only states and institutions and so on are powerful, if we refuse the idea that their power resides in their ability to do violence (or to punish), interesting possibilities arise. Think of the two-year-old, an apparently powerless person, determined not to be put into a snowsuit in obedience to the wishes of the larger, stronger adult. Or the even smaller infant who resists a diaper change. Think of a classroomful of sullen students intent on keeping a teacher from lecturing or testing, though the teacher is nominally more powerful.

Think of the fly whose buzzing against windowpane and lightbulb can destroy one's concentration. Think of the bureaucrat unwilling to hustle, and you have some idea of power only rarely articulated.

Gandhi observed to the British, "You can govern us only so long as we remain the governed." He noted simply that leadership, benign or malevolent, requires followers. Hannah Arendt cites instance after instance in which the Nazis were frustrated by the refusal of obedience and cooperation.[8] Totalitarian regimes like Hitler's required massive, widespread cooperation from bureaucrats, citizens, soldiers, shareholders, taxpayers. Even the death camps required not so much a monster to lead as co-operative people to carry out orders. Had resistance been systematic, widespread and purposeful, Hitler could not have achieved his murderous purposes.

In *Moby Dick,* Herman Melville examines the paradox that one man, clearly mad, can bring others, variously sane, under his control, make them carry out his crazy project. Ahab cannot sail the ship, find, pursue, kill and process the whale by himself. He uses every persuasive device, from cajolery to threats, until finally he is able to shriek at the crew, "Ye are not other men, but my arms and legs; and so obey me!" They do. The narrator realizes that "I, Ishmael, was one of that crew; my shouts had gone up with the rest." He and his fellows make Ahab's lunacy possible, but they *need* not. Melville also examined the power that one person has to withhold consent. His pallid law clerk, "Bartleby the Scrivener," informs *his* employer that "I would prefer not to" perform a variety of tasks expected of him. He brings the law office to a halt by his refusal to cooperate. Though the lawyer is boss, Bartleby with his adamant refusal, is powerful to a degree that disarms lawyer and reader.

The power each person has is the power to cooperate, to obey, to be governed—or *not* to cooperate, *not* to obey, *not* to be governed. If one does *not* refuse cooperation, one cooperates: there is no middle ground. Whichever alternative one chooses, one exercises power. The one action never available is no action. One consents to traffic laws by stopping at red lights. One consented to Hitler's policies by not refusing obedience. One consents to the nuclear arms race by paying taxes and not attacking missiles in their silos with hammers. These truths, that each is powerful (and of course, more so acting in concert with others), that none is apolitical, are at the heart of alternatives to military defense and struggle.

This simple diagram shows crudely the range of political actions a person confronts:

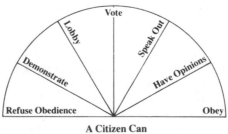

A Citizen Can

Robert Holmes writes:

> Consider a population of 200 million persons committed to non-violent resistance against an invading army bent upon ruling the country. A large industrialized society like ours cannot be run—much less run with the efficiency necessary to make it worthwhile to try to do so—without the cooperation of its population. People are needed to run factories, grow food, collect trash, and to perform thousands of other essential tasks. In fact, it's difficult enough to run the country *with* the cooperation of the people. Deny to an invading army that support—as one can through passive resistance, strikes, boycotts, civil disobedience, and other non-violent techniques—and you render it virtually incapable of attaining its objectives.[9]

A society functions because people cooperate, do their jobs, obey the laws. Minimal and largely symbolic coercion usually suffices—even in ruthless regimes—to persuade people to cooperate most of the time. Most people, even when subjugated in various ways, fear the threat of withdrawn consent, cooperation and obedience because potential chaos is implied. But chaos, carefully organized—that is, mutiny—is precisely what will defeat an oppressor, whether foreign or domestic. To give orders and not be obeyed—a dictator's nightmare—is to be without power. To rely on mechanisms that aren't there—telephones without operators, faucets without water, light switches without electricity, buses without drivers or gas, grocery stores without groceries—is to be powerless.

Most people are unaware of the power they have. Therefore, were we to be invaded tomorrow or to wake up to news of a coup, we would be disorganized and largely ineffectual in resistance. But were training in non-violent means of resistance, in disciplined and systematic refusal of cooperation, to take place, though invasion or dictatorship might not be *initially* forestalled, *government* by invader or dictator could be.

Though power is often equated with violence, the latter may, in fact spring from the perception of powerlessness. Here is my idea of what it's like to feel powerless in the world.

Because Our Hero feels powerless, he is fearful: he has no ability to control his destiny. Therefore, not surprisingly, he is afraid. But fear by itself makes no sense. Therefore he must fear something or someone: he needs enemies on which to project his fear and enemies aren't hard to find. In fact, to the extent that he creates enemies, enemies (also likely to feel powerless and fearful) will exist, fulfilling his fears. To feel powerless and fearful in a world full of enemies leads one (or many) to augment one's strength, to find power in mechanical "arms." It isn't surprising that violence results from being armed among similarly armed enemies, fearful, feeling unable to alter the situation. Though sometimes briefly effective and satisfying, violence rarely solves the problem of powerlessness, which is generally passed along, in child-rearing and policy-making alike. Rulers benefit from citizen powerlessness, which leads to obedience and cooperation and makes those in charge seem powerful. But the rhetoric of leaders is full of the rhetoric of *their* powerlessness. "We have no choice but to . . . ." they say. They speak of themselves as "pitiful, helpless giants."

The sense of powerlessness is transmitted, according to psychoanalyst Alice Miller,[10] by prevailing pedagogies which inflict hurt and humiliation on children as the only available therapy for adults, in their time also hurt and humiliated. Children, taught that they are victims, learn to identify with the aggressor, to associate power with violence, to make their own children victims—the revengers' tragedy preliminary to that of nations'. Powerlessness is also taught by history books and news media, where "important" people are featured, where "important" events are largely wars and administrations, where ordinary individuals are usually newsworthy only when they commit mayhem. Interestingly, until they are dead, "activists" are often subtly denigrated. The same lessons are taught on the job, where the compliant employee is rewarded and the independent punished. The ability to punish, to inflict pain and disgrace, to destroy comes to be synonymous with power, and thus we learn not to see, understand or reason from the evidence of the powerful two-year-old who doesn't want to wear its snowsuit.

But now consider the person who does *not* perceive herself as powerless in the world.

She feels *powerful*. She may attribute this power to a divine or to a human source, but it is the power to consent or to withhold consent. Because she perceives her power, she is not fearful. She is courageous. (Which is just as well, because she likely will be punished for her position in a world in which people are expected to feel and act powerless. Those who feel most powerless are often most outraged by her, since her stance throws their own into doubt.) She may have adversaries, but she does not need enemies to project her fears onto: she does not need to hate and demonize. Since she does not feel powerless, fearful or set about with enemies, she is unlikely to feel the need of augmenting arms and she is far less likely to resort to violence. In her world, those holding office must command her respect through legitimate authority. She is not easily coerced or intimidated, though when she is punished she feels the pain as acutely as anyone else.

Take the propositions explored above and apply them to the matter of defense. Begin with defense against nuclear weapons and despair *is* merited. Without weapons there is no defense against nuclear weapons. *But WITH weapons—any weapons there is similarly no defense.*

It is more likely that we will dismantle and dispose of these weapons and refuse to countenance their use or the threat of their use if we have discovered other means to defend ourselves against the kinds of threats for which there is historic precedent. Therefore, leave aside the nuclear threat: it is safe to do so since our adversaries will not rationally resort to the use of nuclear weapons any more than we will; to do so would threaten their existence and make any target on which they were used valueless. In fact, to persuade our adversaries to lay aside *their* weapons, we would most sensibly reduce the degree to which *they* feel at risk by laying aside our own. We will do this with less anxiety, however, if we've decided what to do when attacked from without or within.

So the best defense against nuclear warfare being disarmament, the best defense against other threats requires thinking about how best to deploy our power. Suppose our adversaries were to invade our territory in the process of taking over the world. It may not be what real Russians really intend, but it is what many Americans believe, and therefore it is a hypothesis to test. Supposing that the requisite number of Russian troops leave home. How many will that be? What will be the domestic consequences of their deployment elsewhere? What will they have to do in order to take over the world? A map of the world suggests that *we* ought not to panic. But supposing our worst fantasies are true and they take over Western Europe? Might we recommend to Europeans, as Franklin Roosevelt did to Germans under Hitler, a policy of non-violent non-cooperation and civil disobedience? Might we travel to Europe to observe and report? Might we be conspicuous in protest? Might we interpose our bodies between attackers and attacked? (See postscript.) Supposing that these wicked and limitless enemies overrun all of Europe, command the Middle East, deploying the necessary forces as they go to maintain control, and, notwithstanding these expenditures, arrive, fresh, ferocious and raring to turn America into a continent of abject slaves. Assuming that they will not meet us one Russian to one American, how will they deploy their troops? What resources will be essential for them to control? How might we go about making that control impossible or unattractive?

Holmes writes that:

> A people who have sought security in arms alone are defenseless once their military forces have been defeated. They are a conquered people. A people committed to non-violence may be deprived of their government, their liberties, their material wealth. But they cannot be conquered!

Non-violent defense against military attack, suggested by the questions above, will have a good deal to do with locality. Pittsburgh's task will be different from New York's and What Cheer, Iowa's. A small, homogeneous country will find different tactics from a large, diverse country. Geography, industry, communication, transportation will determine the appropriate local defense. Clearly the best defense will be highly decentralized. The defending locale will know in advance that the ratio of conquerors to those they wish to conquer will be in favor of the latter. It will be essential to know in advance what the strategic resources of a particular locality are, so as to provide necessities for one's own people while denying them to an invader. It makes sense to plan in advance, not only for strategic purposes, but for purposes of solidarity, discipline and human support.

The invaders will not necessarily be kind when confronted with non-cooperation. They will want to appear invincible. They will attempt to frighten those they wish to conquer with harsh repression. But there are limits on their ability to kill, imprison, torture, etc., because they must have a population to have conquered: they must have drivers to keep the buses running. If genocide is the intent of the aggressor, those carrying it out and those to be destroyed must resist, must refuse cooperation. It takes obedience at many levels to carry out genocide.[12] In fact, repression will backfire *if* the non-violent defenders are prepared for it. It will make clear the *lack* of legitimacy the invaders have, for it will be unmistakable that punitive force is their only power, and the defenders will know such power really manifests weakness.

Gandhi showed that a modern superpower, which had conquered and ruled a "backward" country, could be defeated by unarmed non-cooperation. Gandhi saw that a small number of British ruled by persuading, demoralizing and scaring the Indians into cooperation, convincing them that they were powerless to do otherwise. The Indians did as they were ordered—produced the food, constituted the army, ran the railroads, shuffled the papers, kept the British undershorts laundered and brought their brandy and water—until Gandhi pointed out that the British could be induced to go home by simple refusal to make society work under their aegis. It's sometimes said that the British *could* be persuaded to leave because they were "civilized," an error that comes from overindulging in "Masterpiece Theatre:" when it came to empire, the British were as tough-minded as any other imperial power. It took time and courage for the Indians to expel the British. Unfortunately, Gandhi's success was incomplete.

Reliance on a charismatic leader was a mixed blessing, for while Gandhi left an impressive history of experience in non-violent tactics, his assassination pulled the rug out from under non-violence in India. The same could be said about Martin Luther King, who similarly pioneered domestic revolution, but was too heavily relied on as a leader. For these reasons, it's often said that non-violence failed in both Gandhi's and King's cases. It's true that violence overtook both movements. A part of the dynamic of empowerment explains this phenomenon. Each leader addressed and ended the sense of powerlessness felt by his people. In each case, the aroused sense of power, coupled with impatience *and the prevailing belief that power is inevitably expressed in violence,* ran over the exciting new currents like the faster water that breaks over the top of a wave to crash on the sand. This phenomenon of break-away violence released by empowerment might be controlled *if* advance planning, training and education were to take place so that the civilian citizenry were to learn to construe power and change in non-violent terms.

It can't be said that non-violence has failed: it hasn't been adequately tried. Gene Sharp has compiled excellent accounts of some of the more notable instances of non-violence used as a defensive strategem. He points out that most have been spontaneous. We don't know what would happen if systematic, disciplined education and preparation were made for non-violent defense, though spontaneous instances are encouraging. Part of the problem we face is that so pervasive has been the equation of power and defense with violence, that those who have recorded history, not to mention news, have missed evidence of non-violent power and non-violent defense measures. They have missed what they have not looked for.

Lech Walesa positively chortles as he advises,

> And just take our example, and note that we have not fired a single shot. And we do not know what other means would have to be employed here to win such a victory as ours, except without firing a single shot. I think that the twentieth and twenty-first century should be modeled on a struggle such as the one we have demonstrated. This is a new weapon. Well, not a new one. Actually, an old one. But it is very effective, and tailored exactly to the needs of the twenty-first century.

Solidarity's non-violent battle in Poland is as clearly marked by reverses as a military battle might be. When Solidarity makes gains, the government engages in repression. Sometimes Solidarity has to lie low, to regroup, to repair, but what marks such struggles, unlike military struggles, is that a new civilian order is being created *as the struggle takes place.* War and revolution develop military skills which are inappropriate to civilian government. Further, military engagement always inflicts wounds that anger and embitter some of the population. Aggrieved factions, thus, nearly always spring out of violence and nearly always stimulate repression. Revolution waged Solidarity-style requires the development of trust, community, acceptable policy-making mechanisms and mutually recognized values which will be the sources of post-revolutionary legitimacy. Non-violent revolution, lacking coercive measures, develops other means of gaining and keeping loyalty. Individuals, not required to set aside conscience for the duration, will have greater post-revolutionary integrity: there will be fewer people divided against themselves.

The same advantages should prevail in the case of non-violent defense, some-times called "civilian-based defense," which means that no special part of the population is assigned the task of defense. I've always thought the most extreme discrimination is bringing boys into the world and raising them in the knowledge that in their adolescence they will be called to interrupt their lives, to set aside their plans, to postpone their aspirations, to ignore their particular talents, in order to become soldiers. They are taught, of course, not that they are discriminated against, but that they are accorded high honor. When they become soldiers, they are further indoctrinated and trained to set aside civic virtue and primal conscience in order to be ready killers and victims. They are expected to be heroic in facing what the rest of the population is expected not to have to face. (I sometimes wonder whether rape and incest have anything to do with hidden resentments about the duty to protect women and children at the expense of their own lives.) Just War Theory, in attempting to retain the habit of warfare while minimizing its damage, specifies that soldiers are fair targets for killing, but not civilians. Civilians are considered "innocent," whereas soldiers are apparently not. And yet, soldiers are trained to think that in committing acts of war, they are immunized from ordinary morality. So they find themselves in a bind: taught to override everyday morality, which makes killing and destruction crimes; taught that everyday morality doesn't apply to warriors; yet considered guilty for purposes of protecting those at home who fail to carry their share of the defense burden.

Civilian-based defense allocates the burden of defense more fairly. Those in *need* of defense defend. Women and children are not singled out for preferential treatment, and are thus less likely to be singled out (I suspect) for acts of personal abuse. Communities whose civilian populations defend them must work together, sharing both danger and advantage, reducing the gender-specific division of labor that warfare has promoted.

Nearly all theorists and practitioners of non-violence insist that loving the en-emy is essential. Martin Luther King was careful to point out that to love didn't mean necessarily to like the enemy. But something more radical, a fundamental respect, is associated with non-violence. The psychology of really powerful people is that they do not *need* objects of hatred. But there are also moral and pragmatic reasons for loving the enemy.

To love one's enemy is to recognize the essential humanity of self and enemy, to recognize that while Truth exists, no one or no one camp is privy to it. Because I can change, if the enemy is essentially like me, he too can change: his position contains some element of Truth, which mine does not monopolize. Loving one's enemy gives the enemy an alternative—which he may or may not elect—not to behave brutally, to stop clubbing or commanding police dogs or shooting. Further, recognizing the enemy's humanity is to recognize that his institutions are made up of such persons, each capable of change, of withdrawing consent. The recognition of an enemy's similarity makes it easier to lay plans. It also makes ending a strug-gle easier when one has not made enemies in order to hate them.

Just as in military battle, in nonviolent struggle there comes a time when the war is considered over. The Indian soldiers wearing British uniforms, clubbing

Gandhian troops attempting to take back a salt mine, stop clubbing. Someone realizes either that it will do no good to continue battering the non-violent forces, or that it is undesirable to continue beating them. The grounds for more enduring peace are, thus, laid during "war." Each side has reason for looking more kindly on the other, for one side has refused to injure and the other has ceased to injure.

Detailed application of non-violent defense policies have not yet been worked out. Such application is a rich field for invention in communities determined not to put up with the consequences of being forever faced by the present dilemma— forever, that is, until someone blinks and the bombs go off. Such applications do not require specialists: they yield to practical knowledge of the physical, social and economic community in which one lives. Such principles as I have outlined can interrupt the imperatives of revengers' tragedies—before the fifth act. All that has to happen is for one actor—and then another and another—to declare that we will not go on with a play based on a code that will kill us all.

Postscript

This essay was finished shortly before I left for three weeks in Honduras and Nicaragua, where I travelled with a delegation jointly sponsored by the Fellowship of Reconciliation and Witness for Peace. Witness for Peace is an interesting attempt to use *non-violent* forms of intervention to frustrate a state's *military* intervention.

In Nicaragua, the last dictator of the U.S.-backed Somoza dynasty was overthrown in 1979 in a violent revolution: up to 50,000 were killed, many by Somoza who bombed his own towns and villages. When the dust had settled, the strongest element of the revolutionary coalition, the Sandinistas (named for a nationalist revolutionary of some years earlier) began to implement social changes—land reform, literacy, health, economic measures—which those formerly powerful and privileged bitterly resented. They, along with victims of social rupture and some of those caught in the crossfire, fled into neighboring Honduras and Costa Rica to attempt to harass and topple the new government. The U.S./CIA gave money, arms and training—first in secret, then with congressional consent, then (perhaps) in collaboration with rich U.S. individuals—to these *Contra* forces, who—thus armed and equipped and backed by U.S. military installations and exercises in Honduras—became quite formidable. Some U.S. church people, appalled at what they saw as wanton destruction of civilians and the civilian environment, and at the U.S. fabrication of a totalitarian superpower (where the reality was a struggling, but fairly open, new government in a small, poor country), decided to intervene.

This intervention has (for it is ongoing) two aspects: one is to send U.S. citizens to witness, in the sense of seeing and hearing, and to report more accurately than U.S. news media, who tend to report less critically than newspapers in Nicaragua. These witnesses would use alternative communication techniques (newsletter, Christmas card lists, chain letters, talk shows, newspaper columns, citizen hearings, talks to churches, etc.) to convey reality more truthfully. (In pursuit of this goal, my group was conscientious in talking to many sources of information: critics as well as supporters of the revolutionary process; people encountered in the streets, in shops, driving trucks, American Embassy officials, etc.) We found in both Honduras and Nicaragua, everyone—people on all sides of every question—eager to tell their story for transmission. It was a sort of unspoken reliance on John Milton's theory of an unfettered press: that if many tongues speak freely, something approaching the truth may be known. The second aspect of such intervention as is undertaken by Witness for Peace, is placing our bodies—physically—in areas that have been or are likely to be attacked, thereby confronting attackers with the quandry whether to risk killing U.S. citizens, which might provoke public outcry and diminished support. In other words, Witness for Peace interjects itself in a hostage role, between attackers and attacked. It is an experimental, but promising technique, risky, but less so than allowing warfare to flourish and escalate.

ENDNOTES

1. A recent *Newsweek* poll shows that military officers attribute the increased likelihood of nuclear war to America's "falling behind" in the arms buildup. July 9, 1984.
2. Lifton and Falk, *Indefensible Weapons.* (New York: Basic Books, 1982).
3. *The Fate of the Earth,* (New York: Alfred A. Knopf, 1982).
4. February 27, 1984. His objections can be answered. In short form: non-violent interventions are possible; robustness will develop with attention, energy and practice; non-violence does not require sinless practitioners.
5. "The Sleep of Reason Brings Forth Monsters," (March-April, 1983).
6. *The Politics of Nonviolent Action,* I, (Boston: Porter Sargent, 1973).
7. *Toward a Human World Order,* (New York: Paulist Press, 1977).
8. *Eichmann in Jerusalem,* (New York: Viking Press, 1963).
9. "Sleep of Reason"
10. *For Our Own Good,* (New York: Farrar, Strauss and Giroux, 1983).
11. "Sleep of Reason"
12. Though as Israel Charney points out in *How Can We Commit The Unthinkable?* genocide has not been uncommon in history.

EXTREMISM AND THE PARAMILITARY MOVEMENT

Douglas Mitchell

The image is still vivid. In late 1980, while watching the evening news on the television, I saw ten to twelve Klans-members dressed in military-style camouflage fatigues running and crawling through an obstacle course carrying rifles and shooting at human-form targets. The site is a paramilitary training camp in the woods of northern Alabama near Cullman. The camp is called My Lai after the Vietnamese village where civilians were killed by American soldiers, and it is being run by the Invisible Empire, Knights of the Ku Klux Klan. Alabama Grand Dragon Roger Handley is speaking to the invited media representatives as activity continues in the background. What he says about the people being shown is shocking, "They are training to be prepared to provide security for Klan rallies and marches and to kill black people in the race war that is coming."

This scene was of interest to me for a number of interrelated reasons. I work as a Community Relations Representative for the City of Pittsburgh Commission on Human Relations, and for the last five years anti-Klan work has been a part of my job responsibility. I am a Presbyterian minister who has long been a student of social ethics and whose theological commitments stand foursquare against such displays of militant hatred. Finally, I am originally a Southerner who grew up in Birmingham, Alabama, and for whom the Klan raises memories of the murders of three civil rights workers in Philadelphia, Mississippi, of Viola Liuzzo during the march from Selma to Montgomery, and of the four young black girls who died in the bombing of the Sixteenth Baptist Church in Birmingham. My reactions to the scene were mixed. On the one hand, the "soldiers" were more awkward than imposing, more clumsy than intimidating. They looked like young and middle-aged adults trying unsuccessfully to master the intricacies of a children's game of battle. But on the other hand, they were reported to be carrying high-powered assault weapons and training in attack-and-run techniques, which made their apparent ineptness considerably less comforting. The facts of the scene, however—the camp, the training, the "soldiers" and the weapons are a stark display of a reality that is on the rise in America—the recruitment, maintenance and training of private armies to support and further ideological beliefs.

[275]

Over the last thirty years there have been a substantial number of groups at the extremes of both the right and the left of the American political and social spectrum. On the right have been such well-known groups as the various factions of the Klan, the American Nazi Party, the National States Rights Party and the Liberty Lobby. On the left there have been groups such as the Communist and Socialist Workers Parties, the Progressive Labor Party, the Weather Underground Organization, the Black Liberation Army and the *Fuerza Armadas de Liberacion National Puertoriquena* (FALN). There has been a propensity to violence in many of these groups. The Klans have long been known for their use of terrorism, mutilation and murder against their "enemies." Particularly in the late 1960's and the 1970's the Weather Underground was responsible for a number of bombings and attacks on police and as recently as 1981, members of this group were involved in the highly publicized robbery of a Brinks armored car in which a Brinks guard and two police officers were killed. A pamphlet distributed in 1981 by the International Committee Against Racism proclaims "Only Mass Violence Can Stop the Klan—Join IN-CAR Now!" There are many issues raised by the beliefs and activities of these groups that warrant study and theological reflection by a church which has committed itself to peacemaking as a major thrust. This paper, however, is going to focus specifically on the rise of paramilitary activity as a part of the strategy of ideological groups and parties.

Paramilitary Movement: Definition and Development

This paramilitary movement is characterized by the on-going maintenance of private militias which are organized along military lines, are heavily armed and who receive training in military strategy, discipline and tactics and in the use of a large variety of weapons. These private and at least partially secret armies have no official ties to or sanction from the official United States military systems or from any level of government. In recent history, these quasi-military units have been primarily a phenomenon of the far right and are being maintained by hate groups, survivalist churches and extremist political parties for three primary purposes: to intimidate and control the "enemies" identified by each group, to provide security for meetings and rallies of these groups, and to attempt to guarantee the survival of the white Aryan peoples in a widely expected race war. Details in the level and sophistication of the military training and in the beliefs of different groups vary and will be examined in more detail later, but as a Klanwatch report points out, there does seem to be an elite group of racial and religious bigots forming around these paramilitary units. "Increasingly," they say, "the camouflage uniform, combat boots and assault rifle have supplanted the old symbols of hate—the flaming cross and the Nazi swastika—as the 1980's image of right-wing terror. . ."[1] The cross and swastika are still key symbols of the extreme right, but the increasing militaristic activity does indicate that there has been a significant shift in tactics being followed by such groups.

The historical predecessors of the current paramilitary movement can be traced to around 1960 when groups such as the California Rangers and the Minutemen were founded by William R. Gale and Robert DePugh respectively.[2] A major element of these organizations was an armed militia that stockpiled food and weapons and carried out military-type training for its members. The California Rangers held a violently racist and anti-Semitic ideology, while the Minutemen concentrated more on anticommunism and predictions of the inevitable invasion of the United States by the Communists. According to a 1965 report by the California State Attorney General, the California Rangers were categorized as "a threat to the peace and security of our state," and the report also noted that "the California Rangers were 'closely linked in views, activities and personnel to Dr. Wesley Swift and his 'Identity' church, the Church of Jesus Christ Christian'."[3] This early link with the Identity church movement is very important because the theology of Identity has been adopted widely among current extremist groups. There is also a direct link of personnel between each of these early paramilitary groups and the current vigilante group the Posse Comitatus.

There is a strong element of survivalism in the ideology of the Minutemen that is now a key factor in most of the contemporary paramilitary organizations. This survivalism is a response to the belief that there is to be an imminent apocalyptic fall of the American or worldwide society into anarchy, caused by the "enemies" as defined by each survivalist group. The response is a program of military-type training and stockpiling caches of food, medicines, weapons and other supplies to be ready for the coming strife. The most typically articulated scenario is that the Communists are going to overthrow the country after using blacks and Jews to initiate a cataclysmic race war which will bring on internal collapse. The strategic expectations of these groups range from the mere survival of the group itself to the establishment of interim governments and racial states. Currently, much of the actual instruction in military techniques and weapons proficiency is being done by combat-experienced Vietnam-era veterans who were disillusioned by the American defeat there. Many of these veterans combine an avid anticommunism and a hostility toward the federal government and the "establishment" with a level of expertise and devotion to their cause which increases the seriousness of the potential threat represented by the groups to which they belong.

With this emphasis on survivalism as a consistent element, there were three primary developments within the far-right paramilitary movement through the 1960's and 1970's. First, a number of new groups were founded, including a vigilante association, the Posse Comitatus, and several extremely racist and anti-Semitic survivalist religious communities. Second, many long-established hate groups such as various Klan factions and political parties such as the National Socialist Party of America incorporated paramilitary units and training into their array of extremist activities. And third, a set of theological doctrines called the Identity or Kingdom Identity movement were adopted by almost all the paramilitary groups in order to provide a religious justification for their racist and anti-Semitic views. The development of the Identity movement in its current form was attributed earlier to Minuteman leader Dr. Wesley Swift and his California-based Church of Jesus Christ Christian. The movement takes its name from that church's quarterly newspaper, "Identity,"[4] and it provides an ideological link among a large number of "super-patriot" white supremacy, neo-Nazi and survivalist groups. In a

New York Times article on Identity, there is a description of the much publicized 1983 incident involving a Posse Comitatus member, Gordon Kahl, who was forced underground when he killed two federal marshalls in North Dakota. Kurt Saxon, a former Minuteman and member of the American Nazi Party who is now a widely known survivalist, discusses why people in Arkansas who were not members of Posse Comitatus were willing to shelter Kahl from law enforcement agencies:

"They were members of another right-wing group," he said, "but they were also Identity. Now, the Klan is totally Identity. I don't care what label they use, they are Identity. Most of the Nazi groups are totally Identity. I don't care what label they use, they are Identity."

"It is like one big club," Mr. Saxon continued, "and if you are on the run, a believer will shelter you regardless if he wears the overt label or not. I mean these people who sheltered Gordon were not Posse, they were Identity, therefore, they were obliged to do everything they could for him."[5]

The Identity Movement

This religious system, called Identity or Kingdom Identity by different adherents, had its origin in England in 1837, when the Rev. John Wilson developed a novel interpretation of the Biblical prophecy of glory for the descendants of Jacob: he identified these descendents as the modern English.[6] Anglo-Israelism, as the movement which grew out of Wilson's writing was called, "identifies Anglo-Saxons with the Ten Lost Tribes." Its adherents claim that the promises made to Israel are to be fulfilled with regard to England and America.[7] These teachings came to America later in the nineteenth century as a small sect, but was never of any note until the late 1950's when the teachings of the Aryan races as the true Israel began to be developed into a system of religious legitimation for racist and anti-Semitic beliefs by people like Swift and William Gale. Different self-proclaimed ministers in Identity churches preach some variations in doctrine, but the basic beliefs are that while Adam and Eve are the parents of Abel, the fall came about when Eve had intercourse with Satan and bore Cain. Adam's descendants, through Abel, are the Anglo-Saxon white races while the Jews and all non-white races are descendants of Satan through Cain. The true Israel, God's chosen people, therefore, is the Aryan race, of which Jesus was a member, and not the Jews who are identified with Judah and have been cursed.

This teaching that whites are of the seed of God while Jews and all non-whites are of the seed of Satan is used as the basis for the belief in the inherent superiority of the white race over all others. To let one of the Identity churches speak for itself, the Covenant, the Sword and the Arm of the Lord preaching declares " 'We believe the Scandinavian-Germanic-Teutonic-British-American people to be the Lost Sheep of the House of Israel which Jesus was sent for'," and "that 'Jews of today are not God's chosen people, but are in fact an antichrist race, whose purpose is to destroy God's people and Christianity through its Talmudic teachings, forced inter-racial mixings and perversions'."[8] Throughout the Identity movement there is this satanic conspiracy theory in which Jews are seen as sons of the Devil who are out to destroy the white race. This is paralleled by the teachings that blacks and all non-whites are of an inferior status spiritually because of their origin from Satan's seed and therefore must be controlled and dominated by whites for the good and safety of all. Different leaders emphasize these strains of anti-Semitism and racism with varying prominence, but both are always present to some extent. There is also a general belief that the second coming of Christ will occur in the near future and that Identity members must prepare themselves for the race wars and chaos that will precede it. This provides the theological justification for the survivalist training and militarism which was discussed earlier. One of the major developers and proclaimers of the theology of hate is the Aryan Nations group which is located in Idaho and is led by "the Reverend" Richard Butler, a self-proclaimed Identity minister. It is particularly important because it serves as a communications link for a very large number of extreme racist and anti-Semitic groups both in this country and throughout the neo-Nazi movement in Europe. Butler's preaching of Identity doctrines therefore reaches a very wide audience.

Dr. Rosemary Radford Ruether, a professor of theology at Garrett-Evangelical Theological Seminary, describes a 1981 encounter she had with an Identity group while she and they were both attending conferences at the United Methodist's Lake Junaluska Conference Center in North Carolina. While seeing the "supremacy of the Aryan-white race" being publicly proclaimed in theological and social terms was shocking, Dr. Ruether was more struck by the application of these beliefs to the contemporary political situation—that the election of far-right politicians supported by far-right religious groups was undermining national commitments to social justice and civil rights and "giving sanction to racist extremism to emerge again and claim to represent American values."[9] She gives this reaction to the application of Identity doctrines to the current scene by a group which included President Reagan's inaugural address as a part of its charter:

> Perhaps most startling of all was the way the group is claiming the present Reagan regime as the propitious moment for the emergence and victory of the white Israel. They look forward eagerly to the worsening of the economic status of black and brown Americans that will come about under the present administration. They expect this will lead to renewed urban rioting. But they counsel their people to arm themselves for this development as a holy 'race war' that is being blessed by God. This will be the divinely ordained time for the white Israel to annihilate the evil children of Satan, or the non-white races, and purify the earth.[10]

With this background on the recent history of the far-right paramilitary movement and on the Identity religious movement that provides links of personalities and ideological justification for their activities, we will now turn to an examination of some of the most active groups.

The Invisible Empire, Knights of the Ku Klux Klan

The Invisible Empire is a Klan faction that has been active throughout the eastern half of the United States, and has established at least temporary training camps in Pennsylvania, Illinois and Connecticut as well as the My Lai camp in Alabama and other southern states. The Alabama camp, however, the training site for the Klan "Special Forces," is the most active. Details about the regularity and sophistication of the Special Forces training are sketchy. It is clear that members of the Klan Special Forces were present as a security force at all Klan meetings and rallies through 1980 and 1981 and that they were heavily armed with pistols, shotguns and semi-automatic weapons. In June, 1982, a lawsuit was filed by the Southern Poverty Law Center "on behalf of the NAACP and all black citizens of Alabama" against Bill Wilkinson, the Invisible Empire, Knights of the KKK, and the commander and all individual members of the Klan Special Forces.[11] The result of the suit was a 1984 injunction stating "that the 'defendants and their members, servants, agents, assigns, are hereby enjoined from associating, assembling or congregating together by or under any name in a military capacity for the purpose of drilling, parading or marching at any time or place in Alabama or otherwise take up or bear arms in any capacity'."[12] There was no trial because of the voluntary agreement of all parties to the injunction, but the early fact-finding stages of the investigation clearly indicate there was violation of an Alabama law which prohibits private armies, because it was found that at the training sites, " 'The Klan "soldiers" were armed with high-powered assault weapons, took orders from a "commander-in-chief," and learned rudimentary guerilla warfare techniques'."[13] It appears that paramilitary activity associated with the Invisible Empire in Alabama has in fact fallen off dramatically as a result of the lawsuit. Another feature of the Invisible Empire's program does continue, however. There are several active youth camp programs where the typical athletics and crafts are supplemented by indoctrination of the children in the Klan ideology of hate and by weapons training with legal small-caliber rifles which are given to children eight years old and up.

The Texas Knights of the Ku Klux Klan/Texas Emergency Reserve

Probably the most active and expert Klan paramilitary training has been directed by Louis Beam, Grand Dragon (leader) of the Texas Knights of the KKK and head of a private militia called the Texas Emergency Reserve. Beam is also an active Identity minister, and he holds the post of "ambassador-at-large" for Aryan Nations, a continuation of Wesley Swift's Church of Jesus Christ Christian.[14] The Texas Emergency Reserve made national headlines in February, 1981, when they appeared in camouflage fatigues and fully armed with semi-automatic rifles at a Texas Knights of the KKK rally called to support white shrimp fishermen who were attacking Vietnamese refugees for fishing in competition with them along the Texas Gulf coast. There was a typical cross-burning and during the rally, Beam committed the Reserve to an intensive program of harassment of the immigrant Vietnamese fishermen and anyone who supported them or did business with them. A number of shrimp boats owned by the Vietnamese were burned, threatening phone calls were made and there was an almost continual display of weapons, including several "boat patrols" during which a boatload of heavily armed Klansmen in full robes and regalia cruised the area around Galveston with an effigy of a Vietnamese man hanging from the rigging. This kind of campaign against foreign, non-white immigration into the United States has also led the Texas Knights as well as the California Knights under Tom Metzger to conduct armed "border patrols" along the Mexican border to keep anyone from crossing the border into the U.S.

The history of this Texas Emergency Reserve goes back to 1975 when John Sisente, a former Marine who had fought in Vietnam, founded the Veterans for Victory Over Communism. He established "Camp Puller" near the U.S. Army base, Fort Hood, with the intent of forming a private army unit which would go back to Vietnam and fight to save the government in Saigon.[15] The government declined Sisente's offer of assistance, but he continued to operate Camp Puller as a paramilitary training site. The program soon began to attract a number of Klansmen. In the late 1970's, the Texas Knights of the KKK and some small splinter Klans decided to form a Klan paramilitary unit and they joined Sisente's group to form the Texas Emergency Reserve.[16] Louis Beam moved into the leadership position of the private army and its extensive training program. Klan members and others, most of whom were Vietnam veterans, came from all over the country to be trained in techniques of guerilla warfare, tactical maneuvers and weapons proficiency, including training with Colt AK-15 assault rifles with grenade launching attachments.[17] There were at least four training sites in east Texas, the largest being Camp Puller.

Camp Puller has also been used as a Klan Youth Corps training camp where Youth Corps members and others have been given indoctrination and weapons training. In November, 1980, it was discovered that a Klansman and a Scout leader were giving training in guerilla war tactics and weapons use to a group of Explorer Scouts, ages 13 to 20, and Civil Air Patrol members ages 13 to 19 at Camp Puller.[18] Primarily, however, the camp was used for the training of adult soldiers for the far-right private army which had been harrassing the Vietnamese along the Texas Gulf coast. In April, 1981, the Southern Poverty Law Center filed suit in federal court on behalf of the Vietnamese Fisherman's Association to stop the on-going intimidation and violence by the Texas Emergency Reserve. The next month the complaint was amended to ask the court to enjoin the Klan from operating paramilitary training camps in Texas. In major precedent-setting decisions, U.S. District Judge Gabrielle McDonald issued a preliminary injuction in May, 1982, ordering the Klan and the Texas Emergency Reserve to cease engaging in unlawful acts against the Vietnamese and then in June, 1982, issued an order, based on a Texas law prohibiting private armies, banning all paramilitary training in Texas. Evidence and testimony given at the trial show how closely the Texas Emergency Reserve resembled a regular military reserve unit:

> According to sworn testimony, it has a command structure, its members own or have access to an extensive arsenal of such sophisticated weapons as AR-15 semi-automatic rifles, semi-automatic .12 gauge shotguns known as the Atchisson Assault 12, which resembles a machine gun and is capable of rapidly firing up to 20 magnum shells, and other assorted carbines, rifles and shotguns. The T.E.R. even has a regimental flag. Many of its members are veterans, and film clips of their training exercise demonstrate a high degree of familiarity with military tactics.[19]

Pointing to the threat to individuals' civil rights represented by such training, Judge McDonald wrote, "Regardless of whether it is called 'defense training' or 'survival courses,' it is clear to this court that the proliferation of military/paramilitary organizations can only sow the seeds of future domestic violence and tragedy."[20] A part of the importance of this decision is that there are similar laws prohibiting private armies in at least twenty-four other states. This ruling, for example, was cited as precedent in the court proceedings which led to an injunction against paramilitary activity in Alabama in 1984.

The National Socialist Party of America

Some hate groups are organized into political parties. One of these is the National Socialist Party of America (NSPA) which is best known for its attempts to hold a Nazi rally and march in the village of Skokie, Illinois, in 1977-78. The Chicago office has since become a regional office and under the new leadership of Harold Covington, the central office, "the Office of the Party Leader and Storm Trooper Command," has been moved to Raleigh, North Carolina.[21] A series of incidents in 1979 shows clearly the uses to which formal paramilitary training can be put. One of the unit leaders of the NSPA, who was also a leader in the Carolina Knights of the KKK owns a farm in Johnson County, N.C., which is a NSPA center and has been the site for weapons and tactics training for a number of different racist and anti-Semitic groups. Over the weekend of September 22-23, 1979, there was a meeting in North Carolina for the purpose of forming a "United Racist Front." The three major parties were the Klan—representing several factions including the Carolina Knights—the National States Rights Party and the National Socialist Party of America.[22] All of these groups included members who had received paramilitary training at the Johnson County farm. Just over one month after the United Racist Front was formed, a group of approximately a hundred participants in a legally sanctioned march in Greensboro, N.C., were attacked by about forty Klansmen and Nazis who belonged to groups within the new Front. Five of the demonstrators were killed in the ensuing gunfire. Some of the marchers were found to be carrying handguns, but they proved to be no match for the heavily armed caravan of attackers who were members of groups which had received paramilitary training. Training at the Johnson County NSPA center continues under the banner of defensive and survivalist training, and to date there has been no formal legal challenge to the activities.

Posse Comitatus

Posse Comitatus is a loosely confederated group of survivalist- and vigilante-oriented units which are active in a large number of states, primarily in the Midwest and West. Although it has been in existence since 1969, it had not received much general publicity until the 1983 incident involving Gordon Kahl and federal marshals which was mentioned earlier. The name means "power of the county" in Latin and indicates one of their main beliefs—that there is no legitimate government above the county level. Members often refuse to pay state and federal taxes because they do not recognize these as legitimate levels of government, and it is typical for members to resist such tax collection with armed force as well as to harass and threaten public officials whose job it is to collect taxes. One of their favorite recent targets for armed displays has been sheriff's sales of farms brought on because of the inability of the owner to pay taxes or to meet mortgages.

Two of the national leaders of this coalition are James Wickstrom of Tigerton, Wisconsin, and William Gale of Glendale, California. Both are self-proclaimed Identity ministers and they encourage and assist local Posse groups to form their own Identity churches.[23] There have been a large number of paramilitary training seminars held by Posse Comitatus throughout the areas where they are active such as Colorado, Kansas, Missouri and California. These seminars have involved training in a broad range of military tactics, bomb-making, the administration of poisons, the use of heavy weapons, and techniques for the stockpiling of food, supplies and weapons for later use. There is now fear on the part of federal officials about the level of these activities. "Inspector Kupferer of the Marshals Service said: 'There has been some information that they are into R.P.G.'s—rocket-propelled grenades—mortars, explosive and protective equipment, heavy-duty armor, that type of thing. And so with some of the information we got with some of their training grounds and tactics, it fits.' "[24] Gale, in particular, spends time preaching the racist and anti-Semitic doctrines of the Identity movement. He tapes sermons and other messages spelling out these doctrines and their practical implications of hatred for a radio program, "The National Identity Broadcast," which is carried on a number of stations. Currently, the National Conference of Christians and Jews, the Kansas Attorney General and other individuals and organizations are petitioning the Federal Communications Commission asking that the license of Station KTTL, Dodge City, not be renewed because of their regular broadcasting of Gale's and Wickstrom's extremist sermons.[25]

The Covenant, the Sword and the Arm of the Lord (CSA)

This is one of two major survivalist paramilitary churches that were established in the 1970's and which are associated with the Identity movement. The rhetoric of the CSA is violently racist and anti-Semitic, and it predicts the apocalyptic collapse of the American society which is typical of survivalist groups. It is sometimes difficult to convey the level of hatred represented by such rhetoric, so I will let the CSA present its own vision of the future from the group's journal:

"Russia and possibly China and Japan will attack America, probably with some limited nuclear warfare. Communists will kill white Christians and mutilate them; witches and satanic Jews will offer people up as sacrifices to their gods, openly and proudly; blacks will rape and kill white women, and will torture and kill white men; homosexuals will sodomize whoever they can. Prisoners from Federal and State prisons will be set free to terrorize while Cuban refugees will do the same. Nowhere will be safe without the grace of God."[26]

In order to prepare believers for the coming race war, the CSA maintains a paramilitary program called the "Endtime Overcomer Survival Training School" at its communal settlement, Zarepath-Horeb, which is named for "a Biblical purging place."[27] At this school selected persons are given instruction in the whole range of survivalist, military and weapons training that has been described earlier. The primary use that has been made of these trained CSA members has been to serve as a heavily armed security force for meetings and rallies of other Identity-related groups.

Christian-Patriots Defense League (CPDL)

This is the second major survivalist religious group which carries out paramilitary training and which holds a conspiracy view of history pointing to the inevitable collapse of the society. The CPDL was founded in 1977 by John Harrell as one part of a four-part overall organization designed to establish a huge area in the middle of America which will be secured for patriotic white Christians when the catastrophic fall occurs.[28] A primary on-going activity of the CPDL is the sponsorship of annual "Freedom Festivals." These Freedom Festivals have attracted participants from a large number of racist, anti-Semitic survivalist and mercenary groups. Along with preaching of the whole range of Identity doctrines, the Festivals provide even more than normal variety of paramilitary training in strategy, tactics and weapons proficiency as well as information on gun procurement. In describing the CPDL's purpose, Harrell provides a good list of the "enemies" that white patriots must contend with, " 'humanism, modernism, communism, regionalization, Judaism, integration, taxation, gun-confiscation' and other 'atrocities perpetuated by evil men' among whom are the 'Christ-hating International Jewish Conspiracy.' "[29] Some of the anti-tax, anti-federal-government-policy sentiment that is particularly characteristic of the Posse Comitatus is seen here along with the usual Identity hate list.

Harrell has been active in extreme right-wing politics for over twenty years. In 1959, he founded the Christian Conservative Churches of America "to 'blend Christianity and Patriotism together to effectively oppose Zionism and Communism'."[30] This church has qualified for tax-exempt status, therefore, all of the huge estate and buildings that make up the central compound of the CPDL are exempt from property taxes. Besides the Christian-Patriots Defense League and the Christian Conservative Churches of America, the other two parts of Harrell's organizational complex are the Paul Revere Club, a fund-raising arm, and the Citizens Emergency Defense System (CEDS) which is an extensive private militia. The Defense System includes a series of Christian-Patriots Defense Posts which will be the gathering places for the paramilitary units when the anticipated collapse occurs.[31] The ultimate purpose of this extensive complex of organizations is to create a secure survival area covering most of America's heartland which will be governed by the CPDL and policed by the White Christian militia of the CEDS. As Harrell himself has said:

> "When the collapse of the American government occurs . . . patriots and others like them will gather in the central United States, regroup and start putting the country back together. Their country will need a strong leader and

[284]

we will provide him . . things will be so bad that government will have to be centralized and a single man—a dictator, if you will—will have to take control. Then when things are in order in a few years, we will restore this country to true democracy."[32]

This future democracy, of course, will be established to reflect the white supremacy and anti-Semitic views which are religiously sanctified by Identity doctrine.

This entire fantastic scenario is on its face difficult to take seriously. The examples of Greensboro and the patrols along the Texas Gulf coast, however, are only two of the actual uses to which trained personnel have been put within the last five years. Many more examples of individual and small-unit attacks could also be given. The level to which such personnel are armed and the scope of their training means that this element of the militaristic far right cannot responsibly be ignored.

Mercenaries/Survivalists/Soldiers of Fortune

A brief word needs to be said about a closely related but distinguishable set of activities that also contribute to the militarization of the American society. There are survivalist and mercenary training schools and activities that are less overtly ideological than the kind of groups that have just been examined. They do, however, carry on the same kinds of activities—the training of individuals in combat tactics and techniques, weapons use, and other similar subjects. What are not present are the command-structure and internal, military-style discipline that distinguishes the private militias and the systematic indoctrination in doctrines of bitter racial, ethnic and religious hatred. While they make it perfectly clear that they take no responsibility for the actions of their clients after the training is completed, the leaders of these training schools avoid direct identification with any extremist groups, and they try carefully to operate within the law. There seems, however, to be a nearly universal tendency toward strident anticommunism, a conspiracy view of reality and strong elements of racism in this survivalist/soldier of fortune worldview. The most blatant extension of this view into the general culture are the wide assortment of militarist, weapons-oriented magazines that are sold at virtually every book shop, drug store, airport and sidewalk newsstand with such titles as *Soldier of Fortune: The Journal of Professional Adventurers, Survival Guide,* and *New Breed: The Magazine for the Bold Adventurer.*

In all the groups reviewed here there is a consistent commitment to reliance on military-type force and the use of a wide range of weaponry, from knives and cross-bows to assault rifles and explosives as the only ways to guarantee safety against an assortment of perceived enemies. A set of common beliefs which bind them are that there is much in this world of which to be afraid, and that only by taking extraordinary precautions can one feel any level of safety. Their world is one of fear and suspicion that can only be made secure by force.

The Importance of Religious Legitimation

As members of the United Presbyterian Church in the U.S.A., we affirm a very different worldview than has thus far been described. We recognize that there are indeed threats in the modern world, to peace, to justice, even to survival, but the threats we fear are not understood as normative. We are instructed and encouraged to face the seriousness of such threats head on, but with faith and hope rather than with suspicion and force. The United Presbyterian Church has made clear in its theological and social statements that hatred and unnecessary violence are evils which must be overcome by love. It is true that at the level of congregational action our churches have all too often failed to live up to the commitments of the church as a whole by not taking leadership and speaking out on issues of racial and religious hatred in their own communities. But at least the "party line" is clear for this church.

The party line is clear as well for the extremist groups we have just examined, and in many ways it is no less "church doctrine" for the Klan or the Christian-Patriots Defense League than it is for the Presbyterians. The basic meaning for the Greek term *ecclesia,* which is translated in the Bible as "church," is a group of people who meet together for some commonly understood purpose. It is a group who feel "called out" from others for a purpose and who organize themselves in an on-going structure in order to carry out that purpose. With this understanding, these extremist groups can be seen as *ecclesia,* as churches, in the same way as the normally recognized churches. Some actually call themselves church communities, but all of them function in many of the same ways our congregations do. They provide meaning and doctrine, fellowship, a sense of community and definitions of good and evil.

Many of these groups have a long history of claiming to be Christian (white Christian, of course) communities, and for very important reasons. The Klan is a good example of this. From the time of the rebirth of the modern Klan in 1915, the cross has been a central symbol. For those outside the Klan this has been seen as sacrilege. But as current Klan literature explains it, "The fiery cross is used as a Klan symbol representing the ideals of Christian civilization. In no way does it represent a desecration of the cross, for it actually represents the lighting of the cross, that is, the truth and the light of our sacred doctrine." Klan doctrine has long been cloaked in language of "old-time Protestant religion" as a way to provide theological justification for these beliefs. Because they know their beliefs will be seen by many as outrageous, it is all the more important that they be given legitimacy by Biblical and theological explanations. A burning cross which is used as a tool of terror and intimidation is described among those who use it as a "cross lighting" which is to show the light of the Christian faith to the world. This is racial and religious hatred being packaged and sold in theological terms.

There have always been nagging problems with the support and legitimation provided by such religious language however. It has been difficult to justify white supremacy from a Bible which teaches an ethic of love—and then there is the problem of Jesus being a Jew. The reinterpretations of the old Anglo-Israelism into the current Identity movement have attempted to provide solutions to these problems so that the religious legitimation will fit more smoothly. The Biblical and theological construction of the Identity view of Christianity strikes the outside reader as tortured, but it is extremely important as a report of the testimony from one of the major Klan leaders attests:

> In California, Grand Dragon Tom Metzger says he "encourages" the members of his independent Klan to join the Identity movement.
> Metzger said he had always been "confused" about religion before he heard an Identity minister speak at a "tax protest" meeting in the early 1970's. "It really turned me around," he said. "That was when I became a really formidable racist."[33]

The theological system provides explanation and order for beliefs that otherwise seem unreconcilable, and it allows the believer to justify a dedication to hatred on the basis of a religion that is normally recognized as a religion of love. In other words, it is a system of lies about Christianity with a very important role to play.

Peacemaking vs. Hatemongering

The United Presbyterian Church adopted peacemaking as a primary mission on the basis of the 1980 report, *Peacemaking: The Believers' Calling*. This report provides an excellent Biblical and theological understanding of the church and the society, and I am going to use some of this material as a framework for theological analysis of the contemporary paramilitary movement. It is interesting to note that this report was commissioned by the 187th General Assembly in 1975 in response to certain changes in the world situation. The first major change pointed to is "the United States' defeat in Southeast Asia and the loss of prestige and power in the changing world situation."[34] What is interesting is that at about this same time, from the early to the mid-1970's, many of the extremist groups of the right were responding to this same set of circumstances in a very different way. The events in Vietnam fed the apocalyptic anticommunism of these groups and increased their fears of an invasion of America at the same time as they provided a large number of distressed veterans with combat experience. The Aryan Nations, the Christian-Patriots Defense League, the Texas Emergency Reserve, and the Covenant, the Sword and the Arm of the Lord, for example, each contributed to the development of the Identity movement and to the shift in hate groups to paramilitary training during this period. The church turned to a call for dedication to peacemaking as a way to promote security and safety while the extremists turned to paramilitary training as a way to protect their racist, anti-Semitic ideologies in the collapse of civilization which they saw as both inevitable and imminent. The differences in response reflect basic commitments to faith as opposed to fear, love as opposed to hate, inclusiveness as opposed to exclusiveness, and justice as opposed to oppression.

The call to peacemaking declares the fundamental theological beliefs that, "The body of Christ responds to the world's pain with empathy and anguish, one to another, in our time," and that "Peace is the intended order of the world with life abundant for all God's children."[35] These are again radically different from The Covenant, the Sword and the Arm of the Lord's stated belief in racial separation in which " 'each race is to do as God created that race for, which is for the white race to have dominion over all things and for other races to serve in love.' "[36] Rather than mutuality and community as primary values there is a theology of separateness in which there is racial, ethnic and religious superiority for a specified few who are preparing themselves to respond militarily to any threats from those who they feel were meant to serve them. The effects on a community of this kind of violent presence can be immense. While there are only a small number of individuals who are actually members of these groups, their numbers can have an inordinate impact, at least in part because of the kinds of publicity their radical actions are given. Their presence tends to increase the notion that differences can best be settled by resort to violence, on a massive scale if necessary. The threat of this level of violence increases feelings of fear and distrust in a community and can lead those who feel directly threatened or offended to respond violently as well. The extreme groups also strike a responsive chord in a broader spectrum of people who are alienated or angry about local issues, but who would not actually become a member of such a group. The rhetoric of group hatred provides emotional and ideological support for non-affiliated individuals which can encourage them to act out in imitation of the acts called for by extremist leaders. This escalation of fear, mistrust and defensiveness can make empathetic response and reasoned negotiation around local issues almost impossible. As Rosemary Ruether discovered, this rhetoric of Identity hatred can encourage the analysis of even electoral politics in apocalyptic terms.

The Biblical claims made by these paramilitary groups to justify their actions are particularly inventive. The major themes of reconciliation of enemies, of the equality of all persons before God's love, of the demands for justice as a religious duty are passed over completely and replaced by claims that all non-white races are the result of Eve's intercourse with Satan and therefore must be kept separate and below the white race. Rather than seeing the church as a universal community under Christ which breaks down the former boundaries of race, ethnicity and culture, these groups see themselves as the full extent of the church and these very boundaries are theologically blessed so they cannot be crossed at all. Chauvinism becomes a primary religious value which must be protected by military force if necessary.

A particularly important insight in the report on Peacemaking describes the effects on religious *ecclesia* that result from the abandonment of peacemaking as an essential element of mission:

> The loss of that central purpose threatens the nature of the church and opens doors to the idolatrous service of lesser gods, such as the special interests and purposes of nations, of social and economic systems, of ethnic and racial groups, and of cultural traditions that are of lesser claim than the end to which all creation is directed. Not peace, but strife, is the fruit of idolatrous fanaticism. . . A limited vision tempts us to find peace in the security of these lesser gods, which claim our allegiance, in false confidence in culture, race, economic system, power or nation.

[288]

The quest for peace is easily confused with the quest for security. Fear of what lies around us in the world or ahead of us in time tempts us to exercise power to hold what we have.[37]

The paramilitary *ecclesia* is an extreme example of what results from such loss of purpose. The idolatry of the lesser gods of race, ethnicity, economic system, and nation has indeed resulted in strife rather than peace. Peace has indeed been supplanted by security as a primary value.

For the leaders of these paramilitary groups there is no confidence in the possibility of peace because there is no source of grace. They fear that the conspiracies of their "enemies" will bring them down, and their only available response is the resort to ever-higher levels of militarized security. Their belief system is inadequate to explain the changes they see in the world or to find anything positive in them and therefore they blame their "enemies" for what they can only perceive as increasing disorder. The scapegoats can be blacks, Jews, Communists, school desegregation, welfare, affirmative action, the federal government, taxes or any number of sources for their troubles. The confidence they have placed in institutionalization of racial superiority cannot hold back the slow changes toward equal opportunity, for example, and therefore blacks and liberals become the scapegoats for whatever economic troubles they may have. Many groups have engaged in scapegoating, but now the fear and anger inherent in this process is being backed by private militias. The abandonment of the God of grace for the idolatry of lesser gods even leads these false believers into a dedicated program of turning plowshares into swords: classified ads in the *Survivalist Guide* and *Soldiers of Fortune* magazines offer formulas for sale which use easy-to-obtain and household chemicals for making explosives, and survivalist training includes instruction in this kind of bomb-making. Their paranoia is so strong that they must discover how to turn everyday items with useful purposes into weapons of aggression and defense against the host of their enemies.

The number of individuals who are members of such ideological paramilitary groups is small, but it is growing. No matter how outrageous their beliefs might seem, they must be taken seriously by law enforcement agencies, legal groups, community groups and the media, because the physical and social damage that can be done by even a small number of trained individuals with sophisticated weapons is great indeed. These paramilitary groups must also be taken seriously by the churches which must be strong enough and outspoken enough to unmask the false theology and to stand against idolatry. The mission of peacemaking cannot succeed in communities—local or global—where military might, driven by suspicion is projected as the only source of security, and the church must always stand against this possibility.

ENDNOTES

1. "The Paramilitary Movement: A Klanwatch Report," (Montgomery, Alabama: Klanwatch, 1983), p. 1; hereafter cited as "Paramilitary Report."
2. "Paramilitary Report," p. 2.

3. *Extremism on the Right,* by the Anti-Defamation League of B'nai B'rith (New York: ADL, 1983), p. 86.
4. Wayne King, "Link Seen Among Heavily Armed Rightist Groups," *New York Times,* 11 June 1983, Sect. 1, p. 1.
5. King, P. 5.
6. John Turner, et al., *The Ku Klux Klan: A History of Racism and Violence,* ed. Randall Williams (Montgomery, Alabama: Southern Poverty Law Center, 1981), pp. 45, 47.
7. Extremism, p. 11.
8. Extremism, pp. 7-8.
9. Rosemary Radford Ruether, "The Rise of Bible-Toting Neo-Nazis," *IFCO News,* September-October, 1981, p. 12.
10. Ruether, p. 12.
11. "Paramilitary Unit of KKK is Banned by Judge," *Poverty Law Report,* February, 1984, p. 1; hereafter cited as "Paramilitary Unit."
12. "Paramilitary Unit," p. 2.
13. "Paramilitary Unit," p. 1.
14. *Extremism,* pp. 1, 2.
15. "Paramilitary Report," p. 6.
16. "Paramilitary Report," pp. 6-7.
17. *Hate Groups in America: A record of Bigotry and Violence,* by the Anti-Defamation League of B'nai B'rith (New York: ADL, n.d.), pp. 59-60.
18. "Paramilitary Actions Irk Neighbors of Texas Camp," *New York Times,* 30 November 1980, p. 67; hereafter cited as "Paramilitary Actions."
19. "Klan Paramilitary Activity Banned in Texas," *Poverty Law Report,* September-October, 1982, p. 10; hereafter cited as "Klan Activity."
20. Cindy Horswell, Tom Moran and Nicholas C. Chriss, "Paramilitary Training by Klan is Banned," *Houston Chronicle,* 4 June 1982, p. 1.
21. *Hate Groups,* p. 30.
22. *Hate Groups,* pp. 61, 62.
23. King, p. 5; also see *Extremism,* p. 44.
24. King, p. 5.
25. "Racists Broadcast Calls for Violence," *National Anti-Klan Network Newsletter,* Spring-Summer, 1983, p. 9.
26. *Hate Groups,* p. 51.
27. *Extremism,* p. 7.
28. "Paramilitary Report," p. 17.
29. *Extremism,* p. 5.
30. "Paramilitary Report," p. 16.
31. "Paramilitary Report," pp. 16, 17; for this discussion also see *Hate Groups,* pp. 46-50 and *Extremism,* pp. 5-6.
32. "Paramilitary Report," p. 17.
33. Kirk Loggins and Susan Thomas, " 'There is no Genesis for the Colored or Mongrelized Races. . .'," *The "New" Klan: A Report from the Pages of the Tennessean* (Nashville: The Tennessean, 1978), p. 15.
34. *Peacemaking: The Believers' Calling,* by the General Assembly of the United Presbyterian Church in the U.S.A. (New York: GA, 1980), p. 1.
35. *Peacemaking,* pp. 4, 5.
36. *Hate Groups,* p. 53.
37. *Peacemaking,* p. 18.

A CONCLUDING POSTSCRIPT

The peacemaking struggle is placed between our affirmation of the goodness of God's creation and our hopes for the goodness of God's future. Not all religions affirm the goodness of creation as thoroughly as Christians do. But, the basic beauty and peace of creation is our confession. Likewise neither all religions nor all Christians agree about the shape of God's fulfillment of humanity.

We affirm the goodness with which the Bible concludes as our vision.

> Then I saw a new heaven and a new earth; for the first heaven and the first earth passed away, and the sea was no more. And I saw the holy city, new Jerusalem coming down out of heaven from God prepared as a bride adorned for her husband; and I heard a loud voice from the throne saying: "Behold, the dwelling of God is with humanity. He will dwell with them and they shall be his people, and God himself will be with them;"[1]

Now the way toward that fulfillment is hard. The fulfillment is an apocalyptic image and not political projections. The political context out of which it was projected was the Roman Empire, not the Russian and American imperial struggles.

The way we envisage fulfillment, however, impacts on the way we act now. Even as the recognition that the future is unknown and open is affirmed, our intentions for the future have consequences. The Gospel of Mark has Jesus himself saying that no one knows the time of fulfillment, neither the angels nor the Son, but only God (Mark 13:32-37). Thinking about our world's drift into militarism in conventional armaments, nuclear weapons, and other systems of massive destruction inevitably involves thought about the end of humanity.

No book has had more impact on thinking about nuclear weapons than Jonathan Schell's *The Fate of the Earth*.[2] By providing such an unrelentingly horrible picture of the devastation nuclear war would bring, Schell has penetrated our inclination to deceive ourselves about the character of this weaponry. Surely, as Schell emphasizes, it is not because we are callous about life that we ignore the dangers of nuclear arms. It is because we care so much that we cannot bear the pain or cope with the fear that life might be obliterated. Facing the truth about what the use, accidental or otherwise, of nuclear weapons would mean for God's creation is a fundamental requirement for understanding our situation. Even if one comes to the conclusion that holding nuclear weapons for deterrence is necessary, it can only be credible morally if the consequences of nuclear war are faced with brutal realism. Schell pushes us in such realism not only to face the consequences of mass suicide through nuclear war ("first death") but also death of the future ("second death"), that is the death of unborn generations, of historical memory, of both past and future human creativity. Whereas Schell assumes the probability of an all-out nuclear exchange if the use of such weapons are introduced, Carl Sagan has helped us see the likelihood of a "nuclear winter" in which we would freeze to death by the environmental effects of far fewer nuclear explosions.[3]

What is the theological meaning of this annihilating power that we have brought into the world? What imaginable danger could be greater than that posed by nuclear weapons? Why are we so fascinated by them and attracted to them that we cannot give them up? Is there anything that could be more blasphemous than building a global network of destruction that places God's creation, Earth, at such risk? A scientist theologian has reflected on these questions in words different from, yet also reminiscent of Psalmists:

> It is awesome to contemplate the immense creative investment that has gone into bringing the Earth to her present stage of beauty and fulfillment. The slow but ever-accelerating elaboration of information coded on DNA over an unimaginably vast reach of time has by now produced, suspended in the alien reaches of space, a magic garden and placed within it that strangest achievement of any of the manifold DNA codes—man (humankind). That was possible because of a most delicate balance of gravity, heat, and light realized on the Earth, a balance achieved only very rarely, if at all, on other planets. This uniqueness and the wonder of the creative achievement that it has made possible mean that the Earth is a rare gem of fantastic beauty, and that its desecration or destruction by any being is an act of awful sacrilege against which the heart of all meaning and purpose in the entire universe must cry out in anguish.[4]

Gordon Kaufman, a theologian at the Divinity School of Harvard University, has wondered why religion scholars have not given more attention to the theological significance of nuclear weapons. Certainly, Christians should not rest content with tired cliches about "national security" but ask what this newly developed system of second death means for our views of God, and of human sinfulness and responsibility. Kaufman comments:

> For traditional eschatology there was always some positive meaning—some humanly significant meaning—in the consummating events of history. But our situation is different. The potential catastrophe that we are here called upon to contemplate is empty of any human meaning whatsover."[5]

The time is past when we can expect God to intervene miraculously to stop the nuclear warheads as they leave the launching pad. The capacity to commit planetary holocaust is in human hands—already—and the responsibility is entrusted to us for what happens. The power of God is in our midst for a future different from annihilation if we open our eyes, receive it in faith and respond to it; but God will not intervene to prevent us from engaging in the ultimate act of rebellion through nuclear destruction.

Nuclear destruction is a human possibility, but it is not inevitable. We do not reduce the risk by increased militarism out of our insecurity. To increase the over-kill capacity or to engage in exporting military technology into outer space is like smoking more because we dread lung cancer. Instead we must turn away from the cancer of militarism and the fix of new weapons systems toward the realization of a just peace.

Richard A. Falk has written a paragraph that captures the current reality:

> There are several steps that need to be taken: first we need to understand the inability of the sovereign state to resolve the endangered-planet crisis; second, we need a model of world order that provides a positive vision of the future and is able to resolve this crisis; third, we need a strategy that will transform human attitudes and institutions so as to make it politically possible to bring a new system of world order into being; fourth, we need specific programs to initiate the process, as with learning to walk—we need to learn to walk into the future.

So we have turned away from militarism as represented in the negative theologies and programs of the Secretary of Defense and the President. We read the warning sections of Revelation as projections for the Roman empire and as penultimate to the vision of peace which concludes the book. We read national bellicosity and militarism as characteristic of the present but as a negating program for the future.

The choices between just peace strategies and militarist policies are involved and each person and organization concerned about the future of humanity will be involved in thought and politics over these issues.

The essays on just war theory found that weapons of mass destruction, particularly nuclear weapons, were morally unusable. Debate over the limited-time reliance on nuclear weapons as a deterrent is still an issue on which the country and the churches are divided.

While conventionally thinking of the Soviet Union as a rival or even an enemy, the book has argued for overcoming the walls of animosity. We find no fundamental reasons for these two powers threatening the world with armed bellicosity. Extreme anticommunism leads to the madness of the paramilitary theologies. Those who want to move toward a just peace with human tensions will need to resolve their own feelings about the Cold War conflicts and the politics of their organizations as they relate to overcoming the Cold War. Peacemaking requires answering the question: "What about the Russians?"

There is agreement in Christian thought that justice and peace are inextricably linked. There can be no peace without justice. The cries of injustice are heard from all the flashpoints of the world, particularly South Africa, Central America, and the

Middle East. Similarly the militarism of American society has prevented social justice programs from being funded and has drawn its soldiers disproportionately from the poor. As Allan Boesak reminds us, peacemaking must not be an escape from the social justice struggle. How can our various social justice ministries promote the peacemaking concerns more effectively?

The complexity of the peacemaking struggle has drawn the argument into many problems. The central issue remains, however: Is this the time for the church to declare itself confessionally against present militarist tendencies? Can the "No!" of the church to plans which may destroy all humanity, now be unequivocal? If now is such a time to condemn present militarist tendencies, what tactics of resistance to militarism are required? Can churches now openly discuss and act on questions of the politics of peacemaking, withdrawal of investment funds from war-related industries, withdrawal of vocational allegiance from war-related industries, resistance to military taxes, civil disobedience, sanctuary for refugees and non-violent intervention against military policies?

To what degree can the church as church commit resources and energy to organizations developing the peace movement? How far will the institutional church lead its members in helping them to learn what Christian concerns may discover in these perilous times?

The tactics of resistance need not threaten the tactics of institutional reform. There are tensions but not necessarily contradictions between institutional Christian peacemaking work and resistance. One can both vote and practice civil disobedience. However, the questions of resistance to governmental policies will cause tensions for those committed to working with government. Opposition to Christians in a resistance stand will make other Christian peacemaking work more controversial. Today isn't a time to avoid controversy. Today is a time for deciding on the church's position regarding resistance to militarism.

ENDNOTES

1. *The Revelation to John* 21:1-3 (The Revised Standard Version).
2. Jonathan Schell, *The Fate of the Earth* (New York: Alfred A. Knopf, 1982).
3. See Carl Sagan, *et. al.,* "Nuclear Winter: Global Consequences of Multiple Nuclear Explosions," *Science,* 222 (December 23, 1983), pp. 1283-1292.
4. William G. Pollard, "The Uniqueness of the Earth," *Earth Might Be Fair,* edited by Ian G. Barbour (Englewood Cliffs, New Jersey: Prentice-Hall, Inc., 1972), p. 96.
5. Gordon Kaufman, "Nuclear Eschatology and the Study of Religion," *Harvard Divinity Bulletin* (February-March 1983), pp. 6-10.
6. Richard A. Falk, *This Endangered Planet* (New York: Random House, Inc., 1972), p. 15.